2/20/91

LOCAL AREA NETWORKS

McGraw-Hill Series in Electrical Engineering

Consulting Editor
Stephen W. Director, Carnegie-Mellon University

Circuits and Systems
Communications and Signal Processing
Control Theory
Electronics and Electronic Circuits
Power and Energy
Electromagnetics
Computer Engineering
Introductory
Radar and Antennas
VLSI

Previous Consulting Editors

*Ronald N. Bracewell, Colin Cherry, James F. Gibbons, Willis W. Harman,
Hubert Heffner, Edward W. Herold, John G. Linvill, Simon Ramo, Ronald A. Rohrer,
Anthony E. Siegman, Charles Susskind, Frederick E. Terman, John G. Truxal,
Ernst Weber, and John R. Whinnery*

Communications and Signal Processing

Consulting Editor
Stephen W. Director, Carnegie-Mellon University

Antoniou: *Digital Filters: Analysis and Design*
Candy: *Signal Processing: The Model-Based Approach*
Candy: *Signal Processing: The Modern Approach*
Carlson: *Communications Systems: An Introduction to Signals and Noise in
  Electrical Communication*
Cherin: *An Introduction to Optical Fibers*
Cooper and McGillem: *Modern Communications and Spread Spectrum*
Davenport: *Probability and Random Processes: An Introduction for Applied
  Scientists and Engineers*
Drake: *Fundamentals of Applied Probability Theory*
Guiasu: *Information Theory with New Applications*
Keiser: *Local Area Networks*
Keiser: *Optical Fiber Communications*
Kuc: *Introduction to Digital Signal Processing*
Papoulis: *Probability, Random Variables, and Stochastic Processes*
Papoulis: *Signal Analysis*
Papoulis: *The Fourier Integral and Its Applications*
Peebles: *Probability, Random Variables, and Random Signal Principles*
Proakis: *Digital Communications*
Schwartz: *Information Transmission, Modulation, and Noise*
Schwartz and Shaw: *Signal Processing*
Smith: *Modern Communication Circuits*
Taub and Schilling: *Principles of Communication Systems*

LOCAL AREA NETWORKS

Gerd E. Keiser

GTE

McGraw-Hill Book Company

New York St. Louis San Francisco Auckland Bogotá Caracas
Colorado Springs Hamburg Lisbon London Madrid Mexico Milan
Montreal New Delhi Oklahoma City Panama Paris San Juan
São Paulo Singapore Sydney Tokyo Toronto

This book was set in Times Roman.
The editors were Alar E. Elken and John M. Morriss;
the designer was Albert M. Cetta;
the production supervisor was Denise L. Puryear.
Project supervision was done by Harley Editorial Services.
R. R. Donnelley & Sons Company was printer and binder.

Local Area Networks

Copyright © 1989 by McGraw-Hill, Inc. All rights reserved. Printed in the United States
of America. Except as permitted under the United States Copyright Act of 1976, no part
of this publication may be reproduced or distributed in any form or by any means, or stored
in a data base or retrieval system, without the prior written permission of the publisher.

234567890 DOC DOC 89432109

ISBN 0-07-033561-3

Library of Congress Cataloging-in-Publication Data
Keiser, Gerd.
    Local area networks/Gerd E. Keiser.
        p.   cm.—(McGraw-Hill series in electrical engineering.
    Communications and signal processing)
    Includes bibliographies and index.
    ISBN 0-07-033561-3
        1. Local area networks (Computer networks)   I. Title.
II. Series.
TK5105.7.K44 1989
004.6′8—dc 19   88-8203

ABOUT THE AUTHOR

Gerd E. Keiser received his B.A. and M.S. degrees in mathematics and physics from the University of Wisconsin in Milwaukee, and a Ph.D. degree in solid-state physics from Northeastern University in Boston in 1973. From 1973 to 1974 he carried out research and development of state-of-the-art infrared photo-detectors at the Honeywell Electro-Optics center in Lexington, Massachusetts.

In 1974 Dr. Keiser joined the GTE Government Systems Corporation in Needham Heights, Massachusetts, where he currently is the Engineering Manager of the Communication Equipment Design Department. His work here involves analyzing, designing, and developing fiber optic, microwave, and millimeter-wave information-transmission systems and networks.

Dr. Keiser is also serving as an Adjunct Professor of Electrical Engineering at Northeastern University. In addition, he was the guest editor for the IEEE Communications Magazine in May 1985; he organized an IEEE Lecture Series on Optical Fiber Communications in 1986; and he has presented numerous invited lectures at conferences, local industries, and local professional meetings.

Dr. Keiser has published over 20 technical journal and conference papers and is the author of the book *Optical Fiber Communications*, McGraw-Hill, 1983.

To
Ching-yun and Nishla

CONTENTS

Appendices

Index

PREFACE

This book has been written specifically as a textbook with the purpose of providing the basic material for an introductory senior or first-year graduate course in the analysis and modeling of local area networks. It will also serve well as a working reference for practicing engineers dealing with local area network design and applications. To aid students in learning and applying it to practical designs, a collection of 150 homework problems is included. These problem sets are an important and integral part of this book. They are intended not only to help readers test their comprehension of the material covered, but also to extend and elucidate the text. A solutions manual to the problems is available to the instructor from the publisher.

The background required to study the book is only that of typical senior-level engineering students. Specifically, it is assumed that the student has been introduced to electromagnetic theory, calculus and elementary differential equations, the basic concepts of physics, and the basic concepts of electronics. Courses in communication theory and statistics are not essential, but would be helpful for gaining a full understanding of the material in this book. As an aid to students, I have included brief overviews of relevant units, probability theory, and useful mathematical formulations as appendices at the end of the book.

The book is organized to give a clear and logical sequence of topics. It progresses systematically from descriptions of local area network (LAN) architectures to signaling types and techniques, and ends with discussions on the applications of a variety of popular local area networking schemes. The introductory chapter gives a brief historical background on the evolution of communication systems and how this naturally led to the concept of a LAN. It also sets the stage for the rest of the book by describing what the key elements of a LAN are, and how LANs fit into the overall communications picture that includes computer buses, metropolitan area networks (MANs), and long-haul or wide area networks (WANs). In addition, Chapter 1 addresses some of the functions and general applications of the rapidly growing LAN field.

For two systems to communicate, they must share a common set of rules for generating and interpreting the messages they send or receive. To achieve this, a seven-layer model for network architecture has been established. This widely recognized model, which is known as the Open System Interconnection (OSI) model, is the initial topic of Chapter 2. Next Chapter 2 discusses the relationships of protocols in this model, and the chapter ends with a presentation on the meaning and implementation of each of the seven individual layers.

Chapter 3 provides an introduction and overview of communication theory, particularly as it applies to layers 1 and 2 of the OSI Model. It begins by examining signal types and the modulation techniques used to match the signal properties with the transmission characteristics of the channel. Also included are discussions of frequency response limitations, signal distortion, noise limitations, signal formatting, and multiplexing techniques as they apply to baseband and broadband local area networks. Since errors are unavoidable in any real communication system, methods for detecting and compensating for errors in a digital data stream are discussed next. The final topic in Chapter 3 concerns how communications take place between a number of different devices located at various nodes on a network.

Two important parameters of a local area network are its topology and the transmission medium that is used. These are the topics of Chapter 4, where signal power budget calculations are presented for coaxial-cable and optical-fiber media in several network topologies.

Chapter 5 presents the mathematical foundation of queueing theory which is needed to compare the different access schemes utilized in local area networks. The topics discussed will allow the analysis of message throughput, the queue lengths of messages waiting for service, and the mean response time of LAN access schemes.

Access to a LAN can be gained either in a deterministic (controlled) fashion or by a contention (random-access) scheme. These are described and compared in Chapter 6. In these discussions a key LAN performance characteristic is the throughput or channel utilization, which is a measure of the total rate of traffic being transmitted between two nodes. A second performance parameter used to compare LAN access methods is the system delay which measures the mean transfer time from message source to destination.

A local area network as an isolated entity by itself has limited potential and usefulness. Thus Chapter 7 describes how LANs can interconnect to each other and to other wide area networks, thereby allowing the sharing of resources among different networks. The issues here include the general interconnection problem of different types of networks, procedures for routing packets across internetwork boundaries, and flow-control methodologies.

An important issue in a LAN is network reliability and availability. Thus Chapter 8 addresses methods for determining and improving network reliability through redundancy of either transmission lines or nodal equipment.

Owing to the rapidly growing use of local area networks and their interactions with all types of other networks (often on a worldwide basis), the problem of protecting the confidentiality and integrity of the information transmitted on these networks is of concern. Thus Chapter 9 examines network security. The discussions include vulnerablity analysis and mechanisms for achieving security. Particular emphasis is given to encryption since this is a fundamental tool for ensuring information security.

As a final topic, Chapter 10 examines application aspects of some popular LANs which are being widely used in a variety of commercial networks. These include three variations of the IEEE-802.3 standard for baseband CSMA/CD bus LANs (Ethernet, Cheapernet, and StarLAN), optical fiber versions of Ethernet, schemes used for communicating in the factory and office (the IEEE-802.4-based MAP and the IEEE-802.3-based TOP, respectively), token ring LANs as described by IEEE-802.5, and the 100-Mb/s FDDI optical-fiber token ring.

In preparing this book, I am greatly indebted to the many people with whom I had numerous discussions and who supplied me with various materials. Particular thanks go to Margaret Chan, Dr. Tri Ha, Dr. Ching-yun Keiser, and Dr. Stevan Leiden. Special thanks go to several reviewers whose comments enhanced and clarified the content and organization of the book: Pierce Cantrel, Texas A & M University; R. Lee Hamilton, Jr., The Ohio State University; Doug Jacobson, Iowa State University; Vernon Rego, Purdue University; Manos Roumeliotis, West Virginia University; Charles H. Sauer; and John A. Stankovic, University of Massachusetts—Amherst. Since the development of local area networks is the result of the work of many people from a wide variety of disciplines, this book would not have been possible without the many contributions that have appeared in the open literature. My sincerest thanks also go to Suzanne Allison, Ann Miller, Gail Pickett, and Jean-Sampson, all of whom assisted in typing the manuscript and its various drafts in an exceptionally expert fashion. As a final personal note, I am grateful to my wife Ching-yun and my daughter Nishla for their patience and encouragement during the time I devoted to writing this book.

Gerd E. Keiser

LOCAL AREA NETWORKS

CHAPTER
1

OVERVIEW OF LOCAL AREA NETWORKS

Ever since ancient times, people have devised various techniques for communicating their thoughts, needs, and desires to others. In early civilized times, people tended to congregate in geographically localized clusters in which communications were adequately achieved through speech and written messages. As civilizations spread over larger geographical areas, a variety of long-distance communication methods were tried such as smoke signals, optical signals, and carrier pigeons. One of the earliest known optical transmission links,[1] for example, was the use of a fire signal by the Greeks in the eighth century B.C. for sending alarms, calls for help, or announcements of certain events. However, because of environmental and technology limitations it generally turned out to be faster and more efficient to send letter messages by a courier over the road network.

The discovery of the telegraph by Samuel F. B. Morse in 1838 ushered in a new epoch in communications—the era of electrical communications.[2] Messages

1

in the early nineteenth-century telegraphy systems were first encoded into strings of binary symbols, and were then manually transmitted and received. In the ensuing years developments and implementations of communication systems employing electrical signals became increasingly sophisticated leading, in turn, to the birth of telephone, radio, television, radar, and microwave links. Today these communication systems have become an integral part of everyday life with circuits spanning the entire world carrying voice, text, pictures, and many other types of information.

Along with the development of faster and higher-capacity transmission systems, the past several decades have witnessed a phenomenal growth in the computer industry. As recent advances in integrated circuit technology have allowed computers to become smaller, less expensive, and widely available, people have become increasingly interested in connecting them together to form networks. The term *network* is defined as a set of communication links for interconnecting a collection of terminals, computers, telephones, printers, or other types of data-communicating and data-handling devices. We will refer to these devices generically as *stations*. This interconnection allows these elements to exchange information. One such network is the worldwide telephone system which is an example of the so-called *long-haul network* or *wide-area network* (WAN) that interconnects widely dispersed telecommunication elements.

The successful integration and cross-fertilization of communications and geographically dispersed computing facilities has recently resulted in a tremendous demand for and growth in networks which serve a limited geographical area. In the late 1970s and early 1980s these types of networks, which are called *local area networks* (LANs), made a dramatic entrance into the communications scene. The ensuing years showed a tremendous proliferation of LAN equipment vendors who offered a wide variety of products.

Although it might have appeared that local area networking was a new technology, LANs actually evolved from existing methods of networking and communications. The factors that brought about the rapid rise in the popularity of LANs were the dramatic advances in integrated circuit technology that allowed a small computer chip in the 1980s to have the same processing capabilities of a room-sized computer of the 1950s. This allowed computers to become smaller and less expensive, while they simultaneously became more powerful and versatile.

1.1   THE EVOLUTION OF LOCAL AREA NETWORKS

To see how LANs evolved, let us look at the history of communication networks. Data communication networks resulted from the convergence of two different technologies: computers and telecommunications. This convergence is depicted in Figs. 1.1 through 1.4. In the 1950s computers were large complex machines that could only be operated by specially trained personnel. Jobs in the form of punched cards, paper tape, or magnetic tape were manually brought to

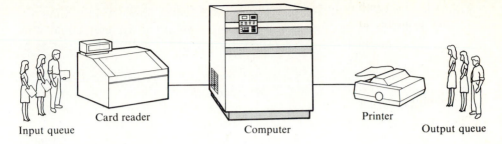

Input queue   Card reader   Computer   Printer   Output queue

FIGURE 1.1
Jobs were processed in batches in the 1950s with no direct user-to-computer interaction.

the machine to be run in single-process batches. Thus, no direct communications were involved between the computer and the user. This batch process was very unwieldy because of the remoteness of the system from the user, and the long time that was often spent between job submission and receipt of the output.

In the 1960s advances in teletypewriter and data transmission technologies led to the development of the interactive terminal. This device allowed users to remotely access a computer directly via a low-speed data line that connected the terminal to the computer. Thus a very simple type of computer network that we see in Fig. 1.2 was established. Users could now interact directly with the

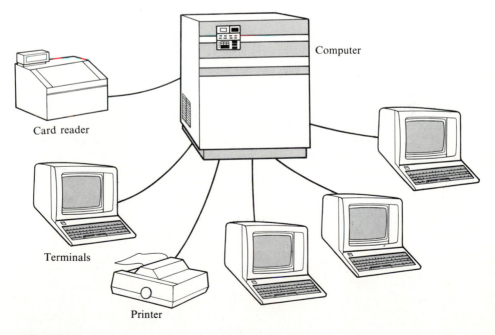

Computer

Card reader

Terminals

Printer

FIGURE 1.2
The interactive terminal allowed direct user-to-computer access.

information processing resources of the computer which provided immediate interactive feedback. In setting up and running a program, the user could now
correct errors immediately instead of having to wait for a printed output as in
the batch-processing case.

As the demand increased for adding more and more peripheral devices to
the computer, it became unwieldy and uneconomical to have a separate long-
distance communication link from the computer to each device. Thus, as we see
in Fig. 1.3, remote multiplexers or concentrators were developed to collect the
outputs from a localized set of peripherals and send this traffic over a common
link to the computer. In addition, to off-load the computer from the need to
handle all the communications to and from the attached equipment, special processors called *front ends* were developed.

Through the increased use of time-sharing, many new applications developed including complex scientific calculations, accounting for banks, generation
of up-to-date business status reports, inventory control, and training in educa-
tional institutions. However, each of these early simple computer networks centered around one computer and provided only a single function. This
centralization tended to limit system flexibility since all the communications

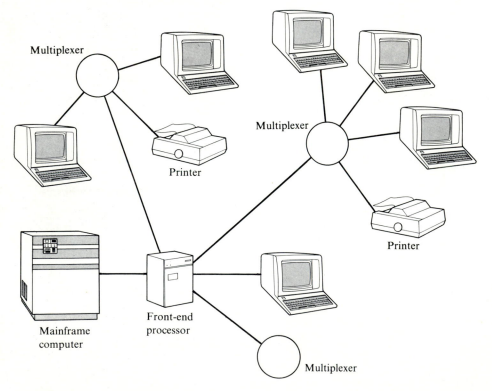

FIGURE 1.3
A network with one centralized computer and transmission lines to a front-end processor.

came to the computer in a starlike configuration. What was missing was the ability to *line share* or *terminal share*. This meant that since a given line and all the terminals on it were part of the access path to only one computer, if the user wanted to access the services of a different computer, another terminal and a separate line to that computer would be needed. In addition the large central computer, which is commonly known as the *mainframe*, is principally designed to provide processing capability, but is generally not flexible enough to handle the demands of highly interactive usage.

The concept of a large-scale, general-purpose network is shown in Fig. 1.4. The network consists essentially of geographically distributed *nodes*, or network

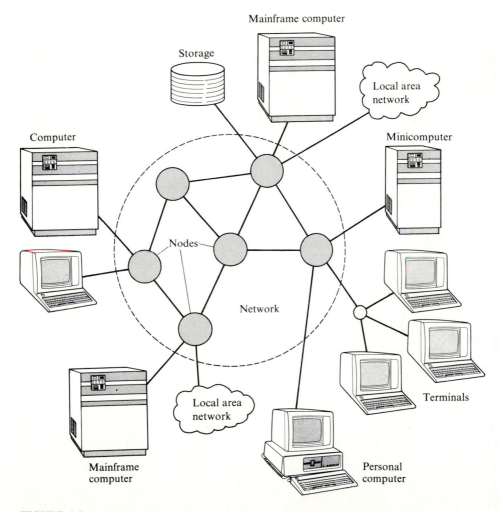

FIGURE 1.4
A generic network consisting of geographically distributed nodes interconnecting various communication equipment, computing elements, and local networks.

switches, interconnected by transmission links. These links can be wire, radio, microwave, fiber-optic, or satellite facilities. Attached to these distributed nodes are various elements such as computers, terminals, databases, or local area networks. Messages originate at the external elements, pass into the network via the nodes, travel from node to node through the network, and arrive at the external destination element via another node. The nodes are generally computers whose primary purpose is to route messages through the network. They are referred to as either *interface message processors* (IMPs) or *switches*.

The dramatic decrease in hardware costs resulting in particular from advances in very large scale integration (VLSI) has led to widely available low-cost intelligent terminals and work stations. Thus, in recent years these types of devices have been installed in large numbers in localized areas such as office buildings and university campuses. However, other expensive resources such as high-quality printers, disk storage, and central files and databases are best utilized on a shared basis. To effectively manage these intelligent devices and resources in a geographically limited area is the function of a local area network which is the main topic of this book. The emphasis here is on the design, implementation, interconnection, and performance of local area networks.

1.2 ELEMENTS OF
A LOCAL AREA NETWORK

As their name implies, local area networks encompass data and computer communication elements which are nominally located less than 10 km but more than 1 m apart. One organization generally controls these elements which could be

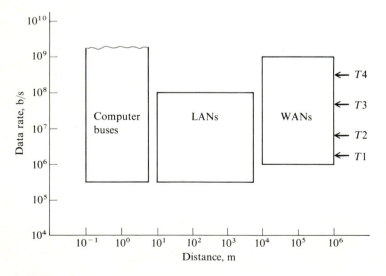

FIGURE 1.5
Comparison of LANs with other networks.

located in facilities such as a university campus, an office building, a manufacturing plant, or several buildings in an industrial complex.

Data rates tend to fall between 100 kb/s (kilobits per second) and 100 Mb/s, so that reliable, high-speed transmission is achieved in a limited geographical area over low-cost links. The applications of LANs thus falls in between long-haul or wide-area networks (WANs) and computer buses, as is generically illustrated in Fig. 1.5.

All data communication networks consist of a collection of circuits, data-switching elements, computing elements, and peripheral devices as shown in Fig. 1.6. The computing elements are often referred to as *hosts*, but in many cases they can be simply treated as terminals attached to the network. Any point in the network at which data is switched is called a *node* or a *switch*. The term *circuit* refers to a point-to-point physical or logical path between two nodes

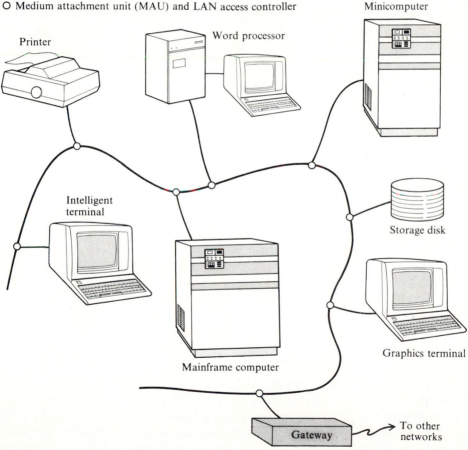

FIGURE 1.6
Elements of a generic local area network.

which can support continuous communications in one or both directions. The peripheral devices include items such as computers, word processors, interactive terminals, graphic terminals, storage elements, printers, and data files.

Access to a network is achieved with a microprocessor-based LAN access controller and a medium attachment unit (MAU). Since the elements attached to a network usually come from several manufacturers, they generally do not conform to a common data transmission protocol. Thus, one of the basic functions of the LAN access controller is to transform the data rate and transmission protocol of the attached device to that of the local area network. Other functions of the LAN access controller include buffering data from the attached equipment until medium access is achieved, scanning each message on the medium to see if it is destined for its attached device, reading messages into its buffer, and monitoring the incoming signals for errors.

1.3   MESSAGES AND PACKETS

From the standpoint of network users, a message in a network is a single unit of communication. For example, in an electronic mail system a message would consist of a document sent from one user to another. In an interactive communication between two or more users, a message is a single unit of communication from one participant to another. A message in an image transmission system could be a single figure, image, or diagram. A critical factor in message transmission is that if the recipient gets only part of the message it is useless.

To transmit a message over a network it is usually represented as a string of binary symbols, that is, ones and zeros. These binary symbols are commonly referred to as *bits*. When transmitting these message bits across a network, control overhead in the form of additional bits must be added to it to ensure factors such as reliable communication, correct routing of the message, and prevention of network congestion. In addition, transmitting long messages as one complete unit is generally not done since this is detrimental to message delay, buffer management, and congestion control. Therefore, long messages are normally broken up into shorter bit strings called *packets*. These packets are then sent through the network as individual units and are reassembled into complete messages at the destination station.

1.4   OVERVIEW OF THE BOOK

In general the equipment which users wish to connect to a LAN consists of many diverse products developed by numerous manufacturers. The difficulty in connecting such a group of heterogeneous machines is that each manufacturer could use different data formats and message-exchange conventions. The only solution to effective communications between such equipment is to have vendors abide by a common set of rules or data-exchange protocols. Chapter 2 addresses this topic in terms of the widely accepted seven-layer network architecture model[3] shown in Fig. 1.7. Included in this are discussions of the following:

1. The basic concepts of layered network architecture
2. The mechanical, electrical, and procedural network interface specifications such as connector types, signal levels, and pin assignments on connectors
3. Methods for establishing, maintaining, and releasing data-link connections among network nodes
4. Character-oriented and bit-oriented data-link protocols
5. Techniques for sending data packets between nodes
6. IEEE-developed standards for LANs
7. A comparison of several network architectures

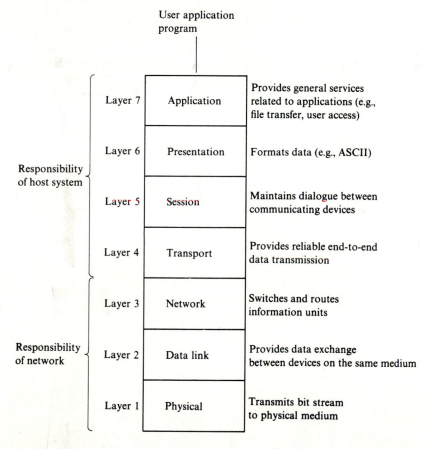

FIGURE 1.7
Seven-layer network architecture model.

To exchange information between any two elements in a LAN, some type of signal has to be transmitted via a communication channel. Chapter 3 gives an overview of the basic functions of information transmission that are applicable to any type of communication system. The topics include:

1. Signal types and modulation techniques
2. Frequency-response limitations and the concept of bandwidth
3. Signal distortion and noise limitations
4. Signal formats used in baseband and broadband LANs
5. Multiplexing techniques
6. Error detection and correction methods

Chapter 4 addresses two important parameters of a LAN. These are the network topology and the transmission medium that is used. The choice of these two parameters determines factors such as the type of data the LAN may handle, the transmission speed, the efficiency of the network, and the degree of flexibility for accommodating a variety of users. The transmission media used in LANs include twisted-pair wire, coaxial cable, and optical fibers. Both the transmission characteristics and detailed examples of link power budget calculations are presented for these media in Chap. 4.

Local area networks are commonly characterized in terms of their topology. The major LAN topologies shown in Fig. 1.8 are the star, bus, and ring networks. Analyses of these networks, with particular emphasis on optical fiber implementations, are also given in Chap. 4.

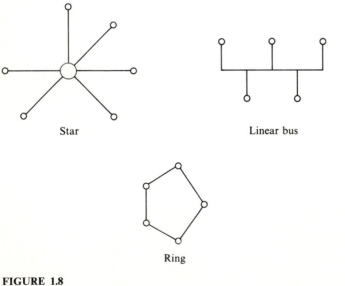

Star

Linear bus

Ring

FIGURE 1.8
The major LAN topologies.

To describe the performance of a local area network, we need some theoretical modeling tools. The mathematical foundations for most analytical models of computer systems and communication networks is queueing theory. As we show in Chap. 5, the purpose of queueing theory is to analyze the contention for network resources by the users, and to determine its effect on the flow of jobs through the system.

One characteristic of a LAN is that its backbone is a shared transmission line which permits all attached users to simultaneously attempt to gain access to the transmission facilities. Thus, when two or more stations try to transmit at the same time their signals interfere and become garbled. As we discuss in Chap. 6, to resolve these conflicts a number of different access protocols have been devised. These fall into the two basic classes of contention (or random-access) methods and deterministic (or controlled) techniques. The performance parameters against which we measure these schemes are the throughput or channel utilization and the delay or mean transfer time of a message through the network.

A local area network which is isolated by itself has limited potential and usefulness. What is desired is the ability of users to also access computing and communication elements in other networks. This is illustrated in Fig. 1.9 and described in Chap. 7. The generic device used for interconnecting any two networks is called a *gateway*. This device must be able to route messages between networks and to control the flow of internetwork information so that a slow network is not swamped with data from a faster network.

An important factor in the usefulness of any network is its reliability. As we show in Chap. 8, reliability is the probability that a network, or element thereof, performs satisfactorily for a given period of time when used under specified operating conditions. One way to achieve high reliability in the event of line failure or nodal equipment malfunction is to require the network to have line

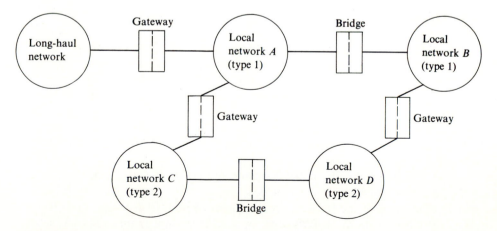

FIGURE 1.9
Connection of different networks via gateways.

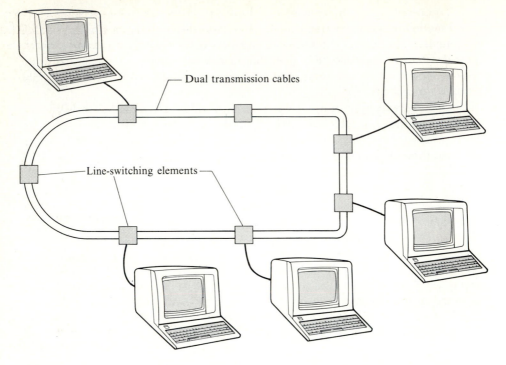

Dual transmission cables

Line-switching elements

FIGURE 1.10
Network reliability enhancement by means of redundancy.

and/or equipment redundancy. Figure 1.10 shows an example that we discuss in detail in Chap. 8. Here a ring network having parallel transmission lines can be easily reconfigured via line-switching elements at the nodes to bypass failed nodes or line segments.

The problem of protecting the confidentiality and integrity of the information on a network is often a major concern of the user. Local area networks are particularly vulnerable to security compromise, since they are by definition designed to provide many user access points. Without proper protection an unauthorized person could use these connections to gain access to proprietary or classified information. Chapter 9 addresses the general issues concerning local area network security. In addition we describe various encryption techniques, since encryption is a fundamental tool for ensuring security in data-transfer systems.

As a final topic, Chap. 10 examines some popular applications of LAN technology. We first discuss the widely popular 10-Mb/s Ethernet scheme[4,5] which follows one of the IEEE LAN standards (ANSI/IEEE 802.3). In this overview we examine both coaxial and optical-fiber implementations. A second popular LAN implementation is the IEEE 802.5 token ring network. This 4-Mb/s architecture evolved from work initiated at the IBM Research Labora-

tory in Zurich, Switzerland. We also examine the Fiber Distributed Data Interface (FDDI) standard.[6] This is a fiber-optic-based token ring LAN with a throughput of 100 Mb/s. It largely follows the IEEE 802.5 standard, deviating only where required to by its higher data throughput rate.

As another topic in Chap. 10 we describe a basic data communication protocol called the Manufacturing Automation Protocol[7] (MAP). This was developed by the General Motors Corporation (Detroit, Michigan) to let intelligent factory entities such as robots, computers, machine tools, and programmable controllers communicate. The MAP activities in turn gave rise to the Technical Office Protocol (TOP) which the Boeing Computer Services Company (Seattle, Washington) developed to interconnect work stations, computers, and peripherals.[8] Developers of the MAP and TOP standards are also devising a common specification that will ensure compatibility between the engineering office and the factory floor.

For the final topic in Chap. 10 we look at the integration of voice and data onto one local area network.[9] Since these two types of traffic have different characteristics, they require different services from the network. Voice is stream traffic that requires real-time delivery, whereas data is bursty traffic that can tolerate long delays.

1.5 NOTES AND FURTHER READING

The following chapters present an introduction to the field of local area networks. The various topics describe the fundamental concepts needed to design and implement a local area network.

Numerous references are given at the end of each chapter as a start for delving deeper into any given topic. Since local area networking brings together research and development efforts from many different scientific and engineering disciplines, there are hundreds of articles in the literature relating to the material covered in each chapter. Even though not all of these articles were cited in the references, the selections represent some of the major contributions to the local area network field and can be considered as a good introduction to the literature. All references were chosen on the basis of easy accessibility and should be available in a good technical library.

Additional references which, in general, are not readily accessible are various conference proceedings. These proceedings can normally be obtained from the organizers of the conferences or through a major technical library. Examples are given in Refs. 10 through 12. A number of review articles and books of reprints are also available for a rapid introduction to local area networks. Among these are Refs. 13 through 15. In addition, supplementary material can be found in the books and journals listed in Refs. 16 through 26.

To help the reader understand and use the material in the book, an overview of units, a listing of mathematical formulas, and discussions of communications theory are given in the appendices.

As is the case for any active scientific and engineering discipline, local area network technology is constantly undergoing changes and improvements. New concepts are presently being pursued and measurement techniques are improving. These changes should not have a major impact on the material presented in this book since it is primarily based on enduring fundamental concepts. The understanding of these concepts will allow a rapid comprehension of any new technological developments that will undoubtedly arise.

REFERENCES

1. V. Aschoff, "Optische Nachrichtenuebertragung im klassichen Altertum," *Nachrichtentechn. Z. (NTZ)*, vol. 30, pp. 23–28, January 1977.
2. H. Busignies, "Communication channels," *Sci. Amer.*, vol. 227, pp. 99–113, September 1972.
3. International Standards Organization, *ISO 7498*, "Basic reference model for Open Systems Interconnection," 1983.
4. J. F. Shoch, Y. K. Dalal, D. D. Redell, and R. C. Crane, "Evolution of the Ethernet Local Computer Network," *Computer*, vol. 15, pp. 10–27, August 1982.
5. ANSI/IEEE Standards 802.1 to 802.6 for Local Area Networks, 1985.
6. S. L. Wallach, "FDDI tutorial," *LAN Magazine*, pp. 44–47, March 1987.
7. G. Kim, "What is MAP?," *LAN Magazine*, pp. 32–36, November 1986.
8. R. Allan, "Factory communication," *Electronic Design*, vol. 34, pp. 102–112, May 15, 1986.
9. O. C. Ibe and D. T. Gibson, "Protocols for integrated voice and data local area networks," *IEEE Commun. Mag.*, vol. 24, pp. 30–36, July 1986.
10. *Proc. of the International Conf. on Commun. (ICC)*, sponsored by IEEE, generally have several sessions devoted to the latest developments in local area networks.
11. *IEEE Computer Networking Symposium*, held annually.
12. *Proc. IEEE Global Telecommun. Conf. (GLOBECOM)*, sponsored annually by IEEE.
13. K. J. Thurber and H. A. Freeman, *Local Computer Networks*, 2d ed., IEEE Comp. Soc. Press, 1981.
14. D. D. Clark, K. T. Pogran, and D. P. Read, "An introduction to local area networks," *Proc. IEEE*, vol. 66, pp. 1497–1517, November 1978.
15. *The Selection of Local Area Computer Networks*, National Bureau of Standards Special Publication 500-96, November 1982.
16. *IEEE J. Select. Areas in Commun.*, Special Issue on Local Area Networks, vol. SAC-1, November 1983.
17. *IEEE J. Select. Areas in Commun.*, Special Issue on Fiber Optics for Local Communications, vol. SAC-3, November 1985.
18. *IEEE Network*, a journal devoted to computer communications, premier issue January 1987.
19. W. Stallings, *Data and Computer Communications*, Macmillan, New York, 1985.
20. A. S. Tanenbaum, *Computer Networks*, Prentice-Hall, Englewood Cliffs, NJ, 1981.
21. M. Schwartz, *Telecommunication Networks*, Addison-Wesley, Reading, MA, 1987.
22. J. L. Hammond and P. J. P. O'Reilly, *Local Computer Networks*, Addison-Wesley, Reading, MA, 1986.
23. D. Bertsekas and R. Gallager, *Data Networks*, Prentice-Hall, Englewood Cliffs, NJ, 1987.
24. J. F. Hayes, *Modeling and Analysis of Computer Communication Networks*, Plenum, New York, 1984.
25. D. G. Baker, *Local Area Networks with Fiber-Optic Applications*, Reston, Englewood Cliffs, NJ, 1986.
26. P. E. Green, Jr., *Computer Network Architectures and Protocols.* Plenum, New York, 1982.

CHAPTER
2

LAYERED
NETWORK
ARCHITECTURE

As we noted in Chap. 1, advances in LSI and VLSI technology in the 1970s and 1980s resulted in continually decreasing costs and sizes of highly functional and powerful computing and communication devices, and progress in human-to-machine interfaces is making these machines easier to use. This has spurred a rapid growth in the number of computers and intelligent devices distributed throughout organizations and has created an associated expanding need for communications among them. In general the equipment which users wish to interconnect consists of many diverse products developed by numerous manufacturers. The difficulty that arises when attempting to interconnect such a group of heterogeneous machines is that the data formats and the data-exchange conventions of the equipment developed by one manufacturer are not necessarily the same as those of another manufacturer. Furthermore, even within a specific manufacturer's product line, different models may not follow the same data-exchange conventions.

How then can two distinct systems exchange information? (Here the word *system* is used to denote a collection of terminals, computers, telephones, printers, and other data-handling devices, together with their associated software, peripheral equipment, and users that are capable of information processing and/or transfer.) The only solution to effective communications among various system components and between networks is to have vendors abide by

15

some common set of rules. This action was started in 1978 when the International Standards Organization (ISO) recognized the importance of and the need for *universality* in exchanging information between and within networks and across geographical boundaries.[1,2]

In this chapter we therefore look at some high-level broad issues that will provide a basis for examining local area network design and implementation. Basically this considers the overall network architecture, which is the structure that determines how the various logical and physical components of a network are interconnected.

To begin let us examine the Open System Interconnection (OSI) Reference Model which is a seven-layer model developed by the ISO for network architecture. We first define some fundamental concepts in Sec. 2.1 and describe the overall functions of the seven layers in Sec. 2.2. In Secs. 2.3 to 2.9 we go into detail on layers 1 through 7, respectively. Having looked at the functions of the various layers, in Sec. 2.10 we then examine how information flows through a network from a data source to a data destination.

An important family of standards for LANs has been developed by the IEEE in order for equipment of a variety of manufacturers to interface. These standards are described in Sec. 2.11. To get a better feeling of how layered network architectures are applied, Sec. 2.12 makes a top-level comparison of some popular network implementations.

2.1 THE OSI REFERENCE MODEL

In 1978 the ISO issued a recommendation for a standard *network architecture* that defines the relationships and interactions between network services and functions through common interfaces and protocols. This recommendation is now widely accepted. It is in the form of a seven-layer model for network architecture and is known as the *Open System Interconnection* (OSI) Reference Model.[3] A simple model of this seven-layer architecture is shown in Fig. 2.1.

Before we get into specifics, let us first look at some terminology. As noted by Day and Zimmermann[4] the term *architecture* can be confusing since it has been used to describe everything from a framework for system development to actual hardware. An architecture is basically a set of rules and conventions by which something is built. For example, Victorian architecture is a set of rules and stylistic conventions that are used to construct a particular form of building. One cannot walk into a Victorian architecture, but one can walk into a Victorian building. The same holds true for network architectures.[5] The network architecture of the OSI Model defines the rules and conventions for various functions within each layer, it specifies the general relations among these functions, and notes the constraints on the types of functions and their relations. Neither the details of the implementation nor the specification of the interlayer interfaces are part of the architecture. Thus, the OSI Reference Model is just that—a model. It cannot be implemented and it does not represent a preferred implementation approach. It serves only as a framework for standards which can be implemented at each layer by a variety of protocols.

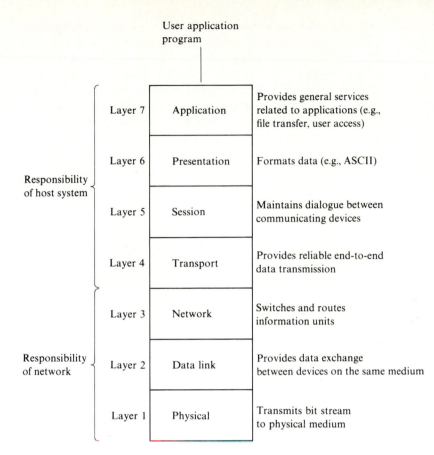

FIGURE 2.1
General representation of the seven-layer ISO network architecture. The bottom three layers (1–3) are specific to local area networks, whereas the top three layers (5–7) are common to all systems. The transport layer (4) resolves physical differences between networks.

The term "open" denotes the ability to transfer information between any two systems that conform to the reference model and the associated standards, and as such it is not concerned with the inner operations of the systems themselves. That is, a system is open to communication with any other system obeying the same standards anywhere in the world.

2.1.1 Basic Concepts of the OSI Model

For two systems to communicate, they must share a common set of rules for generating and interpreting the messages they send or receive. This set of rules is rather complex and many design decisions must be made when setting it up. Since this set of rules is not simple enough to be understood as a whole, a structured modular approach allows the set to be subdivided into a number of individual pieces of manageable and comprehensible size. In carrying out this subdivision, it is advantageous to partition the rules into independent functions. This will allow additions or updating of individual functions to be carried out without destabilizing the entire set of rules.

The OSI Reference Model is an example of such a structured approach. It modularizes a set of system-interconnection rules in a particular way by defining a series of layers of functions. Each layer contains a certain group of functions, and the boundary between the layers represents a demarcation between these groups.[6-8] The basic idea of layering is that each layer adds value to the services provided by lower layers. In this approach a user at the highest layer is offered the full set of services needed to interact with other users and peripheral equipments that are distributed on the network.

The OSI Reference Model is divided into seven layers as is shown in Fig. 2.2. By convention the layers are viewed as a vertical sequence with the numbering starting at the bottom layer. As one progresses up the series of layers, a larger number of functions are provided and the level of abstraction of the service that the user sees increases. The lower layers govern the *communication facilities*: the physical connections, data-link control, and routing and relaying

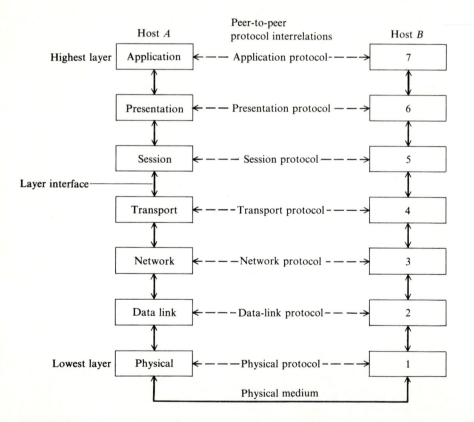

FIGURE 2.2
Information exchange between two systems that follow the seven-layer ISO Model.

functions that support the actual transmission of data. The upper layers support the *user's applications* by structuring and organizing data for the user's needs.

For simplicity in discussing the layers, any layer is referred to as *layer N* or the *N layer*, while its next lower and higher levels are denoted as the $(N - 1)$ layer and the $(N + 1)$ layer, respectively. The same notation is used to designate all concepts relating to layers; for example, entities in the N layer are referred to as *N entities*. We note here that the word *entity* denotes anything which is capable of sending, processing, or receiving information. It can be things such as an application program, a file-transfer package, a database management system, or a terminal.

The same set of layered functions must exist on each system, in order for the two systems to communicate. Layer N on one machine communicates with the corresponding layer N on another machine. The entities that make up the corresponding layers on different machines are called *peer processes*. This information exchange between the two systems is carried out by having the layers on one system communicate with their peer layers in the other system. The orderly exchange of information between peer layers is achieved via protocols. A *protocol* is a set of rules or conventions which governs the format and control of information that is transmitted through a network or that is stored in a database.[9,10] The information may be voice, text, data, or image.

In an actual system, information is not directly transmitted from layer N on one machine to layer N on another machine, except at the lowest level. The real path of the information flow is indicated by the heavy lines in Fig. 2.2. For example, if host A wishes to send a message to host B, each layer at host A passes data and control information to the layer immediately below it. When the lowest layer is reached there is an actual *physical connection* from host A to host B. At host B the information is then passed up from one layer to the next until it reaches layer N.

2.1.2   Services

The term *service* represents a boundary between functions in different layers. In this sense, a service is a statement of the set of capabilities of layer N that is provided to the entities of layer $N + 1$, which are collectively called the *user of the service*. The parts of layer N which provide the set of capabilities to the above layer are called the *provider of the service*, as shown in Fig. 2.3. Also as shown in Fig. 2.3, the N services are offered to the $(N + 1)$ entities via the *service access points* (or SAPs) which represent the logical interfaces between the N entities and the $(N + 1)$ entities.

The service provider need not reside in one particular location, but can be distributed across a number of physically distinct pieces of equipment. This, however, is of no concern to the user who views the services as being provided by a distributed abstract machine.[11]

In defining services, the ISO standard[12] introduces the concept of *service primitives* as abstract, implementation-independent elements of the interaction

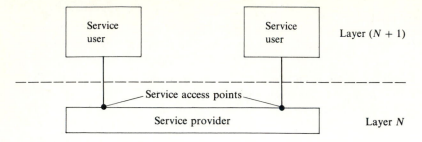

FIGURE 2.3
Service model showing the layered interaction between service user and service provider.

between the service user and the service provider. When an information exchange takes place between two users, the following four service primitives can occur at various instances in the dialogue:

1. *Request.* This primitive is issued by a service user to invoke some procedure.
2. *Indication.* A service provider issues this primitive either to invoke some procedure or to indicate that a procedure has been invoked by the service user at the peer service access point.
3. *Response.* This primitive is issued by a service user to complete, at a particular service access point, some procedure previously invoked by an indication at that service access point.
4. *Confirm.* A service provider issues this primitive to complete, at a particular service access point, some procedure previously invoked by a request at that service access point.

The following two service types occur repeatedly in an information exchange between users:

Unconfirmed. In this service element a request at one service access point produces only an indication at the other.

Confirmed. In this service element a request at one service access point produces an indication at the other access point; this indication leads the service user into issuing a response, which in turn leads to a confirm at the originating service access point.

The occurrence of a service primitive is a logically instantaneous and indivisible event. This event occurs at a specific instance, which cannot be interrupted by another event. Each primitive has a particular direction. This can be either from the service user to the service provider, or vice versa, as is shown in the example in Fig. 2.4. As illustrated here, the order in which related service primitives can occur is conventionally depicted in a *time-sequence diagram*. Each diagram is divided into three parts. The central field represents the service provider and the other two side parts represent the two service users. The passage of time increases downward, so that the position of events along the vertical

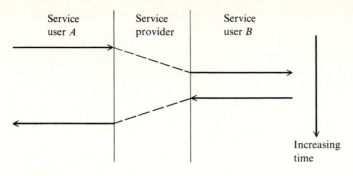

FIGURE 2.4
Time-sequence diagram showing order in which related service primitives can travel.

lines indicates their relative time sequence. Arrows in the user-service areas denote the propagation direction of the primitives, either to or from the service provider.

Example 2.1. An example of a protocol executing the layer 2 (*data-link*) service is given in Fig. 2.5. The users are system *A* and system *B*, and the protocols which

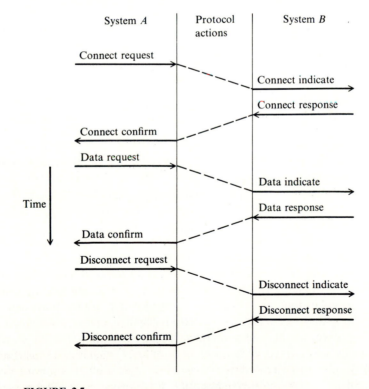

FIGURE 2.5
Example of a protocol executing a layer-2 (data-link) service.

support the services are indicated by dashed lines. (The dashed lines represent generic protocol actions. The specific actions of the dashed lines depend on the particular data-link protocol that is implemented.) As shown here, a *connection request* is first issued by user *A*. User *B* then issues a *connect indicate* and a *connect response*, which in turn is confirmed by user *A*. Similar procedures are then followed for data exchange and link disconnect.

2.2 LAYERS OF THE OSI MODEL

We now turn our attention to some of the details of the seven layers of the OSI Model.[3,4,7,13] A tabulation of these seven layers and their basic functions is given in Table 2.1.

Let us first take a general look at what the various layers do and then examine the specifics. The first three layers (i.e., the *physical, data-link,* and *network layers*) apply specifically to the architecture of local networks. They are concerned with the transmission, framing, and routing of messages between adjacent machines. Protocols at these levels encompass different transmission technologies (such as satellites, coaxial cables, and fiber optics), a variety of network topologies (such as star, ring, and bus configurations), and different accessing methods (including both deterministic and random-access schemes). Since the protocols must deal with physical phenomena, such as propagation delay and message routing, they vary with the type of network.

Whereas the lower three layers are technology-dependent, the top three layers are technology-independent. In moving from the lower to the higher levels in the OSI Model, the emphasis shifts from hardware and software functions, that ensure proper signal flow, to services associated with application processes running in host computers or user devices.

Layer 4, the *transport layer*, serves as the boundary between the data-communication functions of the lower three layers and the data-processing functions of the upper three layers.[14–15] Functionally the middle layer handles error detection and recovery, message sequencing, end-to-end addressing, and multiplexing. A basic function of the transport layer is to subdivide long messages passed down from the *session layer* into smaller units (called *packets*), if this is necessary, and to ensure that the smaller units are properly transmitted to the intended destination.[16–22]

Above the transport layer is the session layer, which deals with the logical functions that are needed to perform orderly data-exchange interactions.[23,24] Its basic task is to take the bare transport-level service, which merely moves raw data bits from one machine to another, and add user-oriented services to it. The session-layer functions include as a minimum a means for two presentation entities to establish, use, and terminate a connection which is called a *session*. The session layer thus serves as the user's interface to the network.

Following the session layer is the *presentation layer*, which allows the user to have a variety of services that may be useful to a particular mode of data transfer, but which are not always essential for correct operation of the

TABLE 2.1
Tabulation of the seven OSI-Model layers and their major functions

APPLICATION LAYER
(a) *Common application-service elements (CASE)*
Log-in
Password checks
Peer-association setups
Agreement on semantics of information to be exchanged
Commitment, concurrency, and recovery
(b) *Specific application-service elements (SASE)*
File transfer, access, and management
Basic-class and forms-class virtual terminals
Message handling
Document transfer
Job transfer and manipulation
Database access and transfer
Videotex, teletex, and telefax
Directory service
System management
Industry protocols: banking, purchasing, invoicing, credit-checking, etc.

PRESENTATION LAYER
Establishes concrete transfer syntax (bit encodings) for data types
Handles pass-through of services from session to application layer

SESSION LAYER
Maps addresses to names (users retain same name when moving)
Establishes connections and terminations
Transfers data
Controls dialogue (who speaks, when, how long, half- or full-duplex)
Synchronizes end-user tasks
Invokes graceful and abrupt closure

TRANSPORT LAYER
Establishes reliable end-to-end transport connections
Multiplexes end-user addresses onto network
Provides end-to-end error detection and recovery
Handles flow control
Monitors quality of service
Disassembles and reassembles session messages

NETWORK LAYER
Sets up routes for packets to travel (establishes virtual circuits)
Provides datagram service
Addresses network equipment on packet routes
Divides transport messages into packets and reassembles them at end
Controls network congestion
Recognizes message priorities and sends messages in proper order
Handles internetworking (both connection-oriented and connectionless)

DATA-LINK LAYER
Transfers data reliably across a single link
Adds flags to signify beginnings and ends of messages
Adds error-checking algorithms
Distinguishes data from flags (provides transparency)
Provides access methods for local area networks

PHYSICAL LAYER
Handles voltages and electrical pulses
Specifies cables, connectors, and media-interface components
Provides collision detection for CSMA/CD access method

23

network.[25] Examples of these services are data encryption, text compression, terminal handling, and file transfer.

The *application layer*[26] is the highest of the seven levels in the OSI Model. Anyone who has worked with a personal computer, a graphics machine, or a word processor is familiar with this layer since an application is a task involving word processing, spreadsheets, graphics, communications, or a database. The composition and function of the application layer are almost totally application-dependent, so that the choice of which specific protocols to use is up to the individual user. Thus, the boundary between the presentation layer and the application layer represents a separation of the protocols imposed by the network designers from those being selected and implemented by the network users.

2.3   THE PHYSICAL LAYER

The physical layer[27-35] is concerned with mechanical, electrical, and procedural network interface specifications; that is, it deals with issues such as connector types, signal levels, and pin assignments on the connectors. The function of the physical layer is the transmission of any arbitrary arrangement of data bits (referred to as either a *raw bit stream* or an *unstructured bit stream*) over an arbitrary medium connecting two pieces of communications equipment. Fundamentally it must activate and deactivate physical connections to other entities and it must act as the logical interface mechanism between the transmission medium and the data-link layer.

A variety of protocols exist for the physical layer. Some common ones include the RS-232C and RS-449 standards of the Electronic Industries Association (EIA),[27,28] sections of the X.21 and V.24 recommendations of the Consultative Committee for International Telephone and Telegraph (CCITT),[29-31] portions of the 802-series protocols recommended by the Institute of Electrical and Electronic Engineers (IEEE)[32,33] and military standards in the MIL-STD-188 series.[34] These standards specify factors such as interchange and control circuits, electric voltage levels, impedances, transmission speeds, connector formats, and transmission distances applicable to the interconnection of *data terminal equipment* (DTE) and *data circuit-terminating equipment* (DCE; this is also often referred to as *data communications equipment*), which is the user-to-network interface.

Let us first define what DTE and DCE are. The basic data communication system elements are shown in Fig. 2.6. The DTE is the user's equipment which is joined to a data communication network. It can be anything from a simple terminal to a large computer system. The term DCE is a generic name for elements that provide a network attachment point for user devices. It is the equipment that provides the functions required to establish, maintain, and terminate a connection; additionally it performs any signal-conversion and coding that may be needed to interface the DTE to the network. An example of a DCE is a modem for connecting a computer terminal to the telephone network.

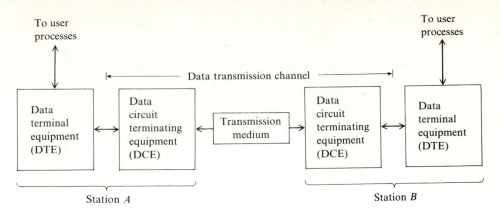

FIGURE 2.6
Basic data-communication system elements showing the interconnection of DTE, DCE, and the transmission medium.

The protocols used by the physical layer should be independent of the transmission medium. This is so that a terminal can be attached to various media such as metallic wire pairs, optical fibers, or radio links. An example of this is shown in Fig. 2.7. Here two systems, for example, a computer and a remote terminal, are connected by a concatenated link consisting of a metallic cable, an optical fiber, and another metallic cable. Within this link there need to be various modems and transducers. The modems provide the network attachment for the user devices and transducers. The transducers are used within the link to convert electrical signals to an optical format and vice versa. These modems and transducers need only serve as relay points that forward the physical data along the line. As such they require very limited intelligence.

If more intelligence is built into the relay devices, they can also use level 1, 2, or 3 protocols to verify that the incoming information stream contains valid data, and they could initiate appropriate line-conditioning actions in case of errors. This is illustrated conceptually in Fig. 2.8. These actions are not of any

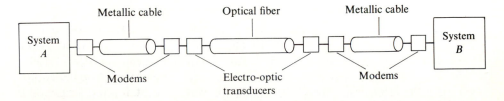

FIGURE 2.7
Example of a physical connection formed by two different media between two systems. The modems and transducers act as simple relay points.

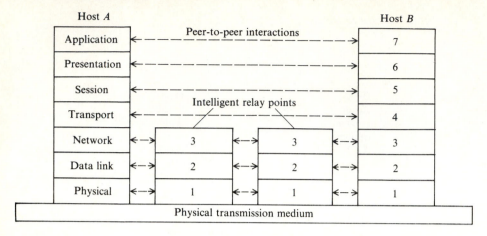

FIGURE 2.8
Schematic representation of intelligent relay points which can invoke level 1, 2, and 3 protocols.

concern to the physical layer, however, since the modem or transducer would still be viewed as a relay point within the transmission line.

Actually no existing protocol fits exactly into the OSI Model layers, but a number of classic specifications and standards deal substantially with the physical layer. We will now look at the general characteristics of some of these protocols. In the United States, the EIA recommends standards for all types of communication equipment and components. Among its activities are recommending interfaces designed for use between manufacturers and purchasers of electronic equipment. Two popular ones for interfacing DTE and DCE are RS-232C "Interface Between Data Terminal Equipment and Data Communication Equipment Employing Serial Binary Data Exchange" (Ref. 27) and RS-449 "General-Purpose 37-Position and 9-Position Interface for Data Terminal Equipment and Data Circuit-Terminating Equipment Employing Serial Binary Data Exchange" (Ref. 28).

2.3.1   EIA RS-232C

RS-232C is an older specification (released in 1969) that uses a 25-pin connector (with 3 pins unassigned and 3 pins reserved for testing). It describes the logical signals carried between the DTE and the DCE over short distances (up to 15 m) at low data rates (maximum of 20 kb/s). The specific interface circuit is a single-ended, bipolar voltage and unterminated circuit. In addition, RS-232C specifies the type of connector and the pin assignments of the logical symbols. The connector configuration is shown in Fig. 2.9. The pin numbers and their corresponding functions are listed in Table 2.2

DTE connector face
25-position plug

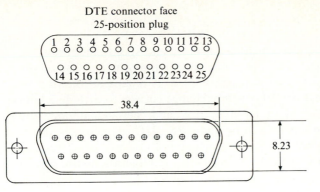

FIGURE 2.9
Connector configuration for
RS-232C signals. Dimensions
are in millimeters.

TABLE 2.2

Pin numbers for RS-232C connectors and their functions

Pin number	Circuit mnemonic	Circuit function	Circuit direction	
1	FG	Frame ground		
2	TD	Transmit data	To	DCE
3	RD	Receive data	From	DCE
4	RTS	Request to send	To	DCE
5	CTS	Clear to send	From	DCE
6	DSR	Data set ready	From	DCE
7	SG	Signal ground		
8	DCD	Data carrier detect	From	DCE
9	—	Pos./neg. DC test voltage	From	DCE
10	—	Voltage	From	DCE
11	—	Equalizer mode	From	DCE
12	SDCD	Secondary data carrier detect	From	DCE
13	SCTS	Secondary clear to send	From	DCE
14	STD	Secondary transmitted data	To	DCE
15	TC	Transmitter clock	From	DCE
16	SRD	Secondary received data	From	DCE
17	RC	Receiver clock	From	DCE
18	DCR	Divided clock, receiver	From	DCE
19	SRTS	Secondary request to send	To	DCE
20	DTR	Data terminal ready	To	DCE
21	SQ	Signal quality	From	DCE
22	RI	Ring indicator	From	DCE
23	—	Data rate selector	To	DCE
24	ETC	External transmit clock	To	DCE
25	—	Busy	To	DCE

2.3.2   EIA RS-449

The RS-449 standard is newer (issued in 1977) than RS-232C. This standard was developed to supplant RS-232C which has distance and speed limitations. As its title implies, RS-449 requires a 37-pin connector for the primary channel and a 9-pin connector for the secondary channel, if used. It retains all the functional capabilities of RS-232C, and has 10 new interchange circuits to include additional functional features such as "terminal-in-service" and "new-signal" indications. RS-449 offers greater immunity to noise than RS-232C, it increases the data signaling rate to 2 Mb/s, and it permits an increase of up to 60 m (200 ft) in the length of the interconnecting cable. The connector configurations are shown in Fig. 2.10 and the pin assignments are listed in Table 2.3.

    The major benefits of RS-449 are the increased cable distance permitted and improved diagnostic capabilities. RS-449 gives the host computer and terminal much more conrol over the modem than is permitted by RS-232C. Most of the control involves diagnostic and reliability issues in terms of checking out

DTE connector face 37-position plug

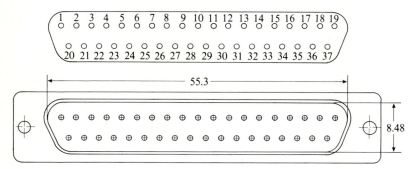

DTE connector face 9-position plug

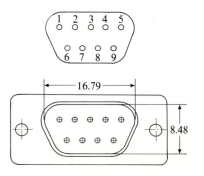

FIGURE 2.10
Connector configuration for RS-449 signals. Dimensions are given in millimeters.

TABLE 2.3
Pin numbers for RS-449 connectors and their functions

Pin numbers	Circuit mnemonic	Circuit function	Circuit direction		Circuit type	
19	SG	Signal ground			Common	
37	SC	Send common	To	DCE		
20	RC	Receive common	From	DCE		
28	IS	Terminal in service	To	DCE	Control	
15	IC	Incoming call	From	DCE		
12, 30	TR	Terminal ready	To	DCE		
11, 29	DM	Data mode	From	DCE		
4, 22	SD	Send data	To	DCE	Data	
6, 24	RD	Receive data	From	DCE		
17, 35	TT	Terminal timing	To	DCE	Timing	
5, 23	ST	Send timing	From	DCE		
8, 26	RT	Receive timing	From	DCE		Primary channel
7, 25	RS	Request to send	To	DCE	Control	
9, 27	CS	Clear to send	From	DCE		
13, 31	RR	Receiver ready	From	DCE		
33	SQ	Signal quality	From	DCE		
34	NS	New signal	To	DCE		
16	SF	Select frequency	To	DCE		
16	SR	Signaling rate selector	To	DCE		
2	SI	Signaling rate indicator	From	DCE		
10	LL	Local loopback	To	DCE	Control	
14	RL	Remote loopback	To	DCE		
18	TM	Test mode	From	DCE		
32	SS	Select standby	To	DCE	Control	
36	SB	Standby indicator	From	DCE		
1	—	Frame ground				
3, 21	—	Spare				

9-pin connector

3	SSD	Secondary send data	To	DCE	Data	
4	SRD	Secondary receive data	From	DCE		
7	SRS	Secondary request to send	To	DCE	Control	Secondary channel
8	SCS	Secondary clear to send	From	DCE		
2	SRR	Secondary receiver ready	From	DCE		
1	—	Frame ground				
5	SG	Signal ground			Common	
6	RC	Receive common	From	DCE		
9	SC	Send common	To	DCE		

29

TABLE 2.4

Equivalency table of EIA RS-232C, EIA RS-449, and CCITT Recommendation V.24. The "Circuit direction" column indicates going to or coming from the DCE

EIA RS-449		EIA RS-232C		CCITT Recommendation V.24		Circuit direction
SG	Signal ground	AB	Signal ground	102	Signal ground	
SC	Send common			102a	DTE common	To
RC	Receive common			102b	DCE common	From
IS	Terminal in service					To
IC	Incoming call	CE	Ring indicator	125	Calling indicator	From
TR	Terminal ready	CD	Data terminal ready	108/2	Data terminal ready	To
DM	Data mode	CC	Data set ready	107	Data set ready	From
SD	Send data	BA	Transmitted data	103	Transmitted data	To
RD	Receive data	BB	Received data	104	Received data	From
TT	Terminal timing	DA	Transmitter signal element timing (DTE source)	113	Transmitter signal element timing (DTE source)	To
ST	Send timing	DB	Transmitter signal element timing (DCE source)	114	Transmitter signal element timing (DCE source)	From
RT	Receive timing	DD	Receiver signal element timing	115	Receiver signal element timing (DCE source)	From
RS	Request to send	CA	Request to send	105	Request to send	To
CS	Clear to send	CB	Clear to send	106	Ready for sending	From
RR	Receiver ready	CF	Received line signal detector	109	Data channel received line signal detector	From

a channel in the modem. The drawback is that a 37- and 9-pin connector plus the connector that couples to the data jacks occupy a large space on the unit.

Unlike RS-232C, voltage levels are not specified in RS-449. The signal-level standards for RS-449 are described in EIA standards RS-422 (Balanced Voltage Digital Interface Circuits) and RS-423 (Unbalanced Voltage Digital Interface Circuits).

Table 2.4 shows a list of interchange circuits for RS-449 and the nearest equivalent circuits of RS-232C and CCITT Recommendation V.24 (described below). Also given in Table 2.4 are the circuit mnemonic and the circuit direction (that is, either going to or coming from the DCE).

	EIA RS-449		EIA RS-232C		CCITT Recommendation V.24	Circuit direction
SQ	Signal quality	CG	Signal quality detector	110	Data signal quality detector	From
NS	New signal					To
SF	Select frequency			126	Select transmit frequency	To
SR	Signaling rate selector	CH	Data signal rate selector (DTE source)	111	Data signaling rate selector (DTE source)	To
SI	Signaling rate indicator	CI	Data signal rate selector (DCE source)	112	Data signaling rate selector (DCE source)	From
SSD	Secondary send data	SBA	Secondary transmitted data	118	Transmitted backward channel data	To
SRD	Secondary receive data	SBB	Secondary received data	119	Received backward channel data	From
SRS	Secondary request to send	SCA	Secondary request to send	120	Transmit backward channel line signal	To
SCS	Secondary clear to send	SCB	Secondary clear to send	121	Backward channel ready	From
SRR	Secondary receiver ready	SCF	Secondary received line signal detector	122	Backward channel received line signal detector	From
LL	Local loopback			141	Local loopback	To
RL	Remote loopback			140	Remote loopback	To
TM	Test mode			142	Test indicator	From
SS	Select standby			116	Select standby	To
SB	Standby indicator			117	Standby indicator	From

2.3.3 CCITT X.21

Recommendation X.21 by the CCITT is often referred to as a physical-layer specification, but it actually contains elements of layers 1, 2, and 3. The obvious reason for this is that X.21 was issued in 1976, before the OSI Model was formulated.

In the X.21 approach, both user data and equipment-controlling information are multiplexed on two pairs of connectors. The physical connector has 15 pins, but not all of them are used. The names and functions of the eight wires defined by X.21 are given in Fig. 2.11. The transmit (*T*) circuit conveys data from the DTE to the DCE, while the receive (*R*) circuit transmits from the DCE

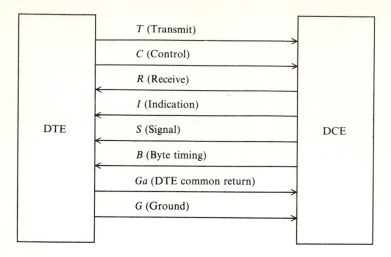

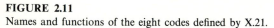

FIGURE 2.11
Names and functions of the eight codes defined by X.21.

to the DTE. In addition, ON and OFF logic levels on the control (C) circuit and on the indication (I) circuit are used in conjunction with encoded data sequences on the T and R circuits to determine the states of the DTE and the DCE. For example, the DTE signals the DCE that it wants to make a call by setting the control circuit to ON and setting the transmit circuit to the zero level. The DCE must then take the appropriate actions necessary to notify the network that a call is being initiated. Depending on the network configuration the actions may include going off-hook in a telephone, turning on a modem carrier, and completing a training sequence.

The signal (S) circuit is used by the DCE to provide timing information so that the DTE knows when each bit interval starts and stops. The B circuit is an option that may be used to group the signal bits into 8-bit frames called *bytes*. These bytes represent either data characters, control information, or synchronization information. The basic function of the B line is to provide byte timing so the DTE knows where each byte begins and ends.

2.3.4   CCITT Rec. V.24

The CCITT V.24 Recommendation is similar to the EIA RS-232C standard. This recommendation, which was first published in 1964, deals with control of the physical medium, and thus does not strictly fall within the OSI Model's definition of the physical layer. It specifies the operation of 39 circuits that may be used by a terminal to control a modem and that may be used by a modem to send indications of its status to the terminal. Its main functions and how they relate to RS-232C and RS-449 are given in Table 2.4.

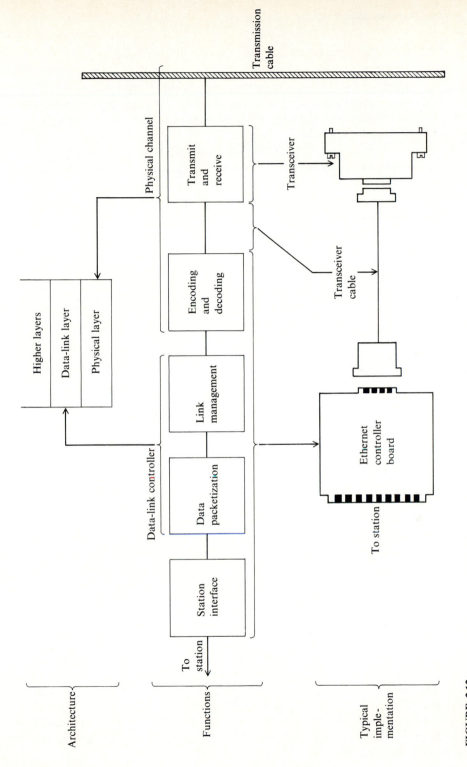

FIGURE 2.12

Architecture and general implementation of Ethernet.

33

2.3.5   Ethernet

Ethernet is a local area network specification that was developed by Digital Equipment Corporation, Intel Corporation, and Xerox Corporation.[36] LANs based on this specification are now in widespread use and are being produced by numerous manufacturers. Because of its popularity, a technical summary of Ethernet is provided in App. C.

Ethernet addresses the physical and the data-link layers. The architecture for this and a typical implementation are shown in Fig. 2.12. The primary physical-layer characters are

Data rate of 10 Mb/s

Maximum station separation of 2.5 km

Maximum of 1024 stations

Medium: shielded coaxial cable with baseband signaling

2.3.6   U.S. Military Interface Standards

Military standards are issued by the United States Department of Defense for application to military communication systems.[34] These standards are more stringent than commercial standards because of the critical missions that military systems must perform under harsh operating environments. In general, however, many equipments which adhere to EIA or CCITT standards may satisfy military requirements.

The military equivalent of RS-232C is MIL-STD-188C. Equipment made to operate under RS-232C can be made to satisfy MIL-STD-188C by use of external waveshaping components on the driver end, plus input resistance and threshold tailoring on the receiver end. An interface circuit diagram for this standard is shown in Fig. 2.13.

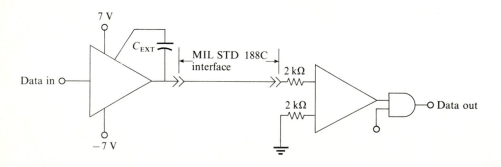

FIGURE 2.13
MIL-STD-188C interface circuit.

2.4   THE DATA-LINK LAYER

The basic purpose of the data-link layer is to establish, maintain, and release data-link connections among network nodes.[37] As shown in Fig. 2.7, a data-link connection between the nodes can consist of one or more physical lines including wire cable, optical fiber cable, microwave links, radio links, or satellite channels.

The devices located at the communicating nodes could be terminals, computers, switching equipment, or any other device which falls under the generic identification of data-communication equipment. The information exchanged between the nodes could be of any form including link-control signals or user data for functions such as inquiry-response, batch processing, time sharing, job entry, or other similar applications.

2.4.1   Basic Link Protocols

The basic structure of a link-control protocol is derived from the nature of the transmission medium being used. As we will see in Chap. 3, any transmission medium can only support a finite data rate, the signals travel over a communication channel at a finite speed, and various types of electrical interference can introduce errors into the transmitted information. Since the integrity of the information being transferred is of paramount importance, the data-link protocol must account for these limitations, plus the finite data-processing speed of the devices connected to the network. In addition to being able to accommodate the characteristics of the transmission medium, the data-link protocol must take into account the application and nature of the information, that is, the user requirements.

These requirements are accomplished through the following set of functions[37] which are common to all data-link protocols:

1. *Initialization.* This function establishes an active connection over an already existing transmission path. How to set up the path and how to move bits over it do not concern the data-link protocol since that is the responsibility of the physical layer processes. To initialize a link, service requests and indications (see Sec. 2.1.2) are exchanged to establish readiness to receive and transmit between two identified parties.

2. *An information segmenting mechanism.* The segmenting mechanism breaks up long streams of data and delimits the beginning and end of the information. This is necessary since extremely long messages are not likely to be transmitted without error through an electrically noisy environment. The data-link layer subdivides the bit stream into structured segments of information called *blocks* or *frames.* As their names imply, blocks or frames consist of data and control bits which are surrounded (that is, the bit group is delimited or "framed") either by reserved bit patterns (an example being 01111110) or reserved character sequences (special bit patterns which are used to define a

particular character or symbol). This segmenting mechanism allows the selection of a block length which is most likely to survive transmission, thereby keeping retransmission of garbled messages to a minimum.

3. *Error checking.* Since errors inevitably occur during transmission, the data-link protocol must have the ability to detect and correct errors to maintain a high degree of information integrity.

4. *Data synchronization.* For the receiver to correctly decode the information that has arrived, a technique for acquiring and maintaining synchronization between the transmitter and receiver is essential. In contrast to the physical layer—which is only responsible for transmitting a raw bit stream without being worried about its meaning or structure, that is, which only deals with bit synchronizing—the data-link layer must align the *character*-decoding mechanism of the receiver with the character-encoding mechanism of the transmitter.

5. *Flow control.* This is a technique for ensuring that a sender does not overwhelm a receiver with data. Flow control functions allow a receiver to regulate the incoming data to an input rate which does not exceed the receiver's capacity to accept and process the data. At the data-link level, flow control is limited to the ability to accept or not to accept information transfers. No overload notification is sent to the transmitter.

6. *Abnormal condition recovery.* This function allows for the detection and recovery from abnormal conditions such as loss of response or cessation of information flow.

7. *Termination.* The termination process consists of those functions associated with relinquishing control of the link following the transfer of the user's information. Link termination does not necessarily mean that the physical path is disconnected (switched off).

2.4.2 Character-Oriented and Bit-Oriented Protocols

Data-link protocols are among the earliest of recognized communication protocols. The evolution of these types has led to two major classes of modern data-link protocols. These are known as *character-oriented protocols* and *bit-oriented protocols.*

Character-oriented data-link control protocols[38] use a defined subset of character structures from a given code set to convey the information necessary to properly format the data and to supervise its interchange across a transmission link. A number of different character code structures have been developed. The codes differ primarily in the number of bits used to represent characters and in the particular bit pattern that corresponds to the characters. Three types of characters are defined. These are *graphic characters* which represent symbols, *control characters* which are used to control a terminal, and *communication characters* which control computer functions such as synchronization and message handling.

Among the numerous presently used character-oriented codes is the 7-bit-plus-parity *American Standard Code for Information Interchange* (ASCII) code shown in Table 2.5. ASCII was introduced by the U.S.A. Standards Institute and has been accepted as the U.S. federal standard. Within any one character the bits are identified as $b_7, b_6, \ldots, b_2, b_1$, where b_7 is the highest order or *most significant bit* and b_1 is the lowest order or *least significant bit*. Any particular entry in Table 2.5 may be identified either by its bit pattern or by its column and row numbers.

Parity checking is an error-detection technique which adds an eighth bit in the most significant bit location. This bit is determined by counting the number of ones in each character. With *odd parity*, if the number of ones in the character is even, then the parity bit is made a 1 to make the number odd. Otherwise the parity bit is a zero. With *even parity*, if the number of ones in the character is odd, then the parity bit is made a 1 to make that number even. Parity checking is done at the receiver which counts the number of ones. For example, if an even

TABLE 2.5

The seven-bit-plus-parity American Standard Code for Information Interchange (ASCII)

Bits $b_4b_3b_2b_1$	Row	Bits $b_7b_6b_3$ 000	001	010	011	100	101	110	111
		Column							
		0	1	2	3	4	5	6	7
0000	0	NUL	DLE	SP	0	@	P	`	p
0001	1··	SOH	DC1	!	1	A	Q	a	q
0010	2	STX	DC2	"	2	B	R	b	r
0011	3	ETX	DC3	#	3	C	S	c	s
0100	4	EOT	DC4	$	4	D	T	d	t
0101	5	ENQ	NAK	%	5	E	U	e	u
0110	6	ACK	SYN	&	6	F	V	f	v
0111	7	BEL	ETB	'	7	G	W	g	w
1000	8	BS	CAN	(	8	H	X	h	x
1001	9	HT	EM	)	9	I	Y	i	y
1010	10	LF	SUB	*	:	J	Z	j	z
1011	11	VT	ESC	+	;	K	[	k	{
1100	12	FF	FS	,	<	L	\	l		
1101	13	CR	GS	—	=	M	]	m	}
1110	14	SO	RS	.	>	N	^	n	~
1111	15	SI	US	/	?	O	—	o	DEL

number of bits shows up in a character when the system is set for odd parity, then an error has occurred.

Another widely used character-oriented code is the *Extended Binary-Coded Decimal Interchange Code* (EBCDIC). This is an eight-level code which is similar to ASCII. The EBCDIC is shown in Table 2.6.

Even though character-oriented protocols have been extensively and successfully used in many applications, they have a number of shortcomings which make them unsuited for modern interactive applications. Thus a whole new family of bit-oriented data-link control procedures[39] was developed in the 1970 time frame. In general bit-oriented protocols are not dependent on control characters, as is the case with character-oriented protocols, but instead rely on the position of bits within specific fields or blocks of bits.

Numerous bit-oriented protocols exist and are known under a variety of names and mnemonics. Two standard ones are the *Advanced Data Communication Control Procedure* (ADCCP)[40] of the American National Standards Institute (ANSI) and the *High-Level Data-Link Control* (HDLC) of the International Standards Organization.[41] Major equipment vendors may also have their own versions, such as the *Synchronous Data-Link Control* (SDLC) of IBM.[42,43] A comparison of these three protocols has been made by Easton[44] to which the interested reader is referred.

Example 2.2. An example of an HDLC bit-oriented frame structure is given in Fig. 2.14. Each frame contains the following six fields:

Address field. Here the source and the destination (sender and receiver) are identified. There are two mutually exclusive address-field options. These are single-octet ($N = 1$) and multiple-octet ($N = 2, 3, \ldots$) addressing. Single-octet addressing allows up to 256 different addresses. Multiple-octet addressing is used if more than 256 addresses are needed.

Control field. This field identifies the function and purpose of the frame. Depending on the protocol this field is either 8 or 16 bits long.

Information field. This field contains the user data to be transmitted, or alternatively, it can be empty. The field could be arbitrarily long, but is usually limited in length since the efficiency of the error-control algorithm (which is used in conjunction with the frame-check field) decreases as the frame length increases. Frames with empty information fields are transmitted continuously on idle point-to-point lines in order to keep the connection alive.

Frame-check-sequence (FCS) field. The 16 bits in this field are used to check the validity of the bits in the frame, that is, it detects if errors have occurred in the transmission and receipt of the bits in the frame. The code used is the 16-bit *cyclic redundancy check* (CRC). The CRC field is a function of the contents of the address, control, and data fields. It is generated by the sender and again by the receiver. If the result generated at the receiver differs from that in the received FCS field, a transmission error has occurred.

Flag. Each frame starts and ends with the special eight-bit sequence 01111110 which is referred to as a *flag*. Since this particular bit sequence could

TABLE 2.6
Table of extended binary-coded decimal interchange code (EBCDIC)

High $B_7B_6B_5B_4$ (Row) \ Low $B_3B_2B_1B_0$ (Column)	0000	0001	0010	0011	0100	0101	0110	0111	1000	1001	1010	1011	1100	1101	1110	1111
	0	1	2	3	4	5	6	7	8	9	A	B	C	D	E	F
0000 / 0	NUL	SOH	STX	ETX	PF	HT	LC	DEL		RLF	SMM	VT	FF	CR	SC	SI
0001 / 1	DLE	DC1	DC2	DC3	RES	NL	BS	IL	CAN	EM	CC		ITS	IGS	IRS	IUS
0010 / 2	DS	SOS	FS		BYP	LF	EOB/ETB	ESC/PRE			3M		DC4	ENR	ACK	BEL
0011 / 3			SYN		PN	RS	UC	EOT						NAK		SUB
0100 / 4	SP										¢	.	<	(	+	|
0101 / 5	&										!	$	*	)	;	¬
0110 / 6	–	/									|	,	%	_	>	?
0111 / 7											:	#	@	'	=	"
1000 / 8		a	b	c	d	e	f	g	h	i						
1001 / 9		j	k	l	m	n	o	p	q	r						
1010 / A		~	s	t	u	v	w	x	y	z						
1011 / B																
1100 / C	{	A	B	C	D	E	F	G	H	I						
1101 / D	}	J	K	L	M	N	O	P	Q	R						
1110 / E	\		S	T	U	V	W	X	Y	Z						
1111 / F	0	1	2	3	4	5	6	7	8	9						

← Frame →

F	*A*	*C*	*I*	*FCS*	*F*
Opening flag 8 bits (01111110)	Address field 8 × *N* bits (*N* = 1 to *K*)	Control field 8 or 16 bits	Information field Variable	Frame check field 16 or 32 bits	Closing flag 8 bits (01111110)

FIGURE 2.14
Example of an HDLC bit-oriented frame structure.

accidentally occur in the data in the information field, special care must be taken when formatting the frame to avoid confusion at the receiving end. For HDLC this is done by *bit stuffing* which is described in Prob. 2.4.

There are three kinds of HDLC frames, each of which has a different control-field format.

Information frames contain the data to be transmitted

Supervisory frames are used for basic link-control functions such as acknowledging or rejecting frames

Unnumbered frames provide supplemental link-control functions such as initializing a station, disconnecting a station, or rejecting a command

2.4.3 LAN Access Protocols

So far we have seen how the data-link layer protocols control the transmission of information over a link. This includes functions such as connection, initialization, data formatting, address recognition, error control, flow control, and connection termination. Within the data-link layer, the IEEE 802 family groups these functions into a sublayer called the *logical link control* (LLC) layer. (See Sec. 2.11)

There is one additional function that must be performed by the data-link layer for networks having many stations that wish to use the network. This function encompasses the management of access to a network. It is treated as a separate sublayer in the IEEE 802 family which is known as the *medium-access control* (MAC) layer. This control is necessary since there is a common medium which is shared by many stations. Without this control several stations could be transmitting simultaneously which, of course, would produce garbled messages.

The various media-access control protocols can be grouped in the following five categories:[45]

1. *Fixed assignment techniques.* These techniques allocate the channel bandwidth
   to the users in a static (fixed) fashion which is independent of their activity.
   Common schemes are time division multiple access (TDMA) and frequency
   division multiple access (FDMA).
2. *Random access techniques.* Here the entire bandwidth is provided to the users
   as a single channel to be accessed randomly. Since collisions of messages from
   two simultaneously transmitting stations can occur in this scheme, a methodology for sensing the activity on the line prior to transmission is often used.
   An example is *carrier sense multiple access (CSMA)* and variations thereof.
3. *Centrally controlled demand-assignment techniques.* The above two techniques
   represent the two extremes in the allocation of the bandwidth spectrum as far
   as the user having control over access right is concerned. At one extreme we
   have the fixed assignment technique which controls the user most rigidly,
   does not adapt dynamically to varying user demand, and can waste network
   capacity if small delays are required. The other extreme is random access
   which involves no control, is simple to implement, is adaptive to varying
   demand, but which can waste capacity when messages from simultaneously
   transmitting users collide. Demand assignment techniques fall in between
   these extremes. In centrally controlled methods an explicit need for transmitting information must be expressed by a user before any channel space is
   allocated for that information. Channel allocation procedures can be done
   either through polling methods where a central controller asks the terminals
   if they have messages to send, or by reservation techniques where the requests
   for channel space are initiated by the user. In either case, a central controller
   allocates channel space or channel time to a user.
4. *Demand assignment with distributed control.* Distributed-control methods are
   advantageous since they have higher reliability and better performance than
   central-control techniques. The higher reliability results from the fact that
   with distributed systems the control functions are not contained within a
   single unit but instead are dispersed among several physical elements. These
   can be either colocated or geographically separated. Distributed control
   yields better performance because direct access to a computer can be provided to small user communities. For example, distributed control can reduce
   the turnaround time in a batch-processing environment or it can provide
   faster response times in a real-time environment.

An important basic factor in all distributed-control algorithms is the need to
either implicitly or explicitly exchange control information among users. With
this control information as a basis, all users can then independently execute the
same algorithm so that there is some coordination in their actions.

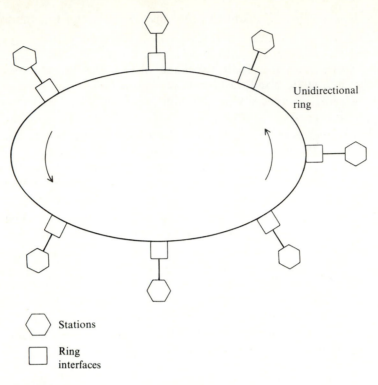

Unidirectional
ring

○ Stations

□ Ring
   interfaces

FIGURE 2.15
In the token passing scheme in a ring topology one station transmits while the others listen.

Example 2.3. As an example of distributed control in a local area network, let us consider the ring topology shown in Fig. 2.15. Here messages and the right to access (i.e., to control) the network are passed from node to node along unidirectional links, until they return to the originating node. The access right could be in the form of a specially formatted 8-bit pattern called a *control token* which is passed sequentially around the ring and universally recognized by each node. When a node which has a message to send receives the control token, it can remove this control token from the ring, send the message, and then pass the control token on to the next node.

5. *Other Techniques.* In certain situations it may be advantageous to have an access strategy that changes its nature according to the traffic demand placed on the network. That is, the access mode should adapt itself to the varying need of the network. As an example, one might have a network that uses a CSMA technique at low traffic loads, but which switches to a token-passing scheme when frequent message collisions occur due to an increased user demand. Discussions of the many adaptive strategies that have been examined can be found in the literature.[45-47]

2.5   THE NETWORK LAYER

The basic function of the network layer is to provide an end-to-end communications capability to the transport layer which lies above it.[48] The OSI Reference Model specifies that this communications capability should relieve the transport layer of the need to know anything about the operational characteristics of the specific transmission facility that underlies it.[49]

The network layer protocols are concerned with the exchange of packets of information between transport layer entities. A *packet* is a group of bits that includes data bits plus source and destination addresses.[50] If a station has a message to send, it can either transmit the complete message as a packet or, as is often the case, if the message is very long it is divided into smaller units which are then transmitted individually as packets. The two techniques for sending these packets from node to node are called *virtual circuit* and *datagram* methods. These are also known as *connection-oriented* and *connectionless network-layer services*, respectively.

2.5.1   Virtual Circuit

The name *virtual circuit* comes from its analogy to a telephone circuit. A route, which consists of a *logical* connection, is first established between two users. During this establishment phase, the two users not only agree to set up a connection between them but also decide upon the quality of service that is to be associated with the connection. For the duration of the connection, sequences of packetized information are transmitted bidirectionally between the two connected nodes. In this process, the information is delivered to the receiver in the same order as transmitted by the sender.

During the data-transfer phase, a virtual circuit facility also has the option of providing other services such as error control and flow control. The error-control service ensures both that the packets are received in the correct sequence and that all packets arrive correctly. If a packet in a certain sequence fails to reach a node or if it arrives incorrectly, the receiving station can request a retransmission of that packet from the transmitting node. The flow-control service may be used to prevent a slow receiver from being overwhelmed with data from a faster transmitter. At the network level if a receiving station finds that it is about to run out of buffer space for incoming messages, it can request the transmitting station to stop sending the messages until further notice. This is in contrast to the data-link layer where flow control is limited to the ability to either accept or not accept the incoming information.

When the stations wish to close down the virtual circuit, one station can terminate the connection with a clear-request packet. The virtual circuit then ceases to exist. It is important to note that the connection that was established is not a dedicated path between stations. The path is generally shared by many other virtual connections, so that packets are usually buffered at intermediate nodes and queued for output over a line which forms part of the virtual circuit.

Even though there may be many different path configurations to choose from when setting up a virtual circuit, once the route has been established for a particular connection the packets will always follow this particular route for the duration of the virtual-circuit setup.

2.5.2 The X.25 Specification

The best-known virtual-circuit protocol is contained in the ISO and CCITT X.25 specification.[51-54] This specification actually covers the lower three levels of the OSI Reference Model. For level 1, X.25 specifies level 1 of X.21. Level 2 of X.25 defines error-control and flow-control functions for the access link between the DTE and the network.

For level 3, X.25 defines the packet formats and control procedures for exchanging information between a DTE and the network. The procedure for establishing a virtual circuit is shown in Fig. 2.16. First a calling DTE sends out

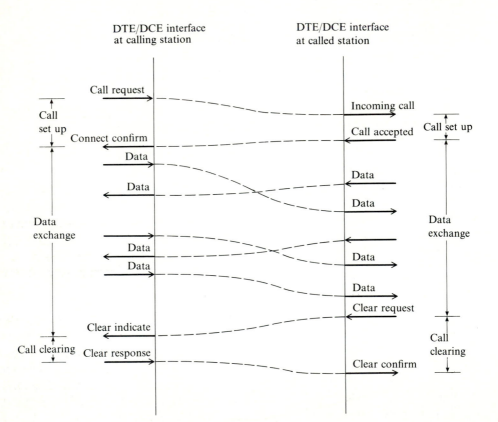

FIGURE 2.16
Time-sequence diagram showing call-establishment, data-transfer, and call-clear phases of a virtual circuit.

a *call-request* packet. Upon arriving at its destination this packet notifies the called DTE that a circuit is being established. If the called DTE wishes to accept the call, it answers by returning a *call-accepted* packet. When the calling DTE receives this packet, the virtual circuit is established. Data packets can then be exchanged between the two DTEs. When the call is completed, the virtual circuit can be disconnected by either side sending a *clear-request* packet to the other side, which then returns a *clear-confirmation* packet as an acknowledgment.

Example 2.4. An example of this is shown in Fig. 2.17. Here we show a network consisting of eight nodes (nodes 1 through 8) where each node can have one or more stations connected to it. These are shown as stations $A, B, \ldots, K$. If two stations, such as stations B and G, wish to communicate, there are a variety of logical paths that the information packets can follow. A particular path is set up as follows: station B first sends a call request packet to node 1 for a connection to station G. Node 1 may then decide to route the request packet to node 4. Node 4 in turn may decide to route the call-request packet to node 5 which then delivers the packet to station G. If station G wishes to accept the call, it sends a call-accepted packet back through nodes 4 and 1 to station B. This establishes the virtual circuit so that stations B and G can now exchange information over the logical connection.

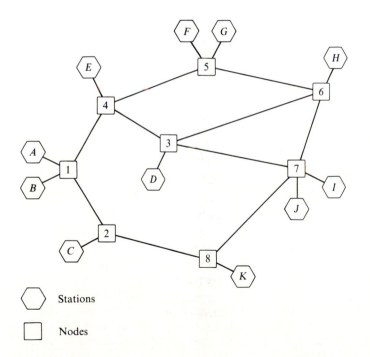

    Stations

☐   Nodes

FIGURE 2.17
Example of an eight-node network with one or more stations connected to each node.

Since other stations can use parts of this same path for their own virtual circuit at the same time, information packets may be buffered and queued for output at any one of the nodes in the path from station *B* to station *G*. Also note that at any time each station can have one or more virtual circuit connections to another station, *and* it can have virtual circuit connections to several stations.

2.5.3   Datagrams

A *datagram* is a self-contained message unit which contains sufficient information to allow it to be routed from source DTE to destination DTE without dependence on previous message interchanges between the source and destination. Thus, in the datagram method each packet is treated independently. The network layer simply accepts messages from the transport layer and sends out each one as an isolated unit.

In contrast to the virtual-circuit method where there is an explicit path setup procedure, followed by a packet transfer phase, and then an explicit circuit shutdown procedure, sequentially transmitted datagrams can follow completely different paths. Thus it is possible that the packets will arrive at the destination in a different sequence from the one in which they were sent. As noted by Tanenbaum,[55] the datagram method is analogous to the postal system. Here each letter is a totally independent message unit which contains a complete destination address. If several different letters are mailed sequentially from the same place to a specific address, each letter can follow a different route from source to destination and they do not necessarily arrive in the same order as they were mailed.

In addition to describing virtual-circuit protocols, the X.25 specification also addresses datagram services. Detailed discussions of these services can be found in the literature.[48,54–57] These references also describe the interaction between two different networks, one of which uses datagrams and the other of which uses a virtual-circuit method.

2.6   THE TRANSPORT LAYER

The first three layers of the OSI Reference Model are concerned with data transmission, framing, and routing functions between machines. In contrast, layer 4, the transport layer, is responsible for providing reliable end-to-end transport services between user processes rather than just between equipment. The transport layer is the first level in the OSI Model that offers a choice between alternative protocols. Users must therefore evaluate the alternatives and choose the protocol which is best suited for their particular local area network application.

The objective of the transport layer is to provide all the functions and protocols needed to satisfy a quality of service requested by the session layer. The quality of service is expressed in terms of parameters such as throughput, transit delay, residual error rate, delay time to establish a connection, cost, security, and priority. For example, if the session layer requests a throughput (the amount of useful information processed or communicated during a specified time period) which is higher than the network access rate, the transport layer would need to establish several network connections and provide a protocol for line-sharing. On the other hand, if the requested throughput is much less than the data-handling capacity of the network line, a protocol for multiplexing several user connections would be needed. In providing these services, the transport layer must know the quality and limitations of the network connection offered by the underlying network layer.

Two widely used transport protocols are the Internet Transport Protocol (ITP) of the Xerox Network Systems[16] and the Internet Protocol/Transmission Control Protocol (IP/TCP) of the Department of Defense.[17-20] Each of these protocols has certain advantages and limitations. The ITP was mainly developed to be used on an Ethernet channel. The following five protocol options exist at the transport layer:[21]

1. The *routing information protocol* updates each node with information needed to allow communications with other nodes on the network.
2. The *error protocol* reports errors in a consistent, predefined manner. When an error is detected, a standard error message is sent to the information source.
3. The *echo protocol* basically asks, "Are you there?" It automatically echoes packets back, thereby allowing the network to verify that the other nodes are operating correctly. This feature is also useful for performing network diagnostics.
4. The *packet-exchange protocol* is used for simple request/reply transactions.
5. The *sequenced-packet protocol* allows users to send many sequenced packets before requesting a response. This is especially useful for reliable high-speed data transfer, such as large files of information.

The IP/TCP protocols were developed by the Defense Advanced Research Projects Agency (DARPA) to connect agency contractors.[20,22] The network is known as Arpanet and interconnects locations ranging from Hawaii to Europe. Arpanet was designed to provide reliable host-to-host communication over potentially noisy, low-quality transmission lines. The level 3 and level 4 protocols of Arpanet are the Internet Protocol (IP) and the Transmission Control Protocol (TCP), respectively. The IP addresses, routes, and delivers packets to the destination network and host. The responsibility of TCP is to assemble packets for transmission and to properly order and reassemble them upon receipt.

TCP is a rather complicated protocol, since it has to deal with lossy subnets. The protocol operates by accepting arbitrarily long messages from user processes, divides them into pieces not exceeding 65K bytes, and sends each piece as a separate datagram. Since there is no guarantee that the network layer will deliver the datagrams in order or at all, it is the task of the TCP to reassemble the pieces in the proper sequence and to request retransmissions as appropriate. In addition to providing a reliable, flow-controlled delivery of data, TCP

also provides commands for initiating a connection, accepting an incoming connection, sending and receiving data, and closing a connection. To ensure reliability, check-summing is required on every packet that is sent and received.

2.7   THE SESSION LAYER

The session layer deals with the logical functions that perform orderly data-
exchange interactions.[23,24] Its basic task is to take the bare transport-level service, which merely moves raw data bits from one machine to another, and add
user-oriented services to it. The session-layer functions include as a minimum a
means for two presentation entities to establish, use, and terminate a connection
which is called a *session*. The session layer may also provide the following additional functions:

Communications dialogue structuring. Here the session layer may determine
whose turn it is to transmit, for how long a user can have the line, and whether
the dialogue type is two-way simultaneous (full duplex), two-way alternate (half-
duplex), or one way (simplex).

Establishing major and minor data-synchronization checkpoints. The purpose
of the checkpoint mechanism is that if an error occurs between checkpoints, the
session service can retransmit all data since the last validly confirmed checkpoint. These checkpoints consist of synchronization marks that are placed in the
data flow. Each mark has an associated serial number which is unique within a
given session connection. There are both major and minor synchronization
marks (checkpoints):

> *Major marks* allow the session-service user to clearly delineate the
> dialogue before and after the mark. The major mark is closely related to
> resynchronization. For example, after it is confirmed by the receiver, the
> major mark prevents any backward penetration of the dialogue; that is,
> the session-service user is not permitted to synchronize to a point earlier
> than the last confirmed major checkpoint.

> *Minor marks* permit the session-service user to place checkpoints in
> the data flow and optionally acknowledge them without being restricted to
> the same clear delineation in the data flow as imposed by major marks.

Resynchronization. The resynchronization function, in conjunction with the
checkpoints, allows the session layer to make higher layers unaware of recovery
from errors or failures that might occur at the transport layer. Whenever a
transport layer connection is broken, the session layer can automatically set up
a new connection, resynchronize both ends of the connection, and then resume
transmission from the last major confirmed checkpoint.

Activity management. The activity-management function allows the session-
service user to break the dialogue into discrete activities. Each activity can be
regarded as a distinct data transfer. The activity-management function also provides a means to allow the session-service user to identify a particular activity,

transfer data, interrupt the activity, and then later on resume the activity on the same or even a different session connection.

Address mapping. Messages arriving at a host typically indicate their origin by giving a machine number and a process number, but not the identity of the actual person sending the message. The address-mapping function provides a way for remote (human) users to identify themselves.

The fundamental session-layer capability is called the *kernel*. The session-layer protocol standards identify a session kernel and three session subsets. The kernel provides the fundamental connect, data-transfer, and disconnect capabilities. The lowest-level subset is called the *basic combined subset* (BCS) which allows full-duplex and half-duplex operation. It also supports optionally expedited data, exception reporting, and negotiated release.

The next subset is the *basic synchronized subset* (BSS), which provides dialogue synchronization and checkpointing. This subset is intended for applications such as reliable file transfer.

The most highly structured set is the *basic activity subset* (BAS), which supports multiple activity subsets. Activity subsets are independent functions that can be operated over the same session connection. In doing this, an activity can be suspended, another begun, and then suspended, after which the first activity can be resumed.

2.8 THE PRESENTATION LAYER

The function of the presentation layer is to give the user a variety of services which may be very useful to a particular mode of data transfer, but which are not always essential for correct operation of the network. Examples of these services are data encryption, text compression, terminal handling, and file transfer. Encryption is a technique whereby data is transformed into a nonintelligible format at the sending end to protect the network resources against unauthorized disclosure, modification, utilization, or destruction. Text compression is a methodology for reducing the total number of bits that must be transmitted to conserve communication bandwidth, which is an expensive resource in most cases. Terminal handling deals with the incompatibilities between different kinds of terminals. A terminal-handling protocol converts the specific characteristics of a user's terminal to a generic model that is used by the application programs in a remote computer.

For application programs and terminal-handling programs to understand the information transferred by computers with different data representations, a common syntax must be used. This syntax represents information such as character codes, alphanumerics, data types, and file formats. The presentation-layer protocol determines what syntax will be used when applications in two different machines exchange information.

Three kinds of syntaxes are needed to exchange information in such a way that it has the same meaning to different end systems and applications. These are the presentation context, an abstract syntax, and a concrete-transfer syntax. The *presentation context* is the category of syntax or data known by names such as ASCII (ANSI) or Alphabet 5 (CCITT).

The *abstract syntax* describes data in an understandable way (e.g., ASCII codes, integers, or floating-point numbers), but it does not say how the data will be encoded for transfer or storage. Typical examples of abstract syntax are "2.3E8" and "Integer 17," which are usually specified in the application layer.

The *concrete-transfer syntax* is bit-level encoding that is used for transferring information. Examples are an ASCII or EBCDIC character string, or a hexidecimal octet string.

To perform its function, the presentation protocol software selects different presentation contexts from its library of contexts. Applications using the selected contexts pass information to the presentation layer in abstract-syntax form. Depending on which two end systems are communicating, the presentation layers in those two systems then negotiate a common concrete-transfer syntax and translate the abstract syntax into it. The presentation protocol can switch from one syntax to another, add syntaxes, or delete them from the set of active syntaxes. However, once the presentation entities of the two end systems agree on a concrete-transfer syntax, they operate with it throughout the information exchange session.

2.9   THE APPLICATION LAYER

The seventh layer contains the applications protocols with which the user gains access to the network. The choice of which specific protocols and their associated functions are to be used at the application level is up to the individual user. Thus the boundary between the presentation layer and the application layer represents a separation of the protocols imposed by the network designers from those being selected and implemented by the network users.

To see how the application layer supports communications, let us first look at some definitions. An *application* is a set of information-processing requirements desired by a user. Examples of applications are airline reservations, credit checking, and inventory control. An *application process* is a logical element within a system that carries out the information processing required for a specific application. If an application is distributed among a number of different system elements, then each distributed portion of the application is an application process.

For two application processes to exchange meaningful information, they must agree on the semantics of all aspects concerning the intended exchange of information. This concept is illustrated in Fig. 2.18. Here the circle on the left encompasses the semantics (or meaning) of all functions relevant to application process 1, and the circle on the right represents the semantics of all functions relevant to application process 2. The shaded area where the two circles intersect represents the semantics of the functions common to both application pro-

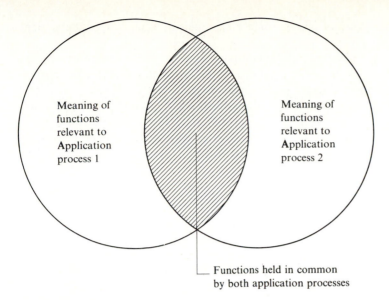

Functions held in common
by both application processes

FIGURE 2.18
The circles represent two application processes. The hatched area represents commonly held functions, which are necessary for meaningful information exchange.

cesses. It is here that the two application processes must agree on the meaning of the information exchange procedures between them.

As an example, application process 1 might refer to all the functions being performed by a travel agency, application process 2 could be concerned with all the operations functions carried out by an airline, and the overlap can represent an airline reservation application, which is common to both processes.

The application-layer protocols are responsible for transferring information between application processes. Some of the tasks of these protocols are as follows:

Allow users to access the network resources and associate them with the right application

Transfer files, messages, and documents electronically

Ensure that users transmit functions such as carriage returns, line feeds, tabs, and subscripts in a commonly understood (among the users) format

Standardize database and operating-system command languages

The application layer contains two types of protocols: the *common application service elements* (CASEs) and the *specific application service elements* (SASEs). Common application service elements provide a general framework and toolkit of service elements for common use by the various specific application protocols. Basically they provide the capabilities required by an application process for information transfer independent of the nature of the application.

User log-in and checking of passwords are examples of application-independent functions.

More general CASE functions encompass what is called *association control*. This is intended primarily for use in distributed enterprises where equipment and applications may communicate autonomously. Here association-control functions would ensure that the communications between two application processes refer to the same information exchange. For example, an airline-reservations application and its communicating counterpart must agree that they are dealing with information relevant to airline reservations (rather than other possible functions such as credit checking or inventory) and they must interpret the exchanged information in that context. Furthermore, association-control protocols must be able to switch from one context to another, such as from airline reservation to credit checking, and they must be able to transfer information in either context.

Specific application service elements (SASEs) provide information-transfer capabilities (e.g., file transfer, database access, and job transfer) or capabilities needed by a particular application process (e.g., banking, order entry, or hotel reservation). Each application-layer entity may consist of service elements from both CASE and SASE categories.

2.10 INFORMATION FLOW THROUGH A NETWORK

Let us now examine how information flows through a network from a data source to a data destination. A typical flow through a layered network is illustrated in Fig. 2.19. Although both ends of the link could be sending and receiving information simultaneously, here we show only a simple one-way flow for illustrative purposes. We will assume further that a logical link has already been created between the data source and destination. This means that the destination has sent a *receive-request* packet to the source and is now waiting for data.

Figure 2.19 shows that as messages from the information source pass down through the hierarchy of layers, each layer adds header information and, where applicable, trailer information to the message. The protocol header contains control and address information for the corresponding peer layer in the destination node. At each layer the message that was received from the higher layer, plus the overhead information (header and trailer) that is added, becomes the data field for the next layer below.

At intermediate nodes the message block that is received on the physical channel is passed up to the data-link layer at that node. The data-link layer uses the cyclic-redundancy-check information (see Sec. 3.6) contained in the data-link trailer to determine if bit errors occurred in the transmission, and it examines the message number contained in the header to see that the data packets arrived in the proper sequence. If errors occurred, a correction procedure will be used by the data-link protocol to receive the correct data packet. If there were no errors, the header and the trailer are removed from the message block and the

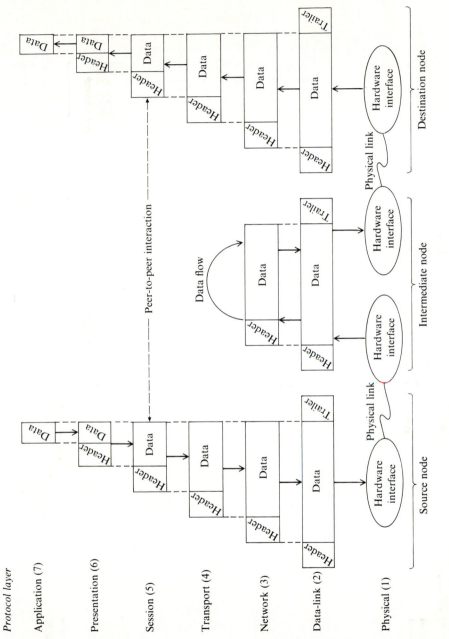

FIGURE 2.19
Flow of information through a typical layered network. The flow is shown by the arrows. The message plus overhead information at each layer becomes the data field for the next lower layer.

53

remainder is passed up to the network layer. There the destination address in the network-layer header is checked to see if this is the destination node. If it is not, the network layer selects its next outgoing channel from its routing table and passes the message back down to the data-link layer. The data-link protocol again adds the appropriate header and trailer information and passes the message block to the physical layer for transmission on the link.

This process will continue until the message finally arrives at the destination node. At the destination node, the various headers and trailers are stripped off of the originating data block which is then interpreted by the destination process according to whatever higher-level protocol is being used.

We should reemphasize here that not all networks contain every layer shown in Fig. 2.19. Individual manufacturers (and even individual products of the same manufacturer) may use different approaches to setting up their particular network architecture. Therefore the reader should consult the literature of the particular network product of interest for details on the specific functions available and their implementation characteristics.[13,58]

2.11   IEEE 802 STANDARDS FOR LANs

A family of standards[32,33,59] for LANs was developed by the IEEE to enable equipment of a variety of manufacturers to interface. This family is called the IEEE 802 Standard family. The standards are in the form of a three-layer communications architecture which functionally encompasses the physical and data-link layers defined by the OSI Reference Model, as is shown in Fig. 2.20. The 802 standards define three types of media-access technologies and the associated physical media, which can be used for a wide range of particular applications or system objectives. The component parts of the IEEE-802 standard are as follows:

802.1   Overview, Internetworking, and Systems Management
802.2   Logical link control
802.3   CSMA/CD bus
802.4   Token bus
802.5   Token ring
802.6   Metropolitan area networks (MANs)
802.7   Advisory group for broadband transmission
802.8   Advisory group for fiber optics
802.9   Integrated voice and data LANs

A comparison of the 802 Standards to the OSI Model is shown in Fig. 2.20.

IEEE Standard 802.1 describes the relationship between the various 802 standards, and their relationship with the OSI Model and higher-level protocols. In addition, this document addresses internetworking and network management issues. Standard 802.2 discusses the logical link control protocol which is common to standards 802.3 through 802.6.

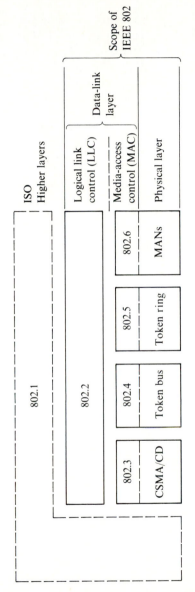

FIGURE 2.20

IEEE family of protocols:

IEEE 802.1 Relationship of 802.X standards to ISO reference model, higher-layer protocols, inter-networking, and management and control

IEEE 802.2 Logical link control protocol standard

IEEE 802.3 CSMA/CD bus access method

IEEE 802.4 Token passing bus access method

IEEE 802.5 Token passing ring access method

IEEE 802.6 Metropolitan area network (MAN) access method

As is noted in Fig. 2.20, the physical layer in the IEEE local area network standard encompasses basically the same features for transmitting and receiving data as does the OSI Model. The difference is that the media-access layer in the IEEE 802 standard includes certain media-access protocol features that are part of the physical layer in the OSI Model.

The IEEE 802 data-link layer is divided into two sublayers for local area networks. These are the *logical link control* (LLC) and the *medium-access control* (MAC). Together they perform the duties of the data-link layer, namely frame exchange between peer data-link layer entities. Frame exchange encompasses frame delimiting, frame transmission, address recognition, error checking, association with a data-link user, and, if desired, link-flow control and assurance of message delivery without loss, duplication, or misordering. The MAC layer is responsible for using either a random or a token (deterministic) procedure for controlling access to the channel (see the discussion on IEEE Standards 802.3 through 802.5 in Sec. 6.4). In addition to the basic access procedures, the MAC layer also handles the frame-delimiting, address-recognition, and error-checking functions.

The LLC layer is above the MAC layer. The LLC layer provides two types of user services: an *unacknowledged connectionless service* and a set of *connection-oriented services*. The unacknowledged connectionless service allows the user to initiate the transfer of service data units with a minimum of protocol overheads. Typically, this service is used when such functions as error recovery and sequencing are being provided in a higher-protocol layer and hence need not be replicated in the LLC layer. Alternatively, the connection-oriented services provide the user with the means to first establish a link-level logical connection before initiating the transfer of any service data units and, should it be required, to then implement error recovery and sequencing of the flow of these units across an established connection.

2.12   APPLICATIONS OF LAYERED NETWORK ARCHITECTURES

To get a better feeling of what layered network architecture is, let us make a top-level comparison of some popular implementations. Table 2.7 lists several widely used network implementations and shows their degree of compatibility with the OSI Model. Note that because of the way that various networks were developed by major computer manufacturers in parallel with the evolution of the OSI Model, not every OSI-Model layer is necessarily represented in a particular network.

2.12.1   Comparison of Network Architectures

In implementing any type of network, a major factor to consider is a *network management service*. This service decides which software to use when the system

TABLE 2.7

Several popular network implementations and their compatibility with the OSI Model

OSI Layer	Xerox	IBM SNA	DEC DNA	DoD	ISO
7 Application	Clearing house service; file transfer; printer server	Transaction services	Network management ———— Network application	File transfer protocol; virtual terminal; voice	2-station, file-transfer protocol
6 Presentation	Courier protocol	Presentation services; function management	—	—	Presentation protocol
5 Session	—	Data-flow control	Session control	—	Session protocol
4 Transport	Internet transport protocol (ITP) with 5 subprotocols	Transmission control	End-to-end communication services	Transmission control protocol (TCP)	Transport protocol (5 classes)
3 Network	Internet datagram protocol ————	Path control	Adaptive routing	Internet protocol (IP) ———— 1822 for Arpanet	Internet protocol
2 Data Link	Ethernet	Synchronous data-link control (SDLC)	Digital data communication message protocol (DDCMP); X.25; Ethernet	Variable (network-dependent)	High-level data link control (HDLC)
1 Physical	Ethernet	IBM physical	DDCMP; X.25; Ethernet	Variable (network-dependent)	

is turned on, it informs nodes of existing peers, it notifies the appropriate network authorities when a particular node has failed, it executes diagnostic and recovery operations on erratically functioning nodes, and it performs various other low-level functions.

Regardless of how it is implemented, network management must deal with all protocol levels. Of all the ISO levels, the transport level is the most difficult one in which to define network management because of the two diverse approaches to networking. These are the connection-oriented virtual circuit and the connectionless datagram methods that we discussed in Sec. 2.5. Recall that in the virtual-circuit technique, connections are established in advance and all transmitted data flows over these paths. In the datagram approach, no relationship exists between currently transmitted messages, prior messages, or subsequent messages, so that datagram packets can travel along different routes to the same destination.

The question that arises is where to put transport-level reliability controls for these two methods. To resolve various problems in implementing these controls, the ISO has defined five classes of transport-level protocols,[15,25] as is noted in Table 2.7. These are designated as class 0 through class 4.

Classes 0 and 1 are very simple protocols which are designed for use in nonmultiplexed, single-network environments. They are used primarily for services like Teletex, or for a single connection from a personal computer to a mail service. Class 0 has no error-recovery capability, whereas class 1 can recover from reported errors. Class 2 assumes there is a reliable lower-level network service (such as X.25) and therefore does not provide most error-detection or recovery functions. Class 3 offers error recovery over networks that report errors (such as X.25) but does not provide error detection. The most complex protocol is class 4, which provides both error detection and correction by attaching checksums and verifying that messages are properly delivered to their destination.

To conform to these subprotocols and other ISO protocols, a manufacturer must implement the functions specified for that protocol. This is sometimes difficult because the ISO protocols will continue to evolve as the technology advances and as standards are updated. Although some manufacturers have developed networks that do not exactly track the OSI Model, the general trend is to migrate toward the ISO standards.

2.12.2   Xerox Network Systems

A poular network implementation is the Xerox Network Systems (XNS) architecture.[16,21] The set of protocols adopted by Xerox is depicted in Fig. 2.21. The higher-level protocols conform functionally to the OSI Model, differing only in details like bit encoding and field layout. As noted in Table 2.7 there is no session layer in the XNS. Here the Internet Transport Protocol (ITP) communicates directly with the Courier protocol at the presentation level. The Courier protocol is a remote call procedure which allows a network user to issue a request to any other computer in the network in the same manner that an ordinary subroutine is called. When such a request is issued, the software transparently finds the appropriate computer, accesses it, and returns to the program at the line following the point where the call was initiated.

At the transport level, the sequenced-packet protocol (which is a subsection of the Internet Transport Protocol) is the functional equivalent of the ISO

ISO Reference Model layers

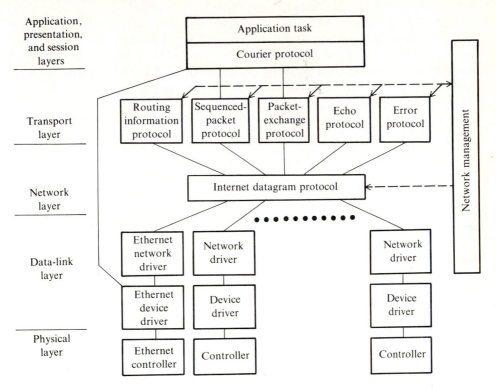

FIGURE 2.21
The Internet Transport Protocol (ITP) of the Xerox Network Systems is made up of five subprotocols. The datagram protocol communicates with the lowest part of the network layer and then with Ethernet.

class-4 protocol. It differs in the format and syntax of its fields but not in their meaning, and it uses a Xerox addressing scheme.

The Internet Datagram Protocol offers level-3 functions. It provides an internetwork communication service that addresses packets, and routes and delivers them from one data link to another. The lower two levels and part of level 3 use the Ethernet protocols.

2.12.3   IBM's System Network Architecture

The seven layers of IBM's System Network Architecture (SNA) are quite similar to those of the OSI Model. This architecture was announced by IBM in 1974. It represents both the philosophy and the detailed directions for how IBM teleprocessing products must communicate with one another.[60,61]

At the top of the architectural structure, the *transaction-services* layer provides application services such as distributed database access and document interchange. The next level is the *presentation-services* (PS) layer. Here the port of the end user is defined in terms of code and data format for different media. Its basic function is to coordinate resource sharing; for example, the PS layer has the job of accommodating the totally different interfaces seen by an end user and the application that is being accessed.

The *data-flow control* has the function of synchronizing flow between end users (for example, whether a user wants to communicate duplex or half-duplex), correlating message exchanges, and grouping related data into units. As an example of the latter, different message packets, called *request units* (RU), might represent different lines of text that make up a single display screen of text.

The *transmission control* elements lie on each end of a link between communicating users (that is, on each end of a session) and ensure isolation of sessions from each other. Transmission control elements also provide session flow control and session-level data encryption, if needed for security.

Path control routes data packets between source and destination and controls traffic in the network. It allows alternate path routing between nodes and the use of several sets of parallel data-link control facilities between a pair of nodes for better reliability and throughput.

The task of the *data-control* protocols is to convert the specific physical facilities which connect two adjacent SNA nodes into a reliable, efficient, full-duplex transmission path. The *data-link control* protocol for bit-serial transmission is known as the *synchronous data-link control* (SDLC) in SNA.

2.12.4   DEC's Digital Network Architecture

The Digital Network Architecture (DNA) of the Digital Equipment Corporation (DEC) is the architectural model from which the DECnet family of network component products was designed.[62] It was originally developed for computer-to-computer communications over private and common-carrier telephone networks, and was subsequently extended to include interfaces with X.25-based public packet-switched networks and Ethernet.

DNA has eight layers. Its two upper layers together map into the OSI application layer. In other aspects DNA and the OSI Model are quite similar.

The *network-management layer* provides the necessary functions to plan, control, and maintain the operation of the network. Its functions include down-line loading of remote nodes and network line testing.

The *network-application* layer controls network functions such as remote file access, file transfers, and remote device access. This layer also defines a universal input/output (I/O) language within DNA so that resource-sharing among heterogeneous systems is simplified.

The *session-control layer* provides system-dependent process-to-process communications functions and performs name-to-address mapping for nodes.

Thus it serves as the point at which network operations start being integrated with an operating system.

The *end-to-end communication services* allow processes in different nodes to exchange data reliably and sequentially. This is done by end-to-end control of addressing, data integrity checking, transaction flows, interrupts, and flow control between communication processes.

The network layer routes data packets to their destination via adaptive routing, controls network congestion, ensures packet lifetime control, and provides a packet datagram service. The lowest two levels use either DEC's Digital Data Communication Message Protocol (DDCMP), X.25, or Ethernet.

2.13 SUMMARY

This chapter gave an overview of the fundamental construction and philosophy of network layering. We first saw that for two computer systems to communicate, they must share a common set of rules for generating and interpreting the messages they send or receive. This can be done by establishing a modularized set of system-interconnection rules that define a hierarchical series of layers of functions. The same set of layered functions must exist on each system in order for the two systems to be able to communicate. The communication between peer layers on two systems is achieved via protocols. A protocol is a set of rules or conventions that govern the format and control of information that is transmitted through a network or that is stored in a database.

An example of functional layering is the seven-layer network architecture defined by the OSI Reference Model. The bottom three layers of this model (the physical, data-link, and network layers) apply specifically to the architecture of individual local networks. Their concern is the transmission, framing, and routing of messages between adjacent machines. Protocols at these levels encompass different transmission technologies (such as satellites, coax. cables, and optical fibers), a variety of network topologies (such as star, ring, and bus configurations), and different accessing methods (including both deterministic and random access schemes).

Layer 4, the transport layer, serves as the boundary between the data-communication functions of the lower three layers and the data-processing functions of the upper three layers. Its functions include error detection and recovery, message sequencing, end-to-end addressing, and multiplexing.

Whereas the lower three levels are technology-dependent, the top three layers are technology-independent. The session layer (No. 5) initiates, ends, synchronizes, and coordinates communications and end-user tasks. At the presentation layer (No. 6) the syntaxes of the different machines on a heterogeneous system are converted into a common syntax for information being exchanged among communicating machines. This eliminates the need for each machine to know the formats of all others. At the top of the OSI Model is layer 7, the application layer, which interprets the meaning of information transferred between application processes.

PROBLEMS

2.1. In a *positive acknowledgment retransmit* (PAR) data-link protocol, framed message blocks are checked at the receiver to ensure that they arrive in the proper sequence. If they arrived correctly, a positive acknowledgment is returned; if errors occurred, the block must be retransmitted. To recover from lost messages, whenever a transmitter sends a message it starts a retransmit timer. If no positive acknowledgment is received at the expiration of the retransmit time, the message is sent out again. To avoid confusion as to which message is acknowledged, the acknowledgments must be numbered to correspond to the messages they verified.

(a) Using this type of protocol, draw a time-sequence diagram for the following message-exchange scenario:

1. Message 1 transmitted and acknowledged
2. Message 2 transmitted and lost on first try
3. Message 3 received incorrectly on first try

(b) What are some pitfalls that must be avoided in this protocol?

2.2. A channel has a transmission capability of 20 kb/s and a propagation delay (time for a bit to travel over the channel) of 20 ms. (a) For what range of frame size does the PAR protocol in Prob. 2.1 have an efficiency of at least 50 percent for error-free transmission? (b) What is the minimum time interval that the retransmit timer can be set at?

2.3. Consider the following frame format for a bit-oriented data-link protocol.

Bits	8	8	8	≤ 1024	16	8
	01111110	Address	Control	Data	Checksum	01111110

(a) What is the maximum data transfer efficiency that is possible?
(b) Consider the PAR data-link protocol described in Prob. 2.1. What is the transmission overhead (bandwidth wasted on headers and retransmission) if the error rate for data frames is 1 percent and the positive acknowledgment (ACK) frames are 40 bits long? Assume the error rate for ACK frames is negligible, and let the message-processing time at the receiver (before the ACK is sent out) be 5 ms. Let the timeout interval be 80 ms.

2.4. To distinguish data from the flag sequence 01111110 in a bit-oriented protocol, a procedure called bit stuffing is used. Whenever the transmitter sees five consecutive ones in the data, it automatically inserts a 0 bit into the outgoing bit stream. At the receiving end, whenever the receiver detects five consecutive 1 bits followed by a 0 bit, it automatically deletes the 0 bit. Determine the data stream appearing on the line for the following original data sequences:

(a) 011011111111111111110010
(b) 011110111110111111010111100

2.5. The utilization U (or efficiency) of a transmission channel depends on the following parameters:

A = the number of bits in an ACK frame
C = the channel capacity in bits per second (b/s)
D = the number of data bits per frame
H = the number of bits in the frame header

$F = D + H$ = total frame length

I = propagation delay time + message processing time at the receiver
   (before an ACK is sent out)

L = the probability that a frame or its ACK is lost or damaged

R = mean number of retransmissions per data frame

T = the time-out interval (set by the transmitter before another message is sent)

(a) Show that the probability of failure L is given by

$$L = 1 - (1 - P_2)(1 - P_1)$$

where P_1 is the probability that a data frame is lost or damaged and P_2 is the probability that an ACK frame is lost or damaged.

(b) Show that $R = L/(1 - L)$

(c) Show that the channel utilization U is given by

$$U = \frac{D}{[L/(1 - L)](F + CT) + (F + A + 2CI)}$$

2.6. Discuss some of the technical differences between virtual circuits and datagrams. Consider factors such as error control, flow control, packet sequencing, and overhead involved in setting up a circuit.

2.7. Flow control is often specified in both the data-link layer and the network layer (e.g., in X.25). Explain the difference between these two functions.

2.8. Gateways are devices that connect nodes and networks of different architectures by performing protocol translations. Discuss some of the functions that gateways would need to perform for

(a) connections between dissimilar LANs (e.g., one supporting datagrams and one supporting virtual-circuit connections)

(b) connections between devices on the same LAN that understand different higher-level protocols.

2.9. Consider the GEK Distributing Corporation which is in the office products distribution business. It receives its products from manufacturers in both the United States and overseas (through importers). The customers are businesses in three geographically separated localities, one of which is near the main business office of GEK. Each geographical location has a warehouse from which deliveries are made once orders are received. Salesmen call in their orders to the appropriate local warehouse using portable ASCII terminals which operate in a remote-job-entry mode. When orders are received at a warehouse, inventories are adjusted for committed stock and shipping invoices are made for the orders. The two remotely located warehouses report their inventory and business activity to the home office on a daily basis.

   In order to remain competitive, the central offices of GEK require access to the mainframe computers of their suppliers for ordering purposes, and they access their remotely located warehouses via Telenet.

(a) Discuss the networking and protocol issues of this corporation with respect to local area networking, mainframe computer access, remote job entry, and electronic mail.

(b) What are some of the applications that would need to be performed by a LAN in the headquarters building?

2.10. A popular application-layer protocol is a file-transfer protocol (FTP). Its purpose is to transfer a file or a portion of a file from one system to another under the command of an FTP user. To carry out a file transfer, a connection must first be established between the sending and receiving nodes. Once this has been made, the following operations are carried out:

1. A READ exchange initiated by the requester
2. One or more DATA exchanges initiated by the file recipient
3. A DATA-END exchange initiated by the file recipient
4. A TRANSFER-END exchange initiated by the requester

What logical sequence of connections is required for a user located at node A to request that a file be exchanged between node B and node C?

2.11. A LAN is to be installed in a 3-story office building. The following devices are to be connected by the LAN: (*a*) 36 terminals from various vendors including IBM, DEC, and Hewlett-Packard (HP); (*b*) 2 IBM 360 computers, 1 HP Series 300 computer, and 2 DEC VAX 11/780 computers; (*c*) A remote X.25 access to public packet networks such as Telenet.

Describe some of the protocol issues that need to be considered when implementing this LAN.

DOCUMENTATION AVAILABILITY

1. ANSI documents are available from the Sales Department, American National Standards Institute, 1430 Broadway, New York, NY 10018, USA.
2. EIA documents are available from Electronic Industries Association, 2001 Eye Street, N.W., Washington, DC 20006, USA.
3. IEEE documents are available from IEEE Service Center, 445 Hoes Lane, Piscataway, NJ 08554, USA.
4. ISO documents are available from:
   (*a*) Sales Department, American National Standards Institute, 1430 Broadway, New York, NY 10018, USA;
   (*b*) ISO Office, 1 rue de Varembe, Case postale 56, CH-1211 Geneve 20, Switzerland.
5. CCITT documents are available from National Technical Information Service, Department of Commerce, 5285 Port Royal Road, Springfield, VA 22161, USA.

REFERENCES

1. A good overview of the ISO, its procedures, and how it relates to other standards organizations is given in E. Loshe, "The role of the ISO in telecommunications and information systems standardization," *IEEE Commun. Mag.*, vol. 23, pp. 18–24, January 1985.
2. ISO/TC97/SC16, "Provisional model of Open Systems Architecture," Doc. no. 34, 1978.
3. (*a*) ISO, *ISO 7498*, "Basic reference model for Open Systems Interconnection," 1983.
   (*b*) CCITT, *Recommendation X.200*, "Reference model of Open System Interconnection," June 1984.
4. J. D. Day and H. Zimmerman, "The OSI Reference Model," *Proc. IEEE*, vol. 71, pp. 1334–1340, December 1983.
5. S. Wecker, "Computer network architecture," *Computer*, vol. 12, pp. 58–72, September 1979.

6. P. F. Linington, "Fundamentals of the layer service definitions and protocol specifications," *Proc. IEEE*, vol. 71, pp. 1341–1345, December 1983.

7. H. Zimmermann, "OSI Reference Model—The ISO model of architecture for Open Systems Interconnection," *IEEE Trans. Commun.*, vol. COM-28, pp. 425–432, April 1980.

8. H. Rudin, "An informal overview of formal protocol specification," *IEEE Commun. Mag.*, vol. 23, pp. 46–52, March 1985.

9. L. Pouzin and H. Zimmermann, "A tutorial on protocols," *Proc. IEEE*, vol. 66, pp. 1346–1370, November 1978.

10. G. V. Bochmann and C. Sunshine, "Formal methods in communication protocol design," *IEEE Trans. Commun.*, vol. COM-28, pp. 624–631, April 1980.

11. S. Schindler, "Distributed abstract machine," *Comput. Commun.*, vol. 3, no. 5, p. 208, 1980.

12. (*a*) ISO/TC97/SC16-N1646, "Information processing systems—Open Systems Interconnection—Service conventions," 1978.
    (*b*) CCITT, *Recommendation X.210*, "OSI layer service definition conventions," June 1984.

13. J. Voelcker, "Helping computers communicate," *IEEE Spectrum*, vol. 23, pp. 61–70, March 1986.

14. K. G. Knightson, "The transport layer standardization," *Proc. IEEE*, vol. 71, pp. 1394–1396, December 1983.

15. (*a*) CCITT, *Recommendation X.214*, "Transport service definition for open systems interconnection," 1984.
    (*b*) CCITT, *Recommendation X.224*, "Transport protocol specification for OSI," 1984.
    (*c*) ISO, *DP8072*, "Transport service definition," 1984.
    (*d*) ISO, *DP8073*, "Connection-oriented transport protocol specification for OSI," 1984.

16. D. R. Boggs, J. F. Shock, E. A. Taft, and R. M. Metcalfe, "Pup: An internetwork architecture," *IEEE Trans. Commun.*, vol. COM-28, pp. 612–624, April 1980.

17. Defense Communications Agency, *MIL-STD-1777: Internet Protocol*, 1983.

18. V. G. Cerf and E. Cain, "The DoD Internet Architecture Model," *Comput. Networks*, vol. 7, pp. 307–318, 1983.

19. V. G. Cerf and R. E. Kahn, "A protocol for packet network intercommunication," *IEEE Trans. Commun.*, vol. COM-22, pp. 637–648, May 1974.

20. B. M. Leiner, R. Cole, J. Postel, and D. Mills, "The DARPA Internet Protocol Suite," *IEEE Comm. Mag.*, vol. 23, pp. 29–34, March 1985.

21. W. E. Seifert, "Choosing a transport protocol," *Systems & Software*, vol. 4, pp. 87–90, June 1985.

22. J. M. McQuillan and D. C. Walden, "The ARPA Network design decision," *Comput. Networks*, vol. 1, pp. 243–289, August 1977.

23. W. F. Emmons and A. S. Chandler, "OSI Session Layer: Services and protocols," *Proc. IEEE*, vol. 71, pp. 1397–1400, December 1983.

24. (*a*) CCITT, *Recommendation X.215*, "Session service definition for OSI," October 1984.
    (*b*) CCITT, *Recommendation X.225*, "Session protocol specification for OSI," 1984.

25. W. B. Rauch-Hindin, "Special series on system integration: upper-level network protocols," *Electronic Design*, vol. 31, pp. 180–194, Mar. 3, 1983.

26. P. D. Bartoli, "The Application Layer of the Reference Model of Open System Interconnection," *Proc. IEEE*, vol. 71, pp. 1404–1407, December 1983.

27. Electronic Industries Association, *Standard RS-232C*, "Interface between DTE and DCE employing serial binary data exchange," 1969.

28. Electronic Industries Association, *Standard RS-449*, "General purpose 37-position and 9-position interface for DTE and DCE employing serial binary data exchange," November 1977.

29. CCITT, *Recommendation X.21*, "Interface between DTE and DCE for synchronous operation on public data networks," November 1980.

30. CCITT, *Recommendation V.24*, "List of definitions for interchange circuits between DTE and DCE," November 1980.

31. Overviews of the CCITT and its functions are given in
    (*a*) E. Hummel, "The CCITT," *IEEE Commun. Mag.*, vol. 23, pp. 8–11, January 1985.
    (*b*) D. M. Cerni, "The United States Organization for the CCITT," *IEEE Commun. Mag.*, vol. 23, pp. 38–42, January 1985.

32. M. Graube, "Local area nets: A pair of standards," *IEEE Spectrum*, vol. 19, pp. 60–64, June 1982.

33. *ANSI/IEEE* Standards 802.1 to 802.6 for Local Area Networks, 1985.

34. P. S. Selvaggi, "The development of communications standards in the DoD," *IEEE Commun. Mag.*, vol. 23, pp. 43–55, January 1985.

35. F. M. McClelland, "Services and protocols of the Physical Layer," *Proc. IEEE*, vol. 71, pp. 1372–1377, December 1983.

36. J. F. Shock, Y. K. Dalal, D. D. Redell, and R. C. Crane, "Evolution of the Ethernet Local Computer Network," *Computer*, vol. 15, pp. 10–27, August 1982.

37. J. W. Coward, "Services and protocols of the Data-Link Layer," *Proc. IEEE*, vol. 71, pp. 1378–1383, December 1983.

38. J. W. Conard, "Character-oriented data link control protocols," *IEEE Trans. Commun.*, vol. COM-28, pp. 445–454, April 1980.

39. D. E. Carlson, "Bit-oriented data link control procedures," *IEEE Trans. Commun.*, vol. COM-28, pp. 455–467, April 1980.

40. ANSI, *Standard X3.66-1979*, "Advanced Data Communication Control Procedures (ADCCP)," American National Standards Institute (ANSI), New York, NY, 1979.

41. ISO, *DIS 3309.2 and DIS 4335*, "High-Level Data Link Control (HDLC)" 1976.

42. J. P. Gray, "Synchronization in SNA networks," in *Protocols and Techniques for Data Communication Networks*, F. F. Kuo (ed.), pp. 319–368, Prentice-Hall, Englewood Cliffs, NJ, 1981.

43. J. P. Gray and T. B. McNeil, "SNA multiple-system networking," *IBM Sys. J.*, vol, 18, pp. 263–297, 1979.

44. M. C. Easton, "Batch throughput efficiency of ADCCP/HDLC/SDLC selective-reject protocols," *IEEE Trans. Commun.*, vol. COM-28, pp. 187–195, February 1980.

45. F. A. Tobagi, "Multiaccess protocols in packet communication systems," *IEEE Trans. Commun.*, vol. COM-28, pp. 468–488, April 1980.

46. B. Dimitriadis, G. Polyzos, N. Alexandridis, and S. Oucheriah, "On a hybrid TDMA/CSMA LAN accessing scheme serving users with variable traffic characteristics," *ICC Conf. Proc.*, pp. 772–776, Boston, Mass., June 1983.

47. K. Kobayashi and K. Watanabe, "A Distributed Adaptive Multiaccess Scheme for Packet Communications," *ICC Conf. Proc.*, pp. 1354–1358, Boston, MA, June 1983.

48. C. Ware, "The OSI Network Layer: Standards to cope with the real world," *Proc. IEEE*, vol. 71, pp. 1384–1387, December 1983.

49. (a) CCITT, *Recommendation X.213*, "Network service definition of open systems interconnection," June 1984.
    (b) ISO, *DIS 8348*, "Network service definition," November 1983.

50. A good overview on packet communications is given in *Proc. IEEE*, "Special Issue on Packet Communication Networks," vol. 66, no. 11, November 1978.

51. M. A. Sirbu and L. E. Zwimpfer, "Standards setting for computer communication: The case of X.25," *IEEE Commun. Mag.*, vol. 23, pp. 35–45, March 1985.

52. CCITT, *Recommendation X.25*, "Interface between DTE and DCE for terminals operating in the packet mode in public data networks," 1978.

53. D. W. Davies, D. L. A. Barber, W. L. Price, and C. M. Solomonides, *Computer Networks and Their Protocols*, Wiley, New York, 1979, pp. 232–257.

54. R. J. Deasington, *X.25 Explained*, Wiley, New York, 1986.

55. A. S. Tanenbaum, *Computer Networks*, Prentice-Hall, Englewood Cliffs, NJ, 1981.

56. H. C. Folts, "X.25 transaction-oriented features—Datagram and Fast Select," *IEEE Trans. Commun.*, vol. COM-28, pp. 496–500, April 1980.

57. A. Rybczynski, "X.25 Interface and end-to-end virtual-circuit service characteristics," *IEEE Trans. Commun.*, vol. COM-28, pp. 500–510, April 1980.

58. I. Groenback, "Conversion between the TCP and ISO transport protocols as a method of achieving interoperability between data communication systems," *IEEE J. Select Areas Commun.*, vol. SAC-4, pp. 288–296, March 1986.

59. IEEE Subcommittees 802.7, 802.8, and 802.9.

60. E. H. Sussenguth, "Systems Network Architecture: A perspective," *Proc. 4th International Conf. on Computer Commun.*, Kyoto, Japan, pp. 353–358, September 1978.
61. J. P. Gray, "Synchronization in SNA networks," in *Protocols and Techniques for Data Communication Networks*, F. F. Kuo (ed.), chap. 8, Prentice-Hall, Englewood Cliffs, NJ, 1981.
62. S. Wecker, "DNA: The Digital Network Architecture," *IEEE Trans. Commun.*, vol. COM-28, pp. 510–526, April 1980.

CHAPTER
3

DATA COMMUNICATION CONCEPTS

To exchange information between any two computer elements in a LAN, some type of signal has to be transmitted from one element to the other via a communication channel. This channel can be either a coaxial cable, radio, microwave, satellite, or optical fiber link. Each of these communication media has unique performance characteristics associated with it. Regardless of its type, the medium degrades the transmitted signal because of an imperfect response of the channel and because of the presence of electrical noise and interference.

Since all communication channels have the same basic function of *information transmission*, this chapter gives an overview of the fundamental analyses and design techniques applicable to any type of communication system.[1-8] In particular we examine how communication theory applies to the lowest layer (the physical layer) in the ISO model hierarchy that we studied in Chap. 2.

We shall first examine signal types and the various modulation techniques used to match the signal properties with the transmission characteristics of the channel. Frequency response limitations of a communication channel are considered next. This leads to the concept of the bandwidth of a channel and its relation to signal bandwidth.

Having examined the properties of an ideal (noiseless) transmission link, we then turn our attention to signal distortion and noise limitations of system performance. In this discussion we shall see how to calculate the probability of errors occurring in a digital system and how the concept of signal-to-noise ratio is used as a figure of merit for measuring the performance of an analog system.

The format of the signal is an important factor in efficiently and reliably sending information through a local area network. This topic is addressed in Sec. 3.5 where we examine signal formats and modulation schemes used in baseband and broadband LANs.

In any type of transmission network, and in particular in a heavily used LAN, many nodes are continuously competing for use of the network. An effective use of the available channel capacity can then be accomplished through multiplexing. This is the topic of Sec. 3.6 where we discuss frequency-division-multiplexing (FDM) and time-division-multiplexing (TDM) schemes. For TDM, both asynchronous and synchronous transmission techniques are addressed, and examples are given for the telephone network.

No matter what type of modulation scheme is used, errors are unavoidable in any real communication system because of noise bursts, data dropouts (e.g., switches temporarily open), or long transient interferences. Thus, the topics of Secs. 3.7 and 3.8 are how to detect and correct errors in a digital data stream. Here we shall see how varying degrees of redundancy introduced into the raw data stream can be used to either simply detect errors or, on a more complex basis, to both detect and correct errors. To correct for errors in LANs, one often uses retransmission techniques which are described in Sec. 3.8.

As a final topic, we look at how communications take place between a number of different devices located at various nodes on a network. The techniques discussed in Sec. 3.9 are switched-network methodologies and broadcast methodologies.

3.1 TYPES OF SIGNALS

A block diagram of a typical communication link is shown in Fig. 3.1. The purpose of such a communication link is to transfer a message from an originating point called a *source* to another point called the *user destination*. We assume that the message output from the source is represented by some type of time-varying electrical waveform. The message waveform can be either a continuous type such as voice or TV signals, or it can consist of discrete information symbols such as numbers from a computer printout or letters of the alphabet generated by a teletype machine. Continuous signals are classified as *analog waveforms*, whereas discrete information symbols are categorized as *digital waveforms*. Although discrete signals can have several different levels, here we shall concentrate on *binary* waveforms, as shown in Fig. 3.2. A binary waveform is represented by a sequence of two types of pulses of known shape, which occur at regularly spaced intervals every $1/R$ seconds, or at a rate of R/second, where R

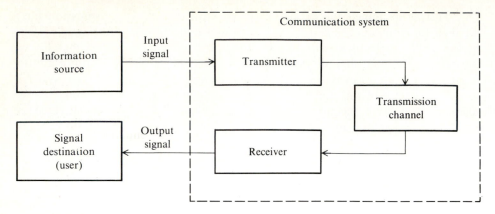

FIGURE 3.1
Block diagram of a typical communication system.

is the *data rate*. The information contained in the signal is given by the particular sequence of the presence (a *one*) and absence (a *zero*) of these pulses, which are commonly known as *bits*. The time slot T in which a bit occurs is called the *bit period*.

The message output of the source shown in Fig. 3.1 serves as the input signal to a transmitter. The function of the transmitter is to couple the message

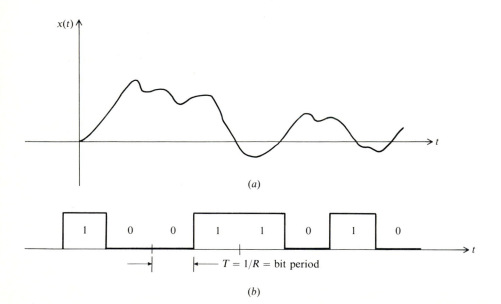

FIGURE 3.2
Two fundamental signal types: (*a*) analog waveforms represent continuous signals; (*b*) digital waveforms represent discrete information symbols.

onto a transmission channel in the form of a signal which matches the transfer properties of the channel. The channel is the medium bridging the distance between the transmitter and the receiver. This can be either a guided transmission line such as a wire or a waveguide, or it can be a nonguided atmospheric or space channel. Regardless of what type of medium is used, as the signal traverses the channel it becomes progressively both attenuated and distorted with increasing distance. For example, electric power is lost through heat generation as an electric signal flows along a wire, and optical power is attenuated through scattering and absorption by air molecules in an atmospheric channel. The function of the receiver is to extract the weakened and distorted signal from the channel, amplify it, and restore it as close as possible to its original form before passing it on to the message destination.

The process of matching the properties of the transmitted signal to the channel characteristics is known as *modulation*. Modulation is the systematic variation of a *carrier waveform* that can be efficiently transmitted over the channel. Depending on the type of message to be sent, these variations can be either the amplitude, phase, or frequency of the carrier waveform. In addition to improving the matching of signal properties to channel characteristics, modulation is used to reduce noise and interference, to simultaneously transmit several independent signals over a single channel, and/or to overcome equipment limitations.[2]

The two fundamental modulation techniques are continuous (carrier) wave (CW) or *analog modulation* and *pulse* or *digital modulation*, each of which can have many different forms. In CW modulation a continuous carrier waveform is transmitted, and a parameter (such as amplitude, phase, or frequency) of the waveform is varied in proportion to the message content of the signal. The carrier in pulse modulation is usually a rectangular pulse waveform, a parameter of which (such as pulse height or width) is changed in accordance with the message signal.

At the receiver the information-bearing signal must be extracted from the modulated carrier. The process of converting a modulated signal back to its original form is known as *demodulation* or *detection*. There are basically two common methods of demodulation. One technique, called *synchronous* or *coherent* detection, simply multiplies the incoming signal at the receiver by a locally generated signal which is the same as the carrier frequency. The resultant multiplied signal is then low-pass filtered to recover the original unmodulated signal. The other method is called *envelope detection*. This consists of passing the modulated carrier through a nonlinear device and then low-pass filtering the nonlinear output to extract the transmitted signal.

3.2 DATA ENCODING TECHNIQUES

To get a better feeling of what these terms mean, let us look at some examples of analog and digital modulation. Depending on the type of modulation used

TABLE 3.1
S/N **required for different signal types**

Analog signal type	Message bandwidth	Signal-to-noise ratio, dB
Telephone quality voice	200 Hz–3.2 kHz	25–35
AM broadcast quality audio	100 Hz–5 kHz	40–50
High fidelity audio	20 Hz–20 kHz	55–65
FM broadcast quality audio:		
Monophonic channel	50 Hz–15 kHz	45–60
Stereophonic channel	23 kHz–53 kHg	
Commercial television video	60 Hz–4.2 MHz	45–55

and the characteristic of the message signal originating at the source, communication systems can be divided into the following three broad categories:

1. Analog messages transmitted using analog modulation schemes
2. Digital messages transmitted using digital modulation methods
3. Analog messages that are periodically sampled and then transmitted using a digital modulation technique

In sending analog signals, two important factors to consider are the message bandwidth required and the signal-to-noise ratio necessary to reproduce the transmitted signal at the receiving end as best as possible. Some typical values are shown in Table 3.1. Note that the signal-to-noise ratio is expressed in decibels (dB) as is described in Prob. 3.1.

The upper limit on the frequency range is the nominal value of the bandwidth. The lower frequency limit is also important since most analog transmission systems cannot operate completely down to direct current, because of the response characteristics of circuit elements such as transformers and coupling capacitors. The requirements for the signal-to-noise ratio are addressed in more detail in Sec. 3.4.

Since pulse modulation is a discontinuous or discrete process in which pulses occur only at certain distinct times, it is naturally used for messages that consist of a sequence of discrete symbols or letters. These include telegraph, teletype, and computer printouts. However, pulse modulation can also be used for transmitting analog data. To do this, a technique called *pulse-code modulation* (PCM) is used.[9] The analog data is first sampled (quantized) at regular intervals and these samples are then coded into discrete binary words.

Example 3.1. An example of PCM is shown in Fig. 3.3. Here the allowed voltage amplitude excursion is divided into eight equally spaced amplitude levels ranging from zero to *V* volts. In this figure samples are taken every second and the nearest discrete amplitude level is chosen as the one to be transmitted, according to the

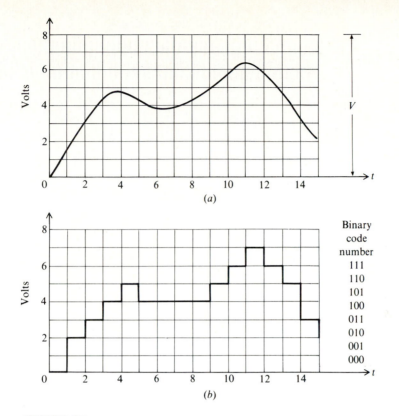

FIGURE 3.3
Digitization of analog waveforms: (*a*) original signal varying between 0 and *V* volts;
(*b*) quantized and sampled digital version.

binary code listed next to the quantizing levels shown in Fig. 3.3. At the receiver
this digital signal is then demodulated.

The resemblance of the reproduced signal to the original signal obviously
depends on the fineness of the quantizing process and on the effect of noise and
distortion added into the transmission system. As we shall see later in this
chapter, if a signal is limited to a bandwidth of *B* hertz, then the signal can be
reproduced without distortion if it is sampled at a rate of 2*B* times per second.
These data samples are represented by a binary code. As noted in Fig. 3.3, eight
quantized levels having upper bounds $V_1, V_2, \ldots, V$ can be described by three
binary digits ($2^3 = 8$). More digits can be used to give finer sampling levels.

Example 3.2. Consider a high-quality color video signal having a 6-MHz bandwidth. To digitize this signal, we sample at 12×10^6 samples per second (twice the
bandwidth). A signal of very high fidelity is created by using eight binary bits per
sample to give $2^8 = 256$ quantizing levels. The resultant digital signal would then
be sent at 96 Mb/s (12×10^6 samples/s $\times$ 8 bits/sample = 96 Mb/s).

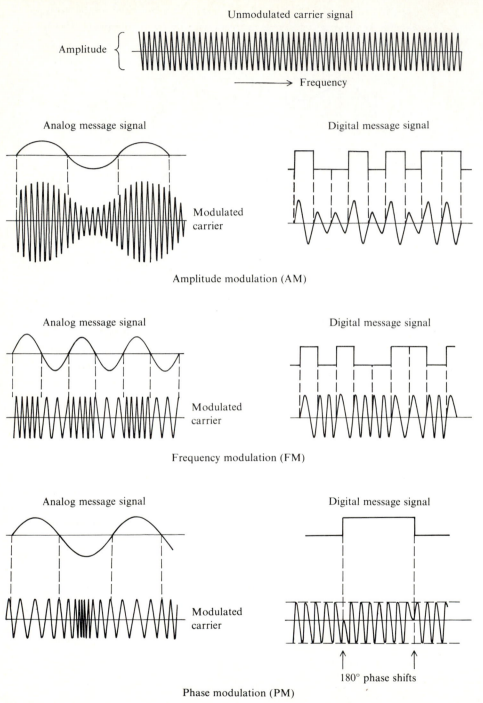

Unmodulated carrier signal

Amplitude

Frequency

Analog message signal

Digital message signal

Modulated carrier

Amplitude modulation (AM)

Analog message signal

Digital message signal

Modulated carrier

Frequency modulation (FM)

Analog message signal

Digital message signal

Modulated carrier

180° phase shifts

Phase modulation (PM)

FIGURE 3.4
Typical AM, FM, and PM waveforms for representative analog and digital waveforms.

Modulating a sinusoidal carrier can be done by varying its amplitude, phase, or frequency in accordance with the signal being transmitted. Mathematically the carrier wave $x_c(t)$ has the form

$$x_c(t) = A_c(t) \cos \left[\omega_c t + \phi(t)\right] \tag{3.1}$$

where $A_c(t)$ is the instantaneous amplitude of the carrier, $f_c = \omega_c/2\pi$ is the carrier frequency, and $\phi(t)$ is the instantaneous phase deviation of the carrier.

If the temporal variation of a message signal $x(t)$ is linearly related to $A(t)$, then we have *amplitude modulation* (AM), an example of which is the familiar commercial AM radio application. When the phase $\phi(t)$ or its time derivative is linearly related to $x(t)$, then we have *phase modulation* (PM) and *frequency modulation* (FM), respectively. Then name *angle modulation* is commonly used to denote both phase and frequency modulation. Figure 3.4 shows typical AM, FM, and PM waveforms for representative analog and digital message waveforms.

An important point to note in Fig. 3.4 is that in the analog case the amplitude, frequency, or phase of the carrier varies continuously in response to the message waveform. However, in the binary digital case, these three parameters switch between one of two possible values, depending on whether a zero pulse or a one pulse is transmitted. For the AM case, the amplitude switches between zero (the *off* state) and a predetermined amplitude level (the *on* state). This type of modulation is referred to as an *on-off-keyed* (OOK) or *amplitude-shift-keyed* (ASK) system. In *phase-shift keying* (PSK), the phase of the carrier is changed by π radians (180°). For the *frequency-shift-keyed* (FSK) case, the signal takes on one of two predetermined frequencies depending on whether a binary one or a zero was sent.

3.3 SIGNAL BANDWIDTH REQUIREMENTS

3.3.1 Transmission Link Capacity

In the analysis of any communication network, an important factor is the amount of information that can be sent across a channel from the message source to the user destination. The phrase "amount of information" refers to the degree of change that a transmitted signal undergoes with time. Rapid information transmission is achieved by using signals that change rapidly with time. However, in any physical electrical system, in order for a signal to vary in time, there must be a corresponding change in stored energy in the circuit components of the system. Thus, depending on the type of circuit components used (TTL logic, ECL logic, microwave transistors, etc.), there is an upper time limit in which the signal can change, since the energy-storage elements (capacitances and inductances) in these circuits do not allow currents or voltages to change instantaneously with time. That is, a certain finite time interval is needed for a voltage to reach a desired amplitude level. Consequently, a limit is imposed on signal speed, since beyond a certain point the system will no longer respond to faster signal changes.

What is this upper limit? To answer this we need to examine in detail the relationship between frequency and time response of a system, since for communications work the analysis of signals is often simpler in the frequency (or steady state sine-wave) domain than in the time domain where we have to deal with transient responses. In fact, as we have already alluded to in Table 3.1, in most cases it is the frequency response that is used to specify the performance of a network.

To carry information a signal must not be a steady state signal (such as a continuous sine wave) but must vary continuously in some manner. Furthermore, these variations occur in an unpredictable manner (if the receiver knew beforehand what the signal variation is, no communication link would be needed!). Thus, a simple steady state sine wave is not sufficient to represent an information-carrying signal. However, they are fundamental in studying communication links since any physical time-varying waveform existing over a finite time interval can be expanded into a Fourier series of sinusoidal functions. This, of course, applies to both analog and digital waveforms.

In the Fourier-series concept a time-periodic function $f(t)$ with period T may be expanded in the form[10,11]

$$f(t) = A_0 + \sum_{n=1}^{\infty} (A_n \cos \omega_n t + B_n \sin \omega_n t) \tag{3.2}$$

where $\omega_n = 2\pi n/T$ is the angular frequency in radians per second. The term A_0 represents the dc term and is simply the average value of the signal over one cycle. The terms A_n and B_n are the cosine and sine amplitudes of the nth harmonics.

Example 3.3. As an example, consider the periodic signal shown in Fig. 3.5. The lowest frequency of the sinusoidal components is $\omega_1 = 2\pi/T$, which is the same as that of the waveform itself. All other frequencies in the signal will be integer multiples of the fundamental. These various components are the harmonics of the system.

The important point to note is that any transmission system must have a sufficiently large bandwidth to allow all *significant* frequencies of the transmitted signal to pass. The trick in communication system designs, then, is to predict the frequency range which contains the major signal components. To do this, we need to select a certain finite bandwidth and assume that the exclusion of all harmonics that fall outside of this range has no noticeable degradation on the signal quality.

For any given function $f(t)$, the amplitudes A_n and B_n are given by

$$A_n = \frac{2}{T} \int_{-T/2}^{T/2} f(t) \cos \omega_n t \, dt$$

$$B_n = \frac{2}{T} \int_{-T/2}^{T/2} f(t) \sin \omega_n t \, dt \tag{3.3}$$

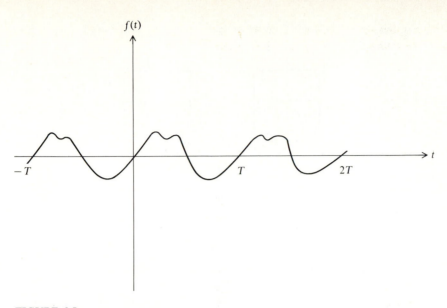

FIGURE 3.5
Example of a periodic analog signal of period T.

The strength of a particular harmonic of a signal is given by the root-mean-square amplitude $(A_n^2 + B_n^2)^{1/2}$ and its phase is $\phi_n = \arctan(-B_n/A_n)$. Alternatively the Fourier series can be written in an exponential form as

$$f(t) = \sum_{n=-\infty}^{\infty} C_n \exp(j\omega_n t) \tag{3.4}$$

where the coefficients C_n are complex numbers called the *spectral components* of $f(t)$ which are defined by

$$C_n = A_n - jB_n = \sqrt{A_n^2 + B_n^2} \exp(j\theta_n)$$
$$= \frac{1}{T} \int_{-T/2}^{T/2} f(t) \exp(-j\omega_n t)\, dt \tag{3.5}$$

A plot of the relative strengths of the various harmonic components as a function of frequency allows a quick visual check of which frequencies are present in the signal and what their relative magnitudes are, that is, the plot shows the relative amount of signal energy transmitted at various frequencies. In the laboratory such a plot is easily obtained with a spectrum analyzer which shows the plot directly on an instrument display screen.

3.3.2 Time-Frequency Correspondence

To see the connection between time and frequency, let us examine the Fourier series analysis of the train of periodic pulses $f(t)$ shown in Fig. 3.6. Here the pulses are of width τ and the origin has been chosen to coincide with one of the

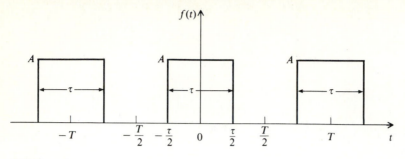

FIGURE 3.6
Example of a periodic pulse train.

pulses. Then

$$C_n = \frac{1}{T} \int_{-\tau/2}^{\tau/2} A_n \exp\left(-j\omega_n t\right) dt = \frac{A\tau}{T} \frac{\sin x}{x} \tag{3.6}$$

where $x = \omega_n \tau/2$ is a normalized, dimensionless variable.

A plot of $(\sin x)/x$ is given in Fig. 3.7 for continuous values of x. This function has a maximum value at $x = 0$, where $(\sin x)/x = 1$. As $x \to \infty$ the function approaches zero, oscillating through positive and negative values along the way. The zero crossings of the function are very important for bandwidth estimations.

The values of the spectral components C_n in Eq. (3.6) are not continuous but take on n discrete values. These values occur at multiples of the fundamental

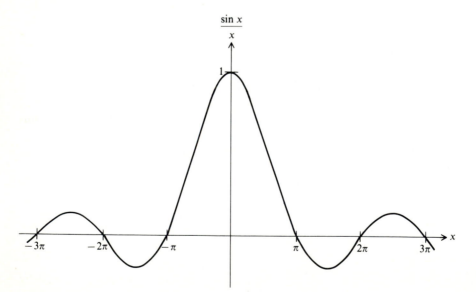

FIGURE 3.7
A plot of the function $(\sin x)/x$ versus x.

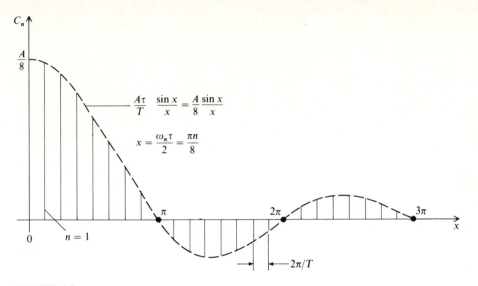

FIGURE 3.8
A plot of the absolute values of the spectral components C_n for a periodic pulse train having a pulse
width $\tau = T/8$, so that $x = \pi n/8$.

frequency $\omega_1 = 2\pi/T$ and the envelope of the plot of C_n will be the curve shown
in Fig. 3.7. A plot of C_n for $\tau = T/8$ is shown in Fig. 3.8. Note that the spacing
between adjacent lines is

$$\Delta\omega_n = \omega_{n+1} - \omega_n = \frac{2\pi}{T}(n+1) - \frac{2\pi n}{T} = \frac{2\pi}{T} \tag{3.7}$$

which is the fundamental angular frequency. The dc component C_0 has an amplitude $A\tau/T$ which is the average value of the pulse train $f(t)$ shown in Fig. 3.6.

A number of interesting points can be noted from Fig. 3.8. A very important and fundamental point is that as we increase the pulse rate by decreasing T,
the frequency lines spread further apart. This shows that as a time-varying signal
changes more rapidly, higher-frequency components start to become more important since the relative amount of energy contained in the higher-frequency
range increases. Conversely, when T becomes larger the frequency lines move
closer together. In this case, most of the energy of the periodic waveform is
concentrated in the lower-frequency range since the lower-frequency lines are
now of higher amplitude than for the small T case.

3.3.3 Nonperiodic Signals and
Fourier Transforms

So far we have considered periodic time functions which can be represented by
Fourier series. However, in an actual communication system an information-
bearing signal must vary in some manner since periodic functions do not carry

information. Thus, to describe an actual signal we must consider nonperiodic time functions.

To examine the time-versus-frequency relationship of nonperiodic signals, we have to introduce the Fourier integral. The procedure is to recognize that a nonperiodic function in a practical communication system is concentrated over a specified time interval T seconds long. Any such signal can be represented in the frequency domain using a Fourier series of base period T. The Fourier integral representation is then introduced by letting the function artificially repeat itself outside of its specified time interval. By increasing the Fourier time period to infinity, the resulting Fourier series transforms into the Fourier integral which is generally much easier to handle mathematically.

Thus the Fourier integral theorem states that a nonperiodic function $f(t)$ can be represented by

$$f(t) = \frac{1}{2\pi} \int_{-\infty}^{\infty} F(\omega) \exp(j\omega t)\, d\omega \tag{3.8}$$

where

$$F(\omega) = \int_{-\infty}^{\infty} f(t) \exp(-j\omega t)\, dt \tag{3.9}$$

is the *Fourier transform* of $f(t)$. The function $F(\omega)$ plays the same role for nonperiodic signals that C_n plays for periodic functions. That is, $F(\omega)$ describes the energy distribution over frequency for the function $f(t)$. Note here that $F(\omega)$ gives a continuous frequency spectrum rather than a line spectrum as in the periodic signal case.

3.3.4   Bandwidth

The beauty of the Fourier transform $F(\omega)$ is that it readily allows us to examine the frequency response of a linear transmission system. In the following chapters we shall often be referring to the *bandwidth* of a communication system, which is a measure of the frequency spread of a signal. The definition of bandwidth for any particular system often depends on the application or on the definition that is desired. However, to see a useful criterion that is often used in practice, let us look at a specific example of a pulse-type signal, since they commonly occur in communication systems.

Example 3.4. Consider the triangular pulse given in Fig. 3.9. Here

$$f(t) = \begin{cases} V - \dfrac{V}{\tau}|t| & \text{for } -\tau < t < \tau \\ \\ 0 & \text{elsewhere} \end{cases} \tag{3.10}$$

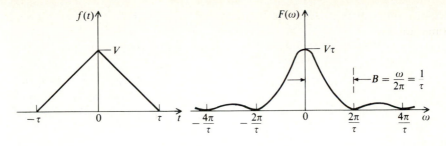

FIGURE 3.9
Triangular pulse and its Fourier transform.

Using Eq. (3.9), its Fourier transform is found to be

$$F(\omega) = V\tau \left[\frac{\sin (\omega\tau/2)}{\omega\tau/2}\right]^2 \tag{3.11}$$

The spectrum of $F(\omega)$ decreases as $1/\omega^2$. The important fact to note here (which is also applicable to all other types of pulse functions) is that as the pulse width τ decreases, the spectral spread moves out in frequency in proportion to $1/\tau$. In addition, note that most of the signal energy lies in the range

$$0 < \omega < \frac{2\pi}{\tau} \tag{3.12}$$

Thus, the first zero crossing of the Fourier transform of a pulse function is frequently taken as a measure of the frequency spread or bandwidth of a signal. An inverse relationship therefore exists between pulse width and bandwidth; as the pulse width τ decreases, the bandwidth B, in hertz, as measured at the first zero crossing, increases as $1/\tau$. In the case of the triangular pulse, the bandwidth in hertz is

$$B = f_1 = \frac{\omega_1}{2\pi} = \frac{1}{\tau}$$

Example 3.5. As another example, let us return to the rectangular pulse case that we examined earlier. For a single pulse

$$f(t) = \begin{cases} V & \text{for } |t| < \dfrac{\tau}{2} \\[2mm] 0 & \text{for } |t| > \dfrac{\tau}{2} \end{cases} \tag{3.13}$$

Using Eq. (3.9), we have

$$F(\omega) = V\tau \frac{\sin (\omega\tau/2)}{\omega\tau/2} \tag{3.14}$$

The pulse $f(t)$ and its Fourier transform are plotted in Fig. 3.10. Again, note the inverse time-frequency relationship between the rectangular pulse and its spectrum;

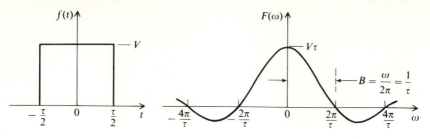

FIGURE 3.10
Rectangular pulse and its Fourier transform.

as the pulse width τ decreases, the spectrum spreads out in frequency in proportion to $1/\tau$. In this case, if we again define the bandwidth B as the first zero crossing of the Fourier transform, then $B = 1/\tau$. Thus, if the pulse width $\tau = 1\,\mu s$ then $B = 1/\tau = 1\,\text{MHz}$; if $\tau = 1\,\text{ms}$, $B = 1\,\text{kHz}$; etc.

The definition of bandwidth we have just seen is one of many that are commonly used. Two other popular definitions of bandwidth are

1. The frequency spacing between the half-power, or 3-dB points, and
2. The rms deviation about the center frequency (this is generally used for gaussian pulses.)

However, no matter which definition is used for bandwidth, it will always be of the form $B = k/\tau$ where k is some proportionality constant. As a practical measure of bandwidth, we can assume that $B = 1/\tau$. Although this is not a precise definition for all cases, we will generally use it in this book for simplicity.

3.3.5 Channel Capacity

A fundamental and important theorem in communications theory is the Shannon-Hartley theorem.[12,13] This theorem states that the maximum data rate capacity C of a channel with bandwidth B and additive gaussian band-limited white noise is

$$C = B \log_2 (1 + S/N) \qquad \text{bits/second} \qquad (3.15)$$

where S and N are the average signal power and noise power, respectively, at the output of the channel.

There are two important aspects of the Shannon-Hartley theorem. First, it gives us the maximum rate at which data can be reliably transmitted over a thermal-noise limited channel. Thus, system designers try to optimize the system to have a data rate as close to C as possible with an acceptable bit error rate.

The second aspect concerns the trade-off between signal-to-noise ratio and bandwidth. For example, suppose we have a channel of 3000-Hz bandwidth and that we need an S/N of 1000 (30 dB) to have an acceptable bit error rate. Then according to Eq. (3.15) the maximum data rate we can transmit at is about 30,000 b/s.

In practice, the ideal system performance predicted by the Shannon-Hartley theorem cannot be achieved, but it does give a good approximation of the upper bound on the channel.

3.4 DISTORTION AND NOISE LIMITATIONS ON SYSTEM PERFORMANCE

Now that we have established what bandwidths are required for a signal, let us see what limitations the physical characteristics of a link impose on the signals.

At the receiving end of any communication link, the signals must be reproduced with a high fidelity if analog information is transmitted, or they must be correctly interpreted as a zero bit or a one bit if they are in a digital format. Thus, a transmission channel must have sufficient bandwidth to pass the communication signals relatively undistorted from the transmitter to the receiver. Unfortunately, noise and distortion are introduced in any communication channel as the signal moves through the link. Both of these factors can cause errors in the signal detection process at the receiver.

Signal distortion arises because transmission channels do not respond uniformly to all frequency components contained in a signal. These band-limiting characteristics of a channel arise from the various RC time constants associated with its circuit and transmission-line components. In general, the result is that energies at individual frequencies are attenuated to different degrees (i.e., each Fourier component is attenuated by a different amount). Transmission channels thus have certain frequency bands within which signals can be efficiently transmitted.

A comparison of the attenuation as a function of frequency for several types of commonly used cables is given in Fig. 3.11 and a tabulation of attenuation at specific frequencies is given in Table 3.2. A change in resistance is the main cause of the increase in attenuation as a function of frequency. For coaxial cables this resistance increase is primarily attributable to the skin effect. This factor plus proximity effects and radiation losses are the major causes of frequency-dependent attenuation variations in twisted-wire pairs.

Noise on a link can generally be classified into two categories.[5,14] The first kind is *gaussian noise* which includes thermal and shot noise in the transmitting and receiving equipment, thermal noise in the channel, and electromagnetic radiation picked up through the channel or the end equipment from various nearby emitters. Gaussian noise is usually *white*. This means that it has a flat power spectral density over a wide range of frequencies. Transmission errors due to *white gaussian noise* are referred to as *random errors* since the occurrence of an error in one particular signaling interval generally does not affect the performance of the system during the following (adjacent) signaling interval.

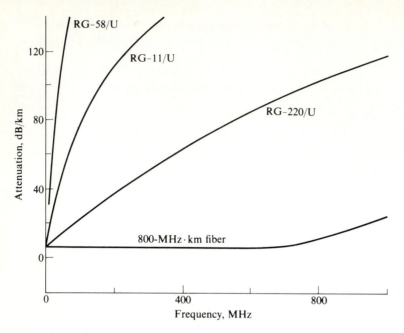

FIGURE 3.11
Attenuation versus frequency for several commonly used cable types.

A second type of noise is called *impulse noise*. This is characterized by long quiet intervals which are then interrupted by high-amplitude noise bursts. This noise can result from either natural or equipment-generated noises such as lightning or transients caused by high-voltage switching. In this case errors in digital systems usually occur in bursts with two or more successive transmitted symbols or bits being affected.

TABLE 3.2
Cable attenuation at specific frequencies

Broadband LAN		Baseband LAN (Ethernet)		
			Attenuation, dB/100 ft	
Frequency, MHz	Attenuation of RG-6/U, dB/100 ft	Frequency, MHz	Coax. trunk	Drop
50	1.5	1	0.2	0.6
100	2.1	5	0.4	1.4
200	3.1	10	0.5	2.0
500	5.0	20	0.65	2.9
900	6.9	50	1.0	4.7

3.4.1 Digital Receiver Performance Calculation

In a digital receiver the amplified and filtered signal is compared to a threshold level once per time slot to determine whether or not a pulse is present in that time slot. Ideally the output signal $v_{out}(t)$ would always exceed the threshold voltage when a 1 is present, and would be less than the threshold when no pulse (a 0) was sent. In actual systems, deviations from the average value of $v_{out}(t)$ are caused by various noises, interference from adjacent pulses, and conditions wherein the signal is not completely extinguished during a zero pulse.

In practice there are several standard ways of measuring the rate of error occurrences in a digital data stream.[15,16] One common approach is to divide the number of errors N_e occurring over a certain time interval t by the number of pulses (ones and zeros) N_t transmitted during this interval. This is called either the *error rate* or the *bit error rate*, which is commonly abbreviated BER. Thus we have

$$\text{BER} = \frac{N_e}{N_t} = \frac{N_e}{Rt} \tag{3.16}$$

where $R = 1/T$ is the bit rate (the pulse transmission rate). The error rate is expressed by a number such as 10^{-6}, for example, which states that on the average one error occurs for every million pulses sent. This error rate depends on the signal-to-noise ratio at the receiver (the ratio of signal power to noise power). The system error rate requirements and the receiver noise levels thus set the lower limit on the signal power level that is required at the receiver.

A typical receiver block diagram is shown in Fig. 3.12. The first section consists of a signal-receiving element (for example, an antenna or a photodetector) and a demodulator. The purpose of the demodulator is to remove the high-frequency sine-wave modulation introduced at the transmitter. The recovered baseband signal is then sent through a filter to eliminate some of the noise introduced during the transmission process, at the expense, however, of further distorting the signal. Finally, the decoder samples the receiver filter output in order to reproduce the original signal message.

To compute the bit error rate at the receiver, we have to know the probability distribution[17,18] of the signal at the decoder input. Knowing the signal probability distribution at this point is important because it is here that the

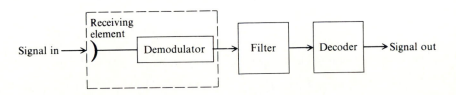

FIGURE 3.12
Block diagram of a typical receiver.

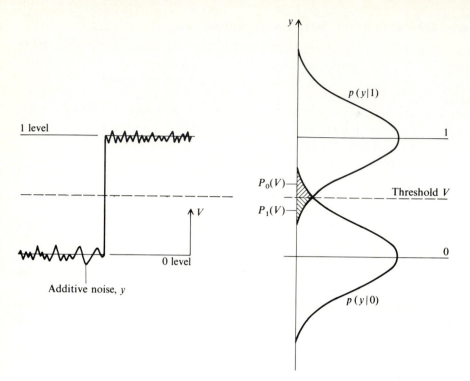

FIGURE 3.13
Probability distribution for 0 and 1 signal levels.

decision is made as to whether a 0 or a 1 was sent. The shapes of two signal probability distributions are shown in Fig. 3.13. These are

$$P_1(v) = \int_{-\infty}^{v} p(y|1) \, dy \qquad (3.17)$$

which is the probability that the filter output voltage is less than v when a 1 pulse was sent, and

$$P_0(v) = \int_{v}^{\infty} p(y|0) \, dy \qquad (3.18)$$

which is the probability that the output voltage exceeds v when a 0 was transmitted. The functions $p(y|1)$ and $p(y|0)$ are the conditional probability distribution functions; that is, $p(y|x)$ is the probability that the output voltage is y, given that an x was transmitted (see App. D).

If the threshold voltage is v_{th} then the error probability P_e is defined as

$$P_e = aP_1(v_{th}) + bP_0(v_{th}) \qquad (3.19)$$

The weighting factors a and b are determined by the *a priori* distribution of the data. That is, a and b are the probabilities that either a 1 or 0 occurs, respectively. For unbiased data with equal probability of 1 and 0 occurrences, $a = b = 0.5$. The problem to be solved now is to select the decision threshold at that point where P_e is minimum.

To calculate the error probability we need to know the noise statistics of the system. In general it is assumed that the noise has a gaussian probability-density function with zero mean. Thus, if we sample the noise voltage $n(t)$ at any arbitrary time t_1, the probability that the measured sample $n(t_1)$ falls in the range n to $n + dn$ is given by

$$f(n) = \frac{1}{\sqrt{2\pi\sigma^2}} e^{-n^2/2\sigma^2} \tag{3.20}$$

where σ^2 is the noise variance.

We can now use this function to determine the probability of error for a data stream in which the pulses are all of amplitude V. Let us first consider the case of a *zero* being sent, so that no pulse is present at the time of decoding. Assuming that we have unbiased data, the probability of error in this case is the probability that the noise will exceed the threshold voltage $v_{th} = V/2$ and be mistaken for a *one* pulse. The probability of error $P_0(v)$ is then simply the chance that the filter output voltage $v(t)$ will fall somewhere between $V/2$ and ∞. Using Eq. (3.18) we have

$$P_0(v_{th}) = \int_{V/2}^{\infty} p(y|0)\, dy = \int_{V/2}^{\infty} f_0(y)\, dy$$

$$= \int_{V/2}^{\infty} \frac{1}{\sqrt{2\pi\sigma^2}} e^{-v^2/2\sigma^2}\, dv \tag{3.21}$$

where the subscript 0 denotes the presence of a *zero* bit.

Similarly we can find the probability of error that a transmitted 1 is misinterpreted as a 0 by the decoder. When a 1 is transmitted, the decoder sees a pulse of amplitude V volts plus superimposed noise. In this case the filter output voltage $v(t)$ will fluctuate around V, so that the probability density function of Eq. (3.20) becomes

$$f_1(v) = \frac{1}{\sqrt{2\pi\sigma^2}} e^{-(v-V)^2/2\sigma^2} \tag{3.22}$$

where the subscript 1 denotes the presence of a *one* bit. The probability of error that a 1 is decoded as a 0 is the likelihood that the sampled signal-plus-noise pulse falls below $V/2$. This is simply given by

$$P_1(v_{th}) = \int_{-\infty}^{V/2} p(y|1)\, dy = \int_{-\infty}^{V/2} f_1(v)\, dv$$

$$= \frac{1}{\sqrt{2\pi\sigma^2}} \int_{-\infty}^{V/2} e^{-(v-V)^2/2\sigma^2}\, dv \tag{3.23}$$

Since we assumed unbiased data, $a = b = 0.5$ in Eq. (3.19) so that we have, substituting Eqs. (3.21) and (3.23) into Eq. (3.19), the probability of error P_e in the decoding of any digit

$$P_e = \frac{1}{2}\left[1 - \text{erf}\left(\frac{V}{2\sqrt{2}\,\sigma}\right)\right] \tag{3.24}$$

where

$$\text{erf } x = \frac{2}{\sqrt{\pi}}\int_0^x e^{-y^2}\,dy \tag{3.25}$$

is the error function which is tabulated in various mathematical handbooks. An important point in Eq. (3.24) is that P_e depends only on the parameter V/σ which is the ratio of the signal amplitude V to the standard deviation σ of the noise. Since σ is usually called the *rms noise*, the ratio V/σ is then the *peak signal-to-rms-noise ratio*. The relationship given in Eq. (3.24) is thus a very fundamental one in communication theory since it relates the bit error probability (or bit error rate denoted by BER) to the signal-to-noise ratio which is often designated by S/N.

A plot of BER versus S/N, in decibels, is given in Fig. 3.14. Recall that (see App. A)

$$\left(\frac{S}{N}\right)_{\text{dB}} = 20\log\frac{V}{\sigma} \tag{3.26}$$

Example 3.6. As an example, Fig. 3.14 shows that for a signal-to-noise ratio of 8.5 (18.6 dB) we have $P_e = 10^{-5}$. In this case on the average 1 out of 10^5 transmitted bits will be interpreted wrong. If this signal is being sent at a standard T1 telephone-line rate (1.544 Mb/s), this BER results in a misinterpreted bit every 0.065 s, which is highly unsatisfactory. However, by increasing the signal strength so that $V/\sigma = 12.0$ (21.6 dB), the BER decreases to $P_e = 10^{-9}$. For the T1 case this means a bit is misinterpreted every 650 s, or 11 min, on the average which, in general, is tolerable.

The above example demonstrates the exponential behavior of the probability of error as a function of the signal-to-noise ratio. Here we saw that by doubling S/N (a 3 dB increase), the BER decreased by 10^4. Thus, there exists a narrow range of signal-to-noise ratios above which the error rate is tolerable and below which a highly unacceptable number of errors occur. The signal-to-noise ratio at which this transition occurs is called the *threshold level*. In general, a performance safety margin of 3 to 6 dB is included in the transmission link design to ensure that this threshold level is not exceeded when system parameters such as transmitter output, line attenuation, or the noise floor vary with time.

3.4.2   Signal-to-Noise Ratios in Analog Systems

We can quite accurately determine the performance of a digital system by calculating the error probability of a signal which has a specific signal-to-noise ratio.

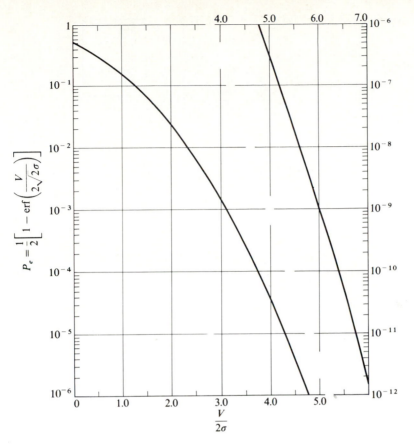

FIGURE 3.14
Bit error rate as a function of signal-to-noise ratio.

A similar approach for an analog system is not readily made because of the continuous nature of an analog signal. However, the concept of signal-to-noise ratio (SNR) is still a useful figure of merit for measuring the performance of an analog system. Although a variety of analog modulation schemes exist, for sake of simplicity we will only consider two detection methods here: the envelope detector in an AM system and the discriminator in an FM system. Furthermore, because of the lengthy complexity of the analyses needed to derive the SNR, we will only examine and discuss the results of the calculation here and refer the interested reader to the literature for the details.

AM ENVELOPE DETECTION. A typical AM receiver is shown in Fig. 3.15. The input to the receiver is an amplitude modulated carrier of the form

$$v(t) = A_c[1 + mf(t)] \cos \omega_c t \qquad (3.27)$$

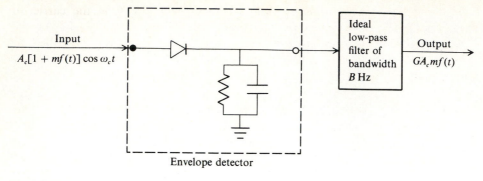

FIGURE 3.15
A typical AM receiver.

Here A_c is the amplitude of the unmodulated carrier of frequency ω_c at the receiver input, m is the modulation index (which states how heavily the carrier is modulated), and $f(t)$ is the modulating signal.

The signal is then passed through a nonlinear device (a common form being the diode half-wave rectifier shown in Fig. 3.15) which is followed by an RC low-pass filter. The output of the envelope detector is given by

$$v_D(t) = GA_c mf(t) \qquad (3.28)$$

where G is a proportionality constant that depends on the particular detector used.

Of interest in the AM case is a comparison of the SNR at the input and output of the envelope detector. This SNR will be denoted by S_0/N_0 and is defined as the ratio of the output signal power in the absence of noise to the mean noise power at the output in the presence of an unmodulated carrier. Under the assumption that only gaussian noise has been added in the detection process, the SNR at the detector output is given by

$$\frac{S_0}{N_0} = \frac{1}{2}\frac{(\text{CNR})^2}{1 + 2\,\text{CNR}} \qquad (3.29)$$

where CNR is the *carrier-to-noise ratio* defined by

$$\text{CNR} = \frac{A_c^2}{2N} \qquad (3.30)$$

with $A_c^2/2$ being the average power in the unmodulated sine-wave carrier.

For high values of CNR, such as are found in AM broadcast systems, for example, Eq. (3.29) reduces to

$$\frac{S_0}{N_0} \approx \frac{1}{4}\,\text{CNR} \qquad (3.31)$$

Thus the output signal-to-noise ratio is linearly dependent on the carrier-to-noise ratio for an AM envelope detection system. From Eq. (3.31) we see that the SNR in an AM system depends only on the CNR. This means that the SNR cannot be improved by increasing the modulation index (increasing the modulating signal strength).

FREQUENCY MODULATION (FM). In a frequency modulation (FM) system, the frequency of the carrier wave is varied in accordance with some specific information-carrying signal. A simplified FM receiver is shown in Fig. 3.16. First a frequency-modulated signal having a transmission bandwidth B_T is passed through a limiter which removes all amplitude variations. Next the signal goes to a discriminator whose output is directly proportional to the instantaneous frequency of the signal. Finally the signal passes through a low-pass filter to eliminate high-frequency distortion terms. The filter bandwidth is $B = f_m < B_T/2$, which is the maximum bandwidth of the actual information signal $f(t)$ being transmitted.

For an FM system the transmitted frequency-modulated carrier can be expressed as

$$v_c(t) = A_c \cos(\omega_c t + \beta \sin \omega_m t) \qquad (3.32)$$

where A_c is the amplitude of the carrier wave of frequency ω_c, ω_m is the rate at which the modulating signal causes the instantaneous radian frequency to vary about the carrier frequency with a maximum deviation of $\Delta\omega$ radians, and

$$\beta = \frac{\Delta\omega}{\omega_m} = \frac{\Delta f}{f_m} \qquad (3.33)$$

is called the *modulation index*. This is defined as the ratio of the *maximum frequency deviation* Δf to the *particular modulating frequency* f_m. Note that the average power S_c of the FM wave given by Eq. (3.32) is just

$$S_c = \frac{1}{2} A_c^2 \qquad (3.34)$$

which is independent of the modulating signal.

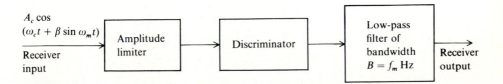

FIGURE 3.16
Block diagram of a simplified FM receiver.

After some lengthy and detailed analysis, it can be shown that the mean SNR at the receiver output is[5]

$$\frac{S_0}{N_0} = 3\beta^2 \frac{S_c}{N_c} \tag{3.35}$$

where S_c/N_c corresponds to the carrier-to-noise ratio of an AM system having the same carrier power and noise spectral density. Note here that, in contrast to the AM case, the output SNR increases with the modulation index or the transmission bandwidth.

3.5 SIGNAL FORMATS USED IN LANs

Here we examine some typical signal formats or modulation schemes that are used in local area networks. In commonly used terminology, local area networks are broadly classified according to the types of signals used. Thus we have either baseband or broadband local area networks. A *baseband* LAN is defined as one that uses digital signals, which are inserted directly on the network transmission line as voltage pulses. Ethernet is a popular implementation of a baseband LAN. In contrast, a *broadband* LAN uses analog signals to transfer data. Here digital signals are passed through a modem and transmitted on a carrier wave over one of the frequency bands of the cable.

3.5.1 Baseband LANs

In baseband LANs the frequency spectrum of the transmitted signal extends from zero hertz to some minimum upper limit which is dictated by the bandwidth requirements of the signal. An important consideration in these networks is the format of the transmitted signal, since the decision circuitry in the receiver must be able to extract precise timing information from the incoming signal stream. This is necessary to properly interpret the message carried in the signal.

Thus a set of *channel* or *line coding* rules is used to arrange the signal symbols in a particular pattern. In selecting the signal format, a trade-off needs to be made between timing and noise bandwidth.[19] From noise considerations, minimum bandwidths are desirable. However, a larger bandwidth may be needed to have timing data available from the bit stream.

Two basic classes of line codes used in baseband LANs are the *nonreturn-to-zero* (NRZ) and the *return-to-zero* (RZ) formats.[6,20-22] In NRZ formats a transmitted data bit occupies a full bit period. For RZ formats the pulse width is less than a full bit period. We note here that the transmitted bit can be either a current or voltage pulse in an electrical line, or an optical power pulse in an optical fiber.

NRZ CODES. A number of different NRZ codes are widely used. Their bandwidths are minimum and serve as references for all other code groups. The simplest NRZ code is NRZ-level (or NRZ-L), shown in Fig. 3.17. For a serial data

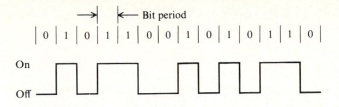

FIGURE 3.17
Example of an NRZ-L data pattern.

stream an on-off (or unipolar) signal represents a 1 by a pulse of current or light filling an entire bit period, whereas for a 0 no pulse is transmitted. These codes are simple to generate and decode, but they possess no inherent error-monitoring or correcting capabilities and they have no self-clocking (timing) features.

A long string of NRZ ones or zeros contains no timing information since there are no level transitions. Thus, unless the timing clocks in the system are extremely stable, a long string of N identical bits could be misinterpreted as either $N-1$ or $N+1$ bits. However, the use of highly stable clocks increases system costs and requires a long system start-up time to achieve synchronization. Two common techniques for restricting the longest time interval in which no level transitions occur are the use of block codes and scrambling.[23,24] *Scrambling* produces a random data pattern by the modulo-2 addition of a known bit sequence with the data stream. At the receiver the same known bit sequence is again modulo-2 added to the received data, and the original bit sequence is recovered. Although the randomness of scrambled NRZ data ensures an adequate amount of timing information, the penalty for its use is an increase in the complexity of the NRZ encoding and decoding circuitry.

RZ CODES. If an adequate bandwidth margin exists, each data bit can be encoded as two line code bits. This is the basis of RZ codes. In these codes a signal level transition occurs during either some or all of the bit periods to provide timing information. A variety of RZ code types exist, some of which are shown in Fig. 3.18. The baseband (NRZ-L) data are shown in Fig. 3.18a. In the unipolar RZ data a 1 bit is represented by a half-period pulse that can occur either in the first or second half of the bit period. A 0 is represented by no signal during the bit period.

A disadvantage of the unipolar RZ format is that long strings of 0 bits can cause loss of timing synchronization. A data format not having this limitation is the biphase-level or Manchester code shown in Fig. 3.18d. The IEEE 802.3 Standard (which is the basis of Ethernet) uses Manchester encoding at the physical level. In this code a positive-going transition at the middle of the bit interval means a logic 0, whereas a negative-going transition indicates a 1 bit. The appearance of the Manchester code is such that when a 1 and a 0 are adjacent to one another, the adjoining pulses appear as a double-width pulse. If a 1 or 0 repeat, normal-width pulses occur at the clock rate. The Manchester code is

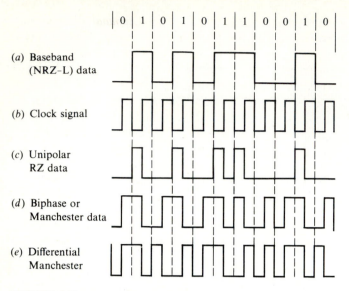

FIGURE 3.18

Examples of RZ data formats. (*a*) NRZ-L baseband data; (*b*) clock signal; (*c*) unipolar RZ data; (*d*) biphase or Manchester; (*e*) differential Manchester data.

simple to generate and decode. Since it is an RZ-type code, it requires twice the bandwidth of an NRZ code. In addition, it has no inherent error-detecting or correcting capability.

Token passing rings as specified by IEEE Standard 802.5 use the differential Manchester encoding scheme shown in Fig. 3.18*e*. In this encoding scheme, when a binary 1 bit cell is compared with the clock period, a transition will occur in the center of the bit cell only. If a binary 0 bit cell is compared with the clock period, transitions occur both at the beginning and the center of the cell.

Coaxial or wire-pair cable systems commonly use the bipolar RZ or alternate mark inversion (AMI) coding scheme. These wire line codes have also been adapted to unipolar optical systems.[25,26] The two-level AMI optical pulse formats require the transmission bandwidth of NRZ codes, but they provide timing information in the data stream, and the redundancy of the encoded information (which is inherent in these codes) allows for direct in-service error monitoring.[27]

BLOCK CODES. An efficient category of redundant binary codes is the *mBnB* block code class.[22,28] In this class of codes, blocks of *m* binary bits are converted to longer blocks of $n > m$ binary bits. These new blocks are then transmitted in NRZ or RZ format. As a result of the additional redundant bits, the increase in bandwidth using this scheme is given by the ratio *n/m*. At the expense of this increased bandwidth, the *mBnB* block codes provide adequate timing and error-monitoring information, and they do not have baseline wander problems since long strings of ones and zeros are eliminated.

A convenient concept used for block codes is the *accumulated* or *running disparity*, which is the cumulative difference between the number of 1 and 0 bits. A simple means of measuring this is with an up-down counter. The key factors in selecting a particular block code are low disparity and a limit in the disparity variation (the difference between the maximum and minimum values of the accumulated disparity). A low disparity allows the dc component of the signal to be canceled. A bound on the accumulated disparity avoids the low-frequency spectral content of the signal and facilitates error-monitoring by detecting the disparity overflow. Generally, one chooses codes that have n even, since for odd values of n there are no coded words with zero disparity.

A comparison of several *mBnB* codes is given in Table 3.3. The parameters shown in this table are:

1. The ratio n/m which gives the bandwidth increase
2. The longest number N_{max} of consecutive identical symbols, where small values of N_{max} allow for easier clock recover
3. The bounds on the accumulated disparity D
4. The percentage W of n-bit words that are not used; the detection of invalid words at the receiver permits character reframing

The most suitable codes for high data rates are the 3B4B, 5B6B, or 6B8B codes. If simplicity of the encoder and decoder circuits is the main criterion, the 3B4B is the most convenient code. The 5B6B code is the most advantageous if bandwidth reduction is the major concern. The 5B6B code is used in the Fiber Distributed Data Interface (FDDI) LAN specification (see Sec. 10.5).

3.5.2 Broadband LANs

Broadband LANs employ analog signaling to transmit information. Here the frequency spectrum of the cable is divided into independent channels or sections of bandwidth. This is the basis of frequency division multiplexing described in Sec. 3.6. These separate channels can be used to transmit independent data signals. The signal structures that can be used include those described in Sec. 3.2

TABLE 3.3

A comparison of several *mBnB* codes

Code	n/m	N_{max}	D	$W\%$
3B4B	1.33	4	± 3	25
6B8B	1.33	6	± 3	75
5B6B	1.20	6	± 4	28
7B8B	1.14	9	± 7	27
9B10B	1.11	11	± 8	24

and shown in Fig. 3.4. They include amplitude shift keying (ASK), phase shift keying (PSK), and frequency shift keying (FSK).

3.6 MULTIPLEXING OF SIGNALS

When many nodes are competing for the use of a network, the capacity or bandwidth of the network channel can be divided, or allocated, in a variety of ways to make the most effective use of the available channel capacity. This is accomplished using multiplexing. The origin of multiplexing came from applications where a large number of data sources were located at a common point and it was desirable to transmit these signals simultaneously over a single communications channel. The two basic multiplexing schemes are *frequency-division multiplexing* (FDM) and *time-division multiplexing* (TDM). In FDM the frequency spectrum is divided into logical channels, with each user having exclusive possession of a particular frequency band. In TDM the users take turns using the entire channel for short bursts of time.

3.6.1 Frequency-Division Multiplexing (FDM)

The concept of FDM is to divide the available bandwidth of a single physical medium into a number of smaller, independent frequency channels. Using modulation, independent message signals are translated to different frequency bands and are then all combined in a linear summing circuit to form a composite signal for transmission, as is illustrated in Fig. 3.19. The carriers used to form the composite signal are referred to as *subcarriers*. The resulting signal can then be transmitted by electromagnetic means.

A general form of the composite signal at the output of the summing circuit is shown in Fig. 3.20. The line in the middle of each channel illustrates possible carrier frequencies, which are designated as $f_{c1}, f_{c2}, \ldots, f_{cN}$. Here each channel is shown as occupying the same bandwidth, but this is not necessary for FDM systems. What is necessary, however, is that some *guard band* exists between successive channels as is illustrated in Fig. 3.20. This is needed to prevent interchannel cross talk that could result from spectral spillover between adjacent channels.

A block diagram of an FDM receiver is shown in Fig. 3.21. The front portion of the system is a radio-frequency (RF) receiver having a sufficiently wide bandwidth to accommodate the FDM signal. The output of the receiver is the composite multiplexed signal whose spectrum has the form shown in Fig. 3.20. This signal is next applied to a bank of bandpass filters that select out the individual frequency channels. There is one filter for each subcarrier frequency, and the center of the passband for a given filter corresponds to the center frequency of the channel band. The bandpass filter outputs are then demodulated by conventional techniques.

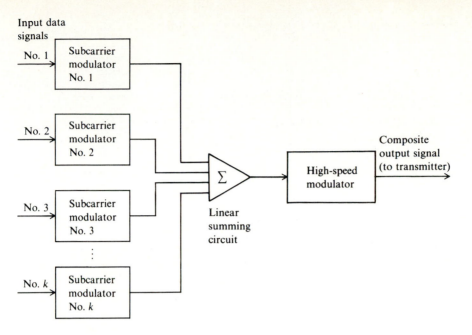

FIGURE 3.19
Concept of frequency-division multiplexing.

If W_i is the bandwidth of the ith frequency channel, including the guard bands between the channels, then the bandwidth B of the composite FDM signal is given by

$$B = \sum_{i=1}^{N} W_i \qquad (3.36)$$

where N is the number of multiplexed signals.

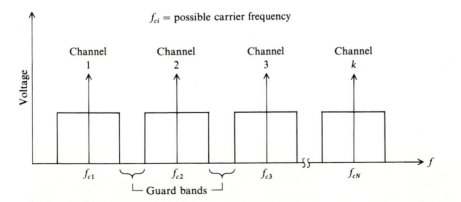

FIGURE 3.20
Composite signal at the output of an FDM transmitter.

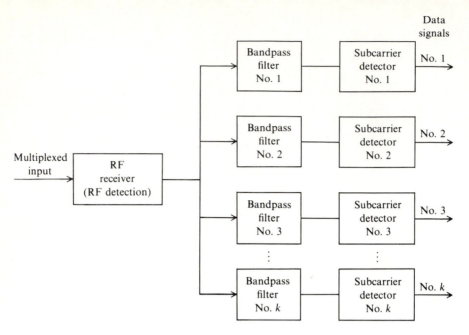

FIGURE 3.21
Block diagram of an FDM receiver.

Well-known examples of FDM are the telephone, radio, and television networks in which a very large number of telephone calls, radio broadcasts, and TV channels are carried in the finite capacity of the available transmission media (wires and unbounded air media). In the telephone network, the standard frequency band used for voice transmission is 4000 Hz. If a particular cable has a usable bandwidth of 48 kHz in the 60- to 108-kHz range, then twelve separate 4-kHz subchannels could be transmitted simultaneously.

Radio and television broadcasts use a similar technique, but employ the atmosphere as the transmission channel. For example, each radio or TV station within a certain broadcast area is assigned a specific broadcast frequency, so that many independent channels can be sent simultaneously within a certain frequency band (for example, 540 to 1600 kHz for AM radio and 88 to 108 MHz for FM radio). Analogous schemes are used in broadband local area networks. These are described in Sec. 4.1.3.

3.6.2   Time-Division Multiplexing (TDM)

In FDM all signals operate at the *same time* with *different frequencies*, whereas in TDM all signals use the *same frequencies* but operate at *different times*. The concept of TDM is best understood by considering Fig. 3.22. Here we have a

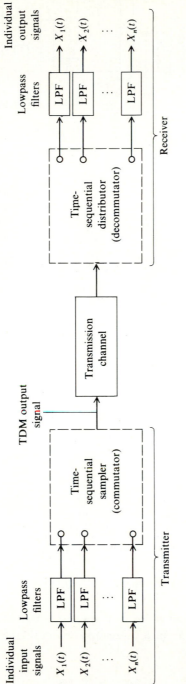

FIGURE 3.22
Block diagram of a time-division multiplexing link.

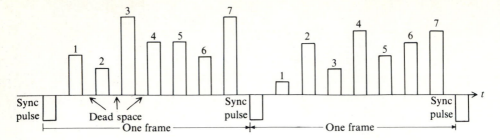

FIGURE 3.23
Composite time-division multiplexed signal.

baseband transmission system in which a number of separate data signals must be transmitted over a single communications link. At the transmitting end, an electronic commutator sequentially samples each data source and interlaces the samples to form a composite baseband signal as is shown in Fig. 3.23.

At the receiving end a second electronic commutator demultiplexes the signal into the appropriate independent message signals. For proper operation the commutator at the receiving end is assumed to be synchronized with the one at the transmitter so that the correct signal can be routed to its desired destination.

The composite signal in Fig. 3.23 shows some unused space ("dead space") between successive sampled pulses. This unused space is needed to prevent inter-channel cross talk which can arise from pulse-spreading in the transmission system. Along with the samples from the data sources (seven in this case), one synchronizing pulse is transmitted with each cycle of sampled pulses. This cycle plus the controlling synchronization pulse (commonly referred to as a *sync pulse*) is known as a *frame*, since, as we saw in Sec. 2.4, a frame is defined as data plus control information.

The minimum bandwidth of a TDM system can be determined by using the *Nyquist sampling theorem*. First assume that no sync pulses are present and that there are N signals to be multiplexed, each of which has a bandwidth W_i. According to the Nyquist theorem, each signal must be sampled no less than $2W_i$ times per second. If the *frame time* is T_f, then the total number of baseband pulses n_s in this time interval is

$$n_s = \sum_{i=1}^{N} 2W_i T_f \qquad (3.37)$$

Assuming that the baseband pulse is a lowpass signal of bandwidth B, the required sampling rate is $2B$. In a T_f-second interval (one frame) we then have $2BT_f$ samples, so that

$$n_s = 2BT_f = \sum_{i=1}^{N} 2W_i T_f \qquad (3.38)$$

or

$$B = \sum_{i=1}^{N} W_i$$

which is the same minimum required bandwidth as obtained for FDM.

3.6.3 Common TDM Schemes

Let us now look at some common TDM schemes. To time-division multiplex digital signals, one must keep the following points in mind:

1. We must define a unit of time called a *frame* within which all signals to be multiplexed have taken at least one turn.
2. The frame is divided in a number of *time slots*, with each signal source having a uniquely assigned slot position.
3. *Control bits* must be added to the frame to enable the receiver to identify the beginning and end of a frame.

The frames can be sent either asynchronously or synchronously.[29] Asynchronous transmission is generally used for slow speed data (up to 1200 b/s) sent at irregular time intervals such as that between a terminal operator and a computer. This type of data is sent in character form, with a character ranging from 5 to 8 bits in length depending on the kind of terminal and code used (five bits for Baudot code, seven with an additional optional parity bit for ASCII code, and eight bits for EBCDIC).

> **Example 3.7.** An example of an asynchronous ASCII-code frame is shown in Fig. 3.24. Here an idle condition (no data being sent) is indicated by having the transmission line be in a 1 state. A START bit, or a transition from 1 to 0, precedes each transmitted character. This notifies the receiver that a character is being transmitted. At the end of the transmitted character, one or more STOP bits return the line to the 1 state where it gets ready for the next character. This process is repeated for each character until the entire message has been sent. The receiver uses the START and STOP bits to synchronize itself to the transmitter on a character-by-character basis.

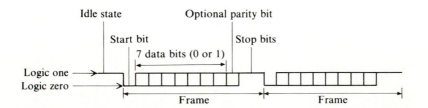

FIGURE 3.24
The synchronous-timing mode is used principally with human-to-machine interfaces.

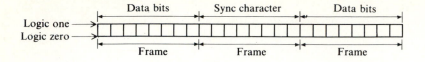

FIGURE 3.25

Synchronous transmission makes use of an internal clocking mechanism to synchronize the transmitter and receiver for high-speed machine-to-machine communication.

For high data rates, we need to use synchronous transmission. This technique does not use START-STOP bits to frame characters and therefore makes more efficient use of the communication channel than asynchronous transmission. Synchronous transmission usually employs a clocking signal which synchronizes the transmitter and receiver. As shown in Fig. 3.25, synchronously formatted data characters are transmitted in frames that start with either one or two uniquely coded synchronization characters. Once such a character has been sensed by the receiving terminal, the incoming stream of data bits is interpreted based on the clock signal generated by the transmitter. Generally this signal is embedded in the data and is derived from the received information signal by means of a phase-locked loop. The receiver continues accepting data until it detects a special ending character which signifies that the message is over. Between messages the communication line may be idle by continuously sending synchronization characters or it may be held in the 1 state.

Example 3.8. An example of a TDM scheme is the digital transmission method used in the telephone network.[30] In the North American digital hierarchy, the fundamental building block is a 1.544 Mb/s transmission rate, known as a T1 rate. This block is formed by time-division multiplexing 24 PCM-encoded voice-frequency channels which are band-limited to the 300- to 3400-Hz range. Each channel is sampled at an 8-kHz rate and each sample is then encoded into 8 bits. This PCM

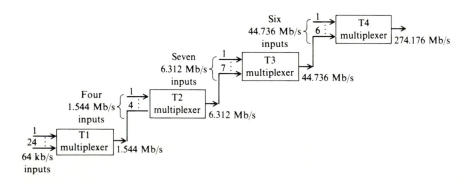

FIGURE 3.26

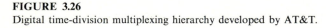
Digital time-division multiplexing hierarchy developed by AT&T.

TABLE 3.4

Standard telephone transmission rates in North America, Europe, and Japan

Hierarchy level no.	North America		Europe		Japan	
	Rate, Mb/s	No. of voice channels	Rate, Mb/s	No. of voice channels	Rate, Mb/s	No. of voice channels
1	1.544	24	2.048	30	1.544	24
2	6.312	96	8.448	120	6.312	96
3	44.736	672	34.368	480	32.064	480
4	274.176	4032	139.264	1920	97.728	1440
5	—	—	560–840	7680–11,520	396.200	5760

conversion process results in a 64 kb/s rate for each voice channel. Framing bits are time-division multiplexed with the 24 digitized voice channels to yield a 1.544 Mb/s data stream.

Figure 3.26 schematically shows the fundamental digital hierarchy used in North America. At any level a data signal at the designated input rate is multiplexed with other input signals at the same rate. The system is not restricted to multiplexing voice signals. For example, at the T1 level, any 64-kb/s signal of the appropriate format could be transmitted as one of the 24 input channels shown in Fig. 3.26. As noted in Fig. 3.26 and Table 3.4, the multiplexed rates are designated as T1 (1.544 Mb/s), T2 (6.312 Mb/s), T3 (44.736 Mb/s), and T4 (274.176 Mb/s). Similar hierarchies, but using different bit rate levels, are employed in Europe and Japan, as Table 3.4 shows.

3.7 ERROR DETECTION

In any digital transmission system, errors are likely to occur even when there is a sufficient signal-to-noise ratio to provide a low bit error rate. To control errors and to improve the reliability of a communication line, first it is necessary to be able to detect the errors and then to correct them.[16,31–34] This is done by the use of *redundancy* in the data stream. With this method, extra bits are introduced into the raw data stream at the transmitter on a regular and logical basis and are extracted again at the receiver. These digits themselves convey no information but allow the receiver to detect and even correct errors in the information-bearing bits. Depending on the amount of redundancy introduced, any degree of error-free transmission of digital data can be achieved, provided that the data rate which includes this redundancy is less than the channel capacity. This last point is a result of the well-known *Shannon channel-coding theory*.

The majority of error-detecting codes are based on the concept of *parity*. The parity of a binary word is *even* when the word contains an even number of one bits, whereas the parity is *odd* if the number of one bits is odd. The simplest example is the single parity-check bit used as the eighth bit in the standard

ASCII data-interchange code. The first seven bits in the frame represent the alphanumeric character being transmitted. The eighth bit is then a one if there are an odd number of ones in the seven data bits, and a zero otherwise. At the receiver this parity check is recalculated to verify whether or not it agrees with the received parity check bit.

Common error-detecting codes having this same structure are the *block codes*. Here the data is transmitted in a sequence of blocks, with each block containing a number of information bits and a number of check bits. The check bits can either follow the information bits or be mixed with them. Here we will view them as following the information bits. These codes are usually described using the notation (n, k) to designate a code containing n total bits in each block, of which k are information bits as illustrated in Fig. 3.27. Since there are k information bits, there are a total of 2^k distinct messages. The encoder transforms each input message block consisting of k information bits into a longer binary sequence of n digits, which is a code word. Therefore, corresponding to the 2^k possible input messages, there are 2^k possible code words at the output of the encoder. This set of 2^k code words constitutes the *block code*. The $n - k$ digits added to each message block by the encoder are the redundant bits.

A second type of encoding is *linear convolutional encoding* of an information sequence. In these convolution codes the encoder operates continuously on the data sequence without breaking it up into independent blocks. At any time unit, the encoder accepts a small block of b information bits (called a *message block*) and produces a block of v code digits (called a *code block*), where $b < v$. The v-digit code block depends not only on the b-bit message block of the same time unit, but also on the previous message blocks. A great deal of effort has been expended on developing such codes, and it is possible to get good improvements in error performance by using relatively short code lengths. Detailed discussions of convolution codes can be found in the works by Michelson and Levesque,[16] Viterbi,[31] and Proakis.[32]

Here we shall concentrate on cyclic codes, which are a particular class of block codes. Relatively simple encoders and decoders exist for cyclic codes, and they are widely used in a variety of applications. Let us first discuss some of the

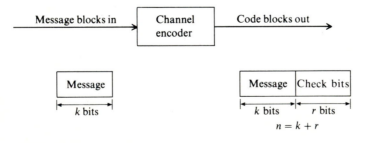

FIGURE 3.27
Block encoding method.

fundamentals of block codes, and then examine the implementation of cyclic codes.

3.7.1 Block Codes

A matrix form is a convenient way of representing a linear block code. If a message of a k-bit data sequence consists of binary (0 or 1) digits $d_1, d_2, \ldots, d_k$, then we denote this by the vector $\mathbf{d}$ which we write as

$$\mathbf{d} = (d_1, d_2, \ldots, d_k) \tag{3.39}$$

The corresponding n-bit code word is denoted by the vector $\mathbf{c}$

$$\mathbf{c} = (c_1, c_2, \ldots, c_k, c_{k+1}, \ldots, c_n) \tag{3.40}$$

where the r parity-check bits $c_{k+1}, \ldots, c_n$ are given by the following weighted modulo-2 sum of the data:

$$
\begin{aligned}
c_{k+1} &= p_{11}d_1 \oplus p_{21}d_2 \oplus \cdots \oplus p_{k1}d_k \\
c_{k+2} &= p_{12}d_1 \oplus p_{22}d_2 \oplus \cdots \oplus p_{k2}d_k \\
&\;\;\vdots \\
c_n &= p_{1r}d_1 \oplus p_{2r}d_2 \oplus \cdots \oplus p_{kr}d_k
\end{aligned}
\tag{3.41}
$$

The coefficients p_{ij} in Eq. (3.41) are either 1 or 0. The symbol $\oplus$ denotes modulo-2 addition which is defined by the standard rules

$$
\begin{aligned}
0 \oplus 0 &= 0 \\
0 \oplus 1 &= 1 \\
1 \oplus 0 &= 1 \\
1 \oplus 1 &= 0
\end{aligned}
\tag{3.42}
$$

Example 3.9. An example of a block code is the (6, 3) code illustrated in Fig. 3.28, where $k = 3$ and $n = 6$. In this code a block of 6 bits contains 3 check bits (c_4, c_5, c_6). Each of the check bits verifies the parity of a particular subset of 2 of the 3 information bits as is shown in Fig. 3.28, to correct any single error over the block of six digits. The eight possible message words for the three data bits and their associated code words are shown in Table 3.5. It is left as an exercise for the reader to verify that these are the correct code words.

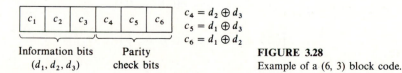

$$
\begin{aligned}
c_4 &= d_2 \oplus d_3 \\
c_5 &= d_1 \oplus d_3 \\
c_6 &= d_1 \oplus d_2
\end{aligned}
$$

Information bits   Parity
(d_1, d_2, d_3) check bits

FIGURE 3.28
Example of a (6, 3) block code.

TABLE 3.5
Message words and code words for a block code with $k = 3$ and $n = 6$

Message words	Code words
000	000000
001	001110
010	010101
011	011011
100	100011
101	101101
110	110110
111	111000

The linear code specified by Eq. (3.41) is referred to as a *systematic parity-check code*. The vector **c** for a linear systematic (n, k) block code can be completely specified by a $k \times n$ matrix operating on the data word **d**:

$$\mathbf{c} = \mathbf{d}G \tag{3.43}$$

where the *code generator matrix* G is given by

$$G = [I_k P] = \begin{bmatrix} 1 & 0 & 0 & \cdots & 0 & p_{11} & p_{12} & \cdots & p_{1r} \\ 0 & 1 & 0 & \cdots & 0 & p_{21} & p_{22} & \cdots & p_{2r} \\ 0 & 0 & 1 & \cdots & 0 & p_{31} & p_{32} & \cdots & p_{3r} \\ \vdots & & \vdots & \vdots & & & & \vdots \\ 0 & 0 & 0 & \cdots & 1 & p_{k1} & p_{k2} & \cdots & p_{kr} \end{bmatrix} \tag{3.44}$$

$$\underbrace{}_{\substack{k \times k \\ \text{identity} \\ \text{matrix } I_k}} \quad \underbrace{\phantom{p_{11} \; p_{12} \cdots p_{1r}}}_{\substack{k \times r \\ \text{parity-bit} \\ \text{matrix } P}}$$

Here the first k columns are an identity matrix I_k which represents the fact that the first k bits of **c** are just the original data bits. The other $r = n - k$ columns of G represent the $k \times r$ matrix P and are the transposed array of the p_{ij} coefficients in Eq. (3.41). When P is specified, it defines the (n, k) block code completely.

To verify that a code word **c** has been generated by the matrix G given by Eq. (3.44), we define the parity-check matrix H which is given by

$$H = \begin{bmatrix} p_{11} & p_{21} & \cdots & p_{k1} & 1 & 0 & \cdots & 0 \\ p_{12} & p_{22} & \cdots & p_{k2} & 0 & 1 & \cdots & 0 \\ \vdots & & \vdots & \vdots & & & & \vdots \\ p_{1r} & p_{2r} & \cdots & p_{kr} & 0 & 0 & \cdots & 1 \end{bmatrix} \tag{3.45}$$

$$= [P^T I_r]$$

Here P^T is the transpose of the matrix P and I_r is an $r \times r$ identity matrix. A code word $\mathbf{c}$ is then valid if it satisfies the condition

$$\mathbf{c}H^T = 0 \tag{3.46}$$

where H^T is the transpose of the matrix H.

Suppose now that errors occur in one or more of the digits of $\mathbf{c}$. Let $\mathbf{r}$ be the received word that has been corrupted by noise in the transmission process. This word may be written as the sum of the original code vector $\mathbf{c}$ and an n-bit vector $\mathbf{e}$ that represents the error pattern

$$\mathbf{r} = \mathbf{c} \oplus \mathbf{e} \tag{3.47}$$

For example, if there are errors in the third and fourth bits, then

$$\mathbf{e} = (0 \ 0 \ 1 \ 1 \ 0 \ \cdots \ 0)$$

The function of the receiver is to decode $\mathbf{c}$ from $\mathbf{r}$, and to derive the message block $\mathbf{d}$ from $\mathbf{c}$. The receiver does the decoding by operating on the word $\mathbf{r}$ with the matrix H^T to determine an r-element vector $\mathbf{s}$ defined as

$$\mathbf{s} = \mathbf{r}H^T = (\mathbf{c} \oplus \mathbf{e})H^T = \mathbf{e}H^T \tag{3.48}$$

The vector $\mathbf{s}$, which is called the *error syndrome* of $\mathbf{r}$, will be nonzero if an error has occurred. It is important to note, however, that the condition $s = 0$ does not guarantee error-free transmission since not all error patterns are detectable by any given code. For example, if noise causes a transmitted code word to be transformed into another valid code word, then the syndrome $s = 0$. In this case the decoder would assume that no transmission errors occurred and would take no action to correct them.

3.7.2 Binary Cyclic Codes

Binary cyclic codes are a subclass of linear block codes. In these codes the code vectors are simple lateral (or cyclic) shifts of one another. For example, if $\mathbf{c} = (c_1, c_2, \ldots, c_{n-1}, c_n)$ is a possible code vector, then so are $(c_2, c_3, \ldots, c_n, c_1)$, $(c_3, c_4, \ldots, c_n, c_1, c_2)$, etc. They are widely used for two reasons. First, encoding and syndrome calculations can be easily implemented using simple shift registers with feedback connections. Second, simple and efficient decoding methods are possible since the codes have a fair amount of inherent algebraic structure.

The cyclic property of the code words places some restrictions on the generator matrix. Consider the kth row (the last row) of the generator matrix G given by Eq. (3.44). If the code is cyclic, the kth row, which has zeros in the first $k - 1$ positions and a 1 in the kth position, must also have a 1 in the nth position. Otherwise a single cyclic shift to the right would create a code word with an all-zero information section and a nonzero parity section, which is not possible. Hence for a systematic cyclic code (that is, one where the first k bits represent the information bits and the remaining $r = n - k$ digits the parity bits), we must have a generator matrix of the form

$$G = \begin{bmatrix} 1 & 0 & 0 & \cdots & 0 & \vdots & \cdots & \cdot \\ 0 & 1 & 0 & \cdots & 0 & \vdots & & \\ 0 & 0 & 1 & \cdots & 0 & \vdots & & \\ & & \vdots & & & \vdots & & \vdots \\ 0 & 0 & 0 & \cdots & 1 & \vdots & \cdots & 1 \end{bmatrix} \tag{3.49}$$

$$\underbrace{\qquad\qquad\qquad}_{I_k}$$

where the last row has a 1 in the last column. Thus the last row must always be representable by a polynomial of degree $n - k$ having the form

$$g(x) = x^{n-k} + g_{n-k-1}x^{n-k-1} + \cdots + g_1 x + 1 \tag{3.50}$$

where the coefficients g_i are 0 or 1, the arithmetic is modulo-2, and the last element must always be a 1.

Equation (3.50), which is called the *generator polynomial* of the code, determines the characteristics of the code. The generator matrix G is derived from $g(x)$ using the following methodology:

1. Use $g(x)$ as the kth row.
2. To form the $(k - 1)$th row, cyclically shift the kth row one column to the left. This corresponds to the operation $xg(x)$. For this row the kth column must be zero to have the standard form of Eq. (3.44). If the kth entry is 1, add the kth row to the cyclically shifted row, so that the $(k - 1)$th row becomes $xg(x) + g(x)$.
3. Similarly, the $(k - j)$th row is formed from the row below it by shifting the entries of the $(k - j + 1)$th row one column to the left. Again if the entry in the kth column is a 1, add $g(x)$ to the shifted row.

Hence every row of G is divisible by $g(x)$, so that $g(x)$ completely specifies every word in the code.

The next task then is how to determine $g(x)$. This turns out to be straightforward according to the following theorem: *the generator polynomial $g(x)$ for an (n, k) cyclic code is a divisor of $x^n + 1$*. For example, for a class of $(7, k)$ codes, the divisors of $x^7 + 1$ are

$$x^7 + 1 = (x + 1)(x^3 + x + 1)(x^3 + x^2 + 1) \tag{3.51}$$

Thus since $g(x)$ is of order $n - k$, Eq. (3.51) has two polynomials of the fourth order that can serve as generators of a $(7, 3)$ code, and two polynomials that can be used for a $(7, 4)$ code.

The syndrome associated with a given cyclic code can be calculated quite easily. Let $c(x)$ and $r(x)$ be the transmitted code polynomial and received polynomial, respectively. Dividing $r(x)$ by the generator polynomial $g(x)$, we have

$$\frac{r(x)}{g(x)} = q(x) + \frac{s(x)}{g(x)} \qquad (3.52)$$

The division results in a quotient polynomial $q(x)$ of degree $(k-1)$ or less and a remainder polynomial $s(x)$. If $s(x) = 0$, the received polynomial $r(x)$ is a multiple of the generator polynomial $g(x)$ and is therefore a valid code word. If $s(x)$ is nonzero, then transmission errors have occurred. Therefore, the remainder $s(x)$ is the syndrome which can be used for error detection and correction.[32-34]

3.8 RETRANSMISSION TECHNIQUES

To control errors in a communcation link, the decoder at the receiver recomputes the check bits to verify whether or not the received 7-digit sequence is an allowable code word. If not then one or more errors must have occurred in the transmission. In this case the receiver uses a feedback channel to the transmitter to request a retransmission of the incorrect message block. The most common retransmission technique is known as *automatic-repeat-request* (ARQ). Three popular versions of ARQ are *stop-and-wait* ARQ, *go-back-N* ARQ, and *selective-repeat* ARQ.

3.8.1 Stop-and-Wait ARQ

The simplest retransmission protocol is stop-and-wait ARQ. With this scheme the transmitter (which we will call station A) sends a frame over the communication line and then waits for a positive or negative acknowledgment from the receiver (which we will call station B). If no errors occurred in the transmission, station B sends a positive acknowledgment (which is called an *ACK*) to station A. An example of this is shown in Fig. 3.29. The transmitter can now start to

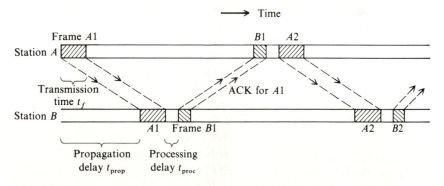

FIGURE 3.29
Timing sequence for stop-and-wait ARQ.

send the next frame. If the frame is received at station B with errors, then a negative acknowledgment (called a *NAK*) is returned to station A. In this case station A must resend the old packet in a new frame.

There is also the possibility that information frames and/or ACKs can be lost. To account for this, the sender is equipped with a timer. If no recognizable acknowledgment is received when the timer expires at the end of the time-out interval t_{out}, then the same frame is sent again. This works fine if information frames are lost, but a refinement is needed if ACKs do not arrive at the sender. In this case if station B correctly receives a packet in the first frame but its ACK is lost on the way to station A, then station B would receive the same packet again in the next frame. To prevent this, a modulo-2 numbering scheme is used wherein frames are alternately labeled with 0 or 1 and positive acknowledgments are of the form ACK0 and ACK1.

The main advantage of stop-and-wait ARQ is its simplicity. However, it is not very useful for modern data networks because of its highly inefficient use of communication links. The major problem is the time spent merely waiting for an ACK, particularly if the link propagation delay is significantly longer than the packet transmission time.

To analyze the efficiency of the stop-and-wait protocol, let us examine Fig. 3.29. Here the *transmission time* t_f is the time required to transmit a frame. For example, a 100-kb/s transmitter needs 0.1 s to send out a 10,000-bit message block. The *propagation delay* t_{prop} is the time needed for a transmitted bit to reach the destination station. This time is on the order of 5 ns/m which is generally negligible for the internodal distances found in local area networks. The *processing delay* t_{proc} is the time required for nodal equipment to perform the necessary processing and switching of data at a node (included here are error detection, address recognition, and input/output queueing delay). The time parameter t_{ack} is the length of an ACK or NAK frame. The minimum time t_T between successive frames then is

$$t_T = t_{prop} + t_f + t_{proc} + t_{prop} + t_{ack} + t_{proc} \tag{3.53}$$

To simplify the analysis and to determine the maximum possible throughput, we shall assume that station A sends information to station B only, and that station B replies with an ACK or a NAK. Furthermore let us assume that the processing time t_{proc} between reception and transmission is negligible, and that the size of the acknowledgment frame is very small. Thus we have

$$t_T \approx t_f + 2t_{prop}$$
$$= t_f + t_{out} \tag{3.54}$$

where we have let $t_{out} = 2t_{prop}$. Thus the system can transmit at most one packet per t_T seconds, which is the maximum possible throughput of information frames that the system can achieve. The actual throughput will always be less than this because of the need to retransmit frames.

To analyze the stop-and-wait protocol in the event of errors, let us assume that p is the probability of a frame being received incorrectly at station B. If we assume that no errors occur in the transmission of ACKs and NAKs, then the probability that it will take i attempts to transmit a frame successfully is $ip^{i-1}(1-p)$. The average time t_c for the correct receipt of a frame is then

$$t_c = \sum_{i=1}^{\infty} ip^{i-1}(1-p)t_T = \frac{t_T}{1-p} = \frac{t_f(1+2a)}{1-p} \tag{3.55}$$

where the parameter $a = t_{prop}/t_f$ has been introduced to relate the information-receipt time to the information frame length.

3.8.2 Go-Back-N ARQ

The most widely used automatic repeat request is go-back-N ARQ, which is also known as *continuous ARQ*. This is used in various data link protocols such as HDLC, SDLC, and ADCCP. In this scheme a series of data frames is sent continuously without waiting for an acknowledgment. This will improve the throughput of the link, especially if the propagation delay is not negligible compared to the frame transmission time.

When the receiving station detects an error in a frame, it sends a NAK to the transmitter for that frame. All further incoming frames at the receiver are then discarded until the frame in error is correctly received. Thus, when the transmitting station receives a NAK, it must retransmit the frame in question plus all succeeding frames. Hence the name *go-back-N*, since the last N previously transmitted frames must be resent when an error occurs. An example of this is shown in Fig. 3.30. Here frames 1 and 2 have been received correctly, but frame 3 is in error. When the NAK for frame 3 arrives at station A, frame 3 plus frames 4, 5, and 6 must be retransmitted.

As in the case with stop-and-wait ARQ, the go-back-N protocol uses a timer mechanism. The number N specifies how many successive packets can be sent in the absence of an acknowledgment. This means that station A cannot send packet $N + i$ before packet i has been acknowledged. Here we shall assume

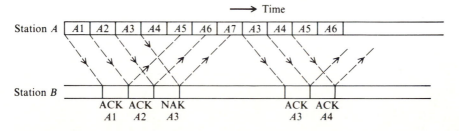

FIGURE 3.30
Timing sequence for go-back-N ARQ. Frame 3 was received in error.

that the length of the time-out window is such that $t_{out} \geq t_f + 2t_{prop}$ so that frames can be sent continuously.

For the go-back-N scheme the minimum time between transmissions is t_f since frames may be sent continuously without waiting for an ACK. Again using the assumptions that the processing and acknowledgment times are negligible, we have from Fig. 3.30 that the average transmission time of a frame is

$$t_c = t_f + \sum_{i=1}^{\infty} ip^i(1-p)t_T = t_f \frac{1+2ap}{1-p} \tag{3.56}$$

where again $t_T = t_f + 2t_{prop}$ and $a = t_{prop}/t_f$.

Figure 3.31 gives a comparison between the stop-and-wait and the go-back-N protocols for the case of one frame out of a thousand being in error ($p = 0.001$). We see that even for small values of a there is a dramatic difference in the two methodologies. We must emphasize here that this figure and Eqs. (3.55) and (3.56) are only approximations, since we have neither taken into account errors that might occur in ACK frames nor, in the case of the go-back-N scheme, that errors can occur in other frames besides the one that was initially incorrect. However, these results are very good approximations to more exact analyses.

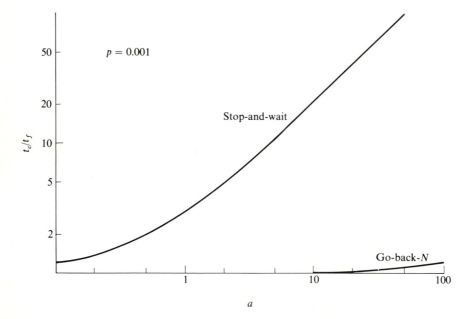

FIGURE 3.31
Comparison of the packet-transmission times for stop-and-wait ARQ and go-back-N ARQ for $p = 0.001$.

3.8.3 Selective-Repeat ARQ

In contrast to the go-back-N scheme, the selective-repeat procedure only needs to retransmit the frame that was negatively acknowledged or for which the timer has expired. Although this is more efficient than the go-back-N scheme, here the receiver requires storage buffers to contain the out-of-order frames until the frame in error is correctly received. The receiver must also have the appropriate logic circuitry needed for reinserting the frames in the correct order. In addition, the transmitter is more complex since it must be able to send frames out of sequence. Consequently, this technique is less commonly used than the go-back-N protocol.

3.9 SWITCHING AND BROADCAST TECHNIQUES

As a final topic in this chapter, we look at how communications take place between a number of different devices on a network. The techniques can be classified as either *switched-network methodologies*[35–38] or *broadcast methodologies*.[39] The three principal types of switched networks are circuit-switched, message-switched, and packet-switched networks. These networks consist of an interconnected set of nodes among which information is transmitted from source to destination by being routed via a switching mechanism through the network of nodes. In a broadcast network there are no intermediate switching nodes. At each node there is a transmitter-receiver pair which is attached to a transmission medium that is shared by all nodes. In the simplest broadcast network, a transmission from any one station is broadcast to and received by all other stations on the network.

3.9.1 Circuit-Switching

In circuit-switching techniques[35] the actual physical electrical path or circuit between the source and destination nodes must be established before data can be transmitted. After the connection is established, the use of the circuit is *exclusive* and *continuous* for the duration of the information exchange. When the exchange is completed, the circuit is disconnected and the physical links between the nodes are ready for use by other connections.

The most predominant use of circuit-switching is in the telephone network. A simple example of this is given in Fig. 3.32. This figure shows that when a call is set up, a dedicated path is established between the two ends and it will continue to exist until the call is completed. In creating such a connection, a certain set-up time is required. This time, which is measured in seconds, does not pose a problem in day-to-day telephone conversations where the set-up time can be offset by the amount of time the channel is used.

However, for information-transmission applications which are on the order of microseconds and which require the total channel capacity to be allocated

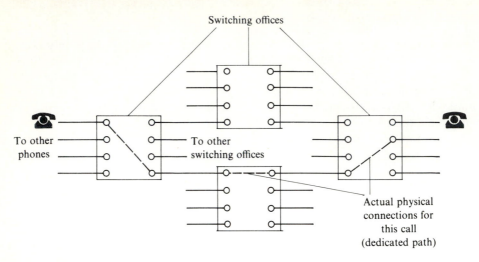

Switching offices

To other phones

To other switching offices

Actual physical connections for this call (dedicated path)

FIGURE 3.32
Circuit-switched connection between two calling parties.

quickly between a number of users, circuit-switching is slow, relatively expensive, and inefficient. Examples of these applications are bursty computer-to-computer transmissions and character-by-character terminal communications. In these cases the channel could be idle for a significant portion of the connection time, yet remain unavailable to other users. On the other hand, once a circuit-switch connection is made, delivery is guaranteed and sequential, delays are small and constant, and communication takes place in real time.

3.9.2 Message-Switching

A different strategy is found in message-switching.[36,37] In this switching method, no dedicated physical path is established in advance between sender and receiver. Instead, it is based on a *store-and forward* technology. When a node has a message block to send, it is stored in the first switching office and then forwarded later on to the next node. That is, the message hops from node to node. At each hop the entire message is received, is inspected for errors, and is temporarily stored in secondary storage until a link to the next node is available.

A model of a message-switching system is shown in Fig. 3.33. Here we want user *A* to send a message to user *B* under the assumption that links 1 and 2 are either down or in use so that they are unavailable for transmission. The message must then be transmitted over links 3 and 4. The following steps will occur:

1. The message is transmitted from user *A* to the data-terminal equipment (DTE) at node 1 where it is stored.

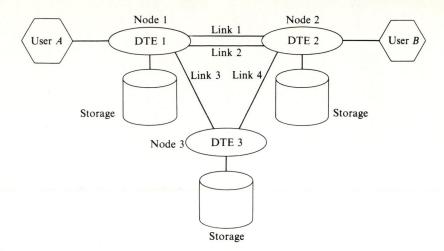

FIGURE 3.33
Message-switching system model.

2. When link 3 is free, the message is read from storage at node 1 and sent in its entirety to node 3 where it is stored.

3. When link 4 is free, the message is read from storage at node 3 and sent in its entirety to node 2 where it is stored.

4. Finally the message is read from storage at node 2 and sent in its entirety to user *B*.

Thus in message-switching no real end-to-end path is created. This makes good use of the communication channels since no resources need to be reserved until the channels are available. However, since message blocks can be very long, large storage capacities must be available at each node to buffer these long blocks. As a result, a single message block can tie up an internodal line for many minutes, thereby making it impossible to have interactive traffic. Because of these limitations, message-switching is not used in local area networks.

3.9.3 Packet-Switching

The principles embodied in packet-switching[38] overcome the long transmission delays inherent in message-switching. Packet-switching is actually very similar to message-switching. A packet-switching system accepts packets from an information source, stores them in buffer memory, and then forwards them to the next packet-switch where the same store-and-forward operation occurs. The only difference between this technique and message-switching is that the maximum length of any packet is generally very short (1000 to 5000 bits) and therefore does not encounter a long transmission delay as it propagates through the store-and-forward network.

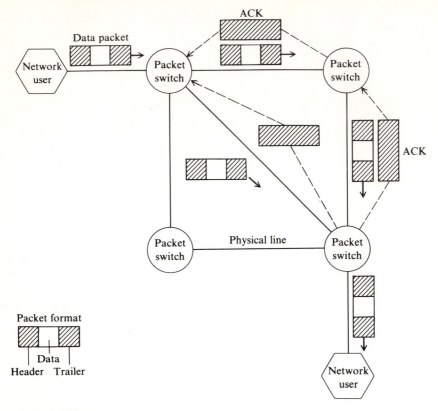

FIGURE 3.34
Packet-switching system model.

The basic concept of packet-switching is shown in Fig. 3.34. Each packet that is sent has both a *header* and a *trailer*. Included in the header is information such as source address, destination address, and packet-sequence number. The trailer is usually a checksum that is used for error control. Typically there is an acknowledgment scheme between adjacent packet switches so that packets can be retransmitted if they are not acknowledged in a certain time frame or if they are negatively acknowledged when an error is detected.

Packet-switching is commonly used for terminal-to-computer and computer-to-computer communications. Here the information exchange can be viewed as a process wherein bursts of information occur with a high peak-to-average rate. Examples of this are point-of-sale systems, inquiry-response systems, remote time-sharing services, and electronic message systems.

The two techniques for sending packets from node to node in a packet-switching system are the *datagram* and *virtual-circuit* methods. A simple comparison of these two techniques with circuit-switching and message-switching is given in Fig. 3.35. This figure shows time-sequence diagrams for the transmission of message from node *A* to node *D* via two intermediate nodes (*B* and *C*).

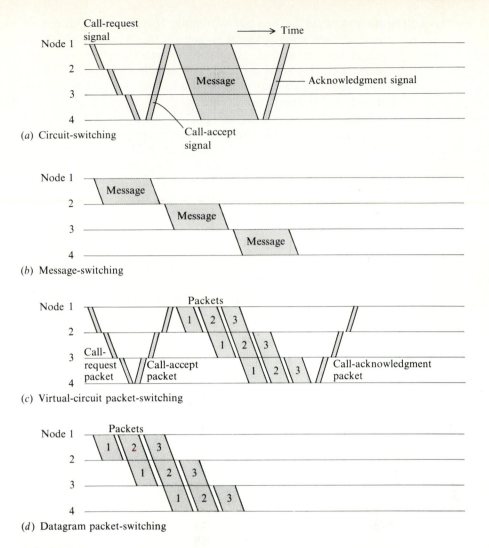

FIGURE 3.35
Comparison of circuit-switching, message-switching, and packet-switching.

As Fig. 3.35 shows, a certain time is required in circuit-switching before a message can be sent. First a call-request signal is sent through the network to the destination node. If this node is prepared to receive a message, a call-accept signal is returned. The time elapsed before the message can be sent thus consists of the propagation time delay through the network and the processing time delay that is required at each node to establish the transmission path during call set-up. Once the connection is set up, the entire message is sent out as a single block with negligible delay occurring at the switching nodes.

No call set-up is required for message-switching. However the entire message must be received at each node before it is sent on to the next node. Since there is no limit on message size, a single message block can tie up an internodal line for many minutes. Thus the total time delay is usually significantly longer than for circuit-switching. Consequently message-switching is not suitable for interactive traffic as is found in local area networks.

Similar to message-switching, datagram packet-switching also does not need a call set-up procedure. In contrast, however, datagram packet-switching is significantly faster than message-switching which makes it ideally suited for interactive traffic in local area networks. There are two key reasons for this difference. First, an upper limit is placed on packet size so that no user can monopolize any transmission line for more than a few tens of microseconds. Secondly, each node along the route can forward any packet of a multipacket message as soon as it arrives; it does not have to wait for the next packet. This reduces delay and improves throughput. Datagram packet-switching is particularly good for short messages and for networks where user flexibility is desirable.

Virtual-circuit packet-switching is similar to circuit-switching in that a circuit route must first be established. This is initiated by a call-request packet which experiences a processing delay at each node analogous to the circuit-switching case. The virtual circuit is established once a call-accept packet from the destination node arrives at the source node. Note that the call-accept packet also incurs processing delays on the return path since at each node the packet must be queued and wait for its turn to be retransmitted. Thus, for comparable networks, the call set-up time is equal to or longer than that occurring in circuit-switching. When the call-accept packet arrives at the source, the message is transmitted in packets. Every packet experiences some processing delay at each node in the path because of the queueing process. This delay is variable and becomes longer when the network gets more heavily used. Nevertheless, virtual-circuit packet-switching is fast enough for interactive traffic. It is especially good for long exchanges of messages and for relieving stations of processing burdens.

3.9.4 Packet Broadcasting

Packets can also be *broadcast* over a medium.[39] This method is commonly used in local area networks. In a packet broadcast network all stations share a common transmission medium and there are no switching devices between them. Thus, a message transmitted by any one station is received by all other stations that are directly connected to the transmission medium. In this case, all stations merely check each packet as it arrives to determine if it is addressed to them, and ignore it otherwise. This approach eliminates the delays that are inherent in systems which route packets from node to node.

Since all the stations share a common transmission medium in a broadcast network, only one station is able to successfully transmit at any given time. Thus some type of medium-access control is needed. This control can be either centralized in one node or distributed among several or all stations. In a centralized scheme a specifically designated controller has the authority to allow a station to access the network. If a station wishes to transmit it must first request and then receive permission to do so from the controller. In a distributed-control scheme all stations collectively share the responsibility of medium-access control. The detailed pros and cons of each method are described in Chap. 6.

3.10 SUMMARY

This chapter described the fundamental principles of how data is transmitted from one element to another over a physical communication channel. To efficiently send a signal over a channel, the properties of the transmitted signal must match the channel characteristics. In this process, which is known as modulation, either the amplitude, phase, or frequency of a carrier waveform is varied systematically in accordance with the message signal. These variations can be of either an analog or a digital nature. In addition to providing matching of signal properties to channel characteristics, modulation is used to reduce noise and interference, to simultaneously transmit several independent signals over a single channel, and/or to overcome equipment limitations.

In analyzing a communication network, an important factor is the rate at which information can be sent over a channel. The physical properties of energy-storage elements (such as capacitors and inductors) limit the speed at which a circuit can respond to time variations of a signal. This limit is related to the bandwidth of the system. The important point to remember is that any transmission system must have a sufficiently large bandwidth to allow all *significant* frequencies of the transmitted signal to pass. To predict the frequency range which contains the major signal components, the Fourier integral representation of a signal and its Fourier transform are extremely valuable when considering nonperiodic time-varying functions (which are essentially information-bearing signals).

Unfortunately, there is no such thing as an ideal transmission line. Noise and distortion are introduced in any communication channel as a signal moves through the link. Both of these factors can cause errors in the signal-detection process at the receiver. Signal distortion arises because transmission channels do not respond uniformly to all frequency components contained in a signal. Two general noise types on a link are gaussian noise and impulse noise. Gaussian noise is usually a white noise (i.e., it has a flat power spectral density) which arises from thermal noise and electromagnetic pickup. Transmission errors due to white gaussian noise are generally random since the occurrence of an error in one particular signaling interval normally does not affect system performance during the following (adjacent) signaling interval. Impulse noise is characterized by long quiet intervals which are then interrupted by high-amplitude noise bursts. Here errors in digital systems usually occur in bursts with several successive transmitted symbols or bits being affected.

To control errors and to improve the reliability of a communication line, it is necessary to detect and correct errors. This is done by the use of redundancy in the data stream. Depending on the amount of redundancy introduced, any degree of error-free transmission of digital data can be achieved, provided that the data rate which includes this redundancy is less than the channel capacity. Numerous types of error-detecting codes exist. A commonly used code is a cyclic-redundancy check code which belongs to the class of block codes. Here the data is transmitted in a sequence of blocks, with each block containing a number of information bits and a number of check bits. Relatively simple encoders and decoders exist for cyclic codes, and they are widely used.

Various schemes can be used to route messages through a network. Viable techniques include circuit-switching, packet-switching, and broadcast methods. With circuit-switching the user is given a dedicated channel from source to destination for the duration of the call. No dedicated circuit exists for packet-switching. Instead the message is broken up into packets of a manageable size. These packets of data are stored and forwarded at each intermediate switching node as they travel through the network from source to destination. No switching devices exist in a packet broadcast network. All stations share a common transmission medium, so that a message transmitted by one station is received by all other stations. This method is commonly used in local area networks.

PROBLEMS

Section 3.2

3.1. An important concept in the communications field is the use of decibels to compare signal powers or voltage ratios. To define this consider the circuit element shown in Fig. P3.1. This could be either an amplifier, an attenuator, a filter, a transmission line, etc. The input signal delivers a power P_1 to the element and the output power is P_2. The power gain G in decibels (abbreviated as dB) for this element is defined as

$$G = 10 \log \frac{P_2}{P_1}$$

where P_2/P_1 is referred to as the absolute power gain. When $P_2 > P_1$, the gain is positive, whereas if $P_2 < P_1$, the gain is negative and there is a power loss in the circuit element.

Alternatively, G can be expressed in terms of a voltage ratio. If the input voltage is V_1, the output voltage is V_2, and the input and output resistances are both R, then

$$G = 10 \log \frac{V_2^2/R}{V_1^2/R} = 20 \log \frac{V_2}{V_1}$$

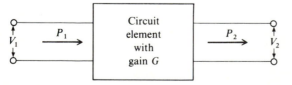

FIGURE P3.1

(*a*) Convert the following absolute power gains P_2/P_1 to decibel power gains: 1, 4, 10, 2^n, 0.3, 10^{-3}, 100, 500.

(*b*) Convert the following decibel power gains to absolute power gains: 0 dB, 30 dB, -30 dB, 13 dB, $10n$ dB.

(*c*) Convert the following absolute voltage gains to decibel power gains: 2, $\sqrt{2}$, 2^n.

3.2. The decibel defined in Prob. 3.1 is not an absolute unit; rather it compares one quantity to another. In actual usage a reference level thus must be established. Commonly used reference levels are often incorporated into the abbreviation for decibels. For example, the abbreviation "dBm" is used to designate power levels relative to 1 mW, and the abbreviation dBW refers to dB values relative to 1 watt (W).

(*a*) Convert the following absolute power levels P_2 to decibel levels referenced to 1 mW; that is, for the following values of P_2, find G in dBm if $P_1 = 1$ mW: 1 mW, 10 mW, 50 mW, 1 W, 13 W, 1 nanowatt (nW), 1 picowatt (pW).

(*b*) Find the values of the power levels P_2 for the following values of G; -13 dBm, 20 dBm, 6 dBm, -6 dBm.

3.3. The use of decibels is particularly important when calculating the overall gain of a cascaded series of amplification and attenuation elements. First, recall that if A, B, and C are some algebraic quantities, then

$$\log (ABC) = \log A + \log B + \log C$$

Thus, considering Fig. P3.3-1, if G_1, G_2, ..., G_n are the gains expressed in dB of n cascaded circuit elements, then the overall gain in dB of those elements is

$$G_{\text{total}} = G_1 + G_2 + G_3 + \cdots + G_n$$

FIGURE P3.3-1

(*a*) Consider the cable system illustrated in Fig. P3.3-2. Calculate the signal levels in both dBm and in volts at points A, B, C, and D.

(*b*) What gain in dB is needed in the final amplification stage so that its nominal output is 3 volts across a 50-ohm load?

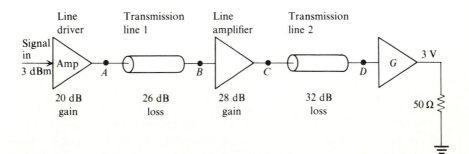

FIGURE P3.3-2

3.4. Consider an analog signal which can range from -4 to $+4$ volts. Assume a PCM scheme will be used to transmit the signal. The sampled values are quantized using 16 equally spaced 0.5-volt steps. Let the quantizing levels be -3.75, -3.25, -2.75, ..., 2.75, 3.25, and 3.75 volts.

(a) Using -3.75 volts as the lowest level, set up a binary code for these 16 levels.

(b) Find the nearest quantizer level for the following sequence of sampled signal values (given in volts): 1.3, 2.3, 2.8, 3.3, 1.4, -1.3, -2.8, 0.1, -1.2.

(c) What are the binary code words associated with each sample?

(d) If the signal is sampled at 2×10^4 samples/second, at what data rate would the resultant signal be sent?

Section 3.3

3.5. Verify that the *dc* component C_0 in the Fourier series representation is the average value of $f(t)$.

3.6. Derive Eq. (3.6) for the coefficients C_n for the periodic pulse train shown in Fig. 3.6.

3.7. Show that the Fourier transform of a gaussian function is also gaussian.

3.8. Derive the Fourier transform of the exponential function

$$\begin{aligned} f(t) &= Ae^{-bt} &&\text{for } t > 0 \\ &= 0 &&\text{for } t < 0 \end{aligned}$$

where $b > 0$.

3.9. Verify Eq. (3.11).

3.10. Find the Fourier transform of $f(t) = A \exp[-\pi(t/\tau)^2]$ for $\tau = 4$ and for $\tau = 1$. Sketch $F(\omega)$ versus ω for each case to verify that smaller values of τ spread the spectrum in the frequency domain.

Section 3.4

3.11. Derive Eq. (3.24).

3.12. A transmission system sends out information at 200,000 b/s. During the transmission process, fluctuation noise is added to the signal so that at the decoder output the signal pulses are 1 volt (V) in amplitude and the rms noise voltage is 0.2 V. (a) Assuming that ones and zeros are equally likely to be transmitted, what is the average time in which an error occurs? (b) How is this time changed if the voltage amplitude is doubled with the rms noise voltage remaining the same?

3.13. A useful approximation to $\frac{1}{2}(1 - \text{erf } x)$ for values of x greater than 3 is given by

$$\frac{1}{2}(1 - \text{erf } x) \approx \frac{\exp(-x^2)}{2\sqrt{\pi}x} \qquad x > 3$$

Using this approximation, consider an on-off binary system that transmits the signal levels 0 and A with equal probability in the presence of gaussian noise. Let the signal amplitude A be K times the standard deviation of the noise.

(a) Calculate the net probability of error if $K = 10$.

(b) Find the value of K required to give a net probability of error of 10^{-5}.

3.14. An audio signal is to be transmitted by either AM or FM. The signal consists of a sine wave at 10 kHz. The amplitude of the signal is such that there is 100 percent modulation in the AM case and a frequency deviation $\Delta f = 75$ kHz in the FM case. The average carrier-power and the noise-power density at the detector input are the same for both the AM and the FM systems.

(a) Given that the carrier-to-noise ratio is 30 dB for the AM system, calculate the output S_0/N_0 for each of the systems.

(b) Find the output S_0/N_0 for both cases if the signal amplitude is reduced by a factor of 2.

Section 3.5

3.15. A popular RZ code used in fiber optic systems is the optical Manchester code. This is formed by direct modulo-2 addition of the baseband (NRZ-L) signal and a double-frequency clock signal as is shown in Fig. 3.18. Using this scheme draw the pulse train for the data string 001101111001.

3.16. Design the encoder logic for an NRZ-to-optical Manchester converter.

3.17. Consider the encoder shown in Fig. P3.17 which changes NRZ data into a PSK waveform. Using this encoder, draw the NRZ and PSK waveforms for the data sequence 0001011101001101.

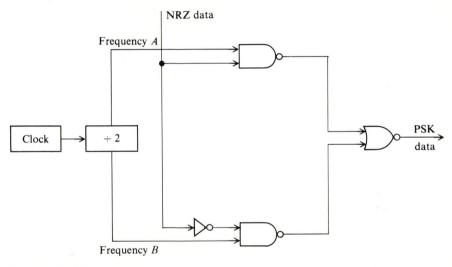

FIGURE P3.17

3.18. A 3B4B code converts blocks of three binary symbols into blocks of four binary digits according to the translation rules shown in Table P3.18. When there are two or more consecutive blocks of three zeros the coded binary blocks 0010 and 1101 are used alternately. Likewise the coded blocks 1011 and 0100 are used alternately for consecutive blocks of three ones.

(a) Using these translation rules, find the coded bit stream for the data input 010001111111101000000001111110

(b) What is the maximum number of consecutive identical bits in the coded pattern?

TABLE P3.18

Original code	3B4B Code	
	Mode 1	Mode 2
000	0010	1101
001	0011	
010	0101	
011	0110	
100	1001	
101	1010	
110	1100	
111	1011	0100

Section 3.6

3.19. A four-channel FDM system is to be implemented using the following design strategy. Channel 1 will be retained directly at baseband. A guard band equal to 25 percent of the bandwidth of channel 1 will be maintained between the upper edge of channel 1 and the lower edge of channel 2. Similarly, a guard band equal to 25 percent of the bandwidth of channel 2 will be maintained beween the upper edge of channel 2 and the lower edge of channel 3. And so on.

   (a) Draw a spectral diagram for the composite baseband spectrum, label the frequencies where the channels begin and end, and compute the total transmission bandwidth for four data channels each having a 4-kHz baseband bandwidth.

   (b) Repeat (a) for four data channels having the following baseband bandwidths:

   Channel 1:   4 kHz
   Channel 2:   6 kHz
   Channel 3: 14 kHz
   Channel 4: 20 kHz

3.20. Consider a PCM system in which 24 signals are to be time-division multiplexed. Each signal has a 3-kHz bandwidth. The sampling rate is 33.3 percent higher than the theoretical maximum, and 8 bits are used for each sample.

   (a) Determine the required bit rate.

   (b) Find the minimum required transmission bandwidth.

3.21. The T1 PCM system shown in Figure 3.26 multiplexes twenty-four 64-kb/s channels. One framing bit is added at the beginning of each T1 frame for synchronization purposes. Draw a frame structure for the T1 system. What is the time span of this frame? Show that the nominal bit rate of the T1 system is 1.544 Mb/s.

Section 3.7

3.22. Verify that the eight code words given in Table 3.5 are correct.

3.23. Consider a (7, 4) block code whose generator matrix is

$$G = \begin{bmatrix} 1 & 0 & 0 & 0 & 1 & 0 & 1 \\ 0 & 1 & 0 & 0 & 1 & 1 & 1 \\ 0 & 0 & 1 & 0 & 1 & 1 & 0 \\ 0 & 0 & 0 & 1 & 0 & 1 & 1 \end{bmatrix}$$

(*a*) Find all the code vectors of this code.

(*b*) Determine the parity check matrix for this code.

3.24. Compute the error syndrome for the message 11001010101 using the polynomial $x^4 + x^3 + x + 1$.

3.25. (*a*) Show that $x^2 + 1$ and $x^4 + x^2 + 1$ are divisors of $x^6 + 1$.

(*b*) What (n, k) code will this give rise to?

(*c*) Find the G matrix.

(*d*) From the G matrix generate all 2^k code words.

Section 3.8

3.26. Data is sent at 1 Mb/s over a transmission line wherein the propagation delay is 5 μs. In the absence of errors, what range of frame sizes gives an efficiency (defined by t_f/t_T) of at least 50 percent for the stop-and-wait ARQ protocol?

3.27. In deriving Eq. (3.56) we assumed $N > 2a + 1$, so that frames can be sent continuously. Show that when $N < 2a + 1$, Eq. (3.56) becomes

$$t_c = \frac{(2a + 1)(1 - p + Np)}{N(1 - p)} t_f$$

REFERENCES

1. R. W. Lucky, J. Salz, and E. J. Weldon, Jr., *Principles of Data Communication*, McGraw-Hill, New York, 1968.
2. A. B. Carlson, *Communication Systems*, 3d ed., McGraw-Hill, New York, 1985.
3. K. S. Shanmugan, *Digital and Analog Communication Systems*, Wiley, New York, 1979.
4. J. G. Proakis, *Digital Communications*, McGraw-Hill, New York, 1983.
5. M. Schwartz, *Information Transmission, Modulation, and Noise*, 3d ed., McGraw-Hill, New York, 1980.
6. S. Haykin, *Communication Systems*, Wiley, New York, 1978.
7. F. Stremler, *Introduction to Communication Systems*, Addison-Wesley, Reading, MA, 1977.
8. A. J. Viterbi and J. K. Omura, *Principles of Digital Communication and Coding*, McGraw-Hill, New York, 1979.
9. K. W. Cattermole, *Principles of Pulse Code Modulation*, American Elsevier, New York, 1975.
10. E. O. Brigham, *The Fast Fourier Transform*, Prentice-Hall, Englewood Cliffs, NJ, 1974.
11. R. Bracewell, *The Fourier Transform and Its Applications*, 2d ed., McGraw-Hill, New York, 1986.
12. C. E. Shannon, "A mathematical theory of communication," *Bell Sys. Tech. J.*, vol. 27, pp. 379–423, July 1948; vol. 27, pp. 623–656, October 1948.
13. A. J. Jerri, "The Shannon sampling theorem—its various extensions and applications: A Tutorial Review," *Proc. IEEE*, vol. 65, pp. 1565–1596, November 1977.
14. A. Van Der Ziel, *Noise: Sources, Characterization, Measurement*, Prentice-Hall, Englewood Cliffs, NJ, 1970.
15. E. A. Newcombe and S. Pasupathy, "Error rate monitoring for digital communications," *Proc. IEEE*, vol. 70, pp. 805–828, August 1982.
16. A. M. Michelson and A. H. Levesque, *Error-Control Techniques for Digital Communication*, Wiley, New York, 1985.
17. A. Papoulis, *Probability, Random Variables, and Stochastic Processes*, 2d ed., McGraw-Hill, New York, 1984.
18. P. Z. Peebles, Jr., *Probability, Random Variables, and Random Signal Principles*, 2d ed., McGraw-Hill, New York, 1987.

19. R. C. Houts and T. A. Green, "Comparing bandwidth requirements for binary baseband signals," *IEEE Trans. Commun.*, vol. COM-21, pp. 776–781, June 1973.
20. W. C. Lindsey and M. K. Simon, *Telecommunication Systems Engineering*, Prentice-Hall, Englewood Cliffs, NJ, 1973.
21. D. Tugal and O. Tugal, *Data Transnmission*, McGraw-Hill, New York, 1982.
22. CSELT Technical Staff, *Optical Fibre Communication*, McGraw-Hill, New York, 1981.
23. J. E. Savage, "Some simple self-synchronizing digital data assemblies," *Bell Sys. Tech. J.*, vol. 46, pp. 449–487, February 1967.
24. R. D. Gitlin and J. F. Hayes, "Timing recovery and scramblers in data transmission," *Bell Sys. Tech. J.*, vol. 54, pp. 569–593, March 1975.
25. Y. Takasaki, M. Tanaka, N. Maeda, K. Yamashita, and K. Nagano, "Optical pulse formats for fiber optic digital communications," *IEEE Trans. Commun.* vol 24, pp. 404–413, April 1976.
26. R. Petrovic, "New transmission code for digital optical communications," *Electron. Lett.*, vol. 14, pp. 541–542, August 1978.
27. E. A. Newcombe and S. Pasupathy, "Error rate monitoring for digital communications," *Proc. IEEE*, vol. 70, pp. 805–828, August 1982.
28. M. Rousseau, "Block codes for optical fibre communication," *Electron. Lett.* vol. 12, pp. 478–479, September 1976.
29. J. J. Stiffler, *Theory of Synchronous Communication*, Prentice-Hall, Englewood Cliffs, NJ, 1971.
30. R. T. James and P. E. Muench, "AT&T Facilities and Services," *Proc. IEEE*, vol. 60, no. 11, pp. 1342–1349, November 1972.
31. A. J. Viterbi, "Convolution codes and their performance in communication systems," *IEEE Trans. Commun.*, vol. COM-19, pp. 751–772, October 1971.
32. J. G. Proakis, *Digital Communications*, McGraw-Hill, New York, 1983, chap. 5.
33. S. Lin and D. J. Costello, Jr., *Error Control Coding: Fundamentals and Applications*, Prentice-Hall, Englewood Cliffs, NJ, 1983.
34. S. Lin, *An Introduction to Error-Correcting Codes*, Prentice-Hall, Englewood Cliffs, NJ, 1970.
35. *Proc. IEEE*, Special Issue on circuit switching, vol. 65, September 1977.
36. P. Schneider, "Switching engineering of switched systems," in D. H. Hamsher, *Communication System Engineering Handbook*, McGraw-Hill, New York, 1967, chap. 7.
37. M. F. Hills, *Telecommunication Switching Principles*, MIT Press, 1979.
38. *Proc. IEEE*, Special issue on packet communication, vol. 66, November 1978.
39. *IEEE J. Selected Areas in Commun.*, Special issue on local area networks, vol. SAC-1, November 1983.

CHAPTER

4

LAN TOPOLOGIES AND TRANSMISSION MEDIA

Two important parameters of a local area network are the topology of the network and the transmission medium that is used. These two factors, together with the medium access control protocol (see Chap. 6), largely influence the nature of a LAN. The particular choices of the various topological and transmission-medium technology alternatives determine factors such as the type of data the LAN may handle, the transmission speed, the efficiency of the network, and the degree of flexibility for accommodating a variety of users.

In this chapter we first discuss the transmission media which are most appropriate for local area networks. This is followed in Sec. 4.2 by an examination of several basic local area network topologies.

4.1 TRANSMISSION MEDIA

The transmission media provide the physical channels that are needed to interconnect nodes in a network. These media can be broadly classified as *bounded* or *unbounded*. Bounded media include twisted-pair wire, coaxial cables, and optical fibers. Unbounded media are the so-called *air waves* over which radio, microwave, and infrared optical signals, for example, are broadcast. Since bounded media are principally used in local area networks, we concentrate on them in this chapter.

4.1.1   Twisted-Pair Wire

As shown in Fig. 4.1, twisted-pair wire has two insulated copper-wire signal conductors per transmission path.[1] The diameters of the wires range from 0.016 to 0.051 inches (26 to 16 gauge). Common wire sizes are 19-, 22-, 24-, and 26-gauge, and in some instances 16-gauge wires are used. The wires are twisted together in pairs in a regular spiral pattern with 2 to 6 inches per 360-degree twist to minimize the interference that is created when adjacent pairs of wires are combined in multipair cables.

Twisted-pair wire was one of the original wire types used in telephone communications, where it still finds widespread usage. In local area networks, twisted-pair wires are mainly used for low-cost, low-performance applications. The advantages are that they are easy to install with commonly available tools, they are often already in place in buildings, and they are relatively inexpensive compared to other transmission media. Maximum transmission distances of around 1 km can be achieved for data rates in the 1-Mb/s range. For signals in the voice frequency range, repeaterless line lengths of up to 6 km are possible.

To examine the transmission properties of a twisted-pair link, let us consider the cross-sectional view of such a line as is shown in Fig. 4.2. Here two wires of radius *a* are separated by a distance *d*. The values of parameters such as the capacitance, inductance, characteristic impedance, resistance, and the response time of the line can be found from standard formulas.[2-4] For example, for the open two-wire line shown in Fig. 4.2, the capacitance in farads per meter is given by

$$C = \frac{\pi\varepsilon}{\text{arc cosh}\,(d/2a)} \tag{4.1}$$

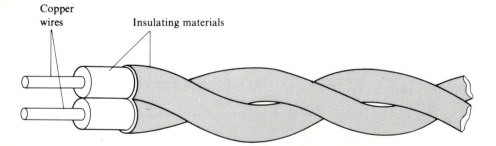

Copper wires

Insulating materials

FIGURE 4.1
Twisted-pair wire configuration.

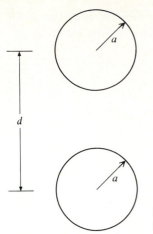

FIGURE 4.2
Cross-sectional view of a twisted-pair line.

and the inductance L in henrys per meter is

$$L = \frac{\mu}{\pi} \text{ arc cosh } \frac{d}{2a} \tag{4.2}$$

In these expressions μ is the permeability of the conductor and ε is the dielectric constant (permittivity) of the insulating material that is between the two wires. The parameter μ for a nonmagnetic material (such as copper) is simply the free-space permeability

$$\mu_0 = 4\pi \times 10^{-7} \text{ H/m}$$

The parameter ε can be expressed in terms of the relative dielectric constant $\varepsilon_r = \varepsilon/\varepsilon_0$ where

$$\varepsilon_0 = 8.854 \times 10^{-12} \text{ F/m}$$

Knowing L and C, the characteristic impedance Z_0 in ohms is given by

$$Z_0 = \sqrt{\frac{L}{C}} = \frac{1}{\pi}\sqrt{\frac{\mu}{\varepsilon}} \text{ arc cosh } \frac{d}{2a} \tag{4.3}$$

For a two-wire line, the resistance R in ohms per meter as a function of the signal frequency f is given by the expression

$$R = \frac{1}{a}\left(\frac{\rho\mu f}{\pi}\right)^{1/2} \tag{4.4}$$

where a is the wire radius (in meters), ρ is the resistivity in ohm-meters, and μ is the permeability of the conductor in henrys per meter. For copper this formula becomes

$$R = 8.34 \times 10^{-6} \frac{\sqrt{f}}{a} \tag{4.5}$$

where a is now the wire radius in *centimeters*.

Another parameter of interest is the response time of the line, since this corresponds to the time constant of an RC network. The response time τ of the line in seconds is given by

$$\tau = \left(\frac{DK}{4Z_0}\right)^2 \tag{4.6}$$

where D is the length of the line in meters, Z_0 is the characteristic impedance defined in Eq. (4.3), and the constant K, which depends on the line parameters, is given in $(\Omega^2 \, s)^{1/2}/m$.

Thus, the response time of a twisted-pair line is proportional to the square of the line length (assuming that the line is properly terminated in its characteristic impedance). Recalling from Sec. 3.3 that the bandwidth B of a line is proportional to the inverse of the response time, we see that the data rate supportable over a twisted-pair line is inversely proportional to the square of the line length.

4.1.2 Coaxial Cables

Coaxial cables offer substantially larger bandwidths than twisted-pair wire. They have the ability to support high data rates with high immunity to electrical interference and a low incidence of errors. A coaxial cable consists of a central carrier wire which is surrounded by an outer conductor as is shown in Fig. 4.3. The inner conductor can be either solid or stranded, and the outer conductor can be either solid or braided. A solid dielectric material is generally used to hold the inner conductor in place and to insulate it from the outer conductor. An outer shield or jacket covers the outer conductor to yield coaxial cable diameters ranging from 0.17 to 1.6 in. Coaxial cables for LAN applications are typically 0.5 in or less in diameter.

As is the case with twisted-pair wire, the values of coaxial-cable parameters such as characteristic impedance, attenuation, and response time of the line can be computed from standard formulas.[2-5] If a and b are the radii of the inner and outer conductors, respectively, then for the special case of low-loss transmis-

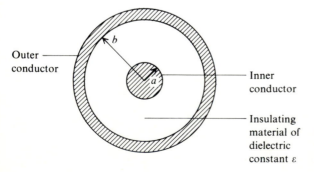

Outer conductor

Inner conductor

Insulating material of dielectric constant ε

FIGURE 4.3
Cross-sectional view of a coaxial cable configuration.

sion lines at radio frequencies, the characteristic impedance Z_0 in ohms for a coaxial cable is

$$Z_0 = \sqrt{\frac{L}{C}} = \frac{1}{2\pi} \sqrt{\frac{\mu}{\varepsilon}} \ln \frac{b}{a} \qquad (4.7)$$

$$= \frac{60}{\sqrt{\varepsilon_r}} \ln \frac{b}{a}$$

where L is the inductance per unit length in henrys per meter, C is the capacitance per unit length expressed in farads per meter, the relative dielectric constant $\varepsilon_r = \varepsilon/\varepsilon_0$ is the ratio of the dielectric constant ε of the insulator to the free-space dielectric constant ε_0, and μ is the permeability.

Coaxial transmission lines have a usable bandwidth of five to six decades of frequency. The upper frequency limit is the frequency whose wavelength is equal to the average circumference of the line. The cutoff frequency f_c in megahertz given by

$$f_c = \frac{7520}{(a+b)\sqrt{\varepsilon_r}} \qquad (4.8)$$

In practical coaxial systems there is always some attenuation in the cable line. For radio-frequency (rf) signals, the following expression for the attenuation α can be derived from Maxwell's equations:

$$\alpha = \frac{1}{2} \left(\frac{R}{Z_0} + GZ_0 \right) = \alpha_c + \alpha_d \qquad (4.9)$$

where the first term α_c refers to the attenuation of the conductor, the second term α_d is the dielectric attenuation, R is the resistance of the coaxial cable, and G is the conductance which is given by

$$G \approx \omega C \tan \phi \qquad (4.10)$$

Here $\tan \phi$ signifies the loss tangent of the insulating material, $\omega = 2\pi f$ is the operating frequency, and

$$C = \frac{2\pi\varepsilon}{\ln (b/a)}$$

is the capacitance of the line, which is given in picofarads (pF) per meter by the expression

$$C = \frac{55.6\varepsilon_r}{\ln (b/a)} \qquad (4.11)$$

For copper conductors the resistance R in ohms per meter is

$$R = 4.2 \times 10^{-6} \sqrt{f} \left(\frac{1}{a} + \frac{1}{b} \right) \qquad (4.12)$$

where a and b are measured in *centimeters*.

For carrier waves less than 400 MHz, which is the range of interest for broadband networks, the dielectric attenuation factor GZ_0 in Eq. (4.9) is much less than the conductor attenuation R/Z_0 (see Prob. 4.4). Thus, from Eqs. (4.9) and (4.12) we see that the attenuation of a coaxial line increases as the square root of the operating frequency.

4.1.3 Coaxial-Cable Application

Coaxial cables are widely used in telephone networks and by the cable TV industry. As a result of this widespread use, coaxial cable is moderate in cost and readily available. Furthermore techniques for installation, connection, and transmission control on coaxial cable are well developed. A variety of cable taps, splitters, couplers, controllers, and repeaters are available so that a cable can be easily extended and branched-off to reach both nearby and remotely located users.

Two types of coaxial cables are used in LAN applications depending on whether a baseband or a broadband network is to be implemented. Although the names *baseband* and *broadband* refer to signaling techniques which are independent of the physical medium, these terms are often used to describe the different varieties of coaxial cables that are used for these two signaling methods.

In a baseband local area network a single baseband signal is transmitted at data rates in the range of 1 to 20 Mb/s. Higher-speed baseband coaxial implementations (up to 50 Mb/s) exist but are expensive. Instead, these higher-speed baseband LANs are usually implemented using optical fibers (see Sec. 4.1.5 and Chap. 10). The coaxial cables used are typically $\frac{3}{8}$ inch in diameter and have a 50-ohm impedance. A very popular baseband LAN is Ethernet[6–8] which operates at 10 Mb/s. Cable runs for baseband LANs are generally 1 to 2 km or less.

For higher data rates and longer distances, broadband coaxial cable is more practical. The transmission medium for broadband LANs is standard $\frac{1}{2}$-inch 75-ohm coaxial cable that is widely used in the telephone and TV industries.[9,10] This cable was chosen because it is readily available, is low cost, offers bandwidths of 300 to 400 MHz, and allows high-speed data transmission with very low bit error rates. Broadband local area networks use frequency division multiplexing (FDM) to divide a single physical channel into a number of smaller independent frequency channels. These smaller channels can be given different bandwidths which allows various forms of information, namely voice, video, and data, to be transmitted simultaneously in different frequency bands on the same cable. Broadband LANs are thus considered to be multifunction networks since they can allow several separate subnetworks to operate simultaneously on one physical network channel.

The transmitted signals in broadband LANs are restricted to travel in only one direction in any particular frequency band. This is in contrast to baseband LANs in which signals may be transmitted in both directions at once. Two-way exchanges of information in a broadband LAN are accomplished either by single-cable or dual-cable schemes. In a dual-cable scheme the coaxial cable

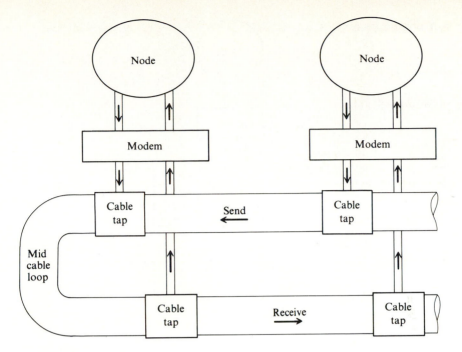

FIGURE 4.4

Dual-cable 300-MHz broadband LAN which has two cable taps per node and a midcable loop to provide both send and receive capabilities on one cable.

simply loops around at one end of the network so that it passes through each node twice, as is shown in Fig. 4.4. The entire bandwidth of the cable is thus available for message transmission in both directions.

In a single-cable scheme the 300-MHz bandwidth of the cable is divided so that there are separate ranges of frequencies for messages being sent and received. The remodulation or translation of Send signals into Receive signals is realized by a device called a *head end* or a *central retransmission facility* (CRF). A schematic of the information flow in such a network is shown in Fig. 4.5.

Three common implementations for a single-cable broadband system are shown in Fig. 4.6. These are known as the midsplit, subsplit, and high-split schemes. In a *midsplit* system, the range from 10 to 110 MHz is dedicated to sending messages. This transmission from the user to the CRF is referred to as either the *inbound* (to the CRF), *upstream*, or *forward information distribution channel*. The 170- to 300-MHz range is used for receiving information. This channel band from the CRF to the user is alternately known as the *outbound* (from the CRF), *downstream*, or *reverse information distribution channel*. The range from 110 to 170 MHz is not used since it serves as a buffer between the inbound and the outbound channels. The midsplit system is most suitable for LANs since it provides equal distribution of bandwidth to inbound and outbound users.

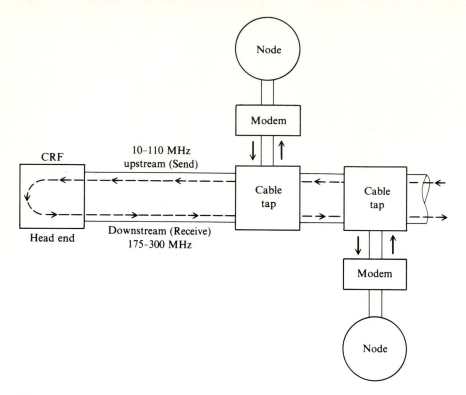

FIGURE 4.5
Path of information flow in a single-cable broadband LAN.

In contrast to the midsplit stream which has equal bandwidth in each direction, a *subsplit system* provides significantly more outbound (downstream) distribution capability than inbound (upstream) capability. This system is commonly used by the CATV industry where there is a need for large central-office-to-subscriber traffic and limited communications from the subscriber to the central office. The inbound frequencies range from 5 to 30 MHz, whereas the outbound frequencies cover the 50 to 300-MHz bandwidth. In this case the 20-MHz buffer from 30 to 50 MHz is unusable for information transferal.

The *high-split scheme* is the opposite of the subsplit scheme. Here there is significantly more inbound than outbound capability. The inbound frequencies vary from 5 to 170 MHz, whereas the outbound frequencies cover the 230- to 300-MHz range. Again there is a buffer bandwidth from 170 to 230 MHz.

It should be noted here that the inbound, outbound, and buffer frequency ranges for these three single-cable systems are not firmly fixed. There are slight variations among various equipment vendors to which the interested reader and applications engineer should refer.

The differences between dual-cable and single-cable LANs are minor. The single-cable system is about 10 to 15 percent less expensive to install, and is also

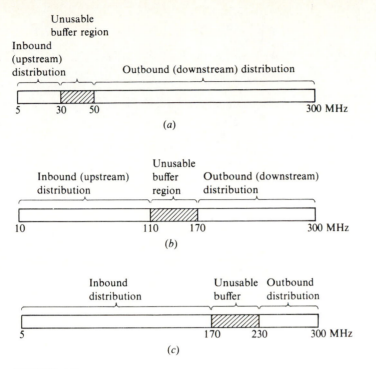

FIGURE 4.6
Common single-cable frequency splits: (*a*) subsplit, (*b*) midsplit, and (*c*) high-split schemes.

advantageous when a single-cable plant already exists in a facility. The dual-cable scheme has twice the capacity of the single-cable midsplit system and it does not require a frequency translator at the head-end.

4.1.4 Coaxial-Cable Link Power Budget

An important application consideration in any network is a power budget or gain-and-loss calculation.[11] A power-budget calculation allows a network designer to properly take into account all loss elements and amplification devices in a network so that appropriate signal levels are present at all receivers. An example of the signal-level specifications for part of a small coaxial-cable network is illustrated in Fig. 4.7. Typically one allows a 40-dB loss accumulation between the central retransmission facility and the interface transceiver of the most-remote user. Included in these loss elements are the various coaxial cable sections, power splitters, user taps, and the reverse loss through bidirectional local amplifiers which are used to boost the signal level in the forward direction. The losses are generally measured at the highest design frequency.

> **Example 4.1.** In Fig. 4.7 we assume a midsplit network. A user sends information upstream to the CRF in the 10- to 110-MHz range. The CRF translates incoming

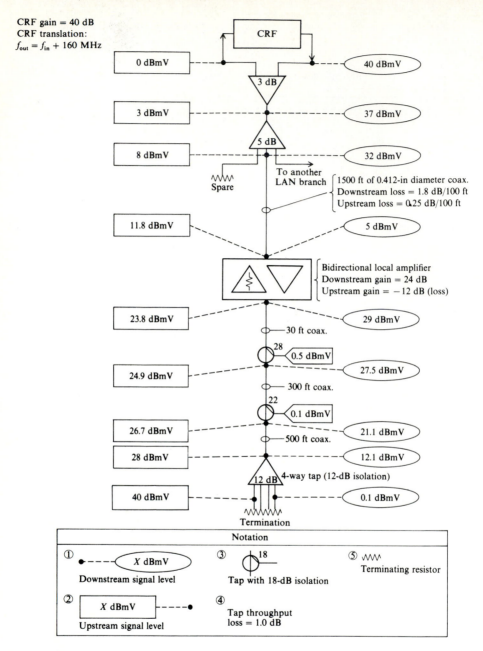

FIGURE 4.7
Signal-level specifications for part of a small broadband coaxial cable network.

signals to outgoing signals by shifting the frequency f_{in} of the incoming signals by 160 MHz; that is, $f_{out} = f_{in} + 160$ MHz. For the transmission line we take a 0.412-in diameter coaxial cable which has a nominal loss of 0.25 dB/100 ft (0.82 dB/100 m) at the upper end of the lower frequencies (the frequencies at which the user transmits) and a nominal loss of 1.8 dB/100 ft (5.9 dB/100 m) at the higher frequencies (the frequencies at which a user receives messages).

The numbers "N dB" shown in the signal-splitter triangles designate the power loss in each leg of the device. For example, a two-way 3-dB splitter divides the incoming power equally into each leg, whereas in a three-way 5-dB splitter the power level in each leg is 5 dB lower than the input power level.

The numbers shown at the user taps denote the degree of isolation that the tap provides between the user and the main signal line. Note that this degree of isolation becomes progressively smaller as users are located further away from the CRF. The reason for this is twofold. First it is desirable to have a received signal level that falls within a certain range, for example, 0.5 to 1.5 mV. Since the signal level on the main transmission line progressively decreases as one gets further away from the CRF, a larger fraction of the available power needs to be tapped off at remote users compared to that fraction needed at users close to the CRF where the signal level is substantially higher. The same argument applies to the signal levels that the users insert into the transmission line. A higher power level must be transmitted at far away users compared to nearby users since the power from distant users must travel further and thus gets more attenuated. For practical purposes and ease of calculations, we assume there is a 1-dB loss at each tap which accounts for both the power tapped off at that point and any additional insertion loss or throughput loss that may be inherent in the tap itself.

Another important factor to consider in doing a coaxial-cable power budget is the fact that signals attenuate more at higher frequencies than at lower frequencies. The difference of the attenuation of the high-frequency signals relative to that of the low-frequency signals increases as the length of the cable system increases. This relationship is called *cable tilt* and must be compensated for or equalized in order to maintain a flat amplitude response throughout the cable system. Amplifiers are thus used to equalize the signals by amplifying the high-frequency signals and by adding attenuation to the lower frequencies. In general, amplifiers must be installed whenever the signal level drops by about 20 dB from the signal level output of the last amplifier, the head-end location (or the CRF), or the last tap point.

In doing the power budget the signal levels being considered are commonly based on peak root-mean-square (rms) video signals measured in dBmV within a 6-MHz bandpass. Note that 1 mV = 0 dBmV into a 75-ohm load which is the impedance of the broadband coaxial cable. Thus in Fig. 4.7 we have set the output voltages from the CRF and from the furthest user at 40 dBmV (100 mV). Allowing a 40-dB loss between the CRF and the furthest user then results in a 0-dBmV nominal signal level at the receiver inputs of the CRF and of the furthest user.

4.1.5 Optical Fibers

The dielectric nature of optical fibers makes them an attractive alternative to wire transmission lines.[12–16] An optical fiber is a dielectric waveguide that operates at optical frequencies. This fiber waveguide is normally cylindrical in form as is shown in Fig. 4.8. The structure consists of a single solid dielectric cylinder of radius a and index of refraction n_1. This is known as the *core* of the fiber. The core is surrounded by a solid dielectric *cladding* having a refractive index n_2 that is less than n_1. Since the core refractive index is larger than that of the cladding, light is made to propagate along the fiber waveguide through internal reflection at the core-cladding interface. The core material is generally glass which is surrounded by either a glass or plastic cladding. In addition, the fibers are encapsulated in an elastic, abrasion-resistant plastic material. This material adds further strength to the fiber and mechanically isolates or buffers the fibers from environmental contaminants and adjacent surface roughnesses.

As is shown in Fig. 4.8, variations in the material composition of the core give rise to two common fiber types known as *step-index* and *graded-index* fibers. In the first case the refractive index of the core is uniform throughout and undergoes an abrupt change (or step) at the core-cladding boundary. In the

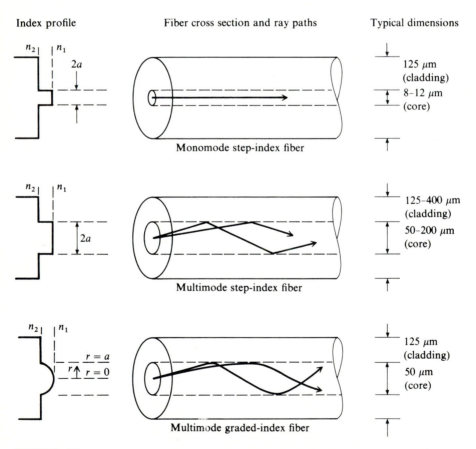

FIGURE 4.8
Schematics of three common optical fiber types: single-mode step-index, multimode step-index, and multimode graded-index structures.

graded-index fiber the core refractive index is made to vary as a function of the radial distance from the center of the fiber. Both step- and graded-index fibers can be further divided into *monomode* and *multimode* classes. As the name implies, a monomode fiber sustains only one mode of propagation, whereas multimode fibers contain many hundreds of modes.

A few typical sizes of monomode and multimode fibers are given in Fig. 4.8 to provide an idea of the dimensional scale. Some popular multimode-core sizes for LAN applications include 50, 62.5, 85, and 100 micrometer diameters. The core size for monomode fibers is 9 μm for operation at a 1300-nm wavelength. Multimode step-index fibers provide bandwidth-distance products of up to 20 MHz-km. Multimode graded-index fibers can have usable bandwidth-distance products of several GHz-km, whereas monomode fibers have capacities well in excess of this.

An important parameter for optical fibers is the numerical aperture (NA), since it is commonly used to describe the light acceptance or gathering capability of a fiber. For a step-index the numerical aperture is defined by

$$NA = (n_1^2 - n_2^2)^{1/2} \approx n_1\sqrt{2\Delta} \tag{4.13}$$

where Δ is the *core-cladding index difference* defined by

$$n_2 = n_1(1 - \Delta)$$

Values of n_2 are chosen so that Δ is nominally 0.01. Since most fibers are constructed of silica (SiO$_2$), n_1 is nominally 1.48.

4.1.6 Optical-Fiber Link Power Budget

The simplest optical-fiber transmission link is a point-to-point line having a transmitter on one end and a receiver on the other, as is shown in Fig. 4.9. This link is used here to examine an optical-fiber link power budget. More complex architectures are considered in Sec. 4.2 when we discuss network topologies.

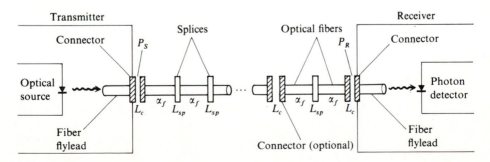

FIGURE 4.9
Optical power loss model for a point-to-point fiber link. The losses occur at connectors (L_c), splices (L_{sp}), and in the fiber (α_f).

The optical source used in the transmitter can be either a semiconductor light-emitting diode (LED) or a laser diode. Of the two devices, an LED is simpler to use and less expensive, but it couples less usable optical power into a fiber than a laser diode and its optical power cannot be modulated as rapidly as that of a laser diode. Although the exact amount of optical power that can be coupled into an optical fiber depends on the specific physical characteristics of the source and the fiber, a practical rule of thumb is that an LED couples approximately 25 microwatts (-16 dBm) into a multimode fiber having a 50-μm core diameter, whereas a laser diode couples 1.0 mW (0 dBm) into a 50-μm-core multimode fiber and 0.5 mW (-3 dBm) into a monomode fiber. Note that these numbers refer to the peak fiber-coupled power.

At the receiving end of the optical link a semiconductor-based photodiode converts the optical power received into an electrical voltage level. The two types of photodiodes used are the *pin* photodetector and the avalanche photo-diode (APD). A comparison of the signal-to-noise ratios for these two devices as a function of the received optical power is shown in Fig. 4.10. Recall from Chap. 3 that for a bit error rate of 10^{-9} (which is often chosen for fiber-optic systems) we need a signal-to-noise ratio of 12 (or approximately 11 dB). Then we see from Fig. 4.10 that for low optical signal levels (less than about -45 dBm) an avalanche photodiode is needed, whereas at larger received optical power levels a *pin* photodiode is adequate.

An optical power loss model for a point-to-point link is shown in Fig. 4.9. The optical power received at the photodetector depends on the amount of light coupled into the fiber and the losses occurring in the fiber and at the connectors and splices. The link-loss budget is derived from the sequential loss contributions of each element in the link. Each of these loss elements is expressed in decibels (dB) as

$$\text{Loss} = 10 \log \frac{P_{\text{in}}}{P_{\text{out}}} \tag{4.14}$$

where P_{in} and P_{out} are the optical powers emanating into and out of the loss element, respectively.

In addition to the link-loss contributors shown in Fig. 4.9, a link power margin is normally provided in the analysis to allow for component aging, temperature fluctuations, and losses arising from components that might be added at future dates. A link margin of 6 to 8 dB is generally used for systems that are not expected to have additional components incorporated into the link in the future.

The link-loss budget simply considers the total optical power loss P_T that is allowed between the light source and the photodetector, and allocates this loss to cable attenuation, connector loss, splice loss, and system margin. Thus if P_S is the optical power emerging from the end of a fiber flylead attached to the light source, and if P_R is the receiver sensitivity, then

$$P_T = P_S - P_R$$

$$= 2L_c + \alpha_f L + \text{system margin} \tag{4.15}$$

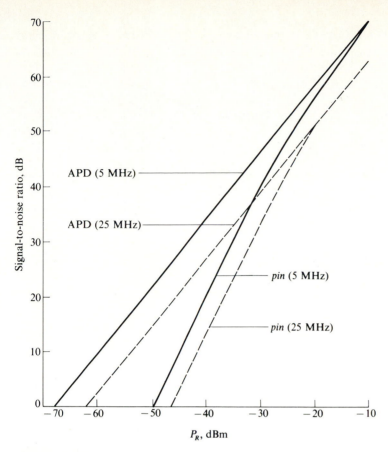

FIGURE 4.10
Comparison of signal-to-noise ratios for *pin* and avalanche photodiodes as a function of received optical power for 5- and 25-MHz bandwidths.

Here L_c is the connector loss, α_f is the fiber attenuation (dB/km), L is the transmission distance, and the system margin is nominally taken as 6 dB. We assume that the cable of length L has connectors only on the ends and none in between. The splice loss is incorporated into the cable loss for simplicity.

Example 4.2. To illustrate how a link-loss budget is set up, let us carry out a specific design example. We begin by specifying a data rate of 20 Mb/s and a bit error rate of 10^{-9} (that is, at most one error can occur for every 10^9 bits sent). For the receiver we choose a silicon pin photodiode operating at 850 nm. Figure 4.11 shows that the required receiver input signal is -42 dBm (42 dB below 1 mW). We next select a GaAlAs LED which can couple a 50-μW (-13-dBm) average optical power level into a fiber flylead with a 50-μm core diameter. We thus have a 29-dB allowable power loss. Assume further that a 1-dB loss occurs when the fiber flylead

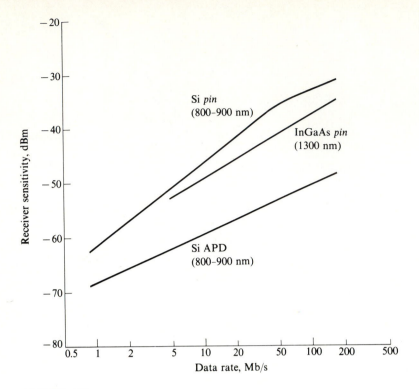

FIGURE 4.11
Receiver sensitivities as a function of bit rate for a 10^{-9} BER.

is connected to the cable and another 1-dB connector loss occurs at the cable-to-photodetector interface. Including a 6-dB system margin, the possible transmission distance for a cable with an attenuation of α_f dB/km can be found from Eq. (4.15):

$$P_T = P_S - P_R = 29 \text{ dB}$$

$$= 2(1 \text{ dB}) + \alpha_f L + 6 \text{ dB} \tag{4.16}$$

If $\alpha_f = 3.5$ dB/km, then a 6.0-km transmission path is possible.

Example 4.3. The link power budget can be represented graphically as is shown in Fig. 4.12. The vertical axis represents the optical power loss allowed between the transmitter and the receiver. The horizontal axis gives the transmission distance. Here we show a silicon pin receiver with a sensitivity of -42 dBm (at 20 Mb/s) and an LED with an output power of -13 dBm coupled into a fiber flylead. We subtract a 1-dB connector loss at each end, which leaves a total margin of 27 dB. Subtracting a 6-dB system margin leaves us with a tolerable loss of 21 dB that can be allocated to cable and splice loss. The slope of the line shown in Fig. 4.12 is the 3.5 dB/km cable (and splice, in this case) loss. This line starts at the -14-dBm point (which is the optical power coupled into the cabled fiber) and ends at the -35-dB level (the receiver sensitivity minus a 1-dB connector loss and a 6-dB

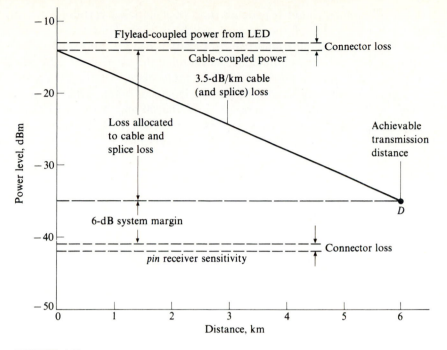

FIGURE 4.12
Graphical representation of an optical fiber link-loss budget.

system margin). The intersect point D then defines the maximum possible transmission path length.

Further design examples for short- and long-wavelength systems can be found in Refs. 12 to 16 and in the problems set at the end of the chapter.

4.1.7 Ethernet Cable Plant

As another example, let us consider an Ethernet cable plant. An important property of the Ethernet physical layer is the *round-trip propagation time* of the physical channel. This time is an implicit part of the interface presented to the data link layer. It represents the maximum time required for a signal to travel from one end of the network to the other, and for a collision signal to propagate back. Thus, to properly implement the collision-detection protocol which depends on the end-to-end propagation delay, the total worst-case round-trip signal propagation is defined to be 450 bit times. This is 45 μs for a 10-Mb/s Ethernet system. This delay time includes the actual propagation time over the network cables, the synchronization time for all intervening electronics, and the signal rise time degradation.

The maximum round-trip delay time thus imposes certain limits on the physical characteristics of the network, such as cable length and interstation distances. To see how the round-trip propagation delay is allocated to the individual components in the channel, let us examine the large-scale Ethernet channel configuration shown in Fig. 4.13. The cable plant is composed of coaxial cable segments that may have a maximum length of 500 m and which are terminated in the characteristic impedance of the 50-ohm cable. A transmitter-receiver pair, called a *transceiver* is closely attached to the coaxial cable for inserting and extracting signals from the broadcast medium. Stations are transformer-coupled to a transceiver via a twisted-pair *transceiver cable* as shown in Fig. 4.14. The length of this twisted-pair cable is 50 m or less. Also shown here is the collision-detection circuitry which is used in conjunction with the receiver. The logic within this unit must detect a collision of signals between two simultaneously transmitting stations within two bit times (200 ns).

Between any two stations there can be up to two repeaters to extend the network topology. These can be located either within or at the end of a coaxial cable segment. The maximum distance between two transceivers is thus 1500 m. Two further restrictions are that the end-to-end length of the Ethernet cable plant is limited to 2.5 km, and the minimum distance between any two transceivers is 2.5 m.

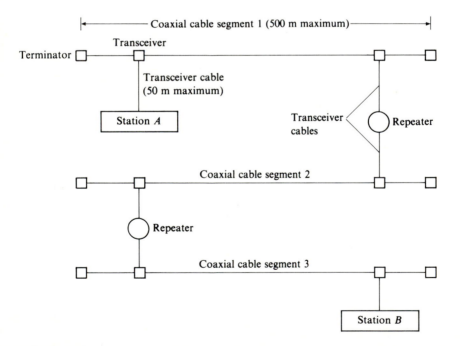

FIGURE 4.13
Example of a large-scale Ethernet channel configuration.

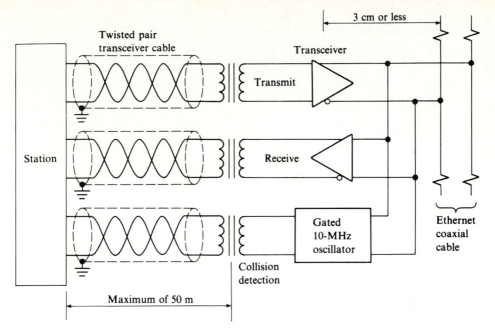

FIGURE 4.14
Station attachment to an Ethernet coaxial cable.

The worst-case round-trip propagation delay can be found by considering Fig. 4.13. Here stations A and B are attached to coaxial-cable segments 1 and 3, respectively, with 50 m of twisted-pair wire. There are two repeaters between the two stations, so that the maximum coaxial distance between transceivers A and B is 1500 m. The propagation velocity in Ethernet coaxial cable is $0.77c$ ($c = 3 \times 10^8$ m/s = speed of light in a vacuum). The total worst-case round-trip delay for all the coaxial cables in the system is thus 13 μs.

For the twisted-pair transceiver cable the propagation velocity is $0.65c$ (5.13 ns/m). Assuming that each station and each repeater is attached to a coaxial cable segment with the maximum allowable 50 m of transceiver cable, then the signal traverses six lengths of twisted-pair cable on a *one-way* trip between stations A and B. The total round-trip delay for the transceiver cables from station A to station B and back is 3.08 μs.

These times and the delays of the other elements in the path are summarized in Table 4.1. Here the propagation delay has been separated into "forward-path" and "return-path" delay. This is done because in one direction a carrier-sense signal traverses the channel, whereas in the other direction it is a collision-detection signal, which has a different propagation delay.

Table 4.1 thus shows how the 45-μs worst-case round-trip propagation delay is allocated among the physical elements of the Ethernet cable plant.

TABLE 4.1
Propagation-delay budget for an Ethernet physical channel

Element	/ Unit steady state delay	+ Unit start-up delay \	× / No. of units in forward path	+ No. of units in return path \	Total delay
Encoder	0.1 μs	0	3	3	0.60 μs
Transceiver cable	5.13 ns/m	0	300 m	300 m	3.08 μs
Transceiver (transmit path)	0.05 μs	0.2 μs	3	3	1.50 μs
Transceiver (receive path)	0.05 μs	0.5 μs	3	0	1.65 μs
Transceiver (collision path)	0	0.5 μs	0	3	1.50 μs
Coaxial cable	4.33 ns/m	0	1500 m	1500 m	13.00 μs
Point-to-point link cable	5.13 ns/m	0	1000 m	1000 m	10.26 μs
Repeater (repeat path)	0.8 μs	0	2	0	1.60 μs
Repeater (collision path)	0.2 μs	0	0	2	0.40 μs
Decoder	0.1 μs	0.8 μs	2	0	1.80 μs
Carrier sense	0	0.2 μs	3	0	0.60 μs
Collision detect	0	0.2 μs	0	3	0.60 μs
Signal rise time (to 70% in 500 m) (Note 3)	0	0.1 μs	3	0	0.30 μs
Signal rise time (50% to 94% in 500 m)(Note 4)	0	2.7 μs	0	3	8.10 μs
Total worst-case round-trip delay					44.99 μs

Note 1. All quantities are worst-case.

Note 2. The propagation delay is separated into "forward-path" and "return path" delay, because in one direction it is *carrier sense* which travels through the channel, and in the return direction it is *collision detect*. The two signals have different propagation delays.

Note 3. In the worst case, the signal must reach 70 percent of its final value to be detected as a valid carrier at the end of 500 m of coaxial cable. This rise time must be included in the propagation delay budget.

Note 4. In the worst case the propagated collision on the return path must reach 94 percent of its final value to be detected as a collision at the end of 500 m of coaxial cable.

4.2 TOPOLOGIES

The manner in which nodes are geometrically arranged and connected is known as the *topology* of the network.[17-19] Local area networks are commonly characterized in terms of their topology. The two major classes of LAN topologies are shown in Fig. 4.15. These include the unconstrained interconnection and the three basic constrained LAN topologies known as the *bus, ring,* and *star* configurations. Each of these methodologies has its own particular advantages and limitations in terms of reliability, expandability, and performance characteristics.

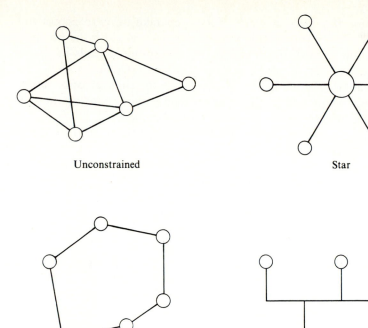

Unconstrained

Star

Ring

Linear bus

FIGURE 4.15
Two major classes of LAN topologies: (*a*) unconstrained interconnection, and (*b*) bus, ring, and star configurations.

Details of the three basic LAN configurations and of an unconstrained topology are presented in the following subsections.

4.2.1 Bus Topology

In a bus topology[20-22] all the network nodes are connected to a common transmission medium. As a result of this, only one pair of users on the network can communicate at the same time. Each network node thus has a unique address which is used when information is transmitted. When a data packet is sent out, it propagates throughout the medium and is received by all stations. To receive messages, each station continuously monitors the medium and copies those messages that are addressed to itself as the data packets go by.

Since the transmission medium in a bus is generally time-shared, there must be some type of control mechanism to prevent several stations from transmitting simultaneously. These mechanisms are generally classified as *polling* or *contention techniques*, the details of which are presented in Chap. 6. Polling techniques are noncontention-access methods that can be either centralized or distributed. In a centralized scheme, a controlling station could use a polling technique to determine the order in which nodes can take turns to access the network. The control station sequentially asks the various users on the bus line if they have information to send. If a node wishes to transmit it sends its information; if not, the control station goes on to poll the next node in the sequence. In this scheme the amount of time that a node can have the channel, once access is gained, is determined by the size of the message that is allowed, or by the size of the time interval allotted to the node by the control station.

Control of access to the network can also be carried out by distributed forms of polling. A popular scheme is a token-passing method wherein a specially formatted code word (which is known as a *token*) is passed from station to station. When a station wishes to transmit, it first removes the token from the line. Possession of the token gives a node exclusive access to the network for transmitting its message, thereby avoiding conflicts with other nodes that wish to transmit. When the message has been sent out, the node puts the token back on the line so that other nodes may gain access to the network.

In contrast to polling schemes which offer a *deterministic* guarantee of channel access to a node, each node in a contention scheme randomly attempts to access the channel. Thus contention schemes are *stochastic* methods for which a statistical guarantee of channel access can be calculated. A common technique is the *carrier sense multiple access with collision detection* (CSMA/CD) scheme. Here any node can send a message immediately upon sensing that the channel is free of traffic. During transmission the node also listens to the channel to sense if another station has also started transmitting at close to the same time. In such an event, a collision would occur between the two messages so that the information sent by each station is garbled. Each node thus ceases transmission, waits for a brief time interval of random duration, and then attempts to transmit again.

As is the case with any network architecture, bus topologies have both advantages and disadvantages. The most significant advantages are that the cable runs are shorter than in other topologies, buses are ideally suited for use with high-performance contention protocols, it is easy to reconfigure the network (add and remove users), and the transmission medium is highly reliable (a failure of any station does not affect operation of the other stations). In addition, the hardware for coaxial-cable buses is widely available since they have been used for some time by the CATV industry and for telephone and data communications.

Limitations of bus networks include transmission distance restrictions in baseband buses, difficulty in implementing delivery priorities, and the signal balancing problem in baseband and dual-cable broadband buses. The balancing problem arises when users on a multiport line wish to communicate. For two distant users the transmitted signal level must be strong enough to provide a minimum signal-to-noise ratio at the far receiver. However, if the same sender wishes to communicate with a neighboring node, the transmitted signal power must not be so strong that it overloads the circuitry of the neighboring receiver. If there are n stations on the network and the signal balancing is done for all permutations of stations taken two at a time, then $n(n-1)$ balances must be done. For a large number of stations this can obviously become a tedious if not unwieldy problem.

The bus topology is widely used in LAN applications. Some of the applications include office automation, industrial process control, laboratory instrumentation sharing, database access, military information transfer, multicomputer interconnections, and the transmission of integrated voice, data, and video.

4.2.2 Optical-Fiber Bus

The bus network topology usually employs coaxial cable as the transmission medium. The primary advantages of such a network are the totally passive nature of the transmission medium and the ability to easily install low-perturbation (high-impedance) taps on the coaxial line without disrupting the operating network. An example of such a network was described in Sec. 4.1.4.

In contrast to a coaxial-cable bus, a fiber-optic-based bus network is more difficult to implement. The impediment is that low-perturbation bidirectional taps which efficiently couple optical signals into and out of the main optical-fiber trunk do not exist to the same extent as coax taps. Access to an optical data bus is achieved by means of a coupling element which can be either active[23–26] or passive[27–29]. An *active coupler* converts the optical signal on the data bus to its electric baseband counterpart before any data processing (such as injecting additional data into the signal stream or merely passing on the received data) is carried out. A *passive coupler* employs no electronic elements. It is used passively to tap off a portion of the optical power from the bus.

ACTIVE OPTICAL-FIBER BUS COUPLERS. Figure 4.16 gives an example of an active coupler. A photodiode receiver converts the optical signal from the bus into an electric signal. The processing element then can remove or copy part of this signal for transmission to the terminal, while the remainder is forwarded to the optical transmitter. The processor can also insert additional information from the terminal into the data stream. The transmitter, in turn, reconverts the electric signal to an optical information stream which gets sent on to the next terminal via the optical fiber bus. Couplers of this type can be easily constructed by using any of a number of commercially available photodiodes and light sources.

The advantage of a linear fiber bus network of this type is that every accessing terminal acts as a repeater. This means that in principle the active bus can accommodate an unlimited number of terminals since the signal is restored to its initial starting value at each node. However, the reliability of each repeater is critical to the operation of the overall network. For example, if one station on a single-fiber bus fails, all traffic will stop. A variety of optical bypassing schemes[24–25] or multifiber bus configurations have been proposed to alleviate this problem.

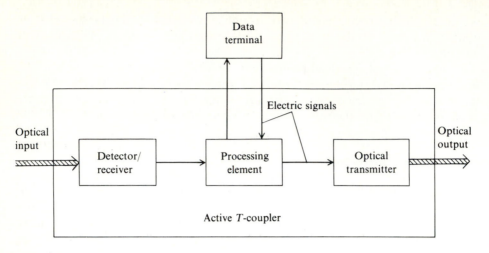

FIGURE 4.16
Example of an active *T*-coupler for a fiber optic bus.

Example 4.4. An example of a passive fiber bypass scheme is shown in Fig. 4.17. Here every station is permanently bypassed with an optical fiber which is connected to opposite sides of a terminal via optical couplers. If one station fails, the bypass thus ensures optical continuity from the former transmitter to the next station. In order not to interfere with a signal being transmitted at the node during normal station operation, the bypassed signal must be sufficiently attenuated (to at least 7 dB below the optical signal at that node to get a 10^{-9} bit error rate) so that it only appears as interfering noise on a normally transmitted signal. This method is simple, reliable, and cost effective, but it reduces the operating margin of the link somewhat.

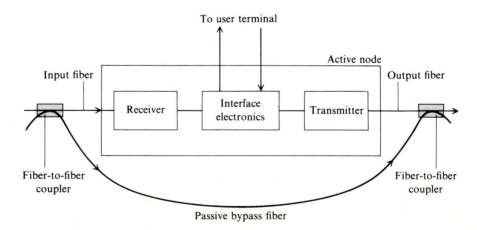

FIGURE 4.17
Example of a passive optical-fiber bypass scheme for a linear data bus configuration.

The bypass function can also be performed with active devices such as electro-optic switches.[26] In this technique no signal is bypassed until the node fails or is turned off. At that time the incoming fiber will be automatically disconnected from the equipment at that node and will be connected to the outgoing fiber by means of an electro-optic switch, thereby circumventing the node.

PASSIVE OPTICAL-FIBER BUS COUPLERS. Passive couplers for an in-line bus are used at each terminal to remove a portion of the optical signal from the bus trunk line or to inject additional light signals onto the trunk. These couplers are known as either *in-line couplers* or *T-couplers*. A major problem of the passive *T*-coupler involves the optical power budget of the network. The difficulty arises from the fact that the optical signal is not regenerated at each terminal node. Insertion and output losses at each tap, plus the fiber losses between taps, limit the network size to a small number of terminals (generally less than 10) when symmetrical couplers are used. However, many more terminals can be attached to the bus by using asymmetric couplers.

A schematic of a generic *T*-coupler is shown in Fig. 4.18. The coupler has four ports: two for connecting the device onto the bus, one for receiving tapped-off data, and one for inserting data onto the bus line. If optical power travels from left to right in Fig. 4.18 then, when a single *T*-coupler is used at a node, signals are injected onto the bus via port *A* and signals extracted from the bus are monitored at port *B*. The arrows in Fig. 4.18 show that some optical power is tapped off the primary fiber bus into the receiver at port *B*.

In many cases with this type of arrangement the transmitter would overload the receiver. To avoid this, two couplers can be put in tandem as shown in Fig. 4.19. Now the receiver port is upstream from the transmitter port and we avoid receiver overloading from the colocated transmitter. Note that there are two unused ports in this configuration.

The coupler shown in Fig. 4.18 can be simply made from two optical fibers by fusing them together over a short distance. This distance, which is designated as Γ_c in Fig. 4.18, is the *coupling length*. Its length and the spacing between the two fiber cores determines the degree of optical power coupling from one fiber

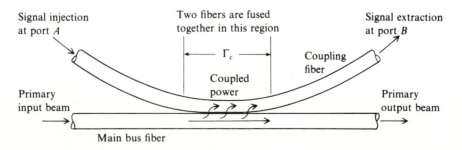

FIGURE 4.18
Schematic of a generic passive optical-fiber *T*-coupler.

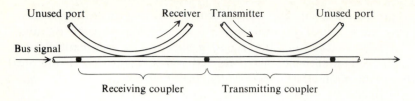

FIGURE 4.19
Use of two optical *T*-couplers in tandem to prevent receiver overload.

to another. When the two fibers are geometrically similar, we have a *symmetric coupler*. An *asymmetric coupler* results when the two fibers are different, for an example, the mainbus fiber could be multimode fiber and the coupling fiber could be a monomode fiber.[30–32]

To evaluate the performance of an in-line bus, let us examine the various sources of power loss along the transmission path. We consider this in terms of the fraction of power lost at a particular interface or within a particular component. First, over an optical fiber of length x (in kilometers), the ratio A of the received-to-transmitted power levels is given by

$$A = 10^{-(\alpha_f x/10)}$$

$$= e^{-(2.3\alpha_f x/10)} \tag{4.17}$$

where α_f is the fiber attenuation in decibels per kilometer.

The losses encountered in a *T*-coupler are shown schematically in Fig. 4.20. For simplicity we do not show the two unused ports here. The coupler thus has four functioning ports: two for connecting the device onto the fiber bus, one for receiving tapped-off data, and one for inserting data onto the line. We assume that a fraction F_c of optical power is lost at each port of the coupler. We take this fraction to be 20 percent, so that the connecting loss L_c is

$$L_c = -10 \log (1 - F_c) \approx 1 \text{ dB} \tag{4.18}$$

That is, the optical power level gets reduced by 1 dB at any coupling junction.

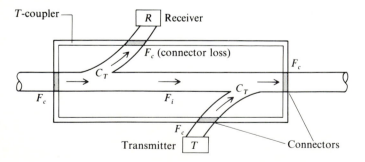

FIGURE 4.20
Optical power losses encountered in two tandem passive *T*-couplers.

Let C_T represent the fraction of power removed from the bus and delivered to the detector port. Note that, in general, the fraction of power removed from the line in a T-coupler is actually $2C_T$, since optical power is extracted at both the receiving and the transmitting taps of the device. The power removed at the transmitting tap is lost from the system. The coupling loss L_T in dB is then given by

$$L_T = -10 \log (1 - 2C_T) \tag{4.19}$$

In addition to connection and tapping losses, there is an intrinsic transmission loss L_i associated with each T-coupler. If the fraction of power lost in the coupler is F_i, then the intrinsic transmission loss L_i in dB is

$$L_i = -10 \log (1 - F_i) \tag{4.20}$$

Generally, an in-line bus will consist of a number of stations separated by various lengths of bus line. However, here for analytical simplicity, we consider an in-line bus of N stations uniformly separated by a distance L. From Eq. (4.17) the fiber attenuation between adjacent stations is

$$A_0 = e^{-(2.3\alpha_f L/10)} \tag{4.21}$$

We use the notation P_{jk} to denote the optical power received at the detector of the kth station from the transmitter of the jth station. For simplicity, we assume that a T-coupler exists at every terminal of the bus including the two end stations.

Because of the serial nature of the in-line bus, the optical power available at a particular node decreases with increasing distance from the source. Thus a performance quantity of interest is the *system dynamic range*. This is the maximum optical power range to which any detector must be able to respond. The smallest difference in transmitted and received optical power occurs for adjacent stations, such as between station 1 and station 2 in Fig. 4.21. If P_0 is the optical power launched from a source flylead and E is the coupling efficiency of optical power onto the bus line, then

$$P_{1,2} = A_0 C_T (1 - F_c)^4 E P_0 \tag{4.22}$$

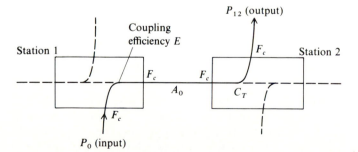

FIGURE 4.21
Optical path between adjacent stations for an in-line bus.

The largest difference in transmitted and received optical power occurs between station 1 and station N. At the transmitting end the fractional power level coupled into the first length of cable is

$$F_1 = (1 - F_c)^2 E$$

At the receiving end the fraction of power from the T-coupler input port that emerges from the detector port is

$$F_N = (1 - F_c)^2 C_T$$

For each of the $N - 2$ intermediate stations the fraction of power passed through each coupler is

$$F_{\text{coup}} = (1 - F_c)^2 (1 - 2C_T)(1 - F_i)$$

Combining these factors and the transmission losses of the $N - 1$ intervening fibers, we find that the power received at station N from station 1 is

$$\begin{aligned}
P_{1N} &= A_0^{N-1} F_1 F_{\text{coup}}^{N-2} F_N P_0 \\
&= A_0^{N-1}(1 - F_c)^{2N}(1 - 2C_T)^{N-2} C_T (1 - F_i)^{N-2} E P_0 \quad (4.23)
\end{aligned}$$

The worst-case dynamic range (DR) is then found from the ratio of Eq. (4.22) to Eq. (4.23)

$$\text{DR} = \frac{1}{[A_0(1 - F_c)^2(1 - 2C_T)(1 - F_i)]^{N-2}} \quad (4.24)$$

4.2.3 Ring Topology

In a ring topology,[33-37] consecutive nodes are connected by point-to-point links which are arranged to form a single closed path as is shown in Fig. 4.22. Information in the form of data packets is transmitted from node to node around the ring which can consist of either twisted-pair wire, baseband coaxial cable, or optical fibers. The interface at each node is an active device that has the ability to recognize its own address in a data packet in order to accept messages. The interface serves not only as a user attachment point but also as an active repeater for retransmitting messages that are addressed to other nodes.

From Fig. 4.22 we see that the interfaces in a ring network can operate either in a listen or a transmit mode, or the node can be bypassed if it is not operational. In the listen mode the bypassing bit stream is monitored for pertinent bit sequences such as a token or an address pattern. The incoming bit stream is thus simply copied to the output with a time delay of about one bit.

When an interface in the listen mode recognizes an address field which specifies it as the information destination, each incoming bit in the packet is

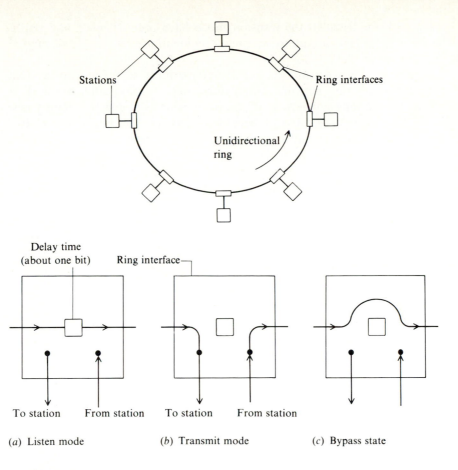

(a) Listen mode   **(b)** Transmit mode   **(c)** Bypass state

FIGURE 4.22
Ring topology and three possible operational modes.

copied and sent to the attached station while simultaneously the bits are also retransmitted to the next station. This, of course, presents the question of when or where are the data packets removed from the ring. For a bus network the signals which travel along the line are absorbed by line terminators once they reach the endpoints of the bus. However, in a ring the packets would continue to circulate indefinitely if they were not removed by some station. This can take place either at the destination station, or it can occur at the sender once the packet has made one complete loop. Removal at the sending station is more advantageous since it allows automatic acknowledgment that a packet has been received and because it allows multicast addressing wherein one packet is simultaneously sent to many stations.

In the transmit mode, the interface breaks the connection between the input and output, and enters its own data onto the ring. A number of methods for switching from the listen to the transmit mode have been designed and implemented. Four popular ones are token rings,[35] contention rings,[17] slotted rings,[35] and insertion rings.[36-37]

A number of implementation considerations must be taken into account when configuring a ring network. First, rings must be physically arranged so that all nodes are fully connected. Whenever a node is added to support new devices, transmission lines have to be placed between this node and its two nearby, topologically adjacent nodes. Thus, it is often difficult to prewire a building for ring networks in anticipation of new nodes to be added in the future. In addition, a break in any line, the failure of a node, or adding a new node will disrupt network operation. A variety of steps can be taken to circumvent these problems, although this generally increases the complexity of the ring interface electronics as well as its cost. Among these methods are node bypass techniques and loop-back schemes used in conjunction with multiple-line cables. We discuss these in more detail in Chap. 8 which deals with network reliability.

4.2.4 Star Architectures

In a star architecture[7,38-41] all nodes are joined at a single point called the *central node* or *hub*. The central node can be an active or a passive device and the transmission medium can be either twisted-pair wire, coaxial cable, or optical fibers.

An active central node is generally used when control of the network is carried out in the central node. In this case the central node performs all routing of messages in the network, whether it is from the central node to outlying nodes, between outlying nodes, or from all nodes to remote points. Point-to-point links connect the central and outlying nodes, so that the outlying nodes are required to have complex network control functions. Star networks with an active central node are most useful when the bulk of the communications is between the central and the outlying nodes. If there is a great deal of message traffic between the outlying nodes, then a heavy switching burden is placed on the central node.

In a star network with a passive central node, a power splitter is used at the hub of the star to divide the incoming signals among all the stations. Power-splitting losses add up as $1/N$ where N represents the number of branches in the splitter. In addition there is always some coupling and throughput loss in each splitter. Thus if there is a large number of terminals, repeater amplifiers may be necessary to boost the power level to meet link power margin requirements. Since a star-coupled network is logically equivalent to a bus network, it offers an attractive implementation of a coaxial bus, because transformers and repeaters are eliminated and network reliability is improved.

Example 4.5. An example of a single-ended coaxial network that employs a power splitter and a power combiner in a star configuration is shown in Fig. 4.23. An

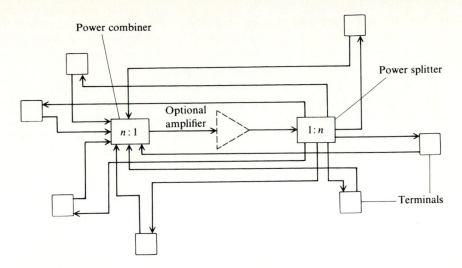

FIGURE 4.23
Single-ended coaxial network that uses power splitters and combiners in a star configuration.

optional amplifier is shown between the combiner and the splitter. This would be used in those cases where the power losses in the splitter are too large to maintain an adequate power margin on all links. For impedance-matched combiners and splitters, any signal path can be treated as a point-to-point link with the additional losses from the couplers added.

A star network is also readily implemented using optical fibers. The couplers in this case can be either the transmission or reflection star couplers shown in Fig. 4.24. These couplers are passive mixing elements, that is, the optical powers from the input ports are mixed together and then divided equally among

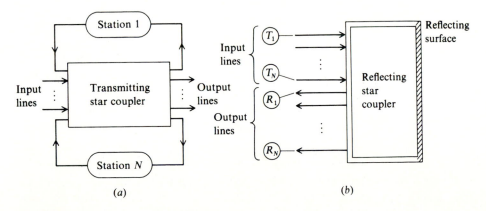

FIGURE 4.24
Transmitting (a) and reflecting (b) type optical-fiber star couplers.

the output ports. They may be used to combine numerous signals together, split a signal into a number of parts, or to tap optical power out of or insert optical power into a fiber-optic link. Either type of star is composed of a set of input fibers, a set of output fibers, and a mixing region.

In general, the reflection star is more versatile because the relative number of input and output ports may be selected or varied after the device has been constructed (the total number of ports, in plus out, being fixed, however). By comparison, the number of transmission star input and output fibers is fixed by initial design and fabrication. The reflection star is usually less efficient since a portion of the light which has entered the coupler is injected back into the input fibers. Given the same number of input and output ports, the transmission star is twice as efficient as the reflection star. Therefore, reflection and transmission star couplers have their own particular advantages and disadvantages, and selection of a star coupler type for a particular application is largely determined by the network topology.

To see how star couplers can be applied to a given network, let us examine the various optical power losses associated with the coupler. The insertion loss L_S of a star coupler is defined as the fraction of optical power lost in the process of coupling light from the input port to all the output ports (see Prob. 4.11 for an example). It is given in decibels by

$$L_S = 10 \log \frac{\sum_{k=1}^{N} P_k}{P_i} \tag{4.25}$$

where the P_k are the output powers from all the ports, P_i is the input power at one port, and for a transmission star coupler N is the number of outputs, whereas for a reflection star coupler N is the number of inputs plus outputs.

The optical power that enters a star coupler gets divided equally among the N output ports. That is, the optical power at any one output port is $(1/N)$th of the total optical power emerging from all the coupler outputs. This is known as the *power splitting factor* L_{sp}, which is given in decibels by

$$L_{sp} = 10 \log N \tag{4.26}$$

If P_S is the fiber-coupled output power from a source in dBm, P_R is the minimum optical power in dBm required at the receiver for a specific data rate, α_f is the fiber attenuation, and L_c is the connector loss in dB, then the balance equation for a particular link having all stations located at the same distance L from the star coupler is

$$P_S - P_R = L_S + 2\alpha_f L + 4L_c + 10 \log N + \text{system margin} \tag{4.27}$$

where we have assumed connector losses at the transmitter, the receiver, and the input and output ports of the star coupler. For a transmission star N is the number of output ports, whereas for a reflection star N is the total number of input plus output ports.

A variety of star coupler types have been proposed[7,42–44] to which the reader is referred for details.

4.2.5 Unconstrained Topology

Unconstrained topologies (also known as *hybrid* or *mesh networks*) have no definite configuration.[45–46] Instead the nodes are connected by point-to-point links in an arbitrary fashion that can vary greatly from one implementation to another. The connections are usually determined by network costs. For example, when transmission line costs are high and there are a few nodes that must communicate with each other, efficiency is gained by choosing only those internodal connections that are needed.

Although an unconstrained topology allows a lot of configuration flexibility, the routing problems associated with such a network are rather difficult to solve. Nodes that make routing decisions must often execute many network-related functions. This is undesirable for LAN nodes since it introduces delay and adds unwanted overhead.

4.3 SUMMARY

The transmission media provide the physical channels that are needed to interconnect nodes in a LAN. These include twisted-pair wire, coaxial cables, and optical fibers. In local area networks, twisted-pair wires are mainly used for low-cost, low-performance applications. Coaxial cables offer substantially larger bandwidths than twisted-pair wire. They have the ability to support high data rates with high immunity to electrical interference and a low incidence of errors. Since coaxial cables are widely used in telephone networks and by the cable TV industry, they are moderate in cost and readily available. The coaxial cables used for baseband LANs that transmit signals in the 1- to 20-Mb/s range are typically $\frac{3}{8}$ inch in diameter and have a 50-ohm impedance. The transmission medium for broadband LANs having bandwidths of 300 to 400 MHz is standard $\frac{1}{2}$-inch 75-ohm coaxial cable.

Optical fibers offer an attractive alternative to wire transmission lines because of their dielectric nature. The two basic classes of optical fibers are multimode and monomode. Some popular multimode core sizes for LAN applications are 50-, 62.5-, 85-, and 100-micrometer diameters. The core size for monomode fibers is 9 μm for operation at a 1300-nm wavelength. Multimode graded-index fibers can have usable bandwidth-distance products of several GHz-km, whereas monomode fibers have capacities well in excess of this.

The manner in which nodes are geometrically arranged and connected is known as the topology of the network. Local area networks are commonly characterized in terms of their topology. The three basic LAN topologies are the bus, ring, and star configurations. Each of these has its own particular advantages and limitations in terms of reliability, expandability, and performance characteristics.

PROBLEMS

Section 4.1

4.1. Show that for copper wires Eqs. (4.1), (4.2), and (4.3) can be written as

$$C = \frac{27.8\varepsilon_r}{\text{arc cosh }(d/2a)} \quad \text{pF/m}$$

$$L = 0.4 \text{ arc cosh } \frac{d}{2a} \quad \mu\text{H/m}$$

and

$$Z_0 = \frac{120}{\sqrt{\varepsilon_r}} \text{ arc cosh } \frac{d}{2a} \quad \text{ohms}$$

4.2. A twisted-pair wire line is composed of two cylindrical 16-gauge copper wires (0.130 cm in diameter) that have a 0.30-cm center-to-center spacing. Assuming the insulating material surrounding the wires has a relative dielectric constant of 2.25, find the capacitance C, the inductance L, the characteristic impedance Z_0, and the resistance of the line at frequencies of 10 kHz, 100 kHz, and 1 MHz.

4.3. Consider a coaxial cable of inner radius a and outer radius b.

(a) Using Ampere's circuital law

$$\oint \mathbf{H} \cdot \mathbf{dl} = I$$

show that the magnetic flux density B is given by

$$B = \mu_0 H = \frac{\mu_0 I}{2\pi r}$$

where $a < r < b$.

(b) The magnetic flux Φ constrained between the conductors in a length Δl is the flux crossing any radial plane extending from a to b within this length element. Using the expression

$$\Phi = \int \mathbf{B} \cdot \mathbf{dA}$$

where dA is an incremental area through which the flux passes, show that

$$\Phi = \frac{\mu_0 I \Delta l}{2\pi} \ln \frac{b}{a}$$

(c) Using the expression $L = \Phi/(I\ \Delta l)$, find the inductance L per unit length of this cable.

(d) The electric field intensity E outside of a cyclindrical conductor of radius a is given by

$$E = \frac{q}{2\pi r \varepsilon}$$

where $r < a$ and ε is the dielectric constant of the material surrounding the conductor. Show that the capacitance C per unit length is given by

$$C = \frac{q}{V} = 2\pi\varepsilon/\ln\ (b/a)$$

(e) Show that the characteristic impedance is given by Eq. (4.7).

4.4. Consider Eq. (4.9) which gives the attenuation for a coaxial cable. On one sheet of log-log graph paper, make separate plots of α_c, α_d, and α for frequencies ranging from 10 MHz to 10^4 MHz to show that α_d is smaller than α_c for broadband LAN frequencies less than 400 MHz. For these calculations let tan $\phi = 0.0002$, $\varepsilon_r = 1.26$, $b/a = 4.07$, and $b = 1.25$ cm.

4.5. Express the high-frequency attenuation given in Eq. (4.9) for a coaxial-cable line in terms of the dimensions a and b. Assuming that b is constant, minimize this expression with respect to a. Show that minimum attenuation is obtained when b/a is approximately 3.6. Show that the corresponding value of Z_0 is $77/\sqrt{\varepsilon_r}$ ohms.

4.6. (a) Verify the values of the upstream and downstream signal levels shown in Fig. 4.7.

(b) Change the signal levels given in dBmV to voltage values.

(c) How many users spaced 50 feet apart can be attached to the spare line coming out of the 5-dB coupler? Assume a 1-dB throughput loss for each tap and assume an 0.412-inch diameter coaxial cable having the loss values shown in Fig. 4.7. Show what the values of the tap isolation should be for each user if the tap level is to be 0.5 ± 0.5 dBmV.

4.7. Make a graphical comparison, as in Fig. 4.12, of the maximum attenuation-limited transmission distance of the following two systems operating at 20 Mb/s:

System 1 operating at 850 nm

(a) GaAlAs laser diode: 0-dBm (1-mW) fiber-coupled power

(b) Silicon avalanche photodiode: −56-dBm sensitivity

(c) Graded-index fiber: 3.5-dB/km attenuation at 850 nm

(d) Connector loss: 1 dB/connector

System 2 operating at 1300 nm

(a) InGaAsP LED: −13-dBm fiber-coupled power

(b) InGaAs *pin* photodiode: −45-dBm sensitivity

(c) Graded-index fiber: 1.5-dB/km attenuation at 1300 nm

(d) Connector loss: 1 dB/connector

Allow a 6-dB system operating margin in each case.

4.8. An engineer has the following components available:

(a) GaAlAs laser diode operating at 850 nm and capable of coupling 1 mW (0 dBm) into a fiber

(b) Ten sections of cable each of which is 500 m long, has a 4-dB/km attenuation, and has connectors at both ends

(c) Connector loss of 2 dB/connector

(d) A *pin* photodiode receiver

(e) An avalanche photodiode receiver

Using these components, the engineer wishes to construct a 5-km link operating at 10 Mb/s. If the sensitivities of the *pin* and APD receivers are −46 and −59 dBm, respectively, which receiver should be used if a 6-dB system operating margin is required?

4.9. Consider a star-coupled optical-fiber network with 16 inputs and 16 outputs operating at 10 Mb/s. Assume this system has the following parameters: $L_c = 1.0$ dB, star coupler insertion loss $L_s = 5$ dB, and a fiber loss of 2 dB/km. Let the sources be InGaAsP LEDs having an output of −16 dBm from a fiber flylead, and assume InGaAsP *pin* photodiodes with a −49 dBm sensitivity are used. Assume that a 6-dB system margin is required.

(a) What is the maximum transmission distance if a transmission star coupler is used?

(b) What is the maximum distance if a reflection star coupler is used?

4.10. Consider an optical-fiber transmission star coupler having seven inputs and seven outputs. Suppose the coupler is constructed by arranging the seven fibers in a circular pattern (a ring of six with one in the center) and butting them against the end of a glass rod which serves as the mixing element.

(a) If the fibers have 50-μm core diameters and 125-μm outer cladding diameters, what is the coupling loss resulting from light escaping between the fiber cores? Let the rod diameter be 300 μm. Assume the fiber cladding is not removed.

(b) What is the coupling loss if the fiber ends are arranged in a row and a 50-μm by 800-μm glass plate is used as the star coupler?

4.11. Repeat Prob. 4.10 for seven fibers having 200-μm core diameters and 400-μm outer cladding diameters. What should the sizes of the glass rod and the glass plate be in this case?

4.12. An engineer wishes to construct an in-line optical-fiber data bus operating at 10 Mb/s. The stations are to be separated by 100 m, for which optical fibers with a 3-dB/km attenuation are used. The optical sources are laser diodes having an output of 1 mW from a fiber flylead and the detectors are avalanche photodiodes with a −58-dBm (1.6-nW) sensitivity. The couplers have a power-coupling efficiency $E = 10$ percent, a power tapoff factor of $C_T = 5$ percent, and a 10 percent fractional intrinsic loss F_i. The power loss at the connectors is 20 percent (1 dB).

(a) Make a plot of P_{1N} in dBm as a function of the number of stations N from 0 to −58 dBm.

(b) What is the system operating margin for eight stations?

(c) What is the worst-case dynamic range for the maximum allowable number of stations if a 6-dB power margin is required?

4.13. A two-story office building has two 10-foot-wide hallways per floor which connect four rows of offices with eight offices per row as is shown in Fig. P4.13. Each office

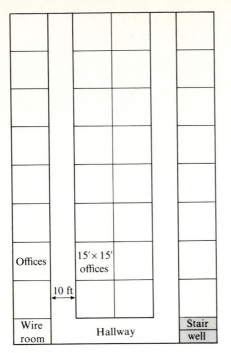

FIGURE P4.13

is 15 feet square. The office ceiling height is nine feet with a false ceiling hung one foot below the actual ceiling. Also, as shown in Fig. P4.13, there is a wiring room for LAN interconnection and control equipment in one corner of each floor. Every office has a local-area-network socket on each of the two walls that are perpendicular to the hallway wall. If we assume that cables can be run only in the walls and in the ceilings, estimate the length of cable (in feet) that is required for the following configurations:

(a) A coaxial cable bus with a twisted-pair wire drop from the ceiling to each outlet.

(b) A fiber-optic star that connects each outlet to the wiring room on the corresponding floor and a vertical fiber-optic riser that connects the stars in each wiring room.

4.14. Consider the M-by-N grid of stations shown in Fig. P4.14 which are to be connected by a local area network. Let the stations be spaced a distance d apart and assume that interconnection cables will be run in ducts that connect nearest-neighbor stations (that is, ducts are not run diagonally in Fig. P4.14). Show that for the following configurations, the cable length for interconnecting the stations is as stated:

(a) $(MN - 1)d$ for a bus configuration

(b) MNd for a ring topology

(c) $1/2\ MN(M + N - 2)d$ for a star topology where each subscriber is connected *individually* to the network hub which is located *in one corner* of the grid.

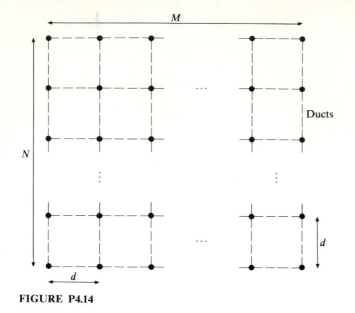

FIGURE P4.14

4.15. Consider the *M*-by-*N* rectangular grid of computer stations shown in Fig. P4.14, where the spacing between stations is *d*. Assume these stations are to be connected by a star-configured LAN using the duct network shown in the figure. Further assume that each station is connected to the central star by means of its own dedicated cable.

(*a*) If *m* and *n* denote the relative position of the star, show that the total cable length *L* needed to connect the stations is given by

$$L = [1/2\, MN(M + N + 2) - Nm(M - m + 1) - Mn(N - n + 1)]d$$

(*b*) Show that if the star is located in one corner of the grid, then this expression becomes

$$L = MN(M + N - 2)d/2$$

(*c*) Show that the shortest cable length is obtained when the star is at the center of the grid.

REFERENCES

1. R. Pickens, "Wideband transmission media III; Guided transmission: Wireline, coaxial cable, and fiber optics," in W. Chou (ed.), *Computer Communications, Vol. 1, Principles,* Prentice-Hall, Englewood Cliffs, NJ, 1983.
2. *Reference Data for Radio Engineers,* H. W. Sams and Co., Indianapolis, IN, 6th ed., 1975.
3. W. C. Johnson, *Transmission Lines and Networks,* McGraw-Hill, New York, 1950, chap. 3.
4. R. E. Matick, *Transmission Lines for Digital and Communication Networks,* McGraw-Hill, New York, 1969.
5. J. Spergel, "Coaxial cable and connector systems," in C. A. Harper (ed.), *Handbook of Wiring, Cabling, and Interconnecting for Electronics,* McGraw-Hill, New York, 1972, chap. 4.

6. R. M. Metcalfe and D. R. Boggs, "Ethernet: Distributed packet switching for local computer networks," *Commun. ACM*, vol. 19, pp. 395–404, July 1976.

7. (*a*) R. V. Schmidt, E. G. Rawson, R. E. Norton, Jr., S. B. Jackson, and M. D. Bailey, "Fibernet II: A fiber optic Ethernet," *IEEE J. Select. Areas Commun.*, vol. SAC-1, pp. 702–711, November 1983.
   (*b*) E. G. Rawson, "The Fibernet II Ethernet-compatible fiber-optic LAN," *IEEE J. Lightwave Tech.*, vol. LT-3, pp. 496–501, June 1985.

8. J. F. Shoch, Y. K. Dalal, and D. D. Redell, "Evolution of the Ethernet local computer network," *Computer*, vol. 15, pp. 10–27, August 1982.

9. E. B. Cooper, "Broadband network design: Issues and answers," *Computer Design*, vol. 22, pp. 209–216, March 1983.

10. M. A. Dineson, "Broadband local area networks enhance communication design," *EDN*, vol. 26, pp. 77–87, Mar. 4, 1981.

11. R. N. Dunbar, "Design considerations for broadband coaxial cable systems," *IEEE Commun. Mag.*, vol. 24, pp. 24–37, June 1986.

12. G. Keiser, *Optical Fiber Communications*, McGraw-Hill, New York, 1983.

13. E. E. Basch, H. A. Carnes, and R. F. Kearns, "Calculate performance into fiber-optic links," *Electron. Design*, vol. 28, pp. 161–166, Aug. 16, 1980.

14. J. Bliss and D. W. Stevenson, "Fiber Optics: A designer's guide to system budgeting," *Electro-Opt. Sys. Design*, vol. 13, pp. 23–32, August 1981.

15. "Special issue on fiber optics for local communications," Special Issue of *IEEE J. Select. Areas Commun.*, vol. SAC-3, November 1985.

16. "Special issue on fiber-optic local area networks," Special issue of *IEEE J. Lightwave Tech.*, vol. LT-3, June 1985.

17. D. D. Clark, K. T. Pogran, and D. P. Reed, "An introduction to local area networks," *Proc. IEEE*, vol. 66, pp. 1497–1517, November 1978.

18. T. V. Feng, "A survey of interconnection networks," *Computer*, vol. 14, pp. 12–27, December 1981.

19. M. M. Nassehi, F. A. Tobagi, and M. E. Marhic, "Fiber-optic configurations for local area networks," *IEEE J. Sel. Areas Commun.*, vol. SAC-3, pp. 941–949, November 1985.

20. V. A. DeMarines and L. W. Hill, "The cable bus in data communications," *Datamation*, vol. 22, pp. 89–92, August 1976.

21. J. C. Naylor, "Data bus design concepts, issues and prospects," *Proc. IEEE Eastcon.*, pp. 34–39, September 1978.

22. A. S. Acampora and M. G. Hluchyj, "A new local area network using a centralized bus," *IEEE Commun. Mag.*, vol. 22, pp. 12–21, August 1984.

23. T. Nishitani, K. Ohasa, K. Tsukada, and Y. Ohgushi, "Optical serial highway for CAMAC system using high-performance optical bus adapters," *IEEE J. Lightwave Tech.*, vol. LT-3, pp. 525–531, June 1985.

24. A. Albanese, "Fail-safe nodes for lightguide digital networks," *Bell Sys. Tech. J.*, vol. 16, pp. 247–256, February 1982.

25. P. A. Bulteel and J. Tillemans. "New directional coupler and connecting device for fiber-optic local area networks," *SPIE Conf. on Fiber Optic Couplers and Connectors*, Arlington, Virginia, May 1–2, 1984.

26. S. F. Su, L. Jou, and J. Lenart, "A review on classification of optical switching systems," *IEEE Commun. Mag.*, vol. 24, pp. 50–55, May 1986.

27. F. A. Tobagi, F. Borgonovo, and L. Fratta, "Expressnet: A high-performance integrated-services local area network," *IEEE J. Select. Areas Commun.*, vol. SAC-1, pp. 898–912, November 1983.

28. J. O. Limb and C. Flores, "Description of Fasnet—A unidirectional local area communications network," *Bell Sys. Tech. J.*, vol. 61, pp. 1413–1440, September 1982.

29. C. W. Tseng and B. U. Chen, "D-Net; A new scheme for high data rate optical local area networks," *IEEE J. Select. Areas Commun.*, vol. SAC-1, pp. 493–499, April 1983.

30. H. H. Witte and V. Kulich, "Branching elements for optical data buses," *Appl. Optics*, vol. 20, pp. 715–718, Feb. 1981.

31. T. H. Wood, "Increased power injection in multimode optical-fiber buses through mode-selective coupling," *IEEE J. Lightwave Tech.*, vol. LT-3, pp. 537–543, June 1985.
32. H. S. Huang, H. C. Chang, and J. S. Wu, "Power transfer between single-mode and multimode optical fibers," *1986 IEEE MTT-S Microwave Symp. Digest*, pp. 519–522, June 2–4, 1986, Baltimore, Maryland.
33. J. H. Saltzer, K. T. Pogran, and D. D. Clark, "Why a ring?," *Computer Networks*, vol. 7, pp. 223–231, 1983.
34. W. Bux, F. H. Closs, K. Kuemmerle, H. J. Keller, and H. R. Mueller, "Architecture and design of a reliable token-ring network," *IEEE J. Select. Areas Commun.*, vol. SAC-1, pp. 756–765, April 1983.
35. J. Pierce, "How far can data loops go?," *IEEE Trans. Commun.*, vol. COM-20, pp, 527–530, June 1972.
36. M. T. Liu, "Distributed loop computer network," in *Advances in Computing*, vol. 17, pp. 163–221, M. C. Yovits (ed.), Academic, New York, 1978.
37. D. E. Huber, W. Steinlin, and P. J. Wild, "SILK: An implementation of a buffer insertion ring," *IEEE J. Select. Areas Commun.*, vol. SAC-1, pp. 766–774, November 1983.
38. M. Schwartz, *Computer-Communication Network Design and Analysis*, Prentice-Hall, Englewood Cliffs, NJ, 1977, chap. 10.
39. S. Moustakas, H. H. Witte, V. Bodlaj, and V. Kulich, "Passive optical star bus with collision detection for CSMA/CD-based local area networks," *IEEE J. Lightwave Tech.*, vol. LT-3, pp. 93–100, February 1985.
40. D. R. Porter, P. R. Couch, and J. W. Schelin, "A high-speed fiber optic data bus for local data communication," *IEEE J. Select. Areas Commun.*, vol. SAC-1, pp. 479–488, April 1983.
41. E. S. Lee and P. I. P. Boulton, "The principles and performance of Hubnet: A 50 Mb/s glass-fiber local area network," *IEEE J. Select. Areas Commun.*, vol. SAC-1, pp. 711–720, November 1983.
42. M. C. Hudson and F. L. Thiel, "The star coupler: A unique interconnection component for multimode optical waveguide communication systems," *Appl. Opt.*, vol. 13, pp. 2540–2545, November 1974.
43. B. S. Kawasaki and K. O. Hill, "Low-loss access coupler for multimode optical fiber distribution networks," *Appl. Opt.*, vol. 16, pp. 1794–1795, July 1977.
44. D. H. McMahon and R. L. Gravel, "Star repeaters for fiber optic links," *Appl. Opt.*, vol. 16, pp. 501–503, February 1977.
45. D. W. Davies, D. L. A. Barber, W. C. Price, and C. M. Solomonides, *Computer Networks and Their Protocols*, Wiley, New York, 1979, chap. 10.
46. H. K. Pung and P. A. Davies, "Fibre-optic local area network with arbitrary topology," *IEE Proc.*, vol. 131, pp. 77–82, April 1984.

CHAPTER
5

BASICS
OF
QUEUEING
THEORY

In the previous two chapters we have studied concepts relating to the physical and data-link layers of the OSI Reference Model outlined in Chap. 2. These topics have included the theoretical basis for reliably sending information from node to node in a local area network, the characteristics of various media over which this information can be sent, and the fundamental types of geometrical patterns (topologies) that can be realized by means of interconnecting the nodes with the different forms of these transmission media.

The next area of interest is how to efficiently gain access to a local area network. This can be done either in a deterministic fashion or by means of a contention method. To compare the different access schemes, we first need to examine the analytical tools that describe the performance of a network.

The mathematical foundation for most analytical models of computer systems and communication networks is queueing theory.[1-9] A *queue* is a waiting line, and *queueing theory* is the study of waiting-line phenomena. Queueing theory is a powerful abstraction for modeling systems that consist of a collection of service resources and a population of customers. The customers arrive at a resource, line up and wait their turn for service, and then depart after having been serviced by the resource. Examples of these systems are supermarket check-outs, airline ticket counters, bank windows, and toll booths.

Queueing theory has also been used very successfully to estimate the performance of computer and communication networks, because it is able to capture the interaction between the workload and the resources of a system. In this case the customers represent jobs or tasks which, depending on the system, correspond to processes in a computer system, users at terminals, messages sent from node to node, etc. The resources can include communication links, terminals, buffers, controllers, and computer-system elements such as processors, memories, disks, and protocol-handling devices.

Within the network the jobs circulate among the resources and line up (queue) at the resources to contend for their use. The individual queues are usually described in terms of the types of resources, the number of distinct resources, the queueing (scheduling) disciplines, and the probability distributions for the service times of jobs at the queues.

The purpose of queueing theory is to analyze the contention for resources and to determine its effect on the flow of jobs through the system. In this chapter we examine the fundamental elements of queueing theory so that we can apply it to calculating message throughput, queue lengths, and the mean response time of various LAN access schemes in Chap. 6.

5.1 OVERVIEW AND DEFINITIONS

This section gives a brief overview of queueing network models and presents definitions of the basic terminology that is used. The theory and application procedures are then developed in the subsequent sections.

5.1.1 Queueing Models

The behavior of a network depends on the interaction of the system workload and the system resources. The simplest view of a queueing model is shown in Fig. 5.1. Here we represent a node that is characterized by what is known as a *single-server queue*. This node has a buffer associated with it in which arriving jobs (messages) queue up and wait for service from a single processing element (a single server). The messages that arrive at the buffer can be coming either from a group of message sources that are directly connected to the node or they can arrive on an external line that is connected to another node. The source of messages can be finite or infinite. A finite-source system cannot have an arbitrarily long service queue, but the number of message sources in the system affects the arrival rate; that is, the larger the number of sources, the higher the message arrival rate. For an infinite-source system the length of the service queue is unlimited, and the arrival rate is not affected by the number of message sources in

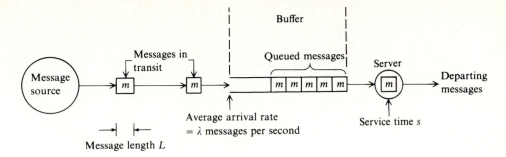

FIGURE 5.1
General overview of a simple queueing model.

the system. If the source population is finite but large, an infinite-source system is usually assumed to simplify the mathematics.

The messages arrive at the buffer at a rate of λ messages per second and they have a length of X data units that could consist of bits, bytes, characters, etc. Here, for ease of calculation, we shall assume that all messages have the same length L.

Functions at a node are characterized by a service rate and a queueing discipline. The *service rate* is expressed as the number of jobs leaving the node per unit servicing time. This service rate may be load-dependent, meaning that the rate at which the node processes jobs may depend on the length of the associated queue. The *queueing discipline* is the rule used to determine the order in which the queued-up jobs receive service. For example, queues in super-markets, banks, or airports process jobs in the order of arrival. This is known as a *first-come-first-served* (FCFS) discipline. In other situations, such as in hospi-tal emergency rooms, for example, there are certain customers (jobs) which obviously have priority over others.

Here we shall assume that the messages are processed on an FCFS basis at a rate of C data units per second, where C is referred to as the *capacity*. If a message arrives and there are n messages ahead of it in the buffer, then the total time T taken to service this message consists of the time w that is spent waiting in the queue plus the message-processing time s, that is,

$$T = \text{waiting time in queue } (w) + \text{service time } (s)$$

$$= \frac{L}{C} + \frac{nL}{C}$$

$$= \frac{1 + n}{\mu} \tag{5.1}$$

where $\mu = C/L$ is the service rate in messages per second. Using this notation, we see a simple model of a single-server queue in Fig. 5.2.

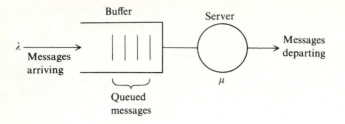

FIGURE 5.2
Model of a single-server queue.

The total waiting time or delay time T is generally a random variable since the state n of the buffer varies with time. Thus, in the next section we look at various statistical models which give rise to an expression for average message time delay in a system.

5.1.2   Poisson Statistics

In studying queueing systems, we need to take into account the randomness of both the message arrival rate and the service time. Since these two parameters are random variables, they are described in statistical terms and thus have a probability distribution associated with them. A brief overview of probability theory is given in App. D.

For the message arrival process the most common description is given in terms of Poisson statistics.[10-13] This assumption is widely used to model telephone traffic and it also agrees well with measurements on message statistics taken in actual computer-communication networks.[14]

Poisson statistics are based on a *discrete* distribution of events. Under the assumption that a system has a large number of independent customers, Poisson statistics state that the probability $P_n(t)$ of exactly n customers arriving during a time interval of length t is given by

$$P_n(t) = \frac{(\lambda t)^n e^{-\lambda t}}{n!} \tag{5.2}$$

where λ is the mean arrival rate and $n = 0, 1, 2, \ldots$.

If $N = \{n | n = 0, 1, 2, \ldots\}$ is the set of the possible number of messages arriving at a node, where the probability of n arrivals is given by Eq. (5.2), then the *average* or *expected number* of message arrivals in a time interval T is given by

$$E[N] = \sum_{n=0}^{\infty} n P_n(t) = \lambda T \tag{5.3}$$

where the notation $E[x]$ denotes the expectation value of the quantity x. [The proof of Eq. (5.3) is left as an exercise.] Thus the expected number of arrivals in the time interval $(0, T)$ is equal to λT.

Using the Poisson arrival process, let us look at the statistics of the message arrival process. First assume that messages enter the queueing system at times t_0, t_1, t_2, ..., t_n where $t_0 < t_1 < t_2 \cdots < t_n$. The random variables $\tau_n = t_n - t_{n-1}$ (where $n \geq 1$) are called the *interarrival times*. These can be assumed to form a sequence of independent and identically distributed random variables. Letting τ represent an arbitrary interarrival time having a probability density function $a(t)$, we can show that Poisson arrivals generate an exponential interarrival probability density.

Consider an infinitesimal time interval Δt. The probability $a(t) \Delta t$ is then the probability that the next arrival occurs at least t seconds but not more than $(t + \Delta t)$ seconds from the time of the last arrival. That is, it is just the probability $P_0(t)$ of no arrivals for a time t multiplied by the probability $P_1(\Delta t)$ of one arrival in the infinitesimal time interval Δt

$$a(t)\Delta t = P_0(t)P_1(\Delta t) \tag{5.4}$$

where from Eq. (5.2), we have $P_0(t) = e^{-\lambda t}$ and $P_1(\Delta t) = \lambda \Delta t e^{-\lambda \Delta t}$. In the limit $\Delta t \to 0$, the exponential term in P_1 approaches unity, so that

$$a(t)\, dt = \lambda e^{-\lambda t}\, dt \tag{5.5}$$

Thus, as is shown in Fig. 5.3, the time τ between arrivals is a continuously distributed exponential random variable. Hence we say that the Poisson arrival process has *exponential arrival times*.

Now let us consider the service time. Here we first have to make an assumption about the message length, since the service time, or time to complete the message transmission, is obviously directly related to how long the message is. Messages that are waiting in a queue are handled by a server which is a fixed-capacity outgoing line that processes messages at a rate of C data units per second. The service time of these messages varies in a statistical manner because the messages themselves vary in length in a random fashion.

To start, we make the simple queueing-theory assumption that the messages are exponentially distributed in length with average length L. For servers having a capacity of C data units per second, a message that is L data units long will be transmitted or serviced in L/C seconds. The *service-time distribution* $S(t)$ can then be written as

$$S(t) = (C/L)e^{-Ct/L} \tag{5.6}$$

which has an expectation value (that is, average message-service or transmission time) of

$$E[S(t)] = \frac{L}{C} = \frac{1}{\mu} \tag{5.7}$$

Since Eq. (5.6) is of the same form as Eq. (5.5), the service-time distribution also obeys Poisson statistics.

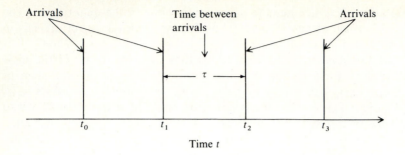

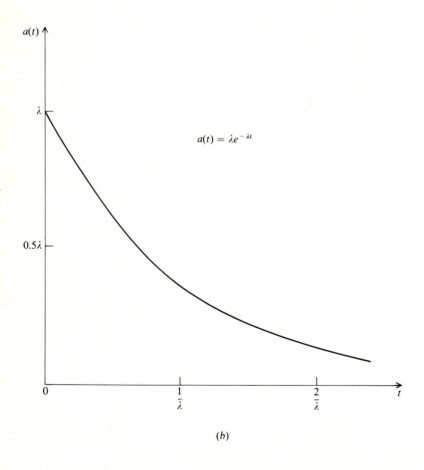

FIGURE 5.3
Representation of (*a*) Poisson arrivals, (*b*) exponentially distributed time between arrivals.

5.1.3 Notation

A notation due to D. G. Kendall[15] is now standardly used to specify queueing systems. In its most general form this notation is given by A/B/c/K/N/Z, where the symbols designate the following conditions:

A The interarrival time distribution
B The service discipline
c The number of servers
K The system capacity (maximum queue length or buffer size)
N The number of potential customers in the given source population
Z The queueing discipline

When there is no limit on the length of the waiting line (the queue), the number of sources is infinite, and the jobs are accepted on an FCFS basis, then the shortened notation A/B/c is generally used. Some of the symbols traditionally used for A and B are

GI General independent interarrival times
G General service time distribution
M Exponential (Markov) interarrival or service time distribution
   (Note: The Poisson process is a Markov process; a brief description of a Markov process is given in App. E.)
D Deterministic (constant) interarrival or service time distribution

An M/G/1 queue would thus have Poisson arrivals, a *general* service distribution (that is, very few assumptions are made about the service time distribution), and one server. A more specific example is an M/D/1 queue where we now have a fixed or constant service time.

In Fig. 5.1 we used the simplest model in queueing theory which is an M/M/1 queue. In this model messages arrive with a Poisson distribution, enter an infinite buffer with an exponential service time distribution, and are handled by a single server on a first-come-first-served basis. The M/M/1 queueing system has been widely applied since the probability distributions which describe the input process and the service process have a rather simple mathematical form. In addition, the M/M/1 model offers a realistic approach to an actual queueing system since customer arrival patterns in many real-world systems (including computer and communications networks) quite often follow a Poisson probability distribution.

5.1.4 Relationships Between the Random Variables

Before we analyze the M/M/1 queue, let us examine the basic relationships between the random variables describing the number of messages in various parts of the system and the random variables describing time (e.g., queueing time, service time, etc.)

Given the random variables

$N(t)$ = the number of messages in the system at time t

$N_q(t)$ = the number of messages in the queue at time t

$N_s(t)$ = the number of messages being processed at time t

the following obvious relationship exists among them at any time t

$$N(t) = N_q(t) + N_s(t) \tag{5.8}$$

When a system is first put into operation, this equation is difficult to solve since it is in a *transient* state. That is, for some time after the system has been turned on, the number of messages in the queue and the number of messages being serviced depend both on how long the system has been in operation and on initial conditions such as the number of messages waiting in the queue at time $t = 0$. However, once the system has been operating for some time the influences of the initial conditions and of the time since the system has started up have damped out. This means that the numbers of messages in the system and in the queue are independent of time. The system is thus described as being in *equilibrium* or *in the steady state*.

In equilibrium Eq. (5.8) becomes

$$\tilde{N} = \tilde{N}_q + \tilde{N}_s \tag{5.9}$$

where, although the steady state quantities $\tilde{N}$, $\tilde{N}_q$, and $\tilde{N}_s$ are independent of time, they are still *random variables*; that is, they are describable by probability distributions. Thus we can write

$$E[\tilde{N}] = E[\tilde{N}_q] + E[\tilde{N}_s] \tag{5.10}$$

which we express as

$$N = N_q + N_s \tag{5.11}$$

where, in equilibrium, N = mean (average) total number of messages in the system (those waiting in line plus those being serviced)
N_q = mean (average) number of messages in the queue alone
N_s = mean (average) number of messages being serviced

Similar relationships can be expressed between the random variables that describe time. If w represents the total time a message spends in the system (queueing time plus service time), q describes the waiting time in the queue, and s is the service time for a message, then clearly

$$w = q + s \tag{5.12}$$

and

$$E[w] = E[q] + E[s] \tag{5.13}$$

In the steady state, Eq. (5.13) becomes

$$T = T_q + T_s \qquad\qquad (5.14)$$

where T = mean (average) time a message spends in the system (includes time spent in the queue plus service time)

T_q = mean (average) time spent waiting in the queue itself

T_s = mean (average) time required to process a message

5.2   M/M/1 QUEUES

5.2.1   State Transitions

Let us now analyze a simple M/M/1 queueing system which is in equilibrium. That is, *in equilibrium* the probability of finding the system in a given state n does not change with time. If a customer arrives, the state changes from n to $n + 1$, whereas when a customer has been served and leaves, the state changes from n to $n - 1$. For a system to be in equilibrium these two processes must occur at the same rate. This principle, which is known as the *principle of detailed balancing*, is used here to analyze the probability states of an M/M/1 queueing system.

In analyzing this system we assume that the only transitions are between adjacent states. If the system is in state n (that is, there are n customers or jobs in the system consisting of queue plus server) and a new customer arrives, the system moves to state $n + 1$. Similarly, when a customer has been served and departs, the system moves down one state to state $n - 1$. Queueing systems in which the only transitions are to adjacent states are known as *birth-death systems*: the arrival of a customer is the birth, whereas the departure is the death.

Such a system can be represented by the *state-transition diagram* shown in Fig. 5.4. Here the circles represent the state of the system, the top arrows represent transitions from a lower state to a higher one, and the left-going arrows indicate transitions from a high to a low state. If the mean arrival rate is λ customers per second, the mean number of transitions per second from state n to state $n + 1$ is λp_n, where p_n is the equilibrium probability that there are exactly n customers in the system (queue plus server). Similarly, if the server is

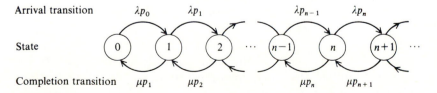

FIGURE 5.4
State-transition diagram for an M/M/1 queueing system.

capable of processing μ customers per second, the transition rate from state $n + 1$ to state n is μp_{n+1}. In either case the transition rate is the arrival rate or service rate times the probability of the system being in the *initial* state, not the final state.

5.2.2   Queue Size

For the M/M/1 queue we would now like to find the probability $p_n(t)$ that n messages are present in the buffer at time t. If we assume that an equilibrium condition exists, then we can say that the rate at which messages arrive must equal the rate at which they depart. This means that in the equilibrium case the message flow into a state n must be equal to the message flow out of state n.

To analyze the M/M/1 queue, we assume that the arrival rate λ_n for any state n is equal to a constant λ and, likewise, we assume that the service rate μ_n for states $n \geq 1$ is equal to a constant μ. For the state $n = 0$, we obviously need to have $\mu_0 = 0$. Since we are dealing with Poisson arrivals and service rates, a simple way to analyze the state of the buffer is to consider the time interval starting at t and ending at $t + \Delta t$, where Δt is an infinitesimal time increment ($\Delta t \rightarrow 0$). During the time interval $(t, t + \Delta t)$, the following possible transitions could occur:

1. A message enters state n from state $n - 1$ with a flow rate λp_{n-1}
2. A message enters state n from state $n + 1$ with a flow rate μp_{n+1}
3. A message leaves state n and enters state $n - 1$ with a flow rate μp_n
4. A message leaves state n and enters state $n + 1$ with a flow rate λp_n

For the system to remain in equilibrium, the flow into state n must equal the flow out of this state. Thus we have

$$\text{Flow into state } n = \lambda p_{n-1} + \mu p_{n+1}$$
$$\text{Flow out of state } n = \lambda p_n + \mu p_n$$

(5.15)

from which we have, for $n \geq 1$,

$$\lambda p_{n-1} + \mu p_{n+1} = (\lambda + \mu)p_n \tag{5.16}$$

To solve Eq. (5.16) we need to specify some boundary conditions. First consider the relationship between states 0 and 1. When a message arrives while the queue is in state 0 (the empty state), the queue moves to state 1. The transition rate for this condition is λp_0. Alternatively, the departure of a message from state 1 moves the queue to state 0. This occurs at a flow rate of μp_1. In the steady state (in equilibrium) these two flows must be equal so that we have the following relationship between p_0 and p_1

$$\lambda p_0 = \mu p_1 \tag{5.17}$$

or

$$p_1 = \frac{\lambda}{\mu} p_0 = \rho p_0 \qquad (5.18)$$

where $\rho = \lambda/\mu$ is known as the *traffic intensity*. The parameter ρ is of importance in that it effectively determines the minimum number of servers required to keep up with the arrival of messages. The unit associated with the traffic intensity ratio is called the *Erlang* after the Danish mathematician A. K. Erlang.[16]

> **Example 5.1.** As an example of this ratio, suppose we have a queueing system where the average interarrival rate $1/\lambda$ is 10 s and the average service rate $1/\mu$ is 5 s. The traffic intensity ratio then is 0.5 Erlangs. If the average service rate were 15 s, then the traffic intensity ratio would be greater than one (1.5 Erlangs) which indicates that messages arrive faster than they can be processed. In that case, two servers would be required to handle the rate of arriving messages.

A general expression can now be found by using Eq. (5.18) and solving Eq. (5.16) recursively. First from Eq. (5.16) with $n = 1$, we have, using Eq. (5.18)

$$p_2 = (\rho + 1)p_1 - \rho p_0 = \rho^2 p_0 \qquad (5.19)$$

Repeating this process recursively, it can easily be shown that the general expression for p_n is given by

$$p_n = \rho^n p_0 \qquad (5.20)$$

One condition on p_n stems from the *probability conservation relation* which is expressed by the equation

$$\sum_{n=0}^{\infty} p_n = 1 \qquad (5.21)$$

What this effectively means is that as $n \to \infty$, p_n must approach zero. Higher states must thus have decreasingly smaller probabilities of occupancy. Since the state probabilities must decrease with n, it is apparent from Eq. (5.21) that we must have $\rho = \lambda/\mu < 1$. This means that the average number of arrivals per unit time λ must be less than the system capacity μ. If this were not the case the queue in the buffer would build up indefinitely, so that a steady state could not be achieved.

From Eq. (5.21) we have

$$\sum_{n=0}^{\infty} p_n = 1 = p_0 \sum_{n=0}^{\infty} \rho^n = \frac{p_0}{1 - \rho} \qquad (5.22)$$

where we have used the mathematical relationship

$$\sum_{n=0}^{\infty} x^n = \frac{1}{1 - x}$$

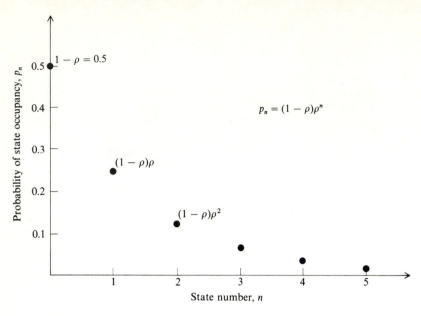

FIGURE 5.5
Probability of state occupancy for $\rho = 0.5$ in an M/M/1 queue.

for $x < 1$. Thus we find that, for $n \geq 0$, the probability of occupancy of the various states of the M/M/1 queue is given by

$$p_n = (1 - \rho)\rho^n \tag{5.23}$$

Note this indicates both that we must have $\rho < 1$ and that, as the traffic intensity ρ increases, the higher states become relatively more probable. As a simple example in Fig. 5.5 we have plotted Eq. (5.23) as a function of n for the case $\rho = 1/2$.

5.3   LITTLE'S FORMULA

Two important parameters in queueing systems are the mean number of waiting customers and the mean time these customers spend in the system waiting for service. There are four different quantities involved here which, for an arbitrary state are denoted by the symbols N, N_q, T, and T_q that were defined in Sec. 5.1.4. A single formula known as *Little's formula* or *Little's theorem* makes it possible to determine any of these quantities given one of them.

5.3.1   Graphical Derivation of Little's Formula

A simple heuristic derivation of Little's formula can be made using the graph shown in Fig. 5.6. Here we assume a system in which messages are processed in

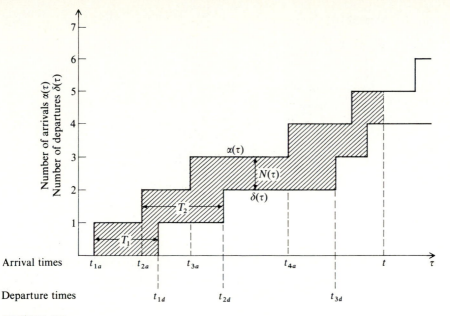

FIGURE 5.6
Graphical aid for heuristically deriving Little's formula.

the order of arrival (i.e., on an FCFS basis). Let $\alpha(\tau)$ denote the number of message arrivals in the interval $[0, \tau]$ and $\delta(\tau)$ the number of messages departing in this interval. These parameters are depicted as the top and bottom lines, respectively, of the shaded area in Fig. 5.6. For example, message i arrives at time t_{ia} and departs at t_{id}. If the system is empty at time $\tau = 0$, the number of messages $N(t)$ in the system at time t is

$$N(t) = \alpha(t) - \delta(t)$$

as is shown in Fig. 5.6. The total time $\gamma(t)$ all messages have spent in the system at time t is the cumulative area in the interval $[0, t]$. This is given by

$$\gamma(t) = \int_0^t N(\tau) \, d\tau \qquad (5.24a)$$

which is also equal to

$$\sum_{i=1}^{\delta(t)} T_i + \sum_{i=\delta(t)+1}^{\alpha(t)} (t - t_i) \qquad (5.24b)$$

where T_i is the time message i spends in the system. Dividing these two expressions by t and equating them, we have

$$N_t = \lambda_t T_t \qquad (5.25)$$

where in the interval $[0, t]$

$$N_t = \frac{1}{t} \int_0^t N(\tau)\, d\tau$$

= average number of messages in the system

$$T_t = \frac{1}{\alpha(t)} \left[\sum_{i=1}^{\delta(t)} T_i + \sum_{i=\delta(t)+1}^{\alpha(t)} (t - t_i) \right]$$

= average time a message spends in the system

$$\lambda_t = \frac{\alpha(t)}{t}$$

= average message arrival rate

Equation (5.25) is Little's formula derived for the special case of FCFS service in the finite interval $[0, t]$. For the equilibrium case t gets very large (that is, $t \to \infty$) and we assume that N_t, λ_t, and T_t all remain finite and approach their equilibrium values N, λ, and T, respectively.

We thus have Little's formula[17]

$$N = \lambda T \tag{5.26}$$

which states that the average number of customers in a queueing system is equal to the average arrival rate of customers to that system, multiplied by the average time spent in the system.

Similarly we have the relationship

$$N_q = \lambda T_q \tag{5.27}$$

which states that the average number of customers in the queue equals the average arrival rate of customers multiplied by the average amount of time that a customer spends waiting in the queue. The relationships given by Eqs. (5.26) and (5.27) are extremely important since they enable all four fundamental quantities of queueing theory to be calculated as soon as any one of them is known.

5.3.2 Application to an M/M/1 Queue

To derive N, N_q, T and T_q for an M/M/1 queue, let us consider Eq. (5.16) which is fundamental for finding all statistical quantities of interest for the queue. One important parameter is the *average number of messages in the system N* which is given by

$$N = E[\tilde{N}] = \sum_{n=0}^{\infty} n p_n = \frac{\rho}{1 - \rho} \tag{5.28}$$

(The proof of this is left as an exercise.) The behavior of the expected number of messages in the system is shown in Fig. 5.7. For ρ less than 0.5, the average

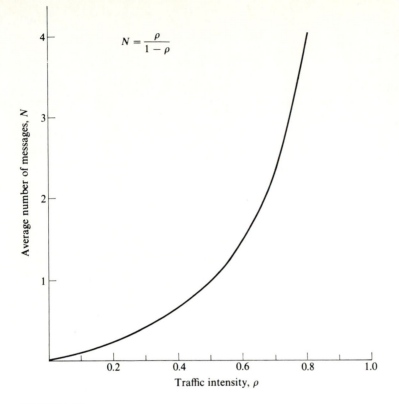

$$N = \frac{\rho}{1 - \rho}$$

Average number of messages, N (vertical axis)

Traffic intensity, ρ (horizontal axis)

FIGURE 5.7
Average number of messages in an M/M/1 queue as a function of the traffic intensity.

number of messages N is less than 1. For larger values of ρ, the number of waiting messages increases rapidly.

Using Little's formula as given by Eq. (5.26) we then find the average waiting time in the system to be

$$T = \frac{N}{\lambda} = \frac{\rho}{\lambda(1 - \rho)} = \frac{1}{\mu(1 - \rho)} = \frac{1}{\mu}(1 + N) \qquad (5.29)$$

As is shown in Fig. 5.8, the behavior of the average time a message spends in the system as a function of the traffic intensity ρ is similar to that exhibited by the average number of messages in the system (Fig. 5.7). When $\rho = 0$ the value of T is exactly the average service time of a message. That is, the message does not have to wait in the queue and is serviced in $1/\mu$ seconds on the average. As the traffic intensity ρ approaches unity, both the average number of messages in the system and the average time spent in the system increase dramatically. Thus we see that for the M/M/1 queue an extreme penalty is paid if we attempt to run the system near its capacity.

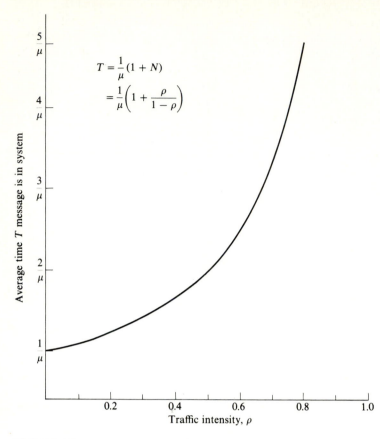

$$T = \frac{1}{\mu}(1 + N)$$

$$= \frac{1}{\mu}\left(1 + \frac{\rho}{1 - \rho}\right)$$

FIGURE 5.8
Average time a message spends in an M/M/1 system as a function of the traffic intensity.

Now let us look at only the queue itself. Since the average service time per message is given by $1/\mu$ and because it is always true that the average time T spent in the system equals the average service time plus the average time T_q the message spends waiting in the queue,

$$T = \frac{1}{\mu} + T_q \qquad (5.30)$$

we have that

$$T_q = T - \frac{1}{\mu} = \frac{\rho}{\mu(1 - \rho)} \qquad (5.31)$$

Applying Little's formula as given by Eq. (5.27) we then have that the average number of messages in the queue is

$$N_q = \lambda T_q = \frac{\rho^2}{1 - \rho} \qquad (5.32)$$

As an additional quantity of interest, let us calculate the probability of finding at least n messages in the system. This can be used to determine the buffer size needed for a specified probability of buffer overflow. From Eq. (5.23) the probability that the number of messages waiting in an M/M/1 queue is greater than some number N is given by

$$P(n > N) = \sum_{n=N+1}^{\infty} p_n = (1 - \rho) \sum_{n=N+1}^{\infty} \rho^n = \rho^{N+1} \tag{5.33}$$

(The proof of this is left as an exercise.) Since $\rho < 1$, we see that the probability of the number of messages in the system exceeding some number N is a geometrically decreasing function of that number.

Example 5.2. An example of this for several values of N and $\rho = 0.5$ is given in the following table:

N	$P(n > N)$
1	0.250
3	0.063
5	0.016
10	4.9×10^{-4}
15	1.5×10^{-5}

From Eq. (5.28) we have that the *average* system occupancy for $\rho = 0.5$ is $E[n] = 1.0$. Thus from the above table we see that the chance of the occupancy exceeding the average buffer occupancy by ten times is less than 10^{-3}. A buffer that is capable of holding 15 messages would then effectively appear like an infinite buffer to this value of ρ.

5.4 M/M/1/K QUEUES

So far we have examined systems having infinite queues. In real life, no system has an infinite amount of buffer space. Thus, let us consider the case of a queueing system in which a maximum number of messages may be stored. The M/M/1/K queue is a model of a system which can hold a limit of K messages including the one being serviced. Once the system contains K messages, any further arriving messages will be refused entry into the system.

Figure 5.9 is a state-transition diagram for this model. Assuming that messages arrive and are processed at constant rates, the transition-rate coefficients are

$$\lambda_n = \begin{cases} \lambda & \text{for } n = 0, 1, 2, \ldots, K - 1 \\ 0 & \text{for } n \geq K \end{cases}$$

and

$$\mu_n = \begin{cases} \mu & \text{for } n = 1, 2, \ldots, K \\ 0 & \text{for } n > K \end{cases}$$

(5.34)

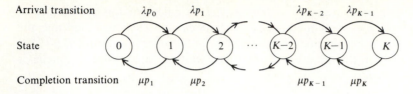

FIGURE 5.9
State-transition diagram for an M/M/1/K queue.

In this model, newly arriving messages will be generated according to a Poisson process, just as in the M/M/1 case, but only those that find the system with strictly less than K messages in it will be allowed to enter.

The steady state probabilities are given by

$$p_n = p_0 \prod_{i=0}^{n-1} \frac{\lambda}{\mu} = \rho^n p_0 \qquad \text{for } n \leq K \tag{5.35}$$

and

$$p_n = 0 \qquad \text{for } n > K \tag{5.36}$$

To solve for p_0, we note that the probabilities of the finite set of states must sum to one. Thus, we have

$$\sum_{n=0}^{K} p_n = 1 = p_0 \sum_{n=0}^{K} \rho^n = p_0 \frac{1 - \rho^{K+1}}{1 - \rho} \tag{5.37}$$

or

$$p_0 = \frac{1 - \rho}{1 - \rho^{K+1}} \tag{5.38}$$

Substituting Eq. (5.38) into Eq. (5.35) then yields

$$p_n = \frac{(1 - \rho)\rho^n}{1 - \rho^{K+1}} \qquad \text{for } 0 \leq n \leq K \tag{5.39}$$

$$0 \qquad\qquad \text{otherwise}$$

We note here that since there are never more than K messages in the system, a steady state is reached for all values of λ and μ. That is, we need not assume that $\lambda < \mu$ for the system to reach equilibrium. If $\lambda = \mu$, then $\rho = 1$ and we have, using L'Hopital's rule,

$$\lim_{\rho \to 1} p_n = \lim_{\rho \to 1} \frac{(1 - \rho)\rho^n}{1 - \rho^{K+1}} = \frac{1}{K + 1} \tag{5.40}$$

to $0 \leq n \leq K$.

For $\rho^K \ll 1$, Eq. (5.39) reduces to the infinite-buffer result of Eq. (5.23). The probability that the buffer is *full* and that messages are turned away or blocked from entering the system is simply the probability that there are K messages in the buffer. Using Eq. (5.39) this is given by

$$p_K = \frac{(1 - \rho)\rho^K}{1 - \rho^{K+1}} \tag{5.41}$$

Similar to the M/M/1-queue case, we can use Little's formula to find the parameters N, T, N_q, and T_q. If $\lambda < \mu$ then the expected number of messages N in the system is

$$N = E[\tilde{N}] = \sum_{n=0}^{K} np_n$$

$$= \frac{\rho}{1 - \rho} - \frac{(K + 1)\rho^{K+1}}{1 - \rho^{K+1}} \tag{5.42}$$

The average number of messages N_q waiting in the queue is given by Eq. (5.11)

$$N_q = N - N_s \tag{5.43}$$

where

$$N_s = E[\tilde{N}_s] = (1 - p_0) \times 1 = 1 - p_0 \tag{5.44}$$

since the average number of messages being serviced is merely the probability that the system is nonempty $(1 - p_0)$ times the average number of messages that are serviced under this condition (which is 1).

Once there are K messages in an M/M/1/K queueing system, any further messages are not allowed into the system until another message has been processed and sent on. This occurs with a probability p_K as given by Eq. (5.41). The probability that a message can enter the system is then $1 - p_K$, so that the average rate λ_a of messages entering the system is given by

$$\lambda_a = \lambda(1 - p_K) \tag{5.45}$$

where λ is the message arrival rate. Using Little's formula as given by Eq. (5.26) we then have that the average time for a message to pass through the system is

$$T = \frac{N}{\lambda_a} \tag{5.46}$$

and the average time a message spends waiting in the queue is

$$T_q = \frac{N_q}{\lambda_a} \tag{5.47}$$

5.5 M/M/m QUEUES

The M/M/1 queueing system that we just examined was mathematically modeled by a Poisson input process and an exponentially distributed service process. The M/M/m queueing system can be similarly modeled, except that here

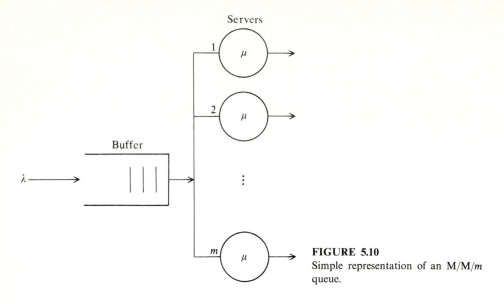

FIGURE 5.10
Simple representation of an M/M/m queue.

the number of servers is greater than one but has a *maximum* of m as is shown in Fig. 5.10. Note that all m servers have the same destination. An example of this is a network node that has several outgoing transmission channels, any one of which could be selected to send out a message to a neighboring node. Here we again consider a system having an infinite buffer and we assume that the arrival rate λ_n for any state n is equal to a constant λ. All m servers are taken to be identical so that each has the same processing capacity C. For the service rates we let

$$
\mu_n = \text{minimum } [n\mu, m\mu]
$$

$$
= \begin{cases} n\mu & \text{for } 0 \leq n \leq m \\ m\mu & \text{for } m \leq n \end{cases} \tag{5.48}
$$

In conjunction with the traffic intensity we can define the *server utilization factor U* for a multiple-server system. This is given by $U = \rho/m$ where m is the number of servers required to handle the incoming traffic rate. The factor U may be interpreted as the expected fraction of busy servers when each server has the same distribution of service time, or alternatively, it can be viewed as the expected fraction of the system capacity that is in use.

The state-transition diagram for the M/M/m queue is shown in Fig. 5.11. When we solve for the state-transition probability p_n, we must separate the solution into two parts since the transition rate is different when $n \geq m$. Thus, for $n \leq m$ we follow the same argument as made in the derivation of Eq. (5.16) to get the detailed-balance equation (since we have again assumed an equilibrium condition)

$$
(\lambda + n\mu)p_n = \lambda p_{n-1} + (n+1)\mu p_{n+1} \qquad \text{for } n \geq 1 \tag{5.49}
$$

Arrival transition $\qquad\quad \lambda p_0 \qquad\qquad \lambda p_1 \qquad\qquad\qquad\qquad \lambda p_{m-2} \qquad \lambda p_{m-1} \qquad \lambda p_m$

State

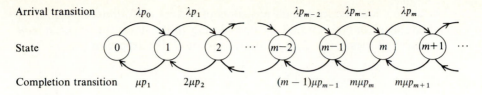

Completion transition $\quad \mu p_1 \qquad\quad 2\mu p_2 \qquad\qquad\qquad\quad (m-1)\mu p_{m-1} \quad m\mu p_m \qquad m\mu p_{m+1}$

FIGURE 5.11
State-transition diagram for an M/M/m queue.

or

$$(\rho + n)p_n = \rho p_{n-1} + (n+1)p_{n+1} \tag{5.50}$$

with $\rho = \lambda/\mu$ again. Analogous to the derivation of Eq. (5.20), we solve Eq. (5.50) recursively to obtain

$$p_n = \frac{\rho^n}{n!} p_0 \qquad \text{for } n \le m \tag{5.51}$$

Similarly, for $n \ge m$, we have the following detailed-balance equation in the equilibrium case

$$(\lambda + m\mu)p_n = \lambda p_{n-1} + m\mu p_{n+1} \tag{5.52}$$

or

$$(\rho + m)p_n = \rho p_{n-1} + m p_{n+1} \qquad \text{for } n \ge m \tag{5.53}$$

Again solving this recursively, we have

$$p_n = \frac{\rho^n p_0}{m! m^{n-m}} \qquad \text{for } n \ge m \tag{5.54}$$

To find the expression for p_0, we use the probability conservation relation given in Eq. (5.21), together with Eqs. (5.51) and (5.54), which then yields

$$p_0 = \left[\sum_{n=0}^{m-1} \frac{\rho^n}{n!} + \sum_{n=m}^{\infty} \frac{\rho^n}{m! m^{n-m}} \right]^{-1}$$

$$= \left[\sum_{n=0}^{m-1} \frac{\rho^n}{n!} + \frac{\rho^m}{m!} \frac{1}{(1 - \rho/m)} \right]^{-1} \tag{5.55}$$

where we have used the relationships

$$\sum_{n=0}^{\infty} x^n = \frac{1}{1-x} \qquad \text{for } x < 1$$

and

$$\sum_{k=1}^{s} aq^{k-1} = \frac{a(q^s - 1)}{q - 1} \qquad \text{for } q \ne 1 \tag{5.56}$$

Let us now find the four main measures of system performance, N_q, T_q, N, and T. The queue length is found by considering those states for which $n \geq m$ since a queue will form only if all m servers are busy. By definition

$$N_q = E[\tilde{N}_q] = \sum_{n=m}^{\infty} (n - m)p_n$$

$$= \sum_{k=0}^{\infty} k p_{m+k}$$

$$= \sum_{k=0}^{\infty} k \frac{\rho^{k+m} p_0}{m!m^k}$$

$$= \frac{(\rho)^m (\rho/m)}{m!(1 - \rho/m)^2} p_0 \qquad (5.57)$$

Then, by Little's formula, we have

$$T_q = \frac{N_q}{\lambda}$$

and

$$N = T\lambda \qquad (5.58)$$

where

$$T = T_q + T_s = T_q + E[s] = T_q + \frac{1}{\mu}$$

since the average message processing time $E[s] = 1/\mu$.

As a final quantity of interest for the M/M/m queue, let us find the probability that all m servers are busy, so that an arriving message has to join the queue. This probability is given by, using Eqs. (5.54) and (5.55),

$$P[\text{queueing}] = \sum_{n=m}^{\infty} p_n$$

$$= \sum_{n=m}^{\infty} p_0 \frac{\rho^n}{m!m^{n-m}}$$

$$= \frac{\dfrac{\rho^m}{m!} \dfrac{1}{(1 - \rho/m)}}{\displaystyle\sum_{n=0}^{m-1} \frac{\rho^n}{n!} + \frac{\rho^m}{m!} \frac{1}{1 - \rho/m}} \qquad (5.59)$$

This expression, which is known as *Erlang's C formula* or *Erlang's delay formula*, is widely used in telephony since it gives the probability that no trunk (i.e., server) is available for an arriving call in a system of m trunk lines.

5.6 M/G/1 QUEUES

In the analyses in the previous sections, we have assumed that arriving messages have exponentially distributed lengths. However, in many data transmission systems the message-length statistics are more accurately represented by nonexponentially distributed lengths. For example, most messages in an inquiry-response network or in a packet-switched network are of a fixed length. This situation can be handled analytically in an M/G/1-queueing representation which involves a general service-time distribution. Since the analysis of an M/G/1 queue is rather involved, we only examine the results here. The interested reader should consult the literature[1,3,8] for detailed derivations.

The basic assumptions for the M/G/1 model are the same as in the previous sections. We assume the system is characterized by a Poisson arrival process with an average rate of λ arrivals per second. Only nearest-neighbor state transitions are allowed and the messages are processed on a first-come-first-served basis. Now, however, the service time distribution has an arbitrary or general form $B(t)$ with a mean service time of $1/\mu$.

Among the most widely used results for the M/G/1 system are the *Pollaczek-Khinchin (P-K) mean-value formulas*[1-3,18-19] for the average number of messages in a queue and the average time delay. Given that σ_b^2 is the variance of the service time (see Prob. 5.19 for a definition of the variance), we define the ratio of σ_b^2 to the mean service time by

$$C_b^2 = \frac{\sigma_b^2}{\mu^2} \tag{5.60}$$

The average number of messages in the system $E[\tilde{N}]$ is then given by the *P-K* mean-value formula

$$N = E[\tilde{N}] = \rho + \rho^2 \frac{1 + C_b^2}{2(1 - \rho)} \tag{5.61}$$

which is given in terms of three known quantities, namely, the traffic intensity factor ρ, the average message length $1/\mu$ (or, alternatively, the average service time $1/\mu$), and the variance σ_b^2 of the service time.

Using Eq. (5.11) we can find the average number of messages in the queue N_q. Given that N_s in Eq. (5.11) is merely ρ (the average message service time $1/\mu$ multiplied by the arrival rate λ), we have

$$N_q = N - N_s = N - \rho$$

$$= \rho^2 \frac{(1 - C_b^2)}{2(1 - \rho)} \tag{5.62}$$

Let us consider two examples.

Example 5.3. First let the message lengths be exponentially distributed. Then $\sigma_b^2 = 1/\mu^2$ and Eq. (5.61) becomes

$$E[\tilde{N}] = \frac{\rho}{1 - \rho} \tag{5.63}$$

which is Eq. (5.28), the average number of messages in an M/M/1 system, as is expected.

Example 5.4. As a second example, let the message length be fixed (or equivalently, the service time be fixed), so that $\sigma_b^2 = 0$. Then we have

$$N = E[\tilde{N}] = \rho + \frac{\rho^2}{2(1 - \rho)}$$

$$= \frac{\rho}{1 - \rho} - \frac{\rho^2}{2(1 - \rho)} \qquad (5.64)$$

Thus in this case the system has $\rho^2/[2(1 - \rho)]$ fewer messages on the average than an M/M/1 system. (This system is referred to as an M/D/1 queue.) This demonstrates that the average number of messages in the system increases in direct proportion to the variance of the service-time distribution.

The average time delay of messages passing through the system can be found by using Little's formula given by Eq. (5.26)

$$T = \frac{1}{\lambda} E[\tilde{N}] = \frac{1}{2\mu(1 - \rho)} [2 - \rho(1 - \mu^2\sigma^2)] \qquad (5.65)$$

Again considering the same examples as above, for exponential message lengths, we have $\sigma^2\mu^2 = 1$, so that $T = 1/[\mu(1 - \rho)]$ for an M/M/1 queue. Similarly for fixed message lengths (fixed service times), we see that the time delay is reduced from that of an M/M/1 queue.

5.7 NETWORKS OF QUEUES

In any communication network, there are many storage devices at which traffic queues can build up. These queues can interact in the sense that messages departing from a node can enter one or more other queues, which in turn can simultaneously be accepting traffic from other queues. The analysis of these networks of queues can become rather involved, and has received much attention.[8,20–25]

There are two generic classes of queueing networks, as shown in Fig. 5.12. These are *open* and *closed queueing systems.* Open systems are characterized by the fact that the number of messages in the system is not fixed, that is, traffic can enter and leave the system. In contrast, closed systems have a fixed number of messages that circulate in the network, and no external arrivals or departures are permitted. In the section we will concentrate on open queueing systems since they are widely used for modeling multiaccess networks.

5.7.1 Modeling Restrictions

To establish a tractable analytical model, we need to make some assumptions and place some restrictions on our model. One difficulty in establishing a model

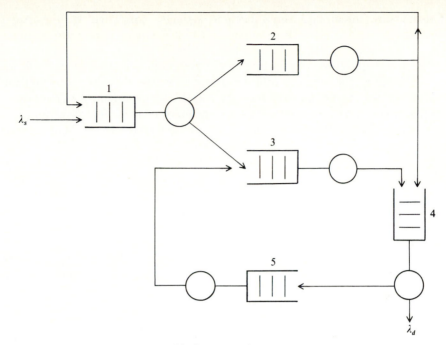

(*a*) Open queueing network

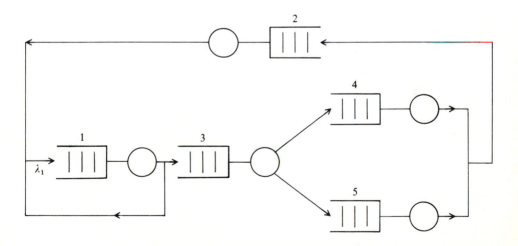

(*b*) Closed queueing network

FIGURE 5.12
Open and closed queueing networks.

is that message interarrival times become strongly correlated with message lengths once the messages have gone past the first queue at their entry point in the network.[8,22]

As an example consider a virtual-circuit system in which a message follows a path consisting of a sequence of links through the network. Suppose that for two tandem transmission links the message lengths are exponentially distributed, are independent of each other, and are independent of the interarrival times at the first queue. The first queue is then M/M/1. However, the length of a message is fixed after it is chosen from a particular exponential distribution. This means that the next node cannot be modeled as an M/M/1 queue since the service times are not independent. To see this, suppose several messages are transmitted in a row at the first queue. The message interarrival time at the second queue between two of these messages then equals the transmission time of the second message. Consequently, at the second queue there is a strong correlation between message length and interarrival time, since long messages have shorter waiting times than short messages. That is, it takes more time to transmit long messages at the first queue, thereby giving the second queue more time to empty out.

To circumvent these difficulties and to set up a simple model wherein each stage of the network can be modeled as a separate M/M/1 queue, we invoke *Kleinrock's independence assumption.*[1,2] This assumption states that if a new choice of message length is made *independently at each queue* (that is, at each outgoing link), then separate M/M/1 queueing models can be used for each communication link between nodes. This is a reasonably good approximation for virtual-circuit systems having Poisson message arrivals at the entry points, message lengths that are exponentially distributed, a densely connected network, and moderate to heavy traffic loads. It also holds if messages join a queue from several different input lines so that there is sufficient mixing of message types at each node.

The modeling of a sequence of links as independent M/M/1 queues gives rise to *Jackson's theorem.*[20–25] This theorem states that a network with first-come-first-served service has solutions which are in a product form. We derive this in Sec. 5.7.2 and give an example in Sec. 5.7.3.

As a final point we note that the M/M/1 approximation does not hold for all networks. In particular, in a datagram network, message packets can follow different routes between a pair of source and destination nodes. For performance purposes in this type of network,[22] each arriving packet is assigned to the queue which currently has the least number of bits in it (the smallest backlog). In this case the network needs to be modeled as an M/M/2 queue, so that the M/M/1 approximation is not accurate.

5.7.2   Jackson's Theorem

To derive Jackson's theorem, let us consider an open network of M queues. A typical queue (queue i) is shown in Fig. 5.13. Here the parameters q_{xy} are the

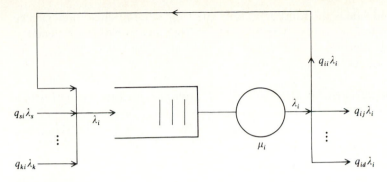

FIGURE 5.13
Typical queue in an open queueing network.

routing or branching probabilities that a message completing service at queue x is routed to queue y. The subscripts d and s denote destination and source, respectively. The arrival rates λ_j are Poisson, and the queue service rate is μ_i. We let the vector $\mathbf{n}$ represent the global state $(n_1, n_2, \ldots, n_M)$, where n_i denotes the state of queue i.

An important requirement for every queue is continuity of flow at the input and the output. Letting λ_i be the total arrival rate at queue i from the source and from all the queues, we have

$$\lambda_i = q_{si}\lambda_s + \sum_{k=1}^{M} q_{ki}\lambda_k \tag{5.66}$$

Jackson's theorem then states that the equilibrium probability $p(\mathbf{n})$ that the network is in state $\mathbf{n}$ is

$$\begin{aligned} p(\mathbf{n}) &= p(n_1, n_2, \ldots, n_M) \\ &= p_1(n_1)p_2(n_2)\cdots p_M(n_M) \end{aligned} \tag{5.67}$$

where $p_i(n_i)$ is the equilibrium probability that queue i is in state n_i. To prove Jackson's theorem we need to verify that a global balance equation is satisfied by a product-form solution as given in Eq. (5.67).

To set up a global balance equation for a state $\mathbf{n}$ we need to equate the total rate of leaving state $\mathbf{n}$ to the rate of entering $\mathbf{n}$. This is given by

$$\left[\lambda_s + \sum_{i=1}^{M} \mu_i\right] p(\mathbf{n}) = \lambda_s \sum_{i=1}^{M} q_{si} p(n_1, n_2, \ldots, n_i - 1, \ldots, n_M)$$

$$+ \sum_{i=1}^{M} q_{id}\mu_i p(n_1, n_2, \ldots, n_i + 1, \ldots, n_M)$$

$$+ \sum_{i=1}^{M} \sum_{j=1}^{M} q_{ij}\mu_j p(n_1, n_2, \ldots, n_i - 1, \ldots, n_j + 1, \ldots, n_M) \tag{5.68}$$

Here the left-hand side is the total departure rate from state **n**, since there can be an arrival with rate λ or a departure at a rate μ_i from any one of the M queues. The total arrival rate into state **n** is given by the right-hand side of Eq. (5.68). The three cases are as follows:

1. The first term accounts for arrivals from the external source at queue i which is in state $n_i - 1$. The arrival rates are $\lambda_s q_{si}$.
2. The second term arises from departures at queue i directly to the destination d. The departure rates from queue i are $q_{id}\mu_i$.
3. The third term describes transitions from queue j, which originally is in state $n_j + 1$, to queue i, which is in state $n_i - 1$.

To solve Eq. (5.68) we use Eq. (5.67) to eliminate the parameter q_{si}. In the resulting expression we then substitute the relationship

$$\lambda_i p(n_1, n_2, \ldots, n_i - 1, \ldots, n_M) = \mu_i p(n_1, n_2, \ldots, n_i, \ldots, n_M) \tag{5.69}$$

and its variations

$$\lambda_j p(n_1, \ldots, n_i - 1, \ldots, n_M) = \mu_j p(n_1, \ldots, n_i - 1, \ldots, n_j + 1, \ldots, n_M) \tag{5.70}$$

and

$$\lambda_i p(n_1, \ldots, n_i, \ldots, n_M) = \mu_i p(n_1, \ldots, n_i + 1, \ldots, n_M) \tag{5.71}$$

Equation (5.69) is based on the concept of *reversibility* introduced by Reich.[26] This states that, in equilibrium, transitions from one state to another in reverse time occur with the same rates as the same transitions in forward time. Thus the original arrival stream is equivalent in all respects to the departure stream in reverse time, which is the essence of Eq. (5.69).

With these substitutions Eq. (5.68) then reduces to the expression

$$\lambda_s = \sum_{i=1}^{M} q_{id}\lambda_i \tag{5.72}$$

which is the condition for flow conservation from source to destination. Thus the balance condition in Eq. (5.68) is satisfied by Eq. (5.69).

We can now find an expression for the joint probability $p(\mathbf{n})$. From Eq. (5.69) we have for queue i

$$p(\mathbf{n}) = \left(\frac{\lambda_i}{\mu_i}\right) p(n_1, n_2, \ldots, n_i - 1, \ldots, n_M) \tag{5.73}$$

Repeating this process n_i times we obtain

$$p(\mathbf{n}) = \left(\frac{\lambda_i}{\mu_i}\right)^{n_i} p(n_1, n_2, \ldots, n_i = 0, \ldots, n_M) \tag{5.74}$$

Following the same steps for all the other queues, we then get

$$p(\mathbf{n}) = \prod_{i=1}^{M} \left(\frac{\lambda_i}{\mu_i}\right)^{n_i} p(\mathbf{0}) \tag{5.75}$$

where $p(\mathbf{0})$ is the probability that all M queues are empty. To find $p(\mathbf{0})$ we let $\rho_i = \lambda_i/\mu_i$, sum Eq. (5.75) over all possible states, and set the result equal to 1:

$$\sum_{\mathbf{n}} p(\mathbf{n}) = p(\mathbf{0}) \left[\sum_{\mathbf{n}} \left(\prod_{i=1}^{M} \rho_i^{n_i} \right) \right] = 1 \tag{5.76}$$

For solutions to exist, the term in brackets must be finite. Thus we can interchange the sums and products to get

$$\sum_{\mathbf{n}} \left(\prod_{i=1}^{M} \rho_i^{n_i} \right) = \prod_{i=1}^{M} \sum_{n_i=0}^{\infty} \rho_i^{n_i} = \prod_{i=1}^{M} (1 - \rho_i)^{-1} \tag{5.77}$$

Thus combining Eqs. (5.75), (5.76) and (5.77) we have

$$p(\mathbf{n}) = \prod_{i=1}^{M} (1 - \rho_i)\rho_i^{n_i} = \prod_{i=1}^{M} p_i(n_i) \tag{5.78}$$

which is Jackson's theorem.

Jackson's theorem given in Eq. (5.67) can also be extended to networks where each queue i has m_i servers rather than a single server. In that case the formula corresponding to $p_i(n_i)$ in Eq. (5.78) is given by Eq. (5.54) which is for the M/M/m_i case.

5.7.3   Application to an Open Queueing Network

As an application of Eq. (5.67), let us consider the *mean network-wide time delay* averaged over all M links. The general problem is depicted in Fig. 5.14. Here an open network in equilibrium consists of a collection of M queues. If γ_s is the arrival rate in messages per second associated with path s, then the total arrival rate in the network is $\gamma = \sum_s \gamma_s$. From Little's formula the network time delay T averaged over the entire network is

$$\gamma T = E[\mathbf{n}] \tag{5.79}$$

Here $E[\mathbf{n}]$, the average number of messages in the network, is

$$E[\mathbf{n}] = \sum_{i=1}^{M} E[n_i] \tag{5.80}$$

where $E[n_i]$ is the average number of messages queued or in service at node i. For an M/M/1 queue from Eq. (5.28) we have

$$E[n_i] = \lambda_i T_i$$

$$= \frac{\lambda_i}{\mu_i - \lambda_i} \tag{5.81}$$

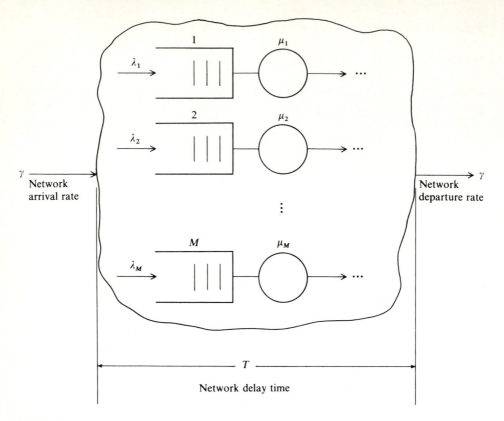

FIGURE 5.14
Average time delay through an open queueing network.

Thus the average time delay is

$$T = \frac{1}{\gamma} \sum_{i=1}^{M} \frac{\lambda_i}{\mu_i - \lambda_i} \tag{5.82}$$

Equation (5.82) neglects propagation delay over the links. If this is included, then for an average propagation delay T_{di} over link i, Eq. (5.82) becomes

$$T = \frac{1}{\gamma} \sum_{i=1}^{M} \left(\frac{\lambda_i}{\mu_i - \lambda_i} + \lambda_i T_{di} \right) \tag{5.83}$$

5.8 SUMMARY

Queueing theory has been used very successfully to quantitatively describe the performance of computer and communication networks. Since the early 1970s system analysts have been using queueing network theory to calculate throughputs, queue lengths, and mean response times for real systems. Numerous experimental studies have shown that these models consistently estimate real throughputs to within 5 percent and real average response times to within 25 percent.

The success of queueing theory was originally somewhat puzzling since the basic assumptions used, namely that the queueing network has time-invariant parameters, is in equilibrium, and has exponential distributions of service times at all FCFS (first-come-first-served) devices, are often seriously violated in practice. However, in 1976 the concept of *operational analysis*[27–29] was introduced, which showed that when the stochastic equations of queueing theory are interpreted as relations among operational or measurable quantities, they can be alternatively derived using assumptions that are commonly satisfied in practice.

The basic queueing models used for computer and communication networks include the M/M/1, M/M/m, and M/G/1 queues, all of which we examined in some detail in this chapter. An important result in all of these queues is Little's formula which allows us to quickly calculate any one of the four important measures of network performance (total average number of messages N in the system, average number of messages N_q in the queue alone, average time T a message spends in the system, and average time T_q spent waiting in the queue) once one of these quantities is known.

PROBLEMS

Section 5.1

5.1. Plot the Poisson distribution $P_n(t)$ in Eq. (5.2) as a function of the parameter $x = \lambda t$ for values of $n = 0, 1, 2, 3, 4$.

5.2. Verify Eq. (5.3) which gives the average number of messages arriving at a node in a time interval T.

Section 5.2

5.3. Verify the steps leading from Eq. (5.16) to Eq. (5.23).

5.4. Given the following state-transition equations for a pure-birth process

$$\frac{dP_n(t)}{dt} = -\lambda P_n(t) + \lambda P_{n-1}(t) \qquad n \geq 1$$

$$\frac{dP_0(t)}{dt} = -\lambda P_0(t) \qquad\qquad n = 0$$

use an induction method to derive the Poisson distribution given in Eq. (5.2).

Hint: Start by assuming that the system begins at time $t = 0$ with zero members.

Section 5.3

5.5. Verify Eq. (5.28) which gives the average number of messages N in an M/M/1 queue.

5.6. Verify Eq. (5.33) which gives the probability that the number of messages waiting in an M/M/1 queue is greater than some number N.

5.7. Consider a computer-disk distribution center with a single server at which engineering students arrive according to a Poisson process. Let the mean arrival rate be one student per minute and assume the serving time is exponentially distributed with an average of 30 seconds per student. (a) What is the average queue length? (b) How long does a student have to wait in the queue? (c) Find the average queue length and waiting time in the queue if the service time increases to 45 seconds per student.

5.8. Consider a network node that has a buffer which is modeled as an infinite M/M/1 queue. Assume a terminal connected to this node generates a 40-bit message every 0.4 s. (a) If the capacity of the outgoing link is 1000 b/s, what is the average buffer occupancy in units of message? (b) What is the average waiting time? (c) If the link capacity is only 500 b/s, find the average buffer occupancy and the total waiting time. (d) What is the time the message spends in the queue in each case?

5.9. A buffer at a network node is modeled as an infinite M/M/1 queue. Suppose 10 terminals are attached to the node and their outputs are time-multiplexed into the buffer. (a) If each terminal transmits 100-bit messages at 300 b/s, what is the required line capacity if the total time delay is to be 50 ms? (b) Now suppose only one such terminal is attached to the node. What line capacity is required in this case?

5.10. Suppose an M/M/1 queue has a state-dependent Poisson arrival rate λ_n and a state-dependent departure rate μ_n. (a) Draw a state-transition diagram for this case. (b) Show that the equation of state after equilibrium has set in is given by

$$(\lambda_n + \mu_n)p_n = \mu_{n+1}p_{n+1} + \lambda_{n-1}p_{n-1} \qquad \text{for } n \geq 1$$

(c) Show that the solution to this equation is given by

$$p_n = \frac{\lambda_0 \, \lambda_1 \, \lambda_2 \, \cdots \, \lambda_{n-1}}{\mu_1 \, \mu_2 \, \cdots \, \mu_n} p_0$$

5.11. Consider a system where arriving messages tend to get discouraged from joining the queue when more and more messages are present in the system. Suppose the arrival and departure coefficients in this case are modeled as follows:

$$\lambda_n = \frac{\alpha}{n+1} \qquad \text{for } n = 0, 1, 2, \ldots$$

$$\mu_n = \mu \qquad \text{for } n = 1, 2, 3, \ldots$$

where α and μ are constants. (a) Draw a state-transition diagram for this case. (b) Find p_n using the equation given in Prob. 5.10. (c) Show that the expected number of messages in the system is given by α/μ. (d) Using Little's formula, find an expression for the average time T spent in the system.

Section 5.4

5.12. Verify that Eq. (5.38) results when the probabilities of the finite set of states given by Eq. (5.35) is summed and set equal to one.

5.13. Derive Eq. (5.42) which gives the expected number of messages in an M/M/1/K queue.

5.14. Plot the parameters p_n and N as given in Eqs. (5.39) and (5.42), respectively, as a function of K for values of K up to 10 for the case $\rho = 0.5$.

5.15. Consider a buffer in an M/M/1/K queue. Compare the probabilities that messages are blocked in each of the following cases: (a) $K = 2$, $\rho = 0.1$; (b) $K = 4$, $\rho = 0.1$; (c) $K = 4$, $\rho = 0.8$; (d) $K = 10$, $\rho = 0.8$. What is the probability in each case that the buffer is empty?

Section 5.5

5.16. Starting from the state equation in Eq. (5.49), derive Eq. (5.51). Similarly, starting with Eq. (5.52), derive Eq. (5.54).

5.17. Verify the expression given Eq. (5.55) for p_0.

5.18. Derive the Erlang C formula given in Eq. (5.59).

Section 5.6

5.19. Given that a continuous random variable x has a density function $f(x)$ over the interval a to b, its variance is defined by

$$\text{Var}\,[x] = \int_a^b (x - E[x])^2 f(x)\,dx$$

where $E[x] = \int_a^b xf(x)\,dx$ is the average value of x. Thus, given a service time which is modeled by the gamma distribution

$$f(x) = \frac{\beta(\beta x)^{k-1} e^{-\beta x}}{\Gamma(k)} \qquad \text{for } x > 0 \text{ and } k > 0$$

where β is a constant and $\Gamma(k)$ is the gamma function, show that $E[x] = k/\beta$ and $\sigma_b^2 = k/\beta^2$.

Section 5.7

5.20. Verify the steps leading from Eq. (5.68) to Eq. (5.72).

5.21. Consider the five-node network shown in Fig. P5.21. The Poisson arrival rates at nodes 1, 2, and 4 are given by $\gamma_1 = \gamma_2 = \gamma_4 = 2$ messages per second. The numbers

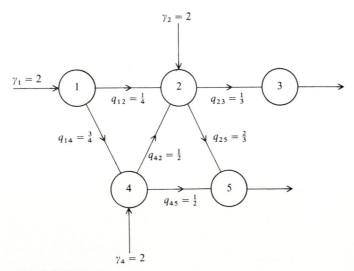

FIGURE P5.21

q_{ij} next to each transmission line give the routing or branching probabilities that a message which completes service at queue i is routed to queue j. For simplicity we assume transmission is in one direction only. (*a*) Find the net message load on each link. (*b*) Find the outgoing message rates at nodes 3 and 5.

5.22. Refer to Fig. P5.21. Assume all links have the same capacity $\mu = 3$ messages per second.

(*a*) Find the network average time delay T.

(*b*) Suppose the branching probabilities are changed to $q_{14} = 0.25$, $q_{12} = 0.75$, and $q_{23} = q_{25} = 0.5$. Find T and compare it with the value found in part *a*.

(*c*) With the branching probabilities given in part *b*, find the outgoing message rates at nodes 3 and 5.

REFERENCES

1. L. Kleinrock, *Queueing Systems, Vol. 1: Theory*, Wiley, New York, 1975.
2. L. Kleinrock, *Queueing Systems, Vol. 2: Computer Applications*, Wiley, New York, 1976.
3. A. O. Allen, *Probability, Statistics, and Queueing Theory with Computer Science Applications*, Academic, New York, 1978.
4. H. Kobayashi and A. G. Konheim, "Queueing models for computer communications system analysis," *IEEE Trans. Commun.*, vol. COM-25, pp. 2–29, January 1977.
5. C. H. Sauer, E. A. MacNair, and J. F. Karose, "Queueing network simulation of computer communication," *IEEE J. Select. Areas Commun.*, vol. SAC-2, pp. 203–220, January 1984.
6. A. O. Allen, "Queueing models of computer systems," *IEEE Commun. Mag.*, vol. 13, pp. 13–24, April 1980.
7. E. Gelenbe and I. Mitrani, *Analysis and Synthesis of Computer Systems*, Academic, New York, 1980.
8. M. Schwartz, *Telecommunication Networks—Protocols, Modeling and Analysis*, Addison-Wesley, Reading, MA, 1987.
9. T. L. Saaty, *Elements of Queueing Theory*, McGraw-Hill, New York, 1961.
10. W. Feller, *An Introduction to Probability Theory and Its Application*, vol. 2, 2d ed., Wiley, New York, 1971.
11. A. Papoulis, *Probability, Random Variables, and Stochastic Processes*, 2d ed., McGraw-Hill, New York, 1984.
12. W. B. Davenport, Jr. and W. Root, *Probability and Random Processes: An Introduction for Applied Scientists and Engineers*, McGraw-Hill, New York, 1970.
13. P. Z. Peebles, *Probability, Random Variables, and Random Signal Principles*, 2d ed., McGraw-Hill, New York, 1987.
14. F. A. Tobagi, M. Gerla, R. W. Peebles, and E. G. Manning, "Modeling and measurement techniques in packet communication networks," *Proc. IEEE*, vol. 66, pp. 1423–1447, November 1978.
15. D. G. Kendall, "Some problems in the theory of queues," *J. Roy. Statis. Soc.*, series B, vol. 13, pp. 151–185, 1951.
16. E. Brockmeyer, H. L. Halstrom, and A. Jensen, "The life and works of A. K. Erlang," *Trans. Danish Academy of Tech. and Science*, vol. 2, 1948.
17. J. D. C. Little, "A proof of the queueing formula $L = \lambda W$," *Operations Research*, vol. 9, pp. 383–387, March-April 1961.
18. F. Pollaczek, "Über eine Aufgabe der Wahrscheinlichkeitstheorie," Parts I–II, *Math. Zeitschrift.*, vol. 32, pp. 64–100, 1930; vol. 32, pp. 729–750, 1930.
19. A. Y. Khinchin, "Mathematical theory of stationary queues," *Mat. Sbornik*, vol. 39, pp. 73–84, 1932.
20. H. Kobayashi, *Modeling and Analysis: An Introduction to System Performance Evaluation Methodology*, Addison-Wesley, Reading, MA, 1978.

21. C. H. Sauer and K. M. Chandy, *Computer Systems Performance Modeling*, Prentice-Hall, Englewood Cliffs, NJ, 1981.
22. D. Bertsekas and R. Gallager, *Data Networks*, Prentice-Hall, Englewood Cliffs, NJ, 1987.
23. J. R. Jackson, "Networks of waiting lines," *Operations Research* vol. 5, no. 4, pp. 518–521, August 1957.
24. J. R. Jackson, "Jobshop-like queueing systems," *Management Sci.*, vol. 10, pp. 131–142, 1963.
25. F. Baskett, K. M. Chandy, R. R. Muntz, and F. C. Palacios, "Open, closed, and mixed networks of queues with different classes of customers," *J. Assoc. Comput. Mach.*, vol. 22, pp. 248–260, April 1975.
26. E. Reich, "Waiting times when queues are in tandem," *Annuls Math. Statistics*, vol. 28, pp. 768–773, 1957.
27. J. P. Buzen, "Fundamental operational laws of computer system performance," *Acta Informatica*, vol. 7, pp. 167–182, 1976.
28. P. J. Denning and J. P. Buzen, "The operational analysis of queueing network models," *Computing Surveys*, vol. 10, pp. 225–261, September 1978.
29. J. P. Buzen and P. J. Denning, "Measuring and calculating queue length distributions," *Computer*, vol. 13, pp. 33–44, April 1980.

CHAPTER
6

LAN
ACCESS
TECHNIQUES

One characteristic of a local area network is that its backbone is a shared transmission link which permits all attached users to simultaneously attempt to gain
access to the transmission facilities. Thus it is possible for two or more stations
to transmit at the same time thereby causing their signals to interfere and become garbled. To resolve these conflicts, a number of different control mechanisms or access protocols have been devised. These all fall into the broad
category of asynchronous time-division multiplexing (TDM), since this mechanism is best suited for handling the bursty nature of LAN traffic. The asynchronous TDM mechanism can be further divided into contention methods (or
random-access schemes) and deterministic (or controlled) techniques.

Among the random-access schemes are the ALOHA (a ground-based radio
packet broadcast network develped in Hawaii), carrier-sense multiple-access
(CSMA), CSMA with collision detection (CSMA/CD), and register-insertion
protocols. (We note here that although ALOHA is not a LAN, its broadcast
concept is applicable to the local networking environment, and as such it is
often compared to other random-access broadcast schemes used in local area
networks. In addition, an understanding of ALOHA will aid the reader in grasp-
ing the concepts behind CSMA and CSMA/CD.)

Controlled access to a LAN can be performed either in a centralized or a distributed fashion. A popular centralized technique is polling, in which a master node decides which node is to access the channel at any one time. Two commonly used distributed controlled-access schemes are token passing and the slotted-ring method, which is a variation of token-passing access in ring networks.

6.1 PERFORMANCE MEASURES AND NOTATION

Before we dive into the details of LAN access methods, let us first see what the performance measures are that we will be using to evaluate the different access techniques. As we saw in Chap. 5, the information input to a system is characterized by its average packet arrival rate λ and its average length or service time $1/\mu$ (μ being the average service rate). In this chapter we analyze access methods in terms of the *average packet delays* versus the channel *throughput*. These analyses are based on the M/G/1 queue wherein packets arrive according to a Poisson distribution, a general service distribution is used, and there is one server (buffer plus processor).

The *throughput* of a local area network is a measure in bits per second of the *successful* traffic being transmitted between stations; that is, since packets can become corrupted in traveling from station to station, it is customary to only count the error-free bits (error-free packets) when measuring throughput. To make the analysis completely independent of the actual channel rate, the throughput S is often expressed in a dimensionless normalized form

$$S = \frac{\lambda K}{R} \qquad (6.1)$$

where K is the packet length in bits, and R is the channel transmission rate in bits per second. The values of S thus range from 0 to 1.

The throughput is expressed in terms of the *offered load G*, which is the actual message load or traffic demand presented to the network. We note that because some packets may need to be retransmitted, the total offered traffic λ_T is the sum of the packets delivered successfully on the first transmission attempt and repetitions of those that were damaged in transit. The normalized offered load G is thus given by

$$G = \frac{\lambda_T K}{R} \qquad (6.2)$$

where $\lambda_T \geq \lambda$. Analogous to the throughput, G is given by a dimensionless number which ranges from 0 to ∞ since λ_T can become arbitrarily large. The maximum achievable throughput for a particular type of access scheme is called the *capacity* of the channel under that access scheme, and is found by maximizing S with respect to G.

Another parameter that is related to throughput is the *channel utilization* or *efficiency* designated by ρ. Channel utilization is defined as the average fraction of time that a channel is busy. In the unlikely case that all packets are transmitted without error and there is no overhead, then throughput and utilization are the same. When overhead is taken into account, channel utilization is sometimes called channel efficiency. Thus, if D and H are the number of data bits and overhead bits, respectively, in a packet then

$$\rho = \frac{SD}{D + H} \tag{6.3}$$

A second performance measure of interest is the *average transfer delay T*, which we will use when making a comparison between random-access and controlled-access protocols. The transfer delay is the time interval from the generation of the last bit of a packet at the information source until the reception of this bit at the destination. Since a packet encounters different elements in its path from source to destination, the time delay likewise consists of different components. The main delay components are (*a*) the queueing delay or waiting time at the source's interface buffer before the packet is processed for transmission, (*b*) processing delays as the protocol interpreter manages the transmission of the packet, (*c*) the propagation time required to transmit a packet through the network (included in here are queueing and processing delays at store-and-forward nodes internal to the network), (*d*) the waiting time at the buffer associated with the destination station, and (*e*) processing delays at the destination station.

6.2   RANDOM-ACCESS METHODS

Random access or *contention* techniques are used in systems where many users try to send messages (typically in the form of packets) to other stations through a common broadcast channel. The term "random access" means that there is no definite or scheduled time when any particular station should transmit. In addition, all stations must *contend* for time on the network since there is no control mechanism for determining whose turn it is to transmit (hence the term *contention*).

The original work in this area resulted in the ALOHA scheme[1,2] where each individual user transmits at any arbitrary time when there is a message to be sent. If more than one user attempts to transmit at the same time, the messages collide and have to be retransmitted later. This scheme is the simplest possible since it is completely asynchronous, that is, there is no coordination among users. However, since there is a high interference possibility between messages from different simultaneously transmitting users, the maximum achievable channel utilization is only about 18 percent.

To improve the efficiency, a scheme called *slotted ALOHA* was proposed[3,4] which doubled the capacity of the ALOHA system. Here the channel is divided into discrete uniform time slots, each interval being equal to one frame transmission time. All users are then synchronized by means of a central clock or other technique so that transmission can only start at the beginning of a time slot. Thus partial overlapping of colliding messages is eliminated and the maximum achievable channel utilization was raised to about 37 percent.

The next improvement in efficiency was made through a scheme in which the user listens to the channel to see if it is free before transmitting a message packet. If the user senses the channel to be ideal, the packet is transmitted; if the channel is sensed to be busy, the packet transmission is delayed to a later time. Through this scheme, which is called *carrier sense multiple access* (CSMA) or *listen before talk* (LBT), the chance of packet collision is greatly reduced.[5]

Although the CSMA scheme is a great improvement over ALOHA methods, packet collisions can still occur. To further improve channel utilization by shortening the collision time duration, a user can listen to the channel while sending out a message and immediately cease transmission before it is completed when a collision with another simultaneously transmitting user is detected. This scheme is called *CSMA with collision detection* (CSMA/CD) or *listen while talk* (LWT) and is the basis of the popular Ethernet protocol.[6-8]

6.3 ALOHA

To set a basis with which to compare various random-access methods, let us first look at ALOHA which is the simplest possible broadcast protocol.[1-3,9-11] The original ALOHA method is often called *pure ALOHA* to distinguish it from the slotted ALOHA scheme.

6.3.1 Pure ALOHA

The basic idea of pure ALOHA is simple since users transmit immediately whenever they have data to send. To determine whether a transmission was successful, a sender waits for an acknowledgment from the receiver for a time period equal to one propagation time (the time it takes a packet to travel from the sender to the receiver and back again). If no acknowledgment is received, the packet will be sent again.

There will obviously be collisions between packets sent within a packet transmission time t_p from different users as is indicated in Fig. 6.1. We first assume that all packets have the same length and that each requires one time unit t_p (called a *slot*) for transmission. Consider an attempt by a user to send packet A starting at time t_0. If another user generates packet B between t_0 and $t_0 + t_p$, the end of packet B will collide with the beginning of packet A. This can occur because, owing to long propagation delays, the sender of packet A did not know that packet B was already under way when the transmission of packet A was started. Similarly, if another user attempts to transmit between $t_0 + t_p$ and $t_0 + 2t_p$ (packet C), the beginning of packet C will collide with the end of packet A. Thus if two packets overlap by even the slightest amount in the vulnerable

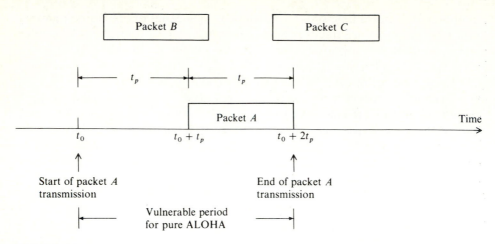

FIGURE 6.1
Vulnerable periods during which packets can collide in the pure ALOHA scheme.

period shown in Fig. 6.1, both packets will be corrupted and will need to be retransmitted later.

Now let S be the channel throughput (the average number of successful transmissions per time period t_p), and let G be the total traffic entering the channel from an infinite population of users (that is, G denotes the number of packet transmissions that are attempted in a time period t_p). To find the throughput, we first assume that the probability p_k of k transmission attempts per packet time follows a Poisson distribution with a mean G per packet time. From Eq. (5.2) this is given by

$$p_k = \frac{G^k e^{-G}}{k!} \tag{6.4}$$

The throughput S is then just the offered load G times the probability of a transmission being successful. Thus

$$S = Gp_0 \tag{6.5}$$

where p_0 is the probability that a packet does not suffer a collision (that is, p_0 is the probability of no other traffic being generated during a vulnerable period which is two packet times long). From Eq. (6.4) the probability of zero packets being generated in an interval two packet times long is

$$p_0 = e^{-2G} \tag{6.6}$$

so that, from Eq. (6.5)

$$S = Ge^{-2G} \tag{6.7}$$

The throughput given by Eq. (6.7) is plotted in Fig. 6.2. The maximum value of S occurs at $G = 0.5$ where $S = 1/(2e)$ which is about 0.184. This means

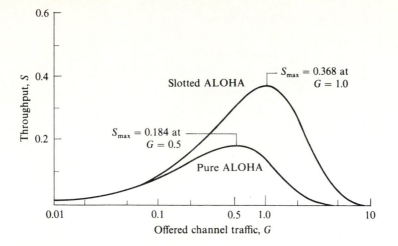

FIGURE 6.2
Comparison of the throughput as a function of offered load for pure and slotted ALOHA.

that the best channel utilization that can be achieved is around 18 percent for the pure ALOHA method.

6.3.2   Slotted ALOHA

To increase the efficiency of the ALOHA method, the slotted ALOHA scheme was introduced.[3] Here the channel is divided into time slots which are exactly equal to a packet transmission time. All users are then synchronized to these time slots, so that whenever a user generates a packet it must synchronize exactly with the next possible channel slot. Consequently, the vulnerable period in which this packet can collide with other data is reduced to *one* packet time period versus *two* for pure ALOHA. Examples of transmission attempts and random retransmission delays for colliding packets are shown in Fig. 6.3 for four network users.

Since the vulnerable period is now reduced by half, the probability of no other traffic occurring during the same time period as the packet we wish to send is $p_0 = e^{-G}$. This in turn leads to a throughput

$$S = Ge^{-G} \tag{6.8}$$

As is shown in Fig. 6.2, the maximum efficiency of the slotted ALOHA system occurs at $G = 1$ where $S = 1/e$ or about 0.368, which is twice that of pure ALOHA.

The curves shown in Fig. 6.2 were obtained for an infinite number of users. Let us now consider a slotted ALOHA system with a *finite* number of users.[12] To start we first examine the relative-frequency concept of probability, so that

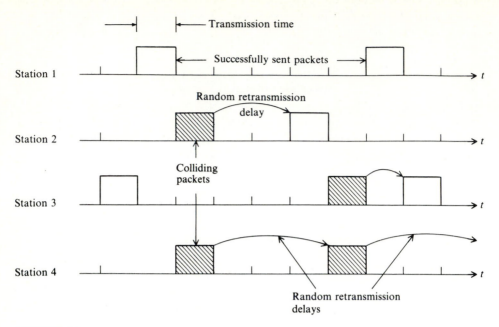

FIGURE 6.3
Transmission attempts and random retransmission delays for colliding packets in slotted ALOHA.

for station i we can redefine the steady state average throughput S_i and the offered traffic G_i by the following:

$$S_i = \frac{\text{number of slots used by station } i \text{ for good transmissions}}{\text{total number of slots}} = \frac{\text{probability that station } i}{\text{successfully transmits}}$$

$$G_i = \frac{\text{number of slots in which station } i \text{ attempts to transmit}}{\text{total number of slots}} = \frac{\text{probability that station } i}{\text{attempts transmission}}$$

For M users, let G_i be the probability that user i transmits a packet in any given slot where $i = 1, 2, \ldots, M$. Since the average traffic per slot due to user i is G_i, the total average channel traffic is

$$G = \sum_{i=1}^{M} G_i \qquad \text{packets per slot} \tag{6.9}$$

Similarly, let S_i be the probability of a successful transmission for a packet generated by user i. This means that the average throughput per slot due to user i is S_i, so that the average total throughput is

$$S = \sum_{i=1}^{M} S_i \qquad \text{packets per slot} \tag{6.10}$$

The probability S_i that user i has a successful transmission in a particular time slot is then merely the probability G_i that user i sends a packet, multiplied by the probability that none of the other $M - 1$ users send packets; thus

$$S_i = G_i \prod_{j \neq i} (1 - G_j) \tag{6.11}$$

As an example, consider the case where all M users are identical. Then each user has a throughput $S_i = S/M$ packets per slot and a total transmission rate of $G_i = G/M$ packets per slot, where G and S are given by Eqs. (6.9) and (6.10), respectively. Substituting these expressions into Eq. (6.11) then yields

$$S = G\left(1 - \frac{G}{M}\right)^{M-1} \tag{6.12}$$

Note that as $M \to \infty$, we have $S = Ge^{-G}$ which is the expected expression of Eq. (6.8) for an infinite population slotted ALOHA system.

6.3.3   Stability of Slotted ALOHA

An important factor in any network is its stability. Let us look at this for slotted ALOHA. We will go into this in some detail here since the results hold for any random access method in general. To study the stability we assume there are N identical stations, each of which can hold at most one packet. Thus if a new packet arrives at a station with a full buffer, the newly arriving message is lost since the station is busy or *blocked*, that is, the station controller prevents any more inputs. We further assume that the station generates new packets according to a Poisson distribution with a mean transfer probability $p \ll 1$ packets per slot when the station is not blocked.

To carry out a tractable analysis, it is necessary to adopt a memoryless model in connection with packet retransmission. Normally in slotted ALOHA a station waits a random integral number of time slots before trying to retransmit. Instead here we assume that a previously collided packet (called a *backlogged* packet) is retransmitted with probability α in every succeeding time slot until a successful transmission occurs. Note that this does not accurately reflect the behavior of a realistic system if a constant interval of time is needed to detect a collision. However, simulation studies[13,14] have shown that this is very good approximation when the condition

$$\frac{1}{\alpha} = R + \frac{K + 1}{2} \tag{6.13}$$

holds, where R is the number of slots that fit into one round-trip propagation time, and K is the number of time slots required for successful retransmission to take place.

The state of the ALOHA system can then be described by determining how many stations are backlogged. First, let state k be the condition wherein k of the N stations are backlogged (that is, the stations contain packets that have undergone collision). Each of these k stations may then decide either to resend its backlogged packet with probability α or skip the present slot with probability $1 - \alpha$. In addition to the mean retransmission attempts of $k\alpha$ packets per slot, the remaining $N - k$ unblocked stations are generating new packets at a collective rate of $(N - k)p$ packets per slot.

There will be a successful transmission in state k only if exactly one packet, either backlogged or new, is sent. Suppose we let n represent the number of new packets generated by the $N - k$ unblocked stations during a given time interval, and let r represent the number of retransmission attempts by the k backlogged stations during the same slot. These parameters obviously need to satisfy the conditions $0 \leq n \leq N - k$ and $0 \leq r \leq k$. Further we let $P\{n = 0\}$ be the probability that no new packets are generated during the present time slot, $P\{n = 1\}$ be the probability that a new packet is generated, and $P\{r \geq 1\}$ be the probability that one or more of the backlogged stations attempts a retransmission. The probability P_k of a successful transmission is then

$$P_k = P\{n = 1\}P\{r = 0\} + P\{n = 0\}P\{r = 1\}$$
$$= [k\alpha(1 - \alpha)^{k-1}][(1 - p)^{N-k}] + [(1 - \alpha)^k][(N - k)p(1 - p)^{N-k-1}]$$
$$= S_{out,k} \tag{6.14}$$

where $S_{out,k}$ is the rate at which packets leave the system when k stations are backlogged. Under the same conditions, the rate at which packets enter the system is

$$S = (N - k)p \tag{6.15}$$

For a large number of stations N and for small transfer probability p, Eq. (6.14) reduces to

$$S_{out,k} = k\alpha(1 - \alpha)^{k-1}e^{-S} + (1 - \alpha)^k Se^{-S} \tag{6.16}$$

When the channel input rate S given by Eq. (6.15) is equal to the channel output rate $S_{out,k}$ for given values of k and α, the network is in *equilibrium*. A plot of an equilibrium contour is given in Fig. 6.4 as a function of the number of backlogged stations k for $\alpha = 0.03$, $N = 200$, and $p = 0.001$. In the shaded region under the curve $S_{out,k}$ is greater than S, so that the number of backlogged stations tends to decrease in the next time slot. Elsewhere $S_{out,k} < S$ which means the network capacity is exceeded. Note that for $k = 0$, we have $S_{out} = 0.164$.

At high transmission rates there will be many collisions between packets and many stations will become backlogged. Since a substantial portion of the traffic then consists of retransmitted messages, there will be many collisions in the succeeding time slots and the throughput will be small, as is shown in Fig. 6.4. By making the retransmission probability α smaller, the shaded area in Fig. 6.4 is increased. Plots of equilibrium contours for various values of α are given in Fig. 6.5. Although this shows that by decreasing α a finite throughput is

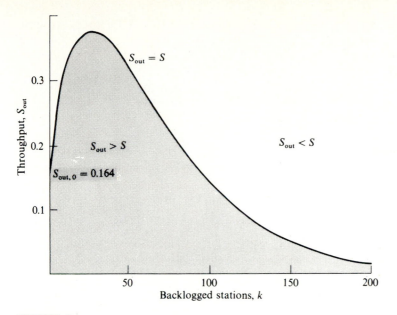

FIGURE 6.4
Equilibrium throughput curve as a function of the number of backlogged stations in slotted ALOHA. At $k = 0$, $S_{out} = 0.164$.

achieved even when the network is heavily backlogged, the result is very long retransmission intervals. This can also be seen from Eq. (6.13), which shows that small values of α correspond to large values of the number of time slots k required for successful retransmission.

When both the number of stations N and the new packet generation probability p are constant in time, we have what is called a *stationary* input. Let us look at the conditions under which a stationary channel is unstable. For this we use Eq. (6.15) for the system input to define the *channel load line*. With N and p constant, Eq. (6.15) defines a straight line in the (k, S) plane. An example is shown in Fig. 6.6 for $N = 200$ and $p = 0.001$. This line has a slope $-p$ and its intercepts on the k and S axes are N and Np, respectively.

The intersection of the load line and the throughput-backlog curve are the points at which the packet input rate S is equal to the packet output rate. These points therefore specify possible operating, or equilibrium, values of throughput. There are three possible equilibrium points. A point is *stable* if operation can remain at or about that point for a finite period of time. Furthermore, if it is the only stable equilibrium point, then it is said to be *globally stable*. If more than one stable equilibrium point exists, each is *locally stable*. An equilibrium point is *unstable* if operation immediately drifts away from it.

There are four possible ways in which the load line and equilibrium curve can intersect. In the first case shown in Fig. 6.7, N is small, the system is lightly loaded, and the backlog is low at the equilibrium operating point D. The input

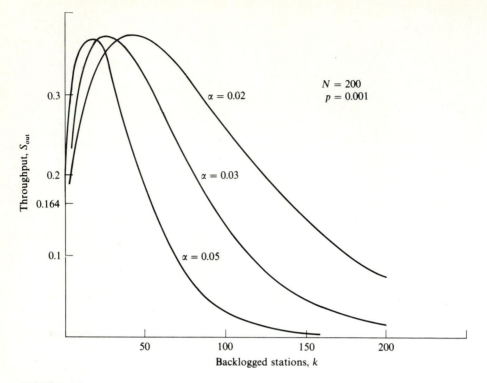

FIGURE 6.5
Equilibrium contours for various values of the retransmission probability α for slotted ALOHA. All curves go to 0.164 at $k = 0$.

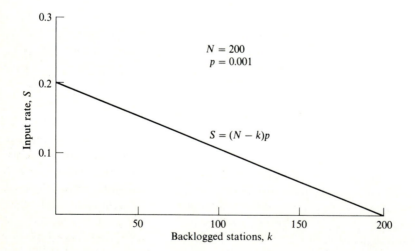

FIGURE 6.6
Example of a channel load line showing the input rate as a function of backlog.

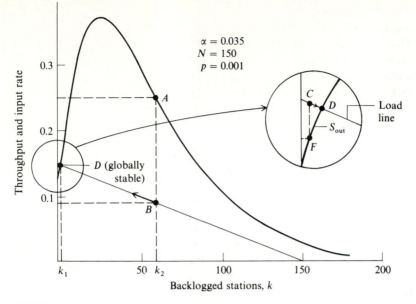

FIGURE 6.7
Example of a globally stable, lightly loaded system.

traffic in this case is so small that packets rarely collide and only a very small backlog builds up (point k_1). However, let us see what happens if a sudden fluctuation in input traffic moves the operation point from D to A where the backlog is much higher (point k_2). The input is now at point B. Since A is higher than B, the throughput is greater than the input rate. The backlog is thus driven back to point D as indicated by the arrow on the load line. Similarly, as shown in the inset in Fig. 6.7, if the input load momentarily moves outside of the equilibrium region to point C (to the left of D on the load line), the throughput decreases sharply to point F and a backlog builds up again. That is, the system is driven back to the equilibrium point D. Thus, point D is a globally stable equilibrium point since it is the only point where the load line crosses the equilibrium curve.

Figure 6.8 shows the case where the number of stations N is increased while keeping α constant. For this example, we take $N = 200$, $p = 0.001$, and $\alpha = 0.035$. The load line then moves up so that it now intersects the equilibrium throughput curve in three places. Although each of these points is a possible equilibrium point, only two of them are stable. Point D_1 is a stable point as we saw in the above argument. The opposite holds at point D_2. If the backlog at this point increases momentarily from k_2, the throughput drops faster than the input rate, thereby making the backlog even greater. This trend increases until the high backlog point D_3 is reached. Here the system is again stable, since the throughput is greater than the input rate.

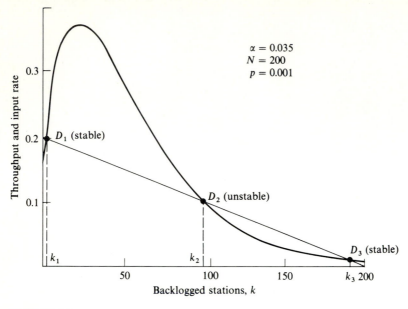

FIGURE 6.8
Bistable system having two locally stable and one unstable equilibrium points.

This operation is thus bistable with two locally stable equilibrium points. The point D_1 gives a large throughput and a small delay, whereas at point D_3 there is almost zero throughput and very large delay so that almost every station is backlogged. This situation is not desirable in a network since the operation can oscillate between the two locally stable points. If the system is operating at point D_1, then a momentary input excursion in which the backlog becomes greater than k_2 will drive the operation to point D_3. Similarly, equilibrium operation changes from D_3 to D_1 when the backlog momentarily becomes less than k_2.

An even further increase in the number of stations N with α held constant yields the condition shown in Fig. 6.9a. Here the channel is completely overloaded. Even though the network is globally stable, the only equilibrium point occurs at channel saturation where both the input rate and the throughput are very close to zero.

Figure 6.9b shows what happens when there are an infinite number of users. As $N \to \infty$, the load line becomes horizontal with two possible equilibrium points (a third one exists at $N = \infty$). Again point D_1 is locally stable (as is the point at infinity) but point D_2 is unstable. If this system happens to get into a high backlog state, the input rate will continue to exceed the throughput and the backlog will grow without bound to the equilibrium point at infinity.

Unstable systems such as shown in Figs. 6.8 and 6.9a can be made stable by decreasing α. By doing so then analogous to Fig. 6.7 there will be a single stable point where the load line and the equilibrium curve meet (see Prob. 6.5).

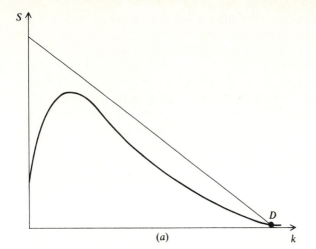

(a)

k

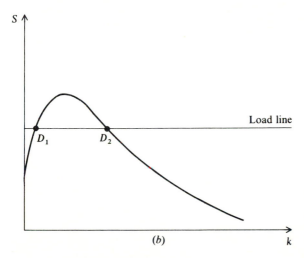

Load line

(b)

k

FIGURE 6.9
Behavior of systems which are
(a) stable but overloaded (N and p
large), (b) unstable with an infinite
number of users.

6.4 CARRIER SENSE MULTIPLE ACCESS (CSMA)

The transmission channels used for local area networks can be characterized as
wideband channels wherein the propagation delay between a sending and a receiving node is small compared to the packet-transmission time. In this case,
when a station sends a packet all the other stations in the network are aware of
it within a fraction of the packet transmission time. This observation led to the
development of the *carrier-sense multiple-access* (CSMA) scheme[5–8,15–18] (also
known as the *listen-before-talk* or **LBT** method). In this scheme a station that
wishes to transmit attempts to avoid collisions by first listening to the medium
to determine if another transmission is in progress.

When the channel is sensed to be idle, a station can take one of three different approaches (depending on the network design) to insert a packet onto the channel. These three protocols are known as *nonpersistent* CSMA, *1-persistent* CSMA, and *p-persistent* CSMA. Actually the 1-persistent protocol is a special case of the *p-persistent* scheme, but we shall consider it separately here. As we shall see below, these protocols differ by the action that a station with a packet to transmit takes after sensing the readiness state of the channel. However, when a station notes that a transmission is unsuccessful, in each protocol the rescheduling of the packet transmission is the same. In these reschedulings the packet is sent again according to a randomly distributed retransmission delay. A comparison of these three CSMA protocols is given in Table 6.1.

Before we analyze the CSMA protocols, let us state the following assumptions on which these analyses are based.[5]

1. A station may not transmit and receive simultaneously.
2. The state of the channel can be sensed instantaneously.
3. All packets are of constant length t_p.
4. The channel is noiseless (this means that message errors resulting from random noise are negligible compared to errors caused by overlapping packets).
5. Any fractional overlap of two packets results in destructive interference so that both must be retransmitted.
6. The propagation delay is the same between all source-destination pairs and is small compared to the packet transmission time.
7. The generation of packets (both new ones and retransmitted ones) from an infinite source of users follows a Poisson distribution. Each user generates traffic at an infinitesimally small rate so that the average channel traffic sums to G packets per packet time t_p.

TABLE 6.1
Characteristics of the three basic CSMA protocols

CSMA protocol	Characteristics
Nonpersistent	If medium is idle, transmit
	If medium is busy, wait random amount of time and resense channel
1-persistent	If medium is idle, transmit
	If medium is busy, continue listening until channel is idle; then transmit immediately
p-persistent	If medium is idle, transmit with probability p
	If medium is busy, continue listening until channel is idle; then transmit with probability p

6.4.1 Nonpersistent CSMA

Let us first consider the nonpersistent CSMA scheme. Here the basic equation for the throughput S is expressed in terms of the offered traffic rate G and the parameter a which is defined as

$$a = \frac{\text{propagation delay}}{\text{packet transmission time}} \tag{6.17}$$

The parameter a corresponds to the vulnerable period during which a transmitted packet can suffer a collision. Since the propagation delay is much smaller than the packet transmission time, a is a small quantity, say on the order of 0.01.

To analyze the nonpersistent CSMA protocol, consider Fig. 6.10, which shows the successful and unsuccessful attempts at transmitting packets. Also shown here is that the activity on the channel may be divided into busy periods during which transmission attempts are made, and idle periods during which no station transmits. (Note that in Fig. 6.10 and in the following discussions, we shall normalize the time scale to units of the packet transmission time t_p.) Now consider the packet that is sent at time $t = 0$ when the channel was sensed to be idle. We let this packet originate at station 1. It will now take a time interval a

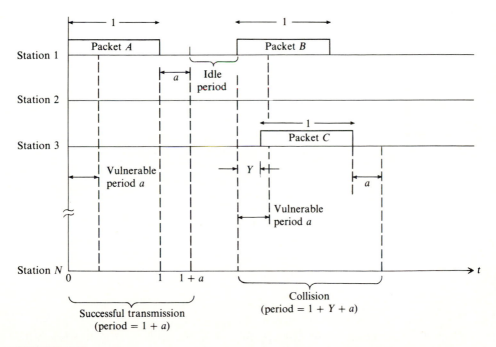

FIGURE 6.10
Successful and unsuccessful transmission attempts for nonpersistent CSMA. Time is measured in units of the packet transmission time t_p.

for all other stations on the channel to become aware that station 1 is transmitting. Thus by the definition of a, if no other station transmits between time $t = 0$ and $t = a$, then the transmission attempt will be successful, because for $t > a$ all other stations will sense the channels to be busy. The busy period for successful transmission is then $1 + a$, which is the propagation delay plus the packet transmission time (in normalized time units). The busy period is followed by an *idle period* during which no station transmits and this, in turn, is immediately followed by another busy period. Thus, we define a *cycle* as consisting of a busy period plus an idle period.

Now assume another station has a packet to send during the time interval a. The station will transmit this packet since it senses the channel to be idle (the packet from station 1 has not arrived yet), and will thereby cause a collision. As shown in Fig. 6.10, we let Y be the arrival time of the last packet which collides with the one sent by station 1, so that $0 \leq Y \leq a$. The transmission of all packets arriving in the time interval Y will be completed after $Y + 1$ time units. Since any station can still transmit during the time period a, the channel will finally be sensed unused at time $Y + 1 + a$. Thus the time duration $Y + 1 + a$ is the busy period for an unsuccessful transmission attempt. It is important to note that there can be at most one successful transmission during a busy period.

To find the channel throughput S, we let $E[B]$ be the expected duration of the busy period, $E[I]$ the expected length of the idle period, and $E[U]$ the average time during the cycle that the channel is used without collisions. The throughput is then given by

$$S = \frac{E[U]}{E[B] + E[I]} \tag{6.18}$$

This equation is based on the facts that all cycles are statistically similar, assuming steady state conditions, and that the throughput is the ratio of the average successful packet transmission time for a cycle to the total cycle time.

To find $E[U]$ we note that having a successful transmission during a busy period is the probability that no station transmits during the first a time units of the period, so that from Eq. (5.2) we have

$$E[U] = e^{-aG} \tag{6.19}$$

The idle period is just the time interval between the end of a busy period and the next arrival to the network. Hence, looking at the end of a busy period and noting that the packet arrivals follow a Poisson distribution, the average duration of an idle period is given by

$$E[I] = \frac{1}{G} \tag{6.20}$$

Now let us examine the busy periods. The time duration B of a transmission attempt is given by the random length

$$B = 1 + a + Y \tag{6.21}$$

where $Y = 0$ for successful transmissions. The average value of B then is

$$E[B] = 1 + E[Y] + a \qquad (6.22)$$

since Y is the only random quantity on the right-hand side of Eq. (6.21).

Equation (6.22) states that the last packet which collides with the one sent from station 1 arrives on the average $E[Y]$ time units after the busy period begins, spends one time unit in transmission, and finally clears the channel a time units later. The probability density function of Y is the probability that no packet arrival occurs in an interval of length $(a - y)$. Thus from Eq. (5.5) we have

$$f(y) = Ge^{-G(a-y)} \qquad \text{for } 0 \le y \le a \qquad (6.23)$$

so that

$$E[Y] = \int_0^a yf(y)\, dy$$

$$= a - \frac{1}{G}(1 - e^{-aG}) \qquad (6.24)$$

The expected duration of the busy period $E[B]$ then becomes

$$E[B] = 1 + 2a - \frac{1}{G}(1 - e^{-aG}) \qquad (6.25)$$

Substituting Eqs. (6.19), (6.20), and (6.25) into Eq. (6.18), we have for nonpersistent CSMA

$$S = \frac{Ge^{-aG}}{G(1 + 2a) + e^{-aG}} \qquad (6.26)$$

In the limit as $a \to 0$, we have

$$\lim_{a \to 0} S = \frac{G}{1 + G} \qquad (6.27)$$

Thus when $a = 0$, a throughput of 1 can theoretically be achieved for an infinitely large offered channel load G. This is shown in Fig. 6.11 where we have plotted the throughput given by Eq. (6.26) as a function of G for various values of a.

6.4.2 Slotted Nonpersistent CSMA

A variation of the nonpersistent CSMA method is *slotted nonpersistent CSMA*. The concept is similar to the slotted ALOHA scheme. Here the time axis is slotted into intervals of length τ as shown in Fig. 6.12. All stations are synchronized and are required to start transmission only at the beginning of a slot. All packets are assumed to be of a length t_p (that is, they require a transmission time t_p), which is an integral number of time slots. When a packet arrives during a time slot, the station senses the state of the channel at the beginning of the

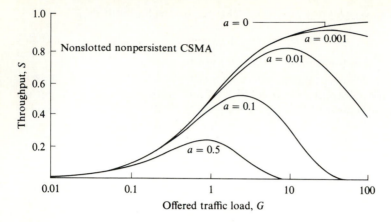

FIGURE 6.11
Throughout S as a function of the offered channel load G for various values of a for nonslotted nonpersistent CSMA.

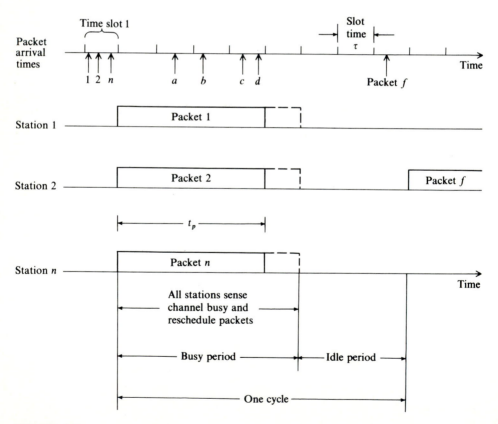

FIGURE 6.12
Example of packet arrivals in busy and idle periods in slotted nonpersistent CSMA.

next slot and then either transmits if the channel is idle or defers to a later time slot if there is traffic present.

An example of this is given in Fig. 6.12. Here packets from stations 1, 2, and n arrive during the first time slot. If the next slot is empty, all three stations will transmit as is shown in the figure. All stations, including the ones at which packets arrive in the busy period (shown as packets a, b, c, and d in Fig. 6.12), will then sense the channel to be busy. These stations thus defer their packets for transmission at a later time. As can be seen in Fig. 6.12, the length of each busy period is exactly $(t_p + \tau)$ or, in normalized time units $(1 + a)$, where $a = \tau/t_p$ as given by Eq. (6.17). The end of the transmission can thus be determined by all stations, since the busy period is longer than the transmission time by the amount τ (or a in normalized time units). Analogous to the unslotted CSMA case, an idle period consisting of an integral number of slots with no arrivals follows a busy period. This is shown as being three slots long in Fig. 6.12. The first two slots are empty and there is an arrival (packet f, which we take as coming from station 2) in the third slot. This packet gets sent in the next slot, thereby ending a cycle.

The analysis for the slotted nonpersistent CSMA case parallels that of the unslotted case in Sec. 6.4.1, in that we calculate S using Eq. (6.18). First let us find $E[U]$, the average time during a cycle that a transmission is successful. In normalized time units this is given by

$$E[U] = P_s \tag{6.28}$$

where the conditional probability P_s is the fraction of time that a transmission is good. This is given by

$$P_s = P\{\text{one packet arrives in slot } a | \text{some arrival occurs}\}$$

$$= \frac{P\{\text{one packet arrives in slot } a \text{ and some arrival occurs}\}}{P\{\text{some arrival occurs}\}}$$

$$= \frac{P\{\text{one packet arrives in slot } a\}}{P\{\text{some arrival occurs}\}} \tag{6.29}$$

Using Poisson arrival statistics we then have

$$P\{\text{one packet arrives in slot } a\} = aGe^{-aG} \tag{6.30}$$

and

$$P\{\text{some arrival occurs}\} = 1 - e^{-aG} \tag{6.31}$$

so that Eq. (6.28) becomes

$$E[U] = \frac{aGe^{-aG}}{1 - e^{-aG}} \tag{6.32}$$

Since, in normalized time units, the busy period is always $1 + a$, its average value is simply

$$E[B] = 1 + a \tag{6.33}$$

Now let us look at the average value of the idle period $E[I]$. First we need to recall the characteristics of the idle period. For slotted nonpersistent CSMA an idle period always consists of an integral number of time slots $I \geq 0$. If a packet arrives during the last time slot of a busy period, then the next slot immediately starts a new busy period so that $I = 0$. When there are no arrivals during the last slot of a busy period, then the next $I - 1$ slots will be empty, until there is an arrival in the final Ith slot. This then marks the beginning of a new busy period .

To find $E[I]$ we first consider the case $I = 0$. The probability p of this occurring is merely the probability of some packet arriving in the interval a, which is given by Eq. (6.31), that is,

$$P\{I = 0\} = p = 1 - e^{-aG} \tag{6.34}$$

Next we look at the case $I = 1$. The probability of this is the joint probability that no arrival occurs in the last slot of the busy period and that some arrival occurs in the next time slot. This is given by

$$P\{I - 1\} = (1 - p)p \tag{6.35}$$

Extending this argument to an idle period of length $I = i$, we have that the probability for no arrivals in i consecutive time slots followed by some arrival in the next slot is

$$P\{I = i\} = (1 - p)^i p \tag{6.36}$$

This describes a geometrically distributed random variable V with a mean value of

$$E[V] = \sum_{i=0}^{\infty} i(1 - p)^i p = \frac{1 - p}{p} \tag{6.37}$$

The average length of the idle period then is a times $E[V]$ so that from Eqs. (6.34) and (6.37)

$$E[I] = aE[V] = \frac{ae^{-aG}}{1 - e^{-aG}} \tag{6.38}$$

Substituting Eqs. (6.32), (6.33), and (6.38) into Eq. (6.18) we have for the slotted nonpersistent CSMA case

$$S = \frac{aGe^{-aG}}{1 - e^{-aG} + a} \tag{6.39}$$

6.4.3   1-Persistent CSMA

The 1-persistent CSMA protocol was devised to avoid situations in which a station has to wait before transmitting even though the channel is idle. As is noted in Table 6.1, the 1-persistent CSMA scheme operates by transmitting a packet with probability one if the channel is sensed idle. If the channel is busy when a station has a packet to transmit, the station waits until the channel goes idle and then transmits immediately with probability one. (This is the reason for the name "1-persistent"; the station persists on transmitting when the channel is busy and then sends its packet with probability one.) When two or more stations are waiting to transmit, a collision is guaranteed since each station will transmit immediately at the end of the busy period. In this case each will wait a random amount of time and will then reattempt to transmit.

As is the case with nonpersistent CSMA, the performance of the 1-persistent CSMA protocol depends on the channel delay time. Suppose that just after a station begins sending, another station has a packet to transmit and checks to see if the channel is idle. If the packet from the first station has not yet arrived at the second station, the latter will assume the channel is idle and will send its packet, thereby creating a collision. As the delay time becomes longer, this effect becomes more important since the performance of the protocol decreases.

The original derivation of the throughput is similar to that for nonpersistent CSMA but is rather lengthy.[5,16,17] A simplified approach using a three-state Markov chain (see App. E) due to Sohraby, Molle, and Venetsanopoulos[18] is given here. We shall refer to this as the SMV model. This model assumes an infinite number of bursty users (users that transmit bursts of information for short periods of time) that collectively generate Poisson traffic at a rate G packets per transmission time. The users are taken to be attached to a worst-case star local area network.

The analysis is based on a sequence of *subbusy periods* that occur within each busy period, as is shown in Fig. 6.13. These correspond to the successful and unsuccessful transmission periods given in Fig. 6.10. All stations that generate packets while they sense the channel busy during the jth subbusy period will transmit them at the start of the $(j + 1)$st subbusy period. A busy period ends

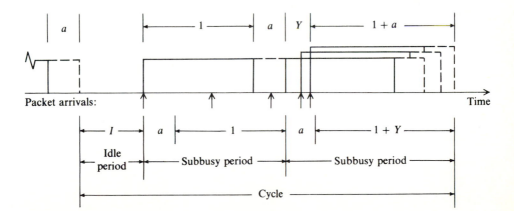

FIGURE 6.13
Channel state in asynchronous 1-persistent CSMA (*reprinted with permission from Sohraby, Molle, and Venetsanopoulos,*[18] © *1987, IEEE*).

and an idle period begins when there are no transmissions at the start of a subbusy period.

The SMV model defines the following three types of subbusy periods:

1. Idle periods which are those having zero packets
2. Subbusy periods having exactly one packet (here a successful transmission results if no further packets arrive during the first a time units of the period)
3. Subbusy periods containing more than one packet, the result being a collision

These periods correspond to states $i = 0$, 1, and 2 for a three-state Markov chain embedded at the start of the subbusy periods. These states and the possible transitions among them are shown in Fig. 6.14. As noted from the criteria in App. E, the chain is finite, aperiodic, irreducible, and therefore ergodic.

Let us look at some of the transition probabilities in more detail. First note that the transition probability P_{01} from state 0 (the idle state) to state 1 is equal to one, since, for 1-persistent CSMA operation the arrival of a packet in the idle state immediately starts a busy period. Because of this, we also have $P_{02} = 0$. As another example, consider the transition probability P_{11}, which gives the change from state 1 back to state 1. What this means is that while the system is in state 1 (that is, a packet has arrived and is being transmitted), there is *one* arrival in the busy period. This packet in turn initiates another busy period after the first packet has been sent out. Similar definitions can be given for the other transition probabilities.

To start the analysis, we let $E[T_i]$ be the average time the protocol spends in state i and let $\pi = \{\pi_0, \pi_1, \pi_2\}$ be the stationary probability distribution of the embedded chain. Then, analogous to Eq. (6.18), the throughput is the ratio of the average successful packet transmission time in a cycle to the total cycle time

$$S = \frac{\pi_1 e^{-aG}}{\sum_{i=0}^{2} E[T_i]\pi_i} \tag{6.40}$$

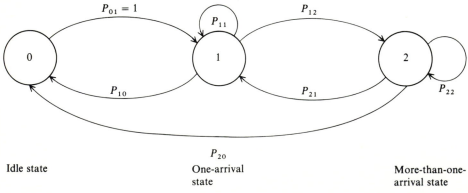

Idle state   One-arrival state   More-than-one-arrival state

FIGURE 6.14
Markov chain representation of 1-persistent CSMA.

Here in the numerator π_1 is the probability of the system being in state 1 during a successful transmission and, from Eq. (6.19), e^{-aG} is the probability of no arrival in the time interval a. The factor in the denominator is the state of the system during an entire cycle time.

Because of the star topology and as a result of the 1-persistent scheduling method, all stations that become ready in jth subbusy period will start transmitting at exactly the same time in the $(j + 1)$st subbusy period. In addition, since there is an infinite population of users, the number of these transmissions in the $(j + 1)$st subbusy period has no influence on the random variable Y, which denotes the *last* packet arriving in the vulnerable period a. Therefore, the duration of subbusy periods starting with one packet (state 1) or with more than one packet (state 2) are identically distributed. Thus we have

$$P_{1i} = P_{2i} \qquad \text{for } 0 \le i \le 2 \tag{6.41}$$

and

$$E[T_1] = E[T_2] \tag{6.42}$$

By noting that $E[T_0]$ is just the mean idle period, which from Eq. (6.20) is given by $1/G$ and using the relationship $\sum_i \pi_i = 1$ from Eq. (E.8), the throughput in Eq. (6.40) becomes

$$S = \frac{\pi_1 e^{-aG}}{\pi_0/G + (1 - \pi_0)E[T_1]} \tag{6.43}$$

To find π_0 and π_1 we make use of Eqs. (E.6) and (6.41) which yield

$$\pi_0 = \frac{P_{10}}{1 + P_{10}} \tag{6.44}$$

and

$$\pi_1 = \frac{P_{10} + P_{11}}{1 + P_{10}} \tag{6.45}$$

The expression of $E[T_1]$ and its derivation are identical to $E[B]$ given by Eq. (6.25). We thus have

$$E[T_1] = 1 + 2a - \frac{1 - e^{-aG}}{G} \tag{6.46}$$

Next we look at P_{10} and P_{11}. First P_{10} is given by the sum of the following joint probabilities

$$P_{10} = P\{\text{no arrival in time interval 1, success}\}$$

$$+ P\{\text{no arrival in time interval } 1 + Y, \text{collision}\}$$

$$= e^{-G}e^{-aG} + \int_0^a e^{-G(1+y)}Ge^{-G(a-y)}\,dy$$

$$= (1 + aG)e^{-G(1+a)} \tag{6.47}$$

Similarly,

$$P_{11} = P\{\text{one arrival during interval 1, success}\}$$

$$+ P\{\text{one arrival during interval } 1 + Y, \text{collision}\}$$

$$= Ge^{-G}e^{-aG} + \int_0^a G(1 + y)e^{-G(1+y)}Ge^{-G(a-y)} \, dy$$

$$= \left\{ G^2 \frac{(1 + a)^2 - 1}{2} + G \right\} e^{-G(1+a)} \tag{6.48}$$

Substituting Eq. (6.44) through (6.48) into Eq. (6.43) then yields

$$S = \frac{Ge^{-G(1+2a)}[1 + G + aG(1 + G + aG/2)]}{G(1 + 2a) - (1 - e^{-aG}) + (1 + aG)e^{-G(1+a)}} \tag{6.49}$$

Similar to the nonpersistent case, a *slotted* version of 1-persistent CSMA can be considered by slotting the time axis and synchronizing the transmission of packets. For the slotted 1-persistent CSMA the throughput equation is given by

$$S = \frac{G(1 + a - e^{-aG})e^{-G(1+a)}}{(1 + a)(1 - e^{-aG}) + ae^{-G(1+a)}} \tag{6.50}$$

In either version, the best performance is achieved when $a = 0$ so that

$$\lim_{a \to 0} S = \frac{Ge^{-G}(1 + G)}{G + e^{-G}} \tag{6.51}$$

Note that at low values of G (very few stations sending), the throughput is low. Also, as G becomes very large, $S \to Ge^{-G}$ which tends to zero. This actually holds for all values of a as is shown in Fig. 6.15, where we have plotted S (for the nonslotted 1-persistent CSMA case) as a function of G for various values of a. The curve for the case $a = 0$ falls almost exactly on top of the curve for $a = 0.01$ and is therefore not shown. For any value of a, the maximum throughput S will occur at an optimum value of G.

6.4.4   *p*-Persistent CSMA

To reduce the interference resulting from collisions and to improve the throughput, the *p*-persistent CSMA scheme was developed. This is a general case of the 1-persistent CSMA protocol and applies to slotted channels. In this protocol, when a station becomes ready to send and it senses the channel to be idle, it either transmits with a probability p or it defers transmission by one time slot (which is typically the maximum propagation delay) with a probability $q = 1 - p$. If the deferred slot is also idle, the station either transmits with a probability p or defers again with probability q. This process is repeated until either the packet is transmitted or the channel becomes busy. When the channel becomes busy, the station acts as though there had been a collision; that is, it waits a random

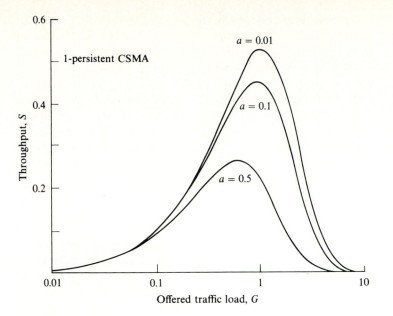

FIGURE 6.15
Throughput as a function of the offered load G for various values of a in the nonslotted 1-persistent CSMA case.

time and then starts the transmission attempt again. In case the channel was originally sensed to be busy, the station waits until the next slot and applies the above procedure.

The analysis and the resulting expression for the throughput of this protocol are rather involved. We will not consider this method further here, since it has no conceptual advantage over nonpersistent CSMA. The interested reader should consult Refs. 5, 16, and 17 for details.

6.5 CSMA WITH COLLISION DETECTION (CSMA/CD): IEEE STANDARD 802.3

A considerable performance improvement in the basic CSMA protocols described above can be achieved by means of the *carrier sense multiple access with collision detection* (CSMA/CD) technique,[6–8,17–26] which is alternatively known as the *listen while talk* (LWT) protocol. As noted in Chap. 2, the development of the CSMA/CD method of randomly accessing a local area network was done at Xerox.[6] This was subsequently developed through a joint effort by Digital Equipment Corporation, Intel, and Xerox into a detailed specification for a system called *Ethernet*.[25] The IEEE 802.3 CSMA/CD Standard[26] for local area networks is based on the Ethernet specification and is almost identical to it.

The CSMA/CD protocols are essentially the same as those for CSMA with the addition of the collision-detection feature. The same variations exist as in CSMA; that is, there are nonpersistent, 1-persistent, and *p*-persistent methodologies, each of which can have a slotted or unslotted version.

When a CSMA/CD station senses that a collision has occurred, it immediately ceases transmitting its packet and sends a brief jamming signal to notify all stations of this collision. Collisions are detected by monitoring the analog waveform directly from the channel. When signals from two or more stations are present simultaneously, the composite waveform is distorted from that of a single station. This is manifested in the form of larger-than-normal-voltage amplitudes on the cable.

6.5.1   Overview of Features

The basic operating characteristics of the CSMA/CD protocol are outlined in Fig. 6.16. Let us first look at the deference mechanism. Even when there is no packet waiting to be transmitted, the CSMA/CD MAC sublayer monitors the physical medium for traffic. When the station becomes ready to transmit, the behavior of the deference mechanism depends on which protocol variation is being used. In particular, suppose the channel is idle. Then the following action is taken:

The packet is transmitted if nonpersistent or 1-persistent CSMA/CD is being used

For *p*-persistent CSMA/CD, the packet is sent with probability *p* or delayed by the end-to-end propagation delay with probability $(1 - p)$

If the channel is busy, then

The packet is backed off and the algorithm is repeated for the nonpersistent case

The station defers transmission until the channel is sensed idle and then immediately transmits in the 1-persistent case

For the *p*-persistent protocol, the station defers until the channel is idle and then follows the idle-channel procedure described above

In each of the channel-busy cases when there is a packet ready to be sent out, the MAC sublayer defers to the passing frame by delaying the transmission of its own waiting packet. After the last bit of the frame from the other station has passed by, the MAC sublayer continues to defer for a certain time period called an *interframe spacing*. Transmission of any waiting packet is initiated at the end of this time. When the transmission is completed (or immediately at the end of the interframe spacing time if no packet is waiting in the transmission buffer), the MAC sublayer resumes monitoring the carrier-sense signal.

Once the deferring at a station is finished and transmission has started, collisions can still occur until acquisition of the network by that station has

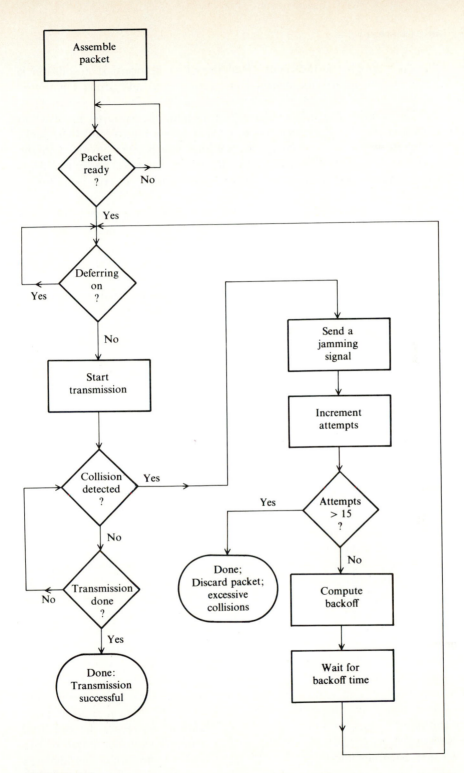

FIGURE 6.16
Flow diagram for the CSMA/CD access scheme.

been achieved through the deference of all the other stations. If a collision is detected, the station aborts the packet being transmitted and sends a jamming signal.

After the jamming signal has been transmitted, the stations involved in colliding packets wait random amounts of time and then try to send their packets again. By using a random delay, the stations which were involved in the collision are not likely to have another collision on the next transmission attempt. However, to ensure that this backoff technique maintains stability, a method known as *truncated binary exponential backoff*[6,8,27,28] is used in Ethernet, for example. In this method a station will persist in trying to transmit when there are repeated collisions. These retries will continue until either the transmission is successful or 16 attempts (the original attempt plus 15 retries) have been made unsuccessfully. At this point (if all 16 attempts fail) the packet is discarded and the event is reported as an error.

The backoff strategy is quite simple. If a packet has been transmitted unsuccessfully n times, the next transmission attempt is delayed by an integer r times the base backoff time (which is often chosen to be twice the end-to-end propagation delay). The integer r is selected as a uniformly distributed integer in the range $0 \leq r \leq 2^k$ where $k = \min(n, 10)$, that is, k is the minimum of the number of presently attempted transmissions n and the integer 10. Thus as the Ethernet load becomes increasingly heavy, the stations automatically adapt to the load.

6.5.2   Throughput Analysis for Nonpersistent CSMA/CD

As is the case with the basic CSMA method, CSMA/CD can use one of the three persistence algorithms described above. A common choice is 1-persistent CSMA/CD which is described in the IEEE-802.3 standard.[26] Thus the analysis of the CSMA/CD method is similar to that of CSMA.

We will first consider the unslotted nonpersistent case. To simplify the analysis we will assume Poisson arrivals from an infinite population, let the collision-detection time δ be negligible compared to the packet propagation time, and treat retransmissions as independent Poisson arrivals. Figure 6.17 shows the sequence of events in a collision. Starting at time $t = 0$, station A transmits a packet. During the vulnerability time period a, station B sends its packet at time $t = y$ since it is unaware as yet that station A is busy. At time $t = a + \delta$, station B detects the message from station A, immediately ceases its packet transmission, and sends out a jamming signal of length b. However, the transmission that was started by station B at $t = y$ will take a time units to reach station A. Thus, at time $t = y + a + \delta$, station A detects the collision, stops sending its packet, and sends out its own jamming signal of length b. The channel then becomes idle at time $t = 2a + y + b + \delta$. In the following analyses we let $\delta \rightarrow 0$.

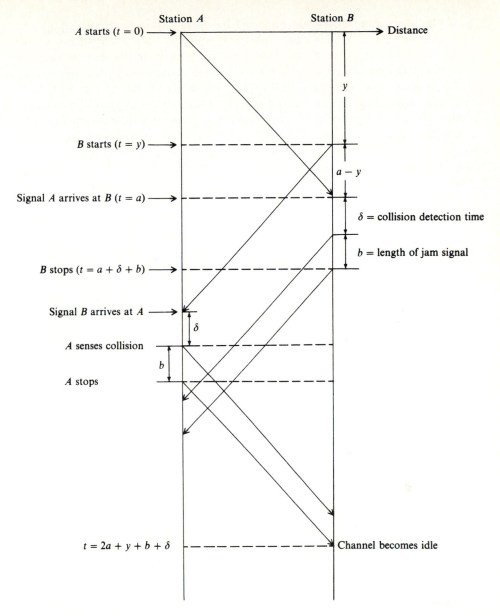

FIGURE 6.17
Sequence of events in a collision using the CSMA/CD protocol.

The throughput can again be found by using Eq. (6.18) where $E[U]$ and $E[I]$ are given by Eqs. (6.19) and (6.20), respectively. Thus it remains to derive $E[B]$, the expected value of the busy period. A busy period can be either a successful transmission period or an unsuccessful contention period when more than one station is attempting to transmit. These are shown in Fig. 6.18. Here when any active station senses a collision, it first broadcasts a jamming tone for a time b to alert all other stations of the collision. As we can see from Fig. 6.17, in this protocol the first station that transmits (station A) is also the last one to stop. Thus for CSMA/CD the random variable Y_1 in Fig. 6.18 is the transmission time of the *first* colliding packet in the vulnerable period of length a, rather than the *last* as in the CSMA case.

As we see from Fig. 6.18, the length of a successful period is $(1 + a)$ whereas that of a contention period is $(2a + b + Y_1)$. Thus the expected duration of the busy period can be found from the expression

$$E[B] = P\{\text{successful transmission}\} \, E[1 + a]$$

$$+ \, P\{\text{unsuccessful transmission}\} \, E[2a + b + Y_1]$$

$$= e^{-aG}(1 + a) + (1 - e^{-aG})(2a + b + E[Y_1]) \tag{6.52}$$

To evaluate $E[Y_1]$ we need to find its probability density function $f(y)$, which is defined as the probability $P\{y \geq Y_1\}$ where $0 \leq y \leq a$. Thus we can write

$$f(y) = P\{y \geq Y_1\} = 1 - P\{y < Y_1\} \tag{6.53}$$

where $P\{y < Y_1\}$ is the probability of no arrivals in the interval $[0, y]$ given that there is at least one arrival in $[0, a]$. Using the basic relationships of conditional probability and independent events (see App. D), this can be written as

$$P\{y < Y_1\} = P\{\text{no arrivals in } [0, y] | \text{at least one arrival in } [0, a]\}$$

$$= \frac{P\{\text{no arrivals in } [0, y]\} \, P\{\text{at least one arrival in } [y, a]\}}{P\{\text{at least one arrival in } [0, a]\}}$$

$$= \frac{e^{-yG}[1 - e^{-G(a-y)}]}{1 - e^{-aG}} \tag{6.54}$$

Thus, from Eq. (6.53) we have

$$f(y) = \frac{1 - e^{-yG}}{1 - e^{-aG}} \qquad 0 \leq y \leq a \tag{6.55}$$

from which we find

$$E[Y_1] = \int_0^a y f(y) \, dy = \frac{1}{G} - \frac{ae^{-aG}}{1 - e^{-aG}} \tag{6.56}$$

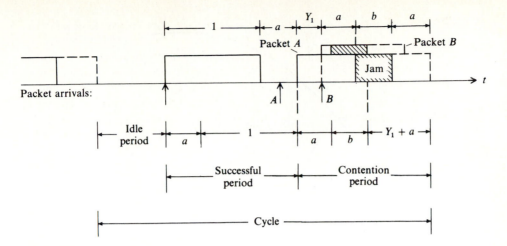

FIGURE 6.18
Successful and unsuccessful transmission periods for nonpersistent CSMA/CD.

Inserting Eq. (6.56) into Eq. (6.52) and substituting the result into Eq. (6.18) together with Eqs. (6.19) and (6.20) then yields for unslotted nonpersistent CSMA/CD

$$S = \frac{Ge^{-aG}}{Ge^{-aG} + bG(1 - e^{-aG}) + 2aG(1 - e^{-aG}) + (2 - e^{-aG})} \quad (6.57)$$

An expression can now readily be found for the *slotted* nonpersistent CSMA/CD case, since its derivation is analogous to that of CSMA given in Sec. 6.4.2. The expressions for P_s, $E[U]$, and $E[I]$ are given by Eqs. (6.28), (6.32), and (6.38), respectively. The only difference in the analysis here is that the collision period needs to be considered. In particular, for slotted nonpersistent CSMA/CD, packets are only sent at the beginning of a slot, the contention period has a constant length $(2a + b)$, and the jamming time b is an integral number of slots. Thus, for the busy period we have

$$E[B] = P\{\text{successful transmission}\} \, E[1 + a]$$

$$+ P\{\text{unsuccessful transmission}\} \, E[2a + b]$$

$$= P_s(1 + a) + (1 - P_s)(2a + b) \quad (6.58)$$

where P_s is given by Eq. (6.32). Substituting Eqs. (6.32), (6.38), and (6.58) into Eq. (6.18) then yields, for slotted nonpersistent CSMA/CD,

$$S = \frac{aGe^{-aG}}{aGe^{-aG} + b(1 - e^{-aG} - aGe^{-aG}) + a(2 - e^{-aG} - aGe^{-aG})} \quad (6.59)$$

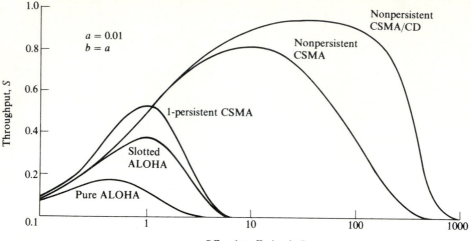

FIGURE 6.19
Performance of unslotted nonpersistent CSMA/CD for $a = 0.01$ and $a = b$ compared to several other channel access methods.

A comparison of Eq. (6.57) with the throughput expressions for pure ALOHA, slotted ALOHA, 1-persistent CSMA, and nonpersistent CSMA is given in Fig. 6.19 for $a = 0.01$ and $b = a$. The improvement in performance for high-offered traffic loads is obvious.

6.5.3 Throughput Analysis for 1-Persistent CSMA/CD

To analyze the throughput for 1-persistent CSMA/CD we again consider the SMV model[18] as described in Sec. 6.4.3. In particular, to find S we will use Eq. (6.40), so that we need to derive expressions for the parameters P_{ik}, π_i, and $E[T_i]$. The state of the channel showing the idle and subbusy periods is illustrated in Fig. 6.20. As in Fig. 6.13, the arrows on the time line indicate possible times for initiating transmissions (i.e., packets arriving at these times either wait for transmission if the channel is busy or transmit immediately otherwise).

First we note that $E[T_0]$ is again just the mean idle period which, from Eq. (6.20), is given by $1/G$. Also the expression for $E[T_1]$ and its derivation are identical to $E[B]$ given by Eq. (6.52). That is,

$$E[T_1] = (1 - e^{-aG})\left(2a + b + \frac{1}{G}\right) + e^{-aG} \qquad (6.60)$$

To derive P_{10} and P_{11} we note from Fig. 6.20 that in the case of a collision, the packets generated in the time interval $a + b + Y_1$ in the current sub-

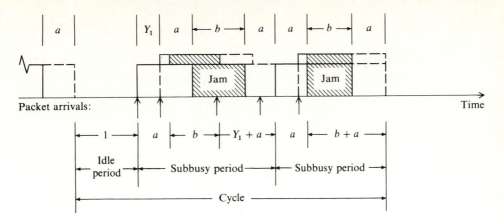

FIGURE 6.20
State of the channel in 1-persistent CSMA/CD *(reprinted with permission from Sohraby, Molle, and Venetsanopoulos,[18] © 1987, IEEE).*

busy period will start in the next subbusy period. Thus, using Eq. (5.2),

$$P_{10} = P\{\text{no arrival during interval 1, success}\}$$

$$+ P\{\text{no arrival in } a + b + y, \text{ collision}\}$$

$$= e^{-G}e^{-aG} + \int_0^a e^{-G(a+b+y)}Ge^{-Gy}\,dy$$

$$= e^{-G(1+a)} + \tfrac{1}{2}e^{-G(a+b)}(1 - e^{-2aG}) \tag{6.61}$$

Similarly, using Eq. (5.2),

$$P_{11} = P\{\text{one arrival during interval 1, success}\}$$

$$+ P\{\text{one arrival in } (a + b + y), \text{ collision}\}$$

$$= Ge^{-G}e^{-aG} + \int_0^a G(a + b + y)e^{-G(a+b+y)}Ge^{-Gy}\,dy$$

$$= Ge^{-G(1+a)} + \tfrac{1}{4}e^{-G(a+b)}\{(1 - e^{-2aG})[1 + 2G(a + b)] - 2aGe^{-2aG}\} \tag{6.62}$$

Now let us consider a subbusy period that is generated by two or more packets (state 2). As shown in the right-hand segment of Fig. 6.20, this subbusy period has a constant length $2a + b$ independent of any further colliding packets. Thus

$$E[T_2] = 2a + b \tag{6.63}$$

The transition probabilities P_{2n} are then merely given by the probabilities $p_n(t)$ in Eq. (5.2) for exactly n packets arriving at a rate G in a time interval t. Thus, for $t = a + b$,

$$P_{20} = e^{-G(a+b)} \tag{6.64}$$

and

$$P_{21} = G(a + b)e^{-G(a+b)} \tag{6.65}$$

To derive π_0, π_1, and π_2 we use Eq. (E.9) for $j = 1$ and 2 together with the relationships given in Eqs. (E.2) and (E.8). This then yields

$$\pi_1 = \frac{P_{20} + P_{21}}{K} \tag{6.66}$$

$$\pi_2 = \frac{1 - P_{10} - P_{11}}{K} \tag{6.67}$$

$$\pi_0 = 1 - \pi_1 - \pi_2 = \frac{(1 - P_{11})P_{20} + P_{10}P_{21}}{K} \tag{6.68}$$

where

$$K = (1 - P_{10} - P_{11})(1 + P_{20}) + (1 + P_{10})(P_{20} + P_{21}) \tag{6.69}$$

Substituting all the appropriate parameters into Eq. (6.40) thus gives us, for unslotted 1-persistent CSMA/CD,

$$S = \frac{(P_{20} + P_{21})e^{-aG}}{\left\{ \frac{(1 - P_{11})P_{20} + P_{10}P_{21}}{G} + (2a + b)(1 - P_{10} - P_{11}) \right.}$$

$$\left. + \left[\left(1 - e^{-aG} \right)\left(2a + b + \frac{1}{G} \right) + e^{-aG} \right](P_{20} + P_{21}) \right\} \tag{6.70}$$

The throughput S as a function of the offered load G is shown in Fig. 6.21 with $a = 0.01$ for several values of b. From this figure we see that the 1-persistent CSMA/CD protocol is able to maintain throughput near capacity over a large range of loads.

6.5.4   Stability of CSMA and CSMA/CD

When analyzing random access protocols, it is common to use the infinite population model to simplify the mathematics. This is a reasonable assumption for the case of a large population of user stations. Various analyses based on the embedded Markov chain model have shown, however, that for the infinite population case both CSMA and CSMA/CD channels are unstable under the assumption of random retransmission delay for blocked terminals. This is in contrast to the finite population case where it is known that the CSMA channel is stable for sufficiently small retransmission probability. The infinite population case thus imposes tighter stability constraints. Meditch and Lea[24] have shown, however, that stabilization can be achieved under distributed retransmission control policies in which the retransmission probability is inversely proportional to the number of blocked stations. (An alternative analysis based on a pseudo-bayesian technique[29] can be found in the book by Bertsekas and Gallager.[28])

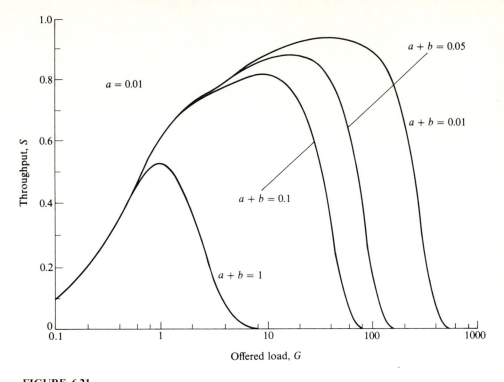

FIGURE 6.21

Throughput as a function of G for $a = 0.01$ and with $b + a = 1.0$, 0.1, 0.05, *and* 0.01 (*reprinted with permission from Takagi and Kleinrock,*[17] © *1987, IEEE*).

The Meditch and Lea analysis (which we will call the ML model) is based on a Markov chain model in which the axis is partitioned into slots of length τ, the one-way propagation delay of the channel. Here we will again normalize time in terms of the packet length, so that the length of the time slot becomes a. The active stations on the network collectively generate new packets in a Poisson stream at a rate λ packets per slot. When there is a collision, a blocked station will reschedule its resensing of the channel in the current slot with a probability $0 < f \le 1$. Channel stability is addressed in the ML model by considering a retransmission control policy of the form $f = \alpha/k$ where $k \ge 1$ is the number of blocked stations and $\alpha > 0$ is a constant. The transmission rate is thus given by α/a.

The ML model covers in detail how to determine ranges of the offered traffic G (and hence of the control parameter α) over which the slotted nonpersistent CSMA and CSMA/CD channels are stable. As a simple variation on their model we consider Eq. (6.59) which gives the throughput S for the slotted nonpersistent CSMA/CD case. Given that the load G offered to the channel consists of traffic from blocked and active stations, that is,

$$aG = \lambda + \alpha \qquad (6.71)$$

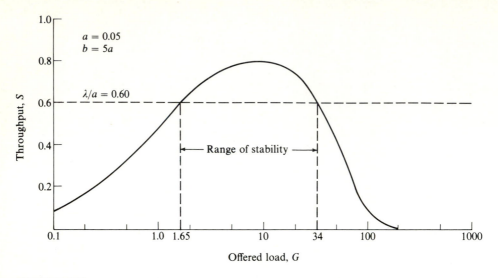

FIGURE 6.22
Stability range example for slotted nonpersistent CSMA/CD with $a = 0.05$ and $b = 5a$ for a desired throughput of 0.6.

where $0 < \lambda < 1$ is the input traffic in packets per slot and $\alpha > 0$ is the retransmission control parameter, then for channel stability we need to have

$$\frac{\lambda}{a} < S \tag{6.72}$$

where, as usual, S is normalized in terms of the packet transmission time t_p.

As an example, we plot Eq. (6.59) for $a = 0.05$ and $b = 5a$ as a function of G in Fig. 6.22. Suppose we wish to have $\lambda/a = 0.60$ over all offered loads as shown by the dashed line. Then for channel stability G must fall between 1.65 and 34. Given that $1.65 \le G \le 34$ and that $\lambda = 0.03$ (since $\lambda/a = 0.6$), from Eq. (6.71) we then find that for channel stability we need to have $0.05 \le \alpha \le 1.67$.

Several points should be noted here. First, the stable range widens if we are willing to accept a lower throughput. Also, what is not shown here but which is left for an exercise, is that the stability range decreases as the jamming interval b increases (see Prob. 6.20). For reasonable values of b, however, the stable range for CSMA/CD is greater than for CSMA.

6.6 CONTROLLED-ACCESS SCHEMES

In contrast to the stochastic nature of contention-based access methods, a controlled-access technique is a deterministic or noncontention method since it employs a specific digital signal to grant permission to transmit to *one station at a time*. Thereby packets from two different stations cannot collide since only one user has the right to send messages at any instance. The responsibility for the control signal can be assigned to one station on the network (centralized control), or it may be distributed among all the nodes.

A common centralized-control method is known as *polling.*[27,30–33] Polling techniques determine the order in which stations can take turns to access the network. This is shown in Fig. 6.23 where we use a commutator analogy to represent a master station cycling among message source buffers. Here messages arrive at N queues with queue k receiving an average rate of λ_k messages per second. Generally we assume the arrival process to be Poisson. The master station queries each station in some prescribed order, asking whether or not the station has a message to send. The polled station then transmits if it has data to send. If it does not have anything to transmit, the station sends back a special negative response. Usually the controller polls the station sequentially, but in special circumstances important terminals may be polled several times per cycle.

Distributed-control access methods are commonly referred to as *token controlled.* These techniques can be employed in ring or bus topologies. Tokens are special bit patterns or packets, usually several bits in length that circulate from node to node when there is no message traffic. When a station wants to send data, it removes the token from the line and holds it. Now the station has exclusive access to the network for transmitting its message. In the meantime, other stations are continuously monitoring the messages that pass by on the network. All stations are responsible for identifying and accepting messages addressed to them. In addition, they must pass on messages that are addressed to other stations.

When a station is finished transmitting its message, it puts the token back into circulation. This indicates to the network that the station has finished sending and gives other stations a chance to transmit.

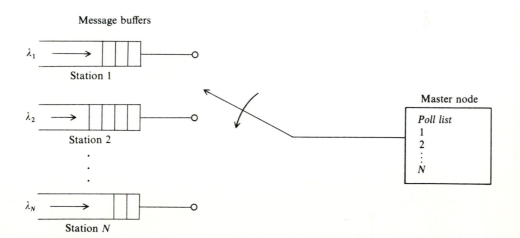

FIGURE 6.23
Schematic representation of a polling technique.

Of the two distributed control techniques, we will only address token methods here, since they are more widely used in local area network applications.

6.6.1 Token Ring: IEEE Standard 802.5

One of the oldest applications is the token ring[34-39] which has been standardized as an access method[40] in the IEEE Standard 802.5. Here we shall mainly examine the throughput characteristics. The details on the frame formats and the token-control access method are given in Sec. 10.4.

In a token ring the stations are connected logically in a ring with each station transmitting to the next sequentially around the ring as is shown in Fig. 6.24. Normally each station simply relays the bit stream received from the previous station on to the next station. This is done with at least a one-bit delay, thereby allowing the station to read and regenerate the incoming information before passing it on. In the token ring scheme, an addressed destination station *copies* the information as it passes, and the originating station *removes* it when it has made a full loop around the ring.

Clearly, when a node wishes to transmit its own information, it must discard the incoming bit stream. Some control mechanism must therefore be used in this case to ensure that what is being received and discarded is not a packet which is still on the way to its ultimate destination. This control is achieved by means of a special eight-bit pattern, such as 11111111. This pattern, which is called a *token*, exists in the network and is passed from station to station.

Bit stuffing is used to prevent this pattern from occurring in the data. Network control is achieved by having the station monitor each bit that passes through the ring interface which attaches the station to the ring. When the station wishes to transmit, it waits for the token to arrive and then changes it into another bit pattern, for example, 11111110. This effectively removes the token from the ring and the station can start transmitting immediately. Upon completing its transmission, the station inserts the token pattern back onto the line.

To see what the throughput of a token ring is, we use the simple analysis of Stallings.[41] As we did in the discussion of contention access, we normalize the

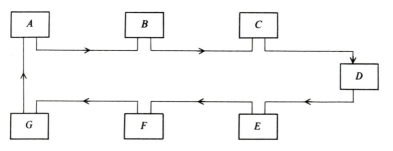

FIGURE 6.24
Station interconnection in a token ring.

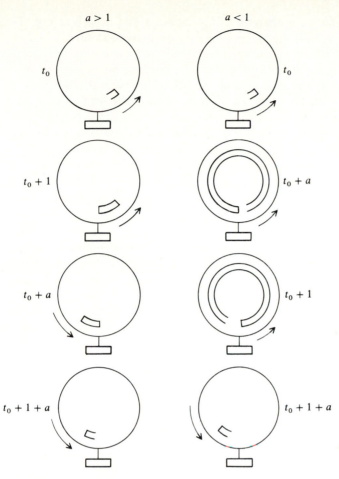

FIGURE 6.25
Operational concept of a ring network. (*Reproduced with permission from Stallings,*[41] © *1984, IEEE.*)

time scale to units of the transmission time. Thus, the packet transmission time equals 1 and the propagation time equals a, as is defined in Eq. (6.17).

An operational concept of a ring network is shown in Fig. 6.25. Here a is the time required for a message bit to leave a particular node, traverse the entire ring, and return. When $a < 1$, which is generally the case, a station starts sending a packet at time t_0, receives the leading edge of this packet on its incoming line at time $t_0 + a$, completes transmission at time $t_0 + 1$, and receives the end of its message at time $t_0 + 1 + a$. When a station finishes transmitting at $t_0 + 1$, it puts a token on the line so that the next station can transmit. If there are N active stations on the network, then on the average the time required to pass a token to the next station is a/N.

In cases where $a > 1$, that is, the propagation time is greater than the packet transmission time, the station does not receive the leading edge of its own message until some time after the entire message has been sent out. This time interval is again a, and the trailing edge again arrives at time $t_0 + 1 + a$. Although the station could emit a token immediately after it finishes its message at time $t_0 + 1$, this is generally not allowed in the $a > 1$ case (particularly in the IEEE 802.5 Standard) in order to simplify control. However, the station is allowed to put its token back on the line once it receives the leading edge of its message at time $t_0 + a$.

By definition, the throughput is the fraction of time that is used to transmit information. Thus, if T_p is the average time required to transmit a data packet, T_e is the time elapsed before a token can be transmitted, and T_t is the average time required to pass a token to the next station on the ring, then the throughput S is given by

$$S = \frac{T_p}{T_e + T_t} \tag{6.73}$$

Since $T_e = T_p = 1$ and $T_t = a/N$ for $a < 1$, the throughput for a token ring is

$$S = \frac{1}{1 + a/N} \qquad \text{for } a < 1 \tag{6.74}$$

For the case $a > 1$, the station can put its token back on the ring once it receives the leading edge of its message. Thus in this case $(a > 1)$, we have $T_e = a$, $T_p = 1$, and $T_t = a/N$ so that, from Eq. (6.73),

$$S = \frac{1}{a(1 + 1/N)} \qquad \text{for } a > 1 \tag{6.75}$$

6.6.2   Token Bus: IEEE Standard 802.4

The token control scheme is also applicable to a bus topology[42-47] as is shown in Fig. 6.26. Here there are m stations with ordered identities, and they are offered service one at a time in a round-robin order. The operation is thus similar to that of a ring except that whereas in a ring the token is passed implicitly (without addressing information), for a bus an explicit token containing a specific node address is used. This results in an ordering of the stations that resem-

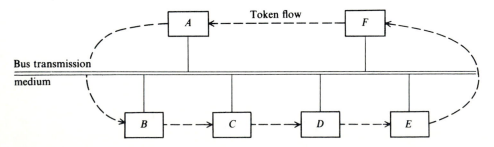

FIGURE 6.26
Station interconnection and token flow in a token bus network.

bles a logical ring. Consequently, the same results apply for the throughput as are found in Eqs. (6.74) and (6.75).

A token bus can be either bidirectional[42] or unidirectional.[43-46] For a bidirectional bus, a logical sequential ordering of the attached stations is achieved by using an addressed idle token. If a station wishes to transmit, it must wait to receive the free token addressed to it before it can access the channel. When the station has finished transmitting, it sends an addressed idle token to the next station that has the access right to the channel.

The address is selected from a predetermined list which is set up in such a way that the stations are assigned positions in an ordered sequence, with the first station in the sequence following the last station once a cycle is completed. Thus the steady state operation consists of alternating data-transfer and token-passing phases.

Unlike the bidirectional token bus, a unidirectional token bus does not use an addressed token. Instead, it uses an implicit token-passing protocol to efficiently utilize channel capacity. Users contend for the transmission medium according to some distributed conflict-free round-robin algorithm. The transmission medium used in these unidirectional broadcast systems consists of an inbound channel and an outbound channel to which the stations are connected. Examples of this for Fasnet[44] and Expressnet[45-46] are shown in Fig. 6.27. The outbound channel is used exclusively for transmitting data, and the

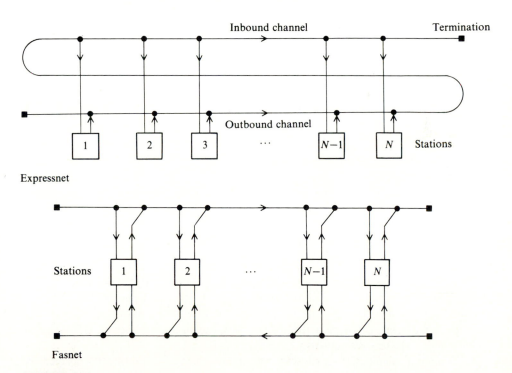

Expressnet

Fasnet

FIGURE 6.27
Topologies of Expressnet and Fasnet unidirectional buses.

inbound channel is designated for reading the transmitted data. The two channels are connected so that all signals transmitted on the outbound channel are
duplicated on the inbound channel, thus achieving broadcast communication
among the stations. All users can read from and write to both channels. The
asymmetry created by the unidirectional signal propagation establishes a natural
ordering among the stations so that a round-robin access protocol can be readily implemented.

6.7 DELAY-THROUGHPUT CHARACTERISTICS

This section presents the results of a performance comparison of two popular
access schemes, namely a random-access bus (CSMA/CD) and a token ring.
This comparison is based on the analyses by Bux[48] and is given in terms of the
delay-throughput characteristics of each type of LAN. *Delay* is measured as the
average interval of time between when a packet is ready for transmission from a
source station until its successful reception at the destination station. This delay
time (which is also called the *transfer time*) thus includes the queueing and access delay at the sender, the transmission time of the packet, and the propagation delay.

The following assumptions are used in the analyses:

There are N stations each of which generates packets at a rate λ_i, $i =
1, 2, \ldots, N$

The aggregate arrival rate of all stations is given by $\lambda = \lambda_1 + \lambda_2 + \cdots + \lambda_N$

The packet lengths L_p are distributed in a general fashion

A header of length L_h which contains control and addressing information
is added to each packet

The transmission rate (in bits per second) is denoted by R

The parameter τ denotes the maximum end-to-end propagation delay for a
bus or the round-trip delay for a ring

The service time of a packet is given by $T_p = (L_h + L_p)/R$

6.7.1 Delay in a Token Ring

The performance model for a token ring is shown in Fig. 6.28. This is a single-
server queueing model where each queue represents a station attached to the
ring. The queues are serviced sequentially as is represented by the rotating
switch which symbolizes the token. The service time of a packet is given by T_p,
and the time required to pass the token from station i to station $i + 1$ is represented by a constant switch-over delay τ_i.

The analysis of Bux starts with the mean-queueing-delay model derived by
Konheim and Meister[33] using a discrete-time approach. In this model equal

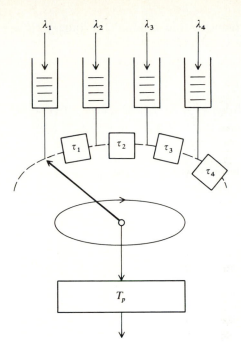

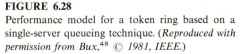

FIGURE 6.28
Performance model for a token ring based on a single-server queueing technique. (*Reproduced with permission from Bux,*[48] © *1981, IEEE.*)

arrival rates λ_i and equal switch-over delays τ_i are assumed. Bux then considers the case of the discrete-time interval approaching zero which results in the mean delay time D given by

$$D = \frac{\rho E[T_p^2]}{2(1 - \rho)E[T_p]} + E[T_p] + \frac{\tau(1 - \rho/N)}{2(1 - \rho)} + \frac{\tau}{2} \tag{6.76}$$

where $\rho = \lambda E[T_p]$ is the traffic intensity and $E[T_p]$ is the average value of T_p.

A basic assumption of Eq. (6.76) is that all stations generate the same amount of traffic. This was made since no explicit analytical expression exists if the stations generate unequal amounts of traffic. However, Eq. (6.76) represents an upper bound on the overall mean transfer delay irrespective of the particular arrival rates from a given station.

6.7.2   Delay in a CSMA/CD Bus

Widely used performance analyses of CSMA/CD networks have been derived by Lam[7] and by Tobagi and Hunt.[8] The access-control comparison of Bux uses a modified result of Lam which, for reasons of analytical tractability, assumes a slotted channel with slot length 2τ. This assumption implies that even if the network utilization approaches zero, packets have to wait an average time τ before they are transmitted. Since this does not occur in a nonslotted system,

Bux modified Lam's delay formula by reducing the mean delay time by the factor τ. This results in a delay time for a CSMA/CD bus given by

$$D_{\text{CSMA/CD}} = \frac{\lambda\{E[T_p^2] + (4e + 2)\tau E[T_p] + 5\tau^2 + 4e(2e - 1)\tau^2\}}{2\{1 - \lambda(E[T_p] + \tau + 2e\tau)\}}$$

$$+ E[T_p] + 2\tau e + \frac{\tau}{2} - \frac{[1 - \exp(-2\lambda\tau)](2/\lambda + 2\tau/e - 6\tau)}{2\{F_p \exp[-(\lambda\tau + 1)] - 1 + \exp(-2\lambda\tau)\}}$$

$$(6.77)$$

where F_p is the Laplace transform of the probability density function of the packet service time T_p.

6.7.3 Performance Comparisons

A comparision of Eqs. (6.76) and (6.77) is given in Fig. 6.29 for a 1-Mb/s transmission rate. In this figure the ordinate represents the mean delay time D relative to the mean packet transmission time $E[L_p]/R$. The abscissa is the traffic load which is given in terms of the ratio of the throughput rate $\lambda E[L_p]$ to the transmission rate R. As noted in this figure, we assume a 2-km cable length, a 5-μs/km propagation delay, 50 stations per network, a 24-bit header, a 1-bit delay per station for the ring network, and exponentially distributed packet

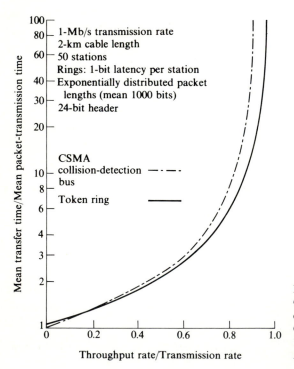

FIGURE 6.29
Comparison of the delay-throughput characteristics of token-ring and CSMA/CD-bus access methods at 1 Mb/s. (*Adapted with permission from Bux,*[48] *© 1981, IEEE.*)

lengths having a mean length of 1000 bits. Under these conditions the performances of the token ring and the CSMA/CD bus are fairly close since the overhead of the two access schemes is virtually negligible.

This similarity in performance changes when the transmission rate is increased. By changing the rate to 10 Mb/s while keeping all other parameters the same, we obtain the result shown in Fig. 6.30. This indicates that for traffic loads less than 0.2, the CSMA/CD bus shows the best performance. However for loads greater than 0.4, the CSMA/CD transfer delay increases dramatically and has an asymptote of about 0.6. This performance results from the fact that for higher throughput rates the frequency of transmission attempts during the vulnerable period of the propagation delay (denoted by a in Fig. 6.17) increases so that more and more transmission attempts end up in collisions. Consequently the transfer delay becomes longer because an increasing number of retransmissions are required.

For the token ring, the slightly higher delay compared to the CSMA/CD bus for low throughput occurs because of the access delay that a station undergoes while it is waiting for the free token to arrive on the ring. For higher transmission loads the overhead becomes insignificant and the token ring still performs very well.

Bux also presents comparisons of a slotted ring, a multilevel, multiple-access bus scheme, and a register insertion technique[49] to which the reader is

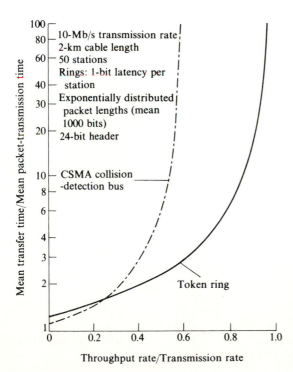

FIGURE 6.30
Comparison of the delay-throughput characteristics of token-ring and CSMA/CD-bus access methods at 10 Mb/s. (*Adapted with permission from Bux,*[48] © *1981, IEEE.*)

referred for details. In addition comparisons of token ring, slotted ring, CSMA/ CD, and register insertion access schemes have been carried out by Liu and coworkers.[50-51] These results and those of Bux are very similar.

A performance study to determine the maximum mean data rate for token rings, token buses, and CSMA/CD networks was also carried out under the sponsorship of the IEEE 802 Local Network Standards Committee.[52] Using a network with 100 stations, two types of message-arrival statistics were investigated. In the first case, only one station out of the one hundred has a message to transmit to one other station. The station is always ready to transmit; that is, as soon as it transmits it has another message waiting to be sent out. In this case it is expected that the limit on the transmission speed would be created by the station and not by the network. In the second case, every one of the 100 stations always has a message ready to transmit to another station. Although this extreme situation, in which all 100 stations are active and generating the same traffic load may never occur in practice, it sets an upper performance bound on the network so that now the network and not the station limits the maximum achievable system transmission rate.

Let us now look at this comparison. For each network, messages consist of 96 control bits and 1000 data bits. Thus the total time T_m required to transmit a message is

$$T_m = T_c + T_d \tag{6.78}$$

where T_c and T_d are the times needed to transmit the control bits and data bits, respectively.

TOKEN RING. A key parameter for the token ring is the propagation time a and the interface time T_{iR} which is the time needed at a station to detect the token and to decide whether to pass it on or hold it. This time is generally equal to one bit transmission time. When only one station is active on the token ring, the maximum mean data rate R_{max} is the reciprocal of the time required to transmit plus the time it takes the token to pass through the 99 idle stations and the active station

$$R_{max} = \frac{1}{T_m + T_{token, R}} \tag{6.79}$$

where

$$T_{token, R} = a + 100 T_{iR} \tag{6.80}$$

When all 100 stations are active, R_{max} is the reciprocal of the time required to transmit plus the time needed to pass the token to the *next* station. In this case, if the stations are equally spaced the token-passing time is $a/100$, so that

$$R_{max} = \frac{1}{T_m + T_{iR} + a/100} \tag{6.81}$$

TOKEN BUS. Unlike the token ring where the interface delay is one bit, on a token bus each station interface has to receive the entire message preamble before it can decide whether to pass the token on to the next station or to hold it for transmitting its own message. As a maximum, this interval is the time needed for a signal bit to travel from one end of the bus to the other, plus the time that a station needs to perform the associated interface signal processing. This bus interface delay T_{iB} is taken to be 4 μs.

When only one of the 100 stations on a token bus is active, the maximum mean throughput rate is the reciprocal of the time required for the station to transmit, plus the time it takes the token to pass through the 99 idle stations and the active station

$$R_{\max} = \frac{1}{T_m + T_{\text{token},B}} \tag{6.82}$$

where

$$T_{\text{token},B} = a + 100T_{iB}$$

Here a is the propagation time from one end of the bus to the other.

When all 100 stations are active, $R_{\max}$ is the reciprocal of the time needed for one station to transmit and pass the token to the next station plus the interface delay

$$R_{\max} = \frac{1}{T_m + T_{iB} + a/100} \tag{6.83}$$

CSMA/CD BUS. On a CSMA/CD bus, a station will not transmit if it senses a carrier waveform on the bus (since this indicates that another station is active). If a carrier is sensed, a station will defer transmission for a time interval called an *interframe gap* T_{if} of 9.6 μs. When a transmitting station detects a collision (a carrier waveform from another station), it stops transmitting information and sends a 48-bit jamming pattern. This pattern requires a transmission time T_{jam}. The interface delay for the CSMA/CD bus is the same as for the token bus, that is, $T_{iB} = 4$ μs.

When only one out of the 100 stations is active, each successful transmission requires a message transmission time T_m plus an interframe gap time T_{if} to allow for circuit and propagation transients. Thus the maximum mean throughput rate is

$$R_{\max} = \frac{1}{T_m + T_{if}} \tag{6.84}$$

When all 100 stations are active we have to consider a parameter called the *slot time* T_{slot}. This is a 512-bit transmission time which is the sum of the time spent by a signal to propagate from one end of the bus and back plus circuit interface transient times. Using the rule of thumb of $2e$ collisions per successful transmission, the maximum mean throughput rate is

$$R_{\max} = \frac{1}{T_m + T_{if} + (2e - 1)(T_{\text{slot}} + T_{\text{jam}})} \tag{6.85}$$

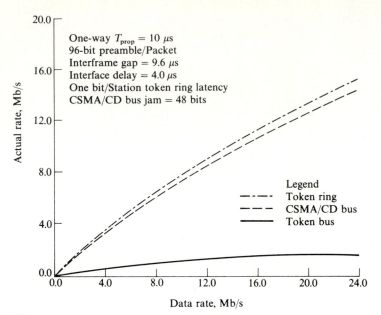

FIGURE 6.31
Comparison of maximum mean data rates versus actual transmission rate for three access schemes when one station out of 100 is active with 500-bit message lengths. (*Reproduced with permission from Stuck,*[52] © *1983, IEEE.*)

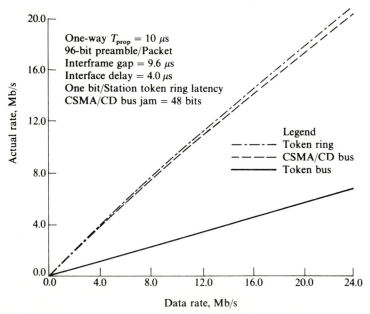

FIGURE 6.32
Comparison of maximum mean data rates versus actual transmission rate for three access schemes when one station out of 100 is active with 2000-bit message lengths. (*Reproduced with permission from Stuck,*[52] © *1983, IEEE.*)

A comparison of the three access schemes for the one-station-busy case is given in Figs. 6.31 and 6.32 for message lengths of 500 and 2000 bits, respectively. Here the abscissa represents the capacity of the medium (that is, its transmission speed), whereas the ordinate is the actual data transmission rate. In the ideal case no transmission capacity would be used for network control. This would be a straight line with unity slope. Deviations from this straight line represent the penalty resulting from using the same network to control access and to transmit messages.

Using the same parameters for all 100 stations active results in the comparison curves given in Figs. 6.33 and 6.34 for message lengths of 500 and 2000 bits, respectively. The conclusions from all of these comparisons figures are that

The token ring is the least sensitive to workload

CSMA/CD has the shortest delay under light-load conditions, but is most sensitive to variations in load when the traffic load is heavy

CSMA/CD is more sensitive to propagation effects than the token bus, whereas the token ring is the least sensitive

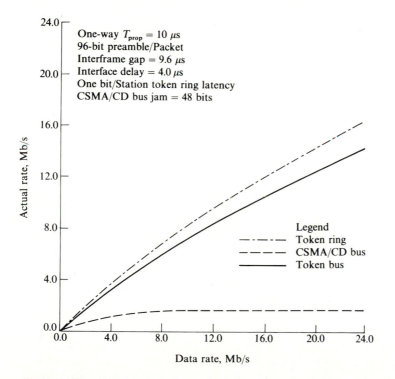

FIGURE 6.33

Comparison of maximum mean data rates versus actual transmission rate for three access schemes when all 100 stations are active with 500-bit message lengths. (*Reproduced with permission from Stuck,*[52] © *1983, IEEE.*)

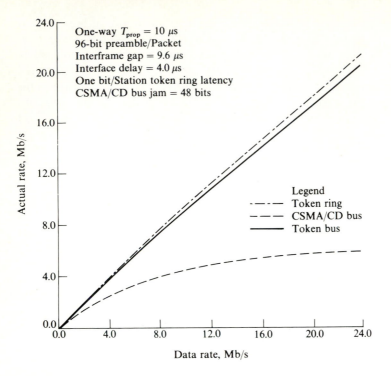

One-way $T_{prop} = 10\ \mu s$
96-bit preamble/Packet
Interframe gap $= 9.6\ \mu s$
Interface delay $= 4.0\ \mu s$
One bit/Station token ring latency
CSMA/CD bus jam $= 48$ bits

Legend
— · — · — Token ring
— — — — CSMA/CD bus
———— Token bus

FIGURE 6.34
Comparison of maximum mean data rates versus actual transmission rate for three access schemes when all 100 stations are active with 2000-bit message lengths. (*Reproduced with permission from Stuck,*[52] © *1983, IEEE.*)

6.8   SUMMARY

A wide variety of schemes for allowing stations to gain access to a local area network have been proposed, analyzed, and implemented by numerous researchers. These schemes can be broadly classified as contention methods (or random-access techniques) and deterministic (or controlled) schemes.

A classic random-access scheme is ALOHA which was used in ground-based radio networks. Although ALOHA is not a LAN, its broadcast concept is applicable to the local networking environment, and as such it is often compared to other random-access broadcast schemes used in local area networks. The evolution of random access schemes eventually led to the *carrier-sense multiple-access with collision detection* (CSMA/CD) method, which is also known as *listen while talk* (LWT). This is the basis of the popular Ethernet protocol.

Controlled access to a LAN can be carried out either in a centralized or a distributed fashion. In contrast to the stochastic nature of contention-based access methods, a controlled-access technique is a deterministic or noncontention method since it employs a specific digital signal to give only one station at a time the permission to transmit. The most common centralized-control method is known as polling. Distributed-control access methods are commonly referred to as token-controlled and can be employed in ring or bus topologies. Tokens are special bit patterns that circulate from node to node when there is no message traffic. When a station wants to send data, it removes the token from the line, sends its data, and then puts the token back into circulation so that the next station may gain access to the transmission medium.

Two key performance considerations for a LAN are the throughput or channel utilization S and the delay characteristics. Throughput is a measure of the successful traffic or the total rate of data being transmitted between nodes. This is expressed in terms of the offered load G which is the actual message load or traffic demand presented to the network. Delay is a measure of the average interval of time between when a packet is ready for transmission from a source station until its successful reception at the destination station.

PROBLEMS

Section 6.3

6.1. Using Eqs. (6.7) and (6.8), show that the maximum values of the throughput S are $(1/2e)$ at $G = 0.5$ for pure ALOHA and $1/e$ at $G = 1.0$ for slotted ALOHA.

6.2. Consider a slotted ALOHA system with a finite number of users M. Assume the M users form two groups so that M_1 of them have a throughput S_1 and $M_2 = M - M_1$ of them have a throughput S_2. Then $S = M_1 S_1 + M_2 S_2$ and $G = M_1 G_1 + M_2 G_2$.

    (a) Using Eq. (6.11) and the condition $G = 1$ for maximum throughput, find expressions for S_1 and S_2 in terms of M_1, M_2, and the offered load G_1.

    (b) For the case $M_1 = 1$ and $M_2 = 1$, show that $S_1 = G_1^2$ and $S_2 = (1 - G_1)^2$. Plot S_1, S_2, and S as a function of G_1 for values of G_1 ranging from 0 to 1.

6.3. Consider a slotted ALOHA system having four stations.

    (a) If the offered loads are $G_1 = 0.1$, $G_2 = 0.5$, $G_3 = 0.2$, and $G_4 = 0.2$ packets per second, find the individual throughput rates for each user and the total throughput.

    (b) What are the individual throughputs and the total throughput if all stations have the same offered load of 0.25 packets per second.

6.4. Show that in the limit as $M \to \infty$, Eq. (6.12) reduces to Eq. (6.8).

6.5. Verify that for $N \to \infty$ and $p \ll 1$, Eq. (6.14) reduces to Eq. (6.16).

6.6. Consider a slotted ALOHA network with 100 stations. Let $p = 0.002$ and $\alpha = 0.05$.

    (a) Plot the equilibrium-throughput curve and the load line to show that the network is stable.

    (b) Suppose we increase the number of stations to 200 and reduce p to 0.001. Keeping $\alpha = 0.05$, plot the load line for this case on the same graph as in part a.

    (c) Show that the network in part b becomes stable if we decrease α to 0.02.

Section 6.4

6.7. Verify the result given in Eq. (6.24).

6.8. The maximum achievable throughput for an access method is called the channel capacity. This is obtained by maximizing S with respect to G. Find the channel capacity for the nonslotted nonpersistent CSMA case with $a = 0.01$.

6.9. Verify the steps leading to the derivation of Eq. (6.38) for the expected value of the idle period in slotted nonpersistent CSMA.

6.10. Similar to the explanations given in the text for P_{01} and P_{11}, give the physical meaning of each of the transition probabilities shown in Fig. 6.14.

6.11. Using Eq. (E.6) from App. E, verify the expressions given for π_0 and π_1 in Eqs. (6.44) and (6.45), respectively.

6.12. Carry out the detailed arguments and analyses needed to derive the results for P_{10} and P_{11} given in Eqs. (6.47) and (6.48), respectively.

Section 6.5

6.13. Verify the steps leading from Eq. (6.52) to Eq. (6.57).

6.14. Make a graphical comparison of the throughput S as given by Eq. (6.57) for the unslotted nonpersistent CSMA/CD access method for values of $a = 0.1, 0.01, 0.001$, and 0. Choose values of G ranging from 0.1 to 100 and let $b = a$.

6.15. Consider an Ethernet system that has N stations which are always ready to transmit. (a) If each station transmits with a probability p during a contention slot, show that the probability P_A that some station acquires the channel during that slot is

$$P_A = Np(1 - p)^{N-1}$$

(b) Show that optimum value of P_A occurs for $p = 1/N$. (c) Find P_A for the cases $p = 0.25, 0.50$, and 0.75 when $N = 4$.

6.16. Before a station can successfully acquire an Ethernet channel, it must wait a mean number of slots W during a contention interval.

(a) Show that the probability that the contention interval has k slots in it is

$$P_k = P_A(1 - P_A)^k$$

where P_A is defined in Prob. 6.15.

   Note: The probability P_0 of immediate transmission or no waiting time is P_A.

(b) Show that the mean number of waiting slots per contention interval is $W = (1 - P_A)/P_A$.

6.17. Verify the expressions given for P_{10} and P_{11} in Eqs. (6.61) and (6.62), respectively.

6.18. Using Eq. (E.9) from App. E together with the relationships given in Eqs. (E.2) and (E.8), derive the expressions for π_1 and π_2 given in Eqs. (6.66) and (6.67), respectively.

6.19. The difference between CSMA/CD and CSMA is that collision detection reduces the time that a station must continue transmitting a packet once a collision has occurred. For slotted CSMA this is a full transmission period $t_p = 1$, whereas for slotted CSMA/CD this time is reduced to $(b + a)$. Thus, letting $b = 1 - a$ in Eq. (6.59), show that the result reduces to the slotted CSMA case given by Eq. (6.39).

6.20. Analogous to Fig. 6.22, plot the slotted nonpersistent CSMA/CD throughput S given by Eq. (6.59) for $a = 0.01$ and the three cases $b = a, 5a$, and $10a$. Also plot the slotted nonpersistent CSMA throughput given by Eq. (6.39) for $a = 0.01$. What are the stability ranges in each case for $\lambda = 0.6$?

Section 6.6

6.21. Consider a token-passing ring network having N stations. On the same graph, make plots of the throughput S as a function of the parameter a for values of $N = 1$, 10, and 100. Let a range from 0.01 to 100.

6.22. Consider a token-passing ring network with N stations. On the same graph plot the throughput S as a function of the number of stations N for values of the parameter $a = 0.1$ and 1.0. Let N range from 1 to 25.

6.23. A token ring transmits at a rate of 5 Mb/s. If the propagation speed on the medium is 2×10^8 m/s, how many meters of cable is a 1-bit delay at a token-ring interface equivalent to?

Section 6.7

6.24. Assume a 2-km-long token ring with 50 stations operating at a 1-Mb/s transmission rate. If the propagation delay is 5 μs/km, the header length is 24 bits, the delay per station is 1 bit, and the packet lengths are exponentially distributed with a mean length of 1000 bits, what is the mean delay time D for a traffic intensity of 0.5?

6.25. Analogous to the curves given in Figs. 6.31 and 6.32 for one active station out of 100, plot the performances of a token ring, a CSMA/CD bus, and a token bus for message lengths of 1000 bits. Use the same network parameters as given in these figures.

6.26. Analogous to the curves given in Figs. 6.33 and 6.34 for all 100 stations active, plot the performances of a token ring, a CSMA/CD bus, and a token bus for message lengths of 1000 bits. Use the same network performance parameters as given in these figures.

REFERENCES

1. N. Abramson, "The ALOHA system—Another alternative for computer communications," *AFIPS Conf. Proc., Fall Joint Computer Conf.*, vol. 37, pp. 281–285, 1970.
2. N. Abramson, "The ALOHA system," in *Computer-Communication Networks*, N. Abramson and F. Kuo (eds.), Prentice-Hall, Englewood Cliffs, NJ, 1973.
3. L. G. Roberts, "ALOHA packet system with and without slots and capture," *ACM SIGCOM Computer Commun. Rev.*, vol. 5, pp. 28–42, April 1975.
4. Y. C. Jenq, "Optimal retransmission control of slotted ALOHA systems," *IEEE Trans. Commun.*, vol. COM-29, pp. 891–895, June 1981.
5. L. Kleinrock and F. A. Tobagi, "Packet switching in radio channels: Part 1—Carrier sense multiple-access modes and their throughput-delay characteristics," *IEEE Trans. Commun.*, vol. COM-23, pp. 1400–1416, December 1975.
6. R. M. Metcalfe and D. R. Boggs, "Ethernet: Distributed packet switching for local computer networks," *Communications of the ACM*, vol. 19, pp. 395–404, July 1976.
7. S. S. Lam, "A carrier sense multiple access protocol for local networks," *Computer Networks*, vol. 4, pp. 21–32, Jan.-Feb. 1980.
8. F. A. Tobagi and V. Hunt, "Performance analysis of carrier sense multiple access with collision detection," *Computer Networks*, vol. 4, pp. 245–259, Oct.-Nov. 1980.
9. H. Kobayashi, Y. Onozato, and D. Huynh, "An approximate method for design and analysis of an ALOHA system," *IEEE Trans. Commun.*, vol. COM-25, pp. 148–157, January 1977.
10. D. Raychandhuri, "ALOHA with multipacket messages and ARQ-type retransmission protocols—throughput analysis," *IEEE Trans. Commun.*, vol. COM-32, pp. 148–154, February 1984.

11. V. C. M. Leung and R. W. Donaldson, "Effects of channel errors on the delay-throughput performance and capacity of ALOHA multiple access systems," *IEEE Trans. Commun.*, vol. COM-34, pp. 497–502, May 1986.

12. N. Abramson, "Packet switching with satellites," *1973 National Computer Conf., AFIPS Conf. Proc.*, vol. 42, pp. 695–702, 1973.

13. S. S. Lam, "Packet switching in a multi-access broadcast channel with application to satellite communications in a computer network," Ph.D. Thesis, Computer Science Dept., University of California, Los Angeles, March 1974.

14. L. Kleinrock, *Queueing Systems, Vol. 2, Computer Applications*, Wiley, New York, 1976.

15. F. A. Tobagi and L. Kleinrock, "Packet switching in radio channels: Part II—The hidden terminal problem in carrier sense multiple access and the busy-tone solution," *IEEE Trans. Commun.*, vol. COM-23, pp. 1417–1433, December 1975.

16. H. Takagi and L. Kleinrock, "Throughput analysis for persistent CSMA systems," *IEEE Trans. Commun.*, vol. COM-33, pp. 627–638, July 1985.

17. H. Takagi and L. Kleinrock, "Correction to 'Throughput analysis for persistent CSMA system'," *IEEE Trans. Commun.*, vol. COM-35, pp. 243–245, February 1987.

18. K. Sohraby, M. L. Molle, and A. N. Venetsanopoulos, "Comments on 'Throughput analysis for persistent CSMA systems'," *IEEE Trans. Commun.*, vol. COM-35, pp. 240–243, Feb. 1987.

19. G. Choudhury and S. S. Rappaport, "Priority access schemes using CSMA-CD," *IEEE Trans. Commun.*, vol. COM-33, pp. 620–626, July 1985.

20. D. P. Heyman, "The effects of random message sizes on the performance of the CSMA/CD protocol," *IEEE Trans. Commun.*, vol. COM-34, pp. 547–553, June 1986.

21. A. N. Netravali and Z. L. Budrikis, "A broadband local area network," *AT&T Tech. J.*, vol. 64, pp. 2449–2465, December 1985.

22. E. J. Coyle and B. Liu, (*a*) "A matrix representation of CSMA/CD networks," *IEEE Trans. Commun.*, vol. COM-33, pp. 53–64, Jan. 1985; (*b*) "Finite population CSMA/CD networks," *IEEE Trans. Commun.*, vol. COM-31, pp. 1247–1251, November 1983.

23. S. Tasaka, "Dynamic behavior of a CSMA-CD system with a finite population of buffered users," *IEEE Trans. Commun.*, vol. COM-34, pp. 576–586, June 1986.

24. J. S. Meditch and C. T. Lea, "Stability and optimization of the CSMA and CSMA/CD channels," *IEEE Trans Commun.*, vol. COM-31, pp. 763–774, June 1983.

25. *The Ethernet: A Local Area Network; Data Link Layer and Physical Layer Specifications*, Digital Equipment Corp., Intel Corp., and Xerox Corp., Version 2.0, November 1982.

26. (*a*) ANSI/IEEE Std. 802.3-1985, "Carrier sense multiple access with collision detection (CSMA/CD)," 1985.
    (*b*) ANSI/IEEE Std. 802.3*a*, *b*, *c*, *e*—1988, "Supplements to Carrier Sense Multiple Access with Collision Detection (CSMA/CD)," 1988.

27. J. L. Hammond and P. J. P. O'Reilly, *Local Computer Networks*, Addison-Wesley, Reading, MA, 1986.

28. D. Bertsekas and R. Gallager, *Data Networks*, Prentice-Hall, Englewood Cliffs, NJ, 1987.

29. R. L. Rivest, *Network Control by Bayesian Broadcast*, Report MIT/LCS/TM-285, MIT, Laboratory for Computer Science, Cambridge, MA, 1985.

30. A. S. Tanenbaum, *Computer Networks*, Prentice-Hall, Englewood Cliffs, NJ, 1981.

31. W. Stallings, *Data and Computer Communications*, Macmillan, New York, 1985.

32. M. Schwartz, *Telecommunication Networks*, Addison-Wesley, Reading, MA, 1987.

33. A. G. Konheim and B. Meister, "Waiting lines and times in a system with polling," *Journal of the ACM*, vol. 21, pp. 470–490, July 1974.

34. W. D. Farmer and E. E. Newhall, "An experimental distributed switching system to handle bursty computer traffic," *Proc. ACM Symp. on Prob. in the Optimization of Data Commun. Systems*, pp. 1–34, Pine Mountain, Georgia, October 1969.

35. B. K. Penny and A. A. Baghdadi, "Survey of computer communications loop networks, Parts 1 and 2," *Computer Commun.*, vol. 2, pp. 165–180, August 1979; vol. 2, pp. 224–241, September 1979.

36. (*a*) N. C. Strole, "A local communications network based on interconnected token-access rings: A tutorial," *IBM J. Res. Develop.*, vol. 27, pp. 481–496, September 1983.

(*b*) N. C. Strole, "The IBM token-ring network—A functional overview," *IEEE Network*, vol. 1, pp. 23–30, January 1987.

37. H. J. Keller, H. Meyr, and H. R. Mueller, "Transmission design criteria for a synchronous token ring," *IEEE J. Select. Areas Commun.*, vol. SAC-1, pp. 721–733, November 1983.

38. W. Bux, F. H. Closs, K. Kuemmerle, H. J. Keller, and H. R. Mueller, "Architecture and design of a reliable token-ring network," *IEEE J. Select. Areas Commun.*, vol. SAC-1, pp. 756–765, November 1983.

39. F. E. Ross, "Fiber Distributed Data Interface (FDDI)—A tutorial," *IEEE Commun. Mag.*, vol. 24, pp. 10–17, May 1986.

40. ANSI/IEEE Standard 802.5-1985, "Token Ring Access Method," 1985.

41. W. Stallings, "Local network performance," *IEEE Commun. Mag.*, vol. 22, pp. 27–36, February 1984.

42. ANSI/IEEE Std. 802.4-1985, "Token-passing bus access method," 1985.

43. C. W. Tseng and B. U. Chen, "D-Net, a new scheme for high data rate optical local area networks," *IEEE J. Select. Areas Commun.*, vol. SAC-1, pp. 493–499, April 1983.

44. D. P. Heyman, "Data-transport performance analysis of Fasnet," *Bell Sys. Tech. J.*, vol. 62, pp. 2547–2560, October 1983.

45. J. O. Limb and C. Flores, "Description of Fasnet—A unidirectional local-area communications network," *Bell Sys. Tech. J.*, vol. 61, pp. 1413–1440, September 1982.

46. F. A. Tobagi, F. Borgonovo, and L. Fratta, "Expressnet: A high-performance integrated-services local area network," *IEEE J. Select. Areas Commun.*, vol. SAC-1, pp. 898–913, November 1983.

47. M. Gerla, C. Yeh, and P. Rodrigues, "Token protocol for high-speed fiber optic local networks," *Proc. 6th OSA/IEEE Opt. Fiber Commun. Conf.*, Paper WF6, pp. 88–89, New Orleans, Feb. 28–Mar. 2 1983.

48. W. Bux, "Local area subnetworks: A performance comparison," *IEEE Trans. Commun.*, vol. COM-29, pp. 1465–1473, October 1981.

49. W. Bux and M. Schlatter, "An approximate method for the performance analysis of buffer insertion rings," *IEEE Trans. Commun.*, vol. COM-31, pp. 50–55, January 1983.

50. M. T. Liu, W. Hilal, and B. H. Groomes, "Performance evaluation of channel-access protocols for local computer networks," *Proc. COMPCON Fall '82*, pp. 417–426, Washington, DC, 1982, IEEE Catalog No. 82CH1796-2.

51. W. Hilal and M. T. Liu, "Analysis and simulation of the register-insertion protocol," *Proc. IEEE Computer Networking Symp.*, Gaithersburg, MD, December 1982.

52. B. W. Stuck, "Calculating the maximum mean data rate in local area networks," *Computer*, vol. 16, pp. 72–76, May 1983.

CHAPTER
7

NETWORK INTERCONNECTIONS

A local area network as an isolated entity by itself has limited potential and usefulness. For example, the maximum number of stations attached to a LAN may be bounded for technical reasons or performance considerations, and the geographical coverage of a LAN is also restricted. What is desired is an ability for users to share not only resources that belong to their own local area network, but also to access devices, mainframes, services, and users on other networks. The concept for achieving this is known as *internetting* and effectively creates a single large loosely coupled network from many different local and wide-area networks.[1–9] The large network is generally known as an *internet* or as an *extended* LAN.

The three basic interconnections of networks are

1. Connections between homogeneous local area networks
2. Connections between heterogeneous local area networks[8]
3. Connections of a local area network to a long-haul public network (wide-area network)[9]

In the first case, geographically dispersed segments of the same network may need to be connected. This could be done by either directly connecting the

LANS to each other, or by means of telecommunication land lines, microwave links, satellite links, or a combination thereof. Interconnections among heterogeneous networks are needed when users or devices in different organizations or in different department networks in the same organization are required to communicate with one another. An example of this is a user attached to an Ethernet LAN desiring access to devices connected to an independently operating IBM SNA-based network. The third interconnection, that is, between a local area network and a long-haul public network provides a user with access to other computer or communication elements all over the world. Examples of this are local area network connections to Telenet or Arpanet.

Since no two types of networks are designed identically, a variety of questions and problems arise when attempting to interconnect not only different LANs but also homogeneous LANs. Thus in this chapter we shall first examine the general interconnection problem, and then we shall analyze implementation issues for routing and controlling the flow of packets from one LAN to another. The latter is of particular importance when different speed networks are interconnected.

7.1 INTERCONNECTION ISSUES

The basic task involved in setting up an interconnection between local area networks is to provide the hardware and software that will allow stations on the two networks to conveniently and efficiently communicate with each other. Devices that interconnect different LANs are known as *relays* and may operate at one of several layers in the OSI model. The terms we will use here and the layers at which they operate are as follows:

1. A *repeater* which operates at the physical link layer
2. A *bridge* interconnecting LANs at the data-link layer
3. A *router* functioning at the network layer
4. *Gateways* which handle higher-level internet protocols

This terminology is fairly standard but not universal. For example, the term *gateway* is often used when discussing a router, and it may also refer to a bridge in the literature.

The relationship of these devices to the OSI model and their related protocols are shown in Fig. 7.1. In this chapter we will address the functions of bridges and repeaters. Before we go into the details on them, let us look at some general internetworking issues. For this purpose only, we shall generically refer to any of these devices as a *gateway*.

A gateway may simply appear as a host node to each network. The gateway accepts messages from the sending (or intermediate) network, translates them from one network-protocol hierarchy to another, and then forwards these newly formatted messages to the receiving (or the next intermediate) network.

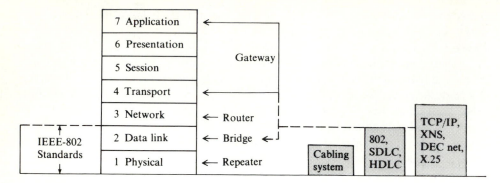

FIGURE 7.1
Relationships of repeaters, bridges, routers, and gateways to the OSI Reference Model.

The question of who owns, operates, and maintains the gateway often arises, particularly when the two networks belong to independent organizations. For this reason each network often operates a *half-gateway*, with the two halves being connected by a transmission line as is shown in Fig. 7.2. Each network is thus responsible only for mapping its own network-dependent protocol to and from a standard internetwork protocol. Since the software of a half-gateway is closely related to the software of its associated local area network, it may be possible to include the device in one of the host computers, thereby avoiding the need for a special independent piece of equipment.

The fundamental issue concerning network interconnection is deciding among alternative methods for translating and forwarding messages in such a way that the gateways are functionally simple, efficient, flexible, and do not require changes in the architecture of any of the network segments being connected. Some of the major considerations that gateway designers are confronted with are the following:

1. *Datagrams versus virtual circuits.* As we noted in Chap. 2, individual networks may provide either a datagram (connectionless) service or a higher-level virtual-circuit (connection-oriented) service. These types of interfaces are related since a virtual circuit interface is usually implemented within a network by the use of datagrams. Local area networks are usually based on a datagram service, whereas long-haul networks tend to use virtual-circuit connections. If there is a datagram-to-virtual-circuit interface, the task of the internet can be significantly simplified if it is required to only transport independent, individually addressed datagrams without having to maintain the connection state needed to support virtual circuits.

2. *Naming, addressing, and routing.* Names, addresses, and routes are three important and distinct concepts in an internetting environment.[4] A *name* identifies some resource (such as a process, device, or service), an *address* indicates the location of the resource, and a *route* specifies a path from the sender to

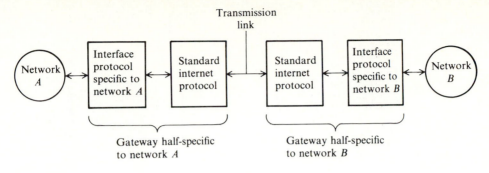

FIGURE 7.2
Gateways represented as two parts, with half belonging to each network they interconnect.

the receiver. In an internet, each of these entities represents a tighter binding of information; that is, names are mapped into addresses, and addresses are mapped into routes. This hierarchy is also used in error recovery which successively falls back to first find an alternate route, then an alternate address, and then an alternate name.

To implement routing, a decision-making algorithm is used to determine the next node a packet will visit on its way through the network. This can be achieved by means of a routing table in each station and gateway that gives, for each possible destination network, the next gateway to which the internetted packet should be sent. Both static (fixed) and adaptive (dynamic) routing strategies exist. In a static method, the same single route is always used to send messages from a given source to a given destination. The route taken by messages in an adaptive strategy does not remain fixed, but changes dynamically as a function of prevailing network conditions. Adaptive strategies are generally used since almost all networks are subject to failures, modifications, and growth.

3. *Fragmentation and reassembly.* Fragmentation[10–11] arises when a gateway connects two networks that have different maximum and/or minimum packet sizes, or when it connects a network that transmits packets with one that transmits messages. Some typical examples of maximum packet lengths are:

a. Arpanet: 1008 bits
b. X.25: generally limited to 1024 bits although packets as long as 8192 bits are permitted
c. Xerox's PUP: 532 bytes
d. Ethernet: 1500 bytes

Since the data units that are transmitted have different sizes, larger units must be broken up (fragmented) and sent as multiple smaller units. These units are then reassembled either at the ultimate destination or at an intermediate gateway, as shown in Fig. 7.3. However, since the reassembly point must have sufficient buffer space to allow for storage of data-unit fragments belonging to

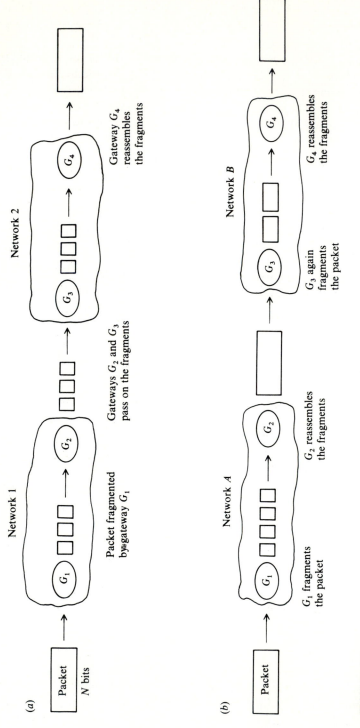

FIGURE 7.3
Fragmentation and reassembly of packets in an internetting environment. (*a*) Packets are fragmented at the first gateway (G_1) and reassembled only at the ultimate destination (G_4). (*b*) Packets are also reassembled and refragmented at intermediate gateways.

the same message, it is generally easier to reassemble the fragments at the ultimate destination. This not only eliminates the need for large buffers at the gateways, but also allows the use of dynamic routing which is otherwise inhibited.

4. *Flow control and congestion control.* The terms *flow control* and *congestion control* are often confused although they refer to two different situations. Flow control is concerned with regulating the flow of messages between a specific source-and-destination pair, so that the source does not send data at a greater rate than the receiver is able to process. In an internet architecture, the responsibility of flow control belongs to the end-to-end protocols. Internet congestion control, on the other hand, is a network-wide mechanism. It is concerned with ensuring that the gateways are not burdened with excessive message traffic. This task is related to internet routing strategies and may involve the rejection of messages by a gateway.

5. *Security.*[12] Since a great deal of information passing through a network may contain proprietary information, internetting can employ encryption to guarantee security of the information being transmitted. This would generally be done at the end process, since otherwise the internet would become rather complex and, in addition, users who are sensitive about the content of their messages would tend not to trust encryption being done exclusively in a gateway. However, the gateway may contain the ability to perform user authentication and access control to protect the networks from unauthorized traffic. Security is addressed separately in Chap. 9.

7.2 BRIDGES

A bridge interconnects two or more LANs (either similar or dissimilar) at the media-access level of the data-link layer, and hence is also called a media-access-control (MAC)-level bridge. The interconnected individual LANs (which are known as *segments*) form what is called a *bridged local network*. The bridge filters or forwards traffic between two electrically independent cable systems attached to it. Because of the high demand for bridges, the IEEE 802 committee has developed two standards to ensure that LANs which are extended by bridges exhibit consistent characteristics.[13-19] The first, which forms Part D of IEEE Standard 802.1, defines a bridge for connecting LAN segments based on any of the IEEE-802 MAC specifications. The second, which is an additional chapter to the 1985 version of IEEE Standard 802.5, defines a bridge that is designed specifically to interconnect token-ring LANs. Bridges that interconnect 802-type local area networks (including Ethernet) directly are called *local bridges*. Bridges in which one or more ports interface to long-haul backbone networks are known as *remote bridges*.

By definition, bridges must operate entirely within the data-link layer (as is shown in Fig. 7.4). Thus if a bridge is to be inserted between two existing LANs, to work correctly for current stations it should not require additional data-link

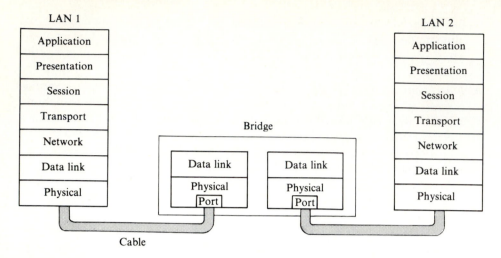

FIGURE 7.4
Bridges between two LANs function at the data-link layer.

headers or additional actions by the stations. To see what information is available in the data-link protocol, let us look at the IEEE-802 standards. As we saw in Chap. 2, the IEEE-802 data-link protocol is divided into two sublayers, the media-access control (MAC) sublayer and the logical link control (LLC) sublayer.

In the MAC sublayers, the services vary depending on which medium access methodology (CSMA/CD, token bus, or token ring) is used. What we need for the bridge to function properly is a generic protocol field that is used by all the MAC sublayers. The only common ones which the bridge can utilize are the source and destination address fields. Care must be taken here to ensure that each station on a bridged local area network has its own unique address; that is, two stations on different LANs cannot have the same address.

As we see from Fig. 2.20, the services provided by the IEEE-802 LLC sublayer are independent of the specific MAC sublayer underneath it. The LLC sublayer provides two types of services. Type 1 is the datagram or connectionless protocol. Here the protocol fields specify service access points and message type. Since these fields are only meaningful to the source and destination stations, they do not give any information to a bridge. Type 2 service encompasses the virtual-circuit or connection-oriented protocols, which provide synchronization, sequential delivery, and error recovery. Here again the fields are specific to a data-link connection and are of no interest to a bridge. Hence it is at the MAC level that bridging is implemented.

Two routing algorithms have been proposed for a bridged LAN environment.[20-21] One is based on dynamically creating a *spanning tree topology*[13,14,22] (also referred to as a *transparent bridge*) and the other takes a *source routing approach.*[22-29] Let us look at these separately.

7.2.1 Transparent or Spanning Tree Bridges

The transparent bridge concept has been selected by the IEEE 802.1 Committee as the standard for interconnecting 802-type LANs. Figure 7.5 shows a flow process for the bridge routing operation. The two main processes are known as *bridge forwarding* and *bridge learning*.

BRIDGE FORWARDING. When a frame is received on a bridge port, the destination address in the frame header is compared to the information contained in a forwarding database. This database contains a list of group and individual station addresses together with information that relates these addresses to one or more of the bridge ports. Note that this information pertains to both source and destination addresses. If the destination address is not in the forwarding database, it is sent out on all ports of the bridge except the one on which the frame was received (called port x in Fig. 7.5). This process is known as *flooding*.

  When the destination address exists in the forwarding database, the port identifier of the stored address is compared with the identifier of the port on which the address was received (port x). If the two identifiers are equal, the frame is not forwarded since it is addressed to a station on the same LAN in which it originated. When the port identifiers are different, the frame is forwarded to the bridge port associated with the address as listed in the forwarding database.

  As an example, consider the network topology shown in Fig. 7.6. Frames sent between stations A and B are discarded by bridge 1 since both stations exist on the same LAN. If station A sends a frame to station C, bridge 1 forwards the frame but bridge 2 discards it (assuming station C is listed in the forwarding database of both bridges). Frames sent from any station on LAN 1 to a station on LAN 3 are forwarded by both bridges. Now suppose station A sends a frame to station H, which is not listed in the forwarding database of bridge 1. This frame is then sent out on ports 2, 3, and 4 of bridge 1.

BRIDGE LEARNING. This takes care of the destination address. Now let us consider actions taken on the source address. These are shown in the *bridge learning box* in Fig. 7.5. When a frame is received at a bridge, its source address is compared against the information residing in the forwarding database. If the source address is not found there, the bridge makes a new entry to the database. This entry consists of the address, the identifier of the port on which the address was received, and a timer value indicating when the address arrived.

  If the address already exists in the database, but it has a different port identifier associated with it, then the entry is modified to account for this new information. No change is made if the information is the same. However, in all cases the timer is reset to indicate that this is an updated entry. When the timer for a particular entry expires, the address information is removed from the database. The timer length can be set by network management and is typically on the order of a few minutes. This action thus removes the addresses of inactive stations or those which have moved to another location.

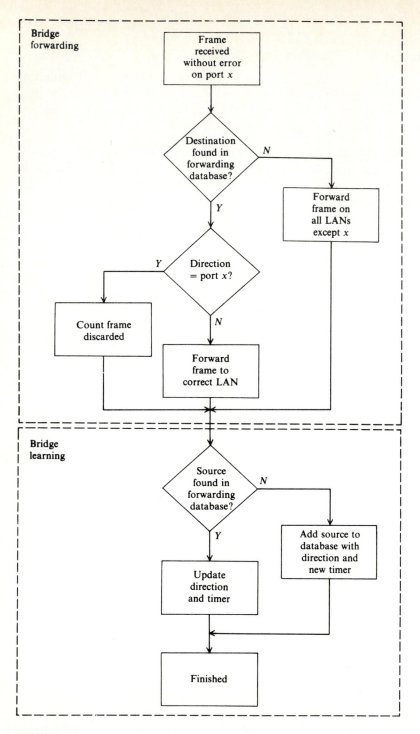

FIGURE 7.5
Logical flow for bridge forwarding and bridge learning in a spanning-tree algorithm. (*Reproduced with permission from Backes,*[13] © *1988, IEEE.*)

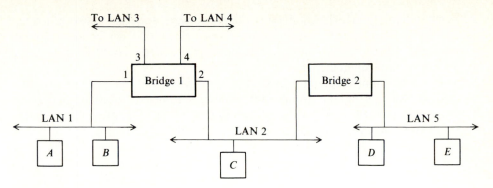

FIGURE 7.6
General topology for bridges connecting LANs.

SPANNING TREE ALGORITHM. For these forwarding and learning processes to operate properly, there must be only one path of bridges and LANs between any two segments in the entire bridged LAN. Such a topology is known as a *spanning tree* and the methodology for setting it up is called the *spanning tree algorithm*. The need for this topology can be seen by examining Fig. 7.7. Here there are redundant bridges between LANs to provide for higher overall

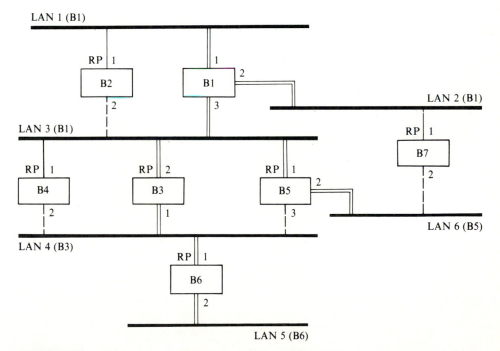

FIGURE 7.7
Topological example of a spanning tree (designated by double solid lines). The single solid lines represent forwarding states and the dashed lines are blocked states.

network reliability. However, if multiple paths were to exist between LANs, packet loops could result and the learning process would get confused about where an end station exists since the same source address could come in to a bridge on several different ports.

For a spanning tree algorithm to work properly, each bridge must have a unique identifier, a unique group address that is received by all bridges on a LAN must exist, and each port within a bridge must have its own distinct identity (called a *port identifier*). To calculate the spanning tree, first a root bridge is selected. Then each bridge selects a port through which the least-cost path to the root bridge is found. This is called a *root port*. A specific *designated bridge* is then chosen for each LAN. Finally each bridge puts its root port and all bridge ports to LANs for which it is designated into a *forwarding* state. The other bridge ports are said to be in a *blocked* state.

As an example, we again look at Fig. 7.7. Here bridge 1 is chosen as the root bridge and it is also the designated bridge for LANs 1, 2, and 3. The selected root ports for each bridge are also shown in the figure. These are identified by the letters RP. The designated bridge for each LAN is given in parentheses next to the name of each LAN (e.g., bridge 3 is the designated bridge for LAN 4). Note that by definition bridge 1 has no root port.

The spanning tree for the network in Fig. 7.7 is shown by the double solid lines connecting bridges and LANs. The single solid lines represent bridge ports in the forwarding state, whereas the dashed lines indicate bridge ports in the blocked state.

When the network is in operation, the spanning tree algorithm exchanges status information between bridges via messages called *bridge protocol data units* (BPDUs). The root bridge typically transmits these BPDUs every 1 to 4 seconds. A designated bridge sends out a BPDU on each of the designated bridge ports every time a BPDU is received on its root port. The BPDUs also allow the network to reconfigure itself in case of topology changes. For example, if bridge 5 were to fail, it would stop sending BPDUs. This would be recognized by bridge 7, which would then take over as the designated bridge for LAN 6 once a designated timer had expired.

7.2.2 Source Routing Bridges

In source routing the transmitter, or source, of the frame specifies which route the frame is to follow. Hence the term *source routing*. The concept of source routing applies to any type of network, not just local area networks. Furthermore, although the major standardization activity has been for token rings, source routing applies to many types of LANs including token rings, token buses, and CSMA/CD buses.

The source routing algorithm operates dynamically. To find a route to a given destination, the source sends out a *discovery* frame which is broadcast over the entire bridged LAN. These frames will thus travel through all possible paths between the source and destination stations. Along the way, each frame records the route it takes. Upon reaching the destination, all the route discovery frames will be returned to the source along the recorded path. The source can then choose which route to use.

Whereas transparent bridges do not modify a frame, a source-routing bridge adds a routing information field to the frame as shown in Fig. 7.8. This field is added immediately after the source address in every frame sent to the destination station. The routing information field can be up to 18 octets in length. It consists of a two-octet routing control (RC) field and a variable number of route designator fields, each of which is two octets long and contains a LAN segment number and a bridge number.

The presence of a routing information field is indicated by a 1 in the most significant bit of the source address in a frame. The bit fields in the routing control segment have the following meaning:

$B =$ broadcast. These bits, when not all zero, indicate that the frame is destined for all rings.

$r =$ reserved (for future use).

$L =$ length. This indicates the total length of the routing information field in octets.

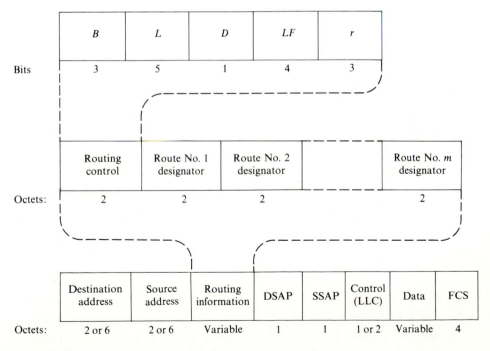

FIGURE 7.8
Frame format for source routing.

D = direction. This tells a bridge whether a frame is coming from or going to the originating station.

LF = largest frame. This field is altered by the bridge on broadcast frames to indicate the largest frame supported by the bridge and the outgoing LAN.

The 16-bit route-designator fields indicate the path between nodes on different physical rings.

7.2.3 Quality of Bridge Services

Since bridging is performed at the MAC layer, the quality of service offered by a bridge should match that of a single local area network. Parameters that define the quality of service include availability, frame mishaps, transit delay, frame lifetime, undetected bit errors, frame size, and priority. Let us briefly look at each of these.

AVAILABILITY. Since the MAC layer does not guarantee delivery of frames, a bridging scheme should minimize any additional unintended frame loss. This is particularly important since higher-level protocols which are designed to guarantee end-to-end integrity usually do not tolerate high frame-loss rates.

FRAME MISHAPS. The bridging scheme should not misorder or duplicate frames of a given service class. Thus the bridging protocol must make sure that multiple paths do not exist. This also means that if new bridges are inserted into the topology, frames may need to be discarded for a limited time to guarantee that they are not duplicated.

TRANSIT TIME. Processing times required by the forwarding and filtering functions cause delays in the transit times of frames. If frames arrive at bridges faster than the processing rate, congestion of links and bridges occurs and frames may be lost unintentionally. Thus care must be taken to properly match the frame arrival rates from a particular link with the processing rate of the local bridge.

FRAME LIFETIME. If frames exist in the network beyond a maximum transit time, a bridge may have to discard them. This is necessary so that higher-level protocols can attempt retransmission with some degree of confidence that duplicate frames are not generated. The bridge system management should thus have some type of forehand knowledge of maximum frame lifetime.

ERROR RATE. The MAC layer provides a very low undetected bit error rate by means of the frame check sequence (FCS) incorporated into a frame. Thus a bridge should discard frames having an incorrect FCS. Also, depending on the MAC scheme, a bridge may need to recalculate the FCS. Since this can lead to further errors, additional frame integrity checks may be necessary within a bridge.

FRAME SIZE. Since different LANs support different maximum frame sizes, a bridge should not attempt to forward a frame which is too big for the next LAN to handle.

PRIORITY. The MAC layer supports the ability of certain frames to have priority relative to other frames sent from the same source address. A bridge may use this priority to determine the order in which frames are forwarded.

7.3 ROUTERS

In contrast to a bridge, the router is not transparent to user protocols. It operates at the network layer where there are protocols such as the DoD Internet Protocol (IP), DNA, XNS, and ISO 8473. A router terminates the MAC and LLC layers of each connected LAN and permits translation between different address domains. Thus routers are used when interfacing 802-type LANs to other networks such as DECnet, XNS, SNA-based networks from IBM, and wide area networks. Because there is a higher protocol-processing overhead, a router generally has a lower throughput than a bridge. However, it provides more efficient routing and flow control than a bridge, since it operates at the network level and can exploit the traffic management procedures which are part of that level.[30–31]

A router offers more sophisticated services than a bridge, since it can select one of many different possible paths to forward a packet. This decision can be based on parameters such as transit delay, congestion at other routers, or the number of routers between the source and destination stations.

To compare bridges and routers, let us look at the same quality-of-service parameters presented in Sec. 7.2.3.

AVAILABILITY. Since a router can readily choose different paths for forwarding packets, it is able to handle failures in links, stations, and other routers.

FRAME MISHAPS. Routers can tolerate misordered or duplicate packets.

TRANSIT TIME. Since it provides a high availability of network routes, a router will introduce transit delay owing to the additional processing overhead associated with the network-layer processing. The network designer should try to keep this delay to a minimum when implementing a router.

FRAME LIFETIME. Packet lifetimes are usually specified within each packet and are typically an integral part of a network-layer specification. Routers attempt to reduce the number of undeliverable or duplicate packets in a network by discarding packets having an expired lifetime. Thus no a priori knowledge of packet lifetime is needed by the router, since this information is contained in each packet.

ERROR RATE. Network layers have error-checking algorithms that examine each received packet. These checks are done either on the entire packet or on the network-layer header only. Erroneous packets are discarded. Since this service is done in addition to the lower-level FCS, it further reduces the probability of undetected bit errors.

FRAME SIZE. As we saw in Fig. 7.3, routers can perform fragmentation on packets from one network that are too large for another network. This property eliminates the need for negotiation of maximum transmitted packet sizes or the discarding of packets that are larger than an attached network can handle.

PRIORITY. Some network protocols also support a high-priority packet delivery service. These urgent packets can be placed ahead of lower-priority traffic on transmit queues. Routing control information is an example of high-priority traffic, since it may contain important control information needed by other routers or host systems on a network.

7.4   FLOW AND CONGESTION CONTROL

The routing procedures discussed above have no direct control over how much traffic is permitted to enter the network. This is the task of flow and congestion control.[32] Their goal is to regulate the amount of data admitted to the network in such a way that resources (for example, logical channels, buffers, transmission bandwidth, processor time, etc.) are efficiently utilized and user performance requirements are met at the same time. This is very critical since in an uncontrolled network there is unrestricted competition for network resources. Problems of inefficiency, unfairness, and congestion can then arise.[33–35]

The term *flow control* refers to the regulation of traffic on an individual connection between a source and a destination station. Thus the flow control procedure is carried out in the source and destination hosts, with the possible participation of intermediate nodes along the path. The main goal of flow control is to prevent overflow of the buffers dedicated to an individual connection.

Congestion control refers to a more global procedure which is exercised by network components such as bridges and routers to prevent network congestion. The controlling action may be applied to many source-destination pairs indiscriminately or simultaneously.

Congestion control in a network consisting of numerous LANs and WANs connected by bridges and/or routers is particularly challenging. For example, there would be a dramatic bandwidth mismatch if network segments consisting of a 10-Mb/s Ethernet, a 100-Mb/s fiber distributed data interface (FDDI), and a 56-kb/s WAN were interconnected. In this case the router would be a major congestion point in the network.

Even if the network consists of similar LANs interconnected by bridges, the load may be unbalanced among the different LANs. Although the MAC layer can effectively control congestion in a single LAN (e.g., round-robin access in token rings and buses, and binary backoff in CSMA/CD schemes), it cannot extend this control from one LAN to another.

7.4.1 Traffic Control Functions

Network operation becomes *inefficient* when resources are wasted. The two network resources that are most commonly wasted are communications capacity and storage capacity. One way this can occur is when a conflicting demand by two or more users ties up the access channel with colliding messages. Inefficiency also arises when some user acquires more resources than are needed, thus preventing their utilization by others. For example, as shown in Fig. 7.9, a high-speed source feeding a low-capacity line can create a backlog of packets in the network thereby preventing other traffic from getting through. Here all nodes are first assumed to be silent. Then let node A, which can send out data at a rate of 100 units per second, transmit to node C. Because of the mismatches between line speeds along the path, the buffer at the intermediate node B is quickly filled. Node D is thereby prevented from transmitting until node A has finished.

The example given in Fig. 7.9 also shows that *unfairness* arises from uncontrolled competition of resources. The relative position of a user in the network or the particular selection of network and traffic parameters may result in one user capturing more resources than other users, thus having an unfair advantage for use of the network.

The third problem of *congestion* is a direct result of resource wastage in an uncontrolled network. A network is defined to be congested if an increment of externally offered traffic causes a decrease in effective throughput. An extreme case of congestion results in a *deadlock*. This occurs when each user in the network has acquired part but not all of the resources necessary to complete a task and does not want to release them, while waiting for the remaining resources to

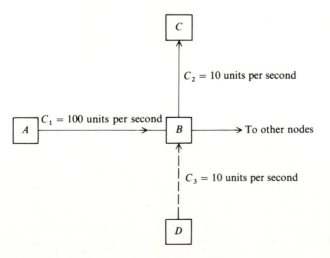

FIGURE 7.9
Competition for resources in an uncontrolled network.

become free. However, since all resources are tied up a deadlock develops and the throughput drops to zero because no task can be completed.

A network can be protected from these types of problems through the implementation of a set of flow and congestion control protocols. We note here that throughput efficiency (expressed in packets per second) is a common quantitative measure of network performance.[22] Careful consideration must be given to the design of flow and congestion control methods, since their requirements for resource reservation together with channel and processor overhead result in a loss in throughput efficiency.

A trade-off between the gain in efficiency, which is due to controls, and the loss in efficiency owing to overhead and resource sharing, is illustrated quantitatively in Fig. 7.10 which shows effective throughput as a function of offered load. Perfect control with no overhead is represented by the curve labeled "ideal." Here throughput increases linearly with the offered load until the maximum theoretical network throughput is reached. Overhead requirements cause the throughput values in an actual system to be lower than the ideal curve. In the uncontrolled case the throughput follows the ideal curve for low offered loads, but degrades quickly to a very low value for high offered loads. If the throughput curve reaches zero, the network is deadlocked. Referring to Fig. 7.10, the network is generally said to be congested when it operates in the region of negative slope.

7.4.2   Traffic Control Modeling

As we noted earlier, traffic control can be applied either on a local basis or by means of a global end-to-end process. However, local control is not by itself sufficient to prevent congestion in a network, so that end-to-end congestion control is necessary to throttle input to the network before saturation is reached.

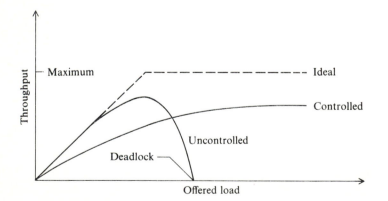

FIGURE 7.10
Comparisons of flow control methods. The network is congested when it operates in the region of negative slope.

A variety of models for flow and congestion control have been considered[34-44] and to some extent validated by simulation and experience. As an example of one of these schemes, let us examine the flow-control simulation carried out by Bux and Grillo[42] on interconnected token-ring LANs. The network topology used in this study is shown in Fig. 7.11. Here several token rings are interconnected through bridges with a backbone token ring serving to interconnect the bridges. The rings follow the operations specified in the ECMA-89 and IEEE-802 Standards[44-46] (see Chap. 2).

Two different kinds of token-ring operation were studied by Bux and Grillo. First the *nonpriority mode* assumes that all stations and the bridges operate at the same ring-access priority level and are only allowed to transmit one frame per token. In the other kind of the operation, the *priority mode*, the bridges operate at a higher ring-access priority level. Here stations transmit only one frame per token, but bridges are allowed to seize the low-priority token, if available, or make a reservation for high-priority access. Once the bridge has the token, it can transmit continuously until its transmit buffer has been emptied. Priority access is only used on the local rings; on the backbone ring each bridge transmits only a single frame per token.

The bridges shown in Fig. 7.11 must be able to provide a high throughput from ring to ring at reasonable costs. To meet these requirements the bridge functions must be simple, thus excluding them from doing any complex flow control or error control. Because of this, when the network becomes momentarily congested, the bridges simply discard packets that they cannot handle. In the

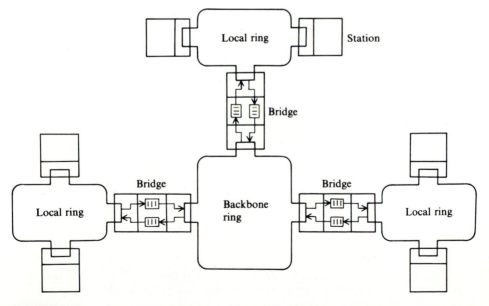

FIGURE 7.11
Network topology for interconnected token-ring LANs. (*Reproduced with permission from Bux and Grillo,*[42] © *1985, IEEE.*)

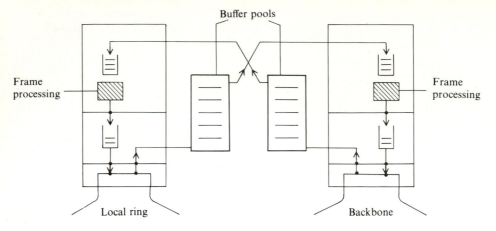

Buffer pools

Frame processing

Frame processing

Local ring

Backbone

FIGURE 7.12
General model of a bridge. (*Reproduced with permission from Bux and Grillo,*[42] © *1985, IEEE.*)

architecture considered here, these discarded packets will be recovered by means of a Type-2 IEEE-802.2 logical-link-control (LLC) end-to-end protocol.[47]

A general schematic model of a bridge is shown in Fig. 7.12. Frames of information are stored in buffers until they can be transmitted on the local or backbone ring. Separate buffer pools are used for each direction of data flow. The separate buffer pools are controlled by independent processors, each of which is modeled as a single server that processes all frames on a first-come-first-served basis.

Let us now look at the characteristics of the stations connected to the network shown in Fig. 7.11. A schematic representation of a station is depicted in Fig. 7.13. Starting at the top in this figure, a traffic source in the sending station represents an application. At the receiving station there is a corresponding message sink. Data units that are provided by users of the LLC service are transmitted in the form of information frames, or I frames. When the total number of I frames and data units being handled by the LLC reaches a threshold value B, a subsequent data unit supplied by a higher-layer entity is not accepted. This data unit together with all further units belonging to the same message are then queued by the higher-layer entity. Simultaneously, no additional messages are generated. When the LLC service can again accept data, the queued units are handled first and the application then resumes generation of new messages.

Flow control in this topology is carried out by means of a *window mechanism*. A sender is allowed to transmit up to a fixed number W (the window size) of I frames without having to wait for an acknowledgment. This acknowledgment is in the form of a receive-ready (RR) frame that is transmitted back for each successfully received I frame. The receiver returns a reject (REJ) frame if the frame sequence number is not the one that is expected. All further I frames

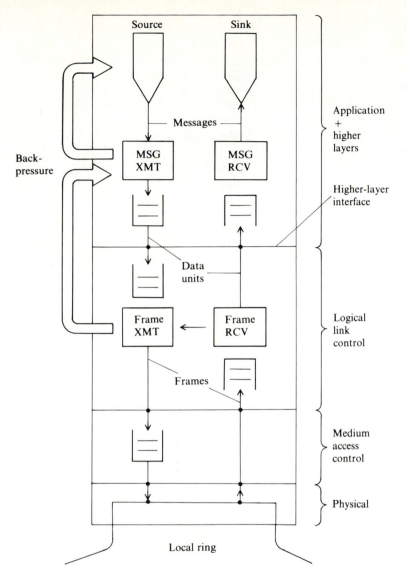

FIGURE 7.13
Conceptual representation of a user station. (*Reproduced with permission from Bux and Grillo,*[42] ©
1985, IEEE.)

are then rejected until the expected one arrives. When the source receives a REJ
frame, it retransmits all I frames starting with the expected number denoted
within the REJ frame.

The model used to evaluate the flow control was the RESQ2 simulation
tool.[48] The values of some of the main simulation parameters are listed in Table
7.1. The two basic performance measures were throughput and end-to-end delay.

TABLE 7.1

Main simulation parameters used for the token-ring analysis

Parameter	Value
Local ring transmission rate	4 Mb/s
Backbone transmission rates	4 or 16 Mb/s
Frame processing time in bridge	300 μs
Bridge buffer size	4 kbytes
Maximum I field length	0.5 kbytes
Framing overhead of I frames	24 bytes
Mean message length	1 kbyte
Processing times	
(*a*) Transmit I frame	2.0 ms
(*b*) Transmit RR frame	2.5 ms
(*c*) Receive RR frame and delete I frame(s)	0.75 ms
Backpressure threshold value B	$W + 4$

These were both measured at the higher-layer interface since data units are delivered there without errors and in the proper sequence.

Let us first look at the simulation results for the nonpriority mode of operation. The network configuration that was examined is shown in Fig. 7.14. There are 12 stations attached to each ring. Each station is assumed to generate the same amount of traffic and to be logically connected to a station on a different ring. The flow of I-frame traffic is bidirectional between logically connected

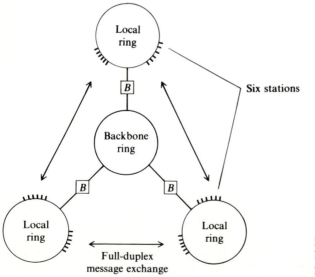

Six stations

Full-duplex
message exchange

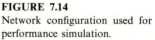

FIGURE 7.14
Network configuration used for performance simulation.

pairs of stations. The transmission speed on the backbone ring is taken to be 4 Mb/s.

The total throughput as a function of the total offered traffic is shown in Fig. 7.15 for different window sizes. At first the throughput increases linearly with the offered data rate. When the backbone starts becoming loaded, queues of frames waiting to enter the backbone build up in the bridges, and buffer overflow eventually occurs. This of course results in I-frame loss and retransmission. The large throughput differences of the various window sizes occurs since the value of W sets an upper limit on the number of frames to be retransmitted per lost frame. Thus the additional traffic resulting from retransmissions decreases with smaller window sizes.

The mean end-to-end delay as a function of the total throughput is illustrated in Fig. 7.16. For small window sizes the message delay is high for low throughput values. This is caused by the window being closed during the times when a station cannot transmit its queued-up I frames. As the throughput rises, the delay also increases because of contention for network resources. The delays increase very sharply when throughput approaches its maximum value. If the offered data rate rises beyond this value, the network experiences both a decrease in throughput and an increase in delay. Note that the curves in Fig. 7.16 for $W = 2$, 5, and 10 need to be interpreted in conjunction with the curves in Fig. 7.15. That is, as the total offered data rate increases, the total throughput decreases and hence the mean end-to-end delay increases.

Very similar network performance characteristics result when the backbone speed is changed from 4 to 16 Mb/s with all other simulation parameters

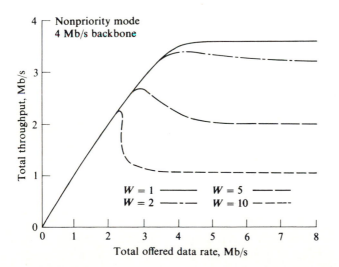

FIGURE 7.15

Total throughput versus total offered data rate for different window sizes in the nonpriority access mode. (*Adapted with permission from Bux and Grillo,*[42] © *1985, IEEE.*)

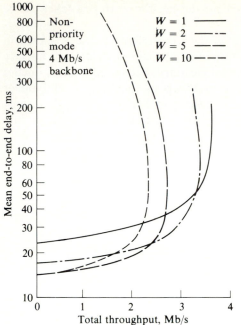
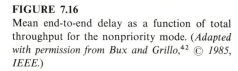

FIGURE 7.16
Mean end-to-end delay as a function of total throughput for the nonpriority mode. (*Adapted with permission from Bux and Grillo,*[42] © *1985, IEEE.*)

remaining the same. The only difference is that now the local rings are the bottleneck, whereas the backbone is the network performance limiter when its speed is 4 Mb/s.

Priority access by the bridges results in a significant performance improvement compared to the nonpriority mode. Using the network configuration in Fig. 7.14 and keeping all simulation parameters the same as above, the total throughput for the priority mode with a 16-Mb/s backbone is shown in Fig. 7.17. The interesting point to note is that there are negligibly few frame losses. This occurs in the priority mode because the access of stations to their corresponding local ring is delayed, thereby slowing down both the introduction of new I frames to the network and the return of acknowledgments. Delayed acknowledgments, in turn, further throttle the transmission of I frames because of the LLC window flow-control protocol. The resulting effect resembles the flow-control schemes suggested for wide-area packet-switching networks in which packets are handled with higher priority the closer they are to their destination.[34,37,42,49]

The delay-throughput characteristic corresponding to the 16-Mb/s priority-mode backbone is given in Fig. 7.18. Again we see a great improvement in performance. It should be noted, however, that this improvement is to a large extent a consequence of the symmetry of the traffic pattern chosen for the simulation. In an asymmetric priority-mode traffic flow pattern, the throughput characteristics shown in Fig. 7.15 appear, indicating congestion in the bridge. Also, the same type of pattern results for a 4-Mb/s priority-mode backbone since

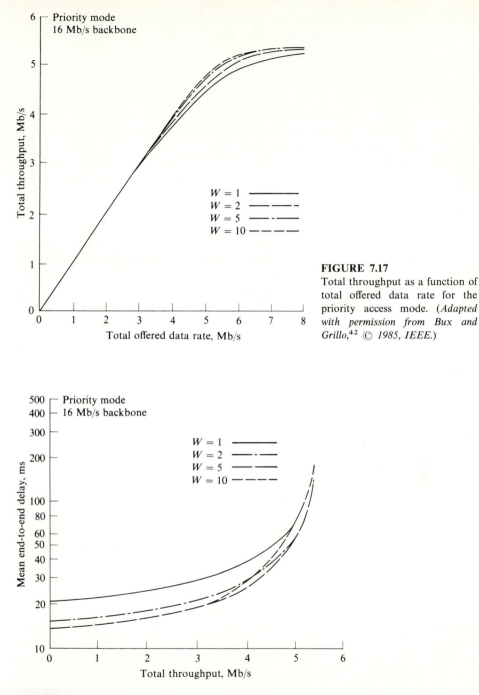

FIGURE 7.17
Total throughput as a function of total offered data rate for the priority access mode. (*Adapted with permission from Bux and Grillo,*[42] © *1985, IEEE.*)

FIGURE 7.18
Mean end-to-end delay versus total throughput for the priority mode. (*Adapted with permission from Bux and Grillo,*[42] © *1985, IEEE.*)

again the backbone is the network bottleneck, so that providing bridges with priority access to their local rings cannot change performance significantly.

7.5   SUMMARY

In this chapter we have studied factors concerned with connecting a particular local area network to other networks, thereby expanding its usefulness and capabilities. The concept for achieving this is known as internetting and effectively creates a single large loosely coupled network from a variety of local and wide-area networks. The three basic network interconnections are between homogeneous LANs, between heterogeneous LANs, and between a LAN and a long-haul public (wide-area) network.

The interconnection between two independent networks is achieved by means of a special device which is generically called a gateway. The gateway accepts messages from a sending network, translates them from this network's protocol hierarchy to that of the connecting network, and then forwards these newly formatted messages to the next network. Devices used for interconnecting LANs at the data-link level are called bridges, whereas at the network level routers are used.

When moving data units from a source node to a destination node in any computer network or between networks, routing and flow-control procedures are required to regulate the movement and the amount of traffic within the network. The objective of routing is to provide the best collection of paths between each source and destination pair, given the traffic requirements and the network configuration. The routing procedure can be fixed (static) or adaptive (dynamic). In static routing, a fixed message path is uniquely determined from only its origin and destination stations. An adaptive routing procedure can assign different paths to a particular message unit depending on the traffic flow and topological fluctuations.

In designing a network and its associated routing methodology, a one-dimensional performance criterion is usually defined and an attempt is made to minimize this quantity to optimize network performance. The simplest criterion is to choose the least-cost route. A common method is to base the cost on the queueing delay in which case the least-cost path minimizes the message delay.

Whereas routing determines which path a message should follow, the tasks of flow and congestion control are to determine how much traffic is permitted to enter the network. A common quantitative measure of flow control performance is throughput efficiency (expressed in packets per second). Flow control is usually realized in a network by allocating an adequate number of buffers to achieve a certain performance level. From queueing analyses we can see that this number depends strongly on the load of the network, and starts to grow rapidly after a certain load threshold has been reached. For a fixed number of buffers, flow-control procedures are thus used to keep the offered traffic below this threshold. Note that this threshold is referred to as the onset of congestion.

Analytical models for flow and congestion control prove to be unfeasible for all but the smallest networks.[50-51] Thus most models have been validated to varying degrees of success by simulation and experience.

PROBLEMS

Section 7.1

7.1. A constraint on a CSMA/CD-based Ethernet system running at 10 Mb/s is that the furthest station-to-station span is limited to 2.5 km. Show how an Ethernet-to-Ethernet bridge can eliminate this limitation. What are some operational requirements of the bridge?

7.2. A message consisting of 1600 bits of data and 160 bits of header is to be transmitted across two networks to a third network. The two intermediate networks have a maximum packet size of 1024 bits which includes a 24-bit header on each packet. If the final network has a maximum packet size of 800 bits, how many bits (including headers) are delivered at the destination? Into how many packets is the original message fragmented?

Section 7.2

7.3. Consider the network shown in Fig. P7.3. Noting that the numbers shown next to the links are transmission distances, set up a central routing table based on the shortest-path route. Assume that the nodal processing time is negligible.

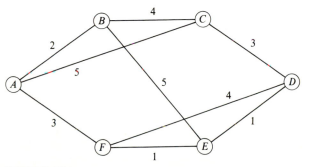

FIGURE P7.3

7.4. For the network shown in Fig. P7.3, assume the distances shown next to the links are given in kilometers and that the propagation time along a link is 5 μs/km. If the message service time at each node is 0.5 ms, set up a routing table for this case, assuming that the optimum route is the one with the shortest end-to-end message-transmission delay.

7.5. Repeat Prob. 7.4 assuming that the message service times are 0.5 ms for nodes A, B, and C, and 1.0 ms for nodes D, E, and F.

Section 7.4

7.6. The simplest form of flow control is based on a stop-and-wait protocol. Here a receiver agrees to accept data either by sending a poll or by responding to a select.

After the reception of transmitted data, the receiver must return an acknowledgment to the source before more data can be sent. Suppose a sequence of data frames f_1, $f_2, \ldots, f_n$ is to be sent using the following polling procedure:

Station S_1 sends a poll to station S_2
Station S_2 replies with f_1
S_1 sends an acknowledgment
S_2 responds with f_2
S_1 acknowledges
$\vdots$
S_2 sends out f_n
S_1 acknowledges

(a) Letting t_{prop} = propagation time between S_1 to S_2
          t_{proc} = message processing time
          t_f = frame transmission time
          t_{poll} = station polling time
          t_{ack} = frame acknowledgment time
find expressions for the time to initiate a sequence (t_I), the time to send one frame (t_f), and the total time needed to send the sequence of n frames.

(b) Assuming that for a long sequence of frames t_I, t_{proc}, and t_{ack} are small and can be ignored, show that the utilization or efficiency of the line is

$$U = \frac{1}{1 + 2a}$$

where $a = t_{\text{prop}}/t_f$.

7.7. (a) Using the following definition for the parameter a

$$a = \frac{\text{propagation time}}{\text{transmission time}}$$

derive an expression for a in terms of the distance d of the link, the propagation velocity v, the frame length L (in bits), and the data rate B.

(b) Using this expression, determine for what range of frame sizes a stop-and-wait protocol gives an efficiency of at least 50 percent for a 4-kb/s channel having a 20-ms propagation delay.

(c) Repeat part b for a 10-Mb/s channel having a 5-μs propagation delay.

REFERENCES

1. V. G. Cerf and P. T. Kirstein, "Issues in packet-network interconnection," *Proc. IEEE*, vol. 66, pp. 1386–1408, November 1978.
2. J. B. Postel, "Internetwork protocol approaches," *IEEE Trans. Commun.*, vol. COM-28, pp. 604–611, April 1980.
3. W. Stallings, *Data and Computer Communications*, Macmillan, New York, 1985, chap. 14.
4. D. R. Boggs, J. F. Shoch, E. A. Taft, and R. M. Metcalfe, "Pup: An internetwork architecture," *IEEE Trans. Commun.*, vol. COM-28, pp. 612–624, April 1980.
5. R. Callon, "Internetwork protocol," *Proc. IEEE*, vol. 71, pp. 1388–1393, December 1983.
6. P. E. Green, Jr., "Protocol conversion," *IEEE Trans. Commun.*, vol. COM-34, pp. 257–268, March 1986.

7. E. Benhamou and J. Estrin, "Multilevel internetworking gateways: Architecture and applications," *Computer*, vol. 16, pp. 27–34, September 1983.

8. R. Hinden, J. Haverty, and A. Sheltzer, "The DARPA Internet: Interconnecting heterogeneous computer networks with gateways," *Computer*, vol. 16, pp. 38–48, September 1983.

9. N. Schneidewind, "Interconnecting local networks to long-distance networks," *Computer*, vol. 16, pp. 15–24, September 1983.

10. J. F. Shoch, "Packet fragmentation in internetwork protocols," *Computer Networks*, vol. 3, pp. 3–8, February 1979.

11. A. S. Tanenbaum, *Computer Networks*, Prentice-Hall, Englewood Cliffs, NJ, 1981.

12. M. D. Abrams and H. J. Powell (eds.) *Computer and Network Security*, IEEE Computer Society, Washington, DC, 1987.

13. F. Backes, "Transparent bridges for interconnection of IEEE 802 LANs," *IEEE Network*, vol. 2, pp. 5–9, January 1988.

14. J. Hart, "Extending the IEEE 802.1 MAC Bridge Standard to remote bridges," *IEEE Network*, vol. 2, pp. 10–15, January 1988.

15. IEEE Project 802 Local and Metropolitan Area Network Standards, "IEEE Draft Standard 802.1: Part D, MAC Bridges," May 1987.

16. C. Cargill and M. Soha, "Standards and their influences on MAC bridges," *IEEE Network*, vol. 2, pp. 87–89, January 1988.

17. A. L. Chapin, "Standards for bridges and gateways," *IEEE Network*, vol. 2, pp. 90–91, January 1988.

18. W. M. Seifert, "Bridges and routers," *IEEE Network*, vol. 2, pp. 57–64, January 1988.

19. R. Perlman, A. Harvey, and G. Varghese, "Choosing the appropriate ISO layer for LAN interconnections," *IEEE Network*, vol. 2, pp. 81–86, January 1988.

20. M. Soha and R. Perlman, "Comparison of two LAN bridge approaches," *IEEE Network*, vol. 2, pp. 37–43, January 1988.

21. L. Zhang, "Comparison of two bridge routing approaches," *IEEE Network*, vol. 2, pp. 44–48, January 1988.

22. B. Hawe, A. Kirby, and B. Stewart, "Transparent interconnection of local networks with bridges," *J. Telecommun. Networks*, vol. 3, pp. 116–130, June 1984; reprinted in *Advances in Local Area Networks*, K. Kummerle, J. Limb, and F. Tobagi (eds.), IEEE Press, New York, 1987.

23. C. A. Sunshine, "Interconnection of computer networks," *Computer Networks*, vol. 1, no. 3, pp. 175–195, 1977.

24. C. A. Sunshine, "Source routing in computer networks," *ACM Computer Commun. Rev.*, vol. 7, pp. 29–33, January 1977.

25. D. A. Pitt, K. K. Sy, and R. A. Donnan, "Source routing for bridged local area networks," reprinted in *Advances in Local Area Networks*, K. Kummerle, J. Limb, and F. Tobagi (eds.), IEEE Press, New York, 1987.

26. R. C. Dixon and D. A. Pitt, "Addressing, bridging, and source routing," *IEEE Network*, vol. 2, pp. 25–32, January 1988.

27. M. C. Hammer and G. R. Samsen, "Source routing bridge implementation," *IEEE Network*, vol. 2, pp. 33–36, January 1988.

28. D. A. Pitt and J. L. Winkler, "Table-free bridging," *IEEE J. Sel. Areas Commun.*, vol. SAC-5, pp. 1454–1462, December 1987.

29. J. W. Wong, A. J. Vernon, and J. A. Field, "Evaluation of a path-finding algorithm for interconnected local area networks," *IEEE J. Sel. Areas Commun.*, vol. SAC-5, pp. 1463–1470, December 1987.

30. M. Willett and R. D. Martin, "LAN management in an IBM framework," *IEEE Network*, vol. 2, pp. 6–12, March 1988.

31. S. M. Klerer, "The OSI Management Architecture: an overview," *IEEE Network*, vol. 2, pp. 20–29, March 1988.

32. M. Gerla and L. Kleinrock, "Congestion control in interconnected LANs," *IEEE Network*, vol. 2, pp. 72–76, January 1988.

33. M. Gerla, "Routing and flow control," in *Protocols and Techniques for Data Communication Networks*, F. F. Kuo (ed.), Prentice-Hall, Englewood Cliffs, NJ, 1981, chap. 4.
34. M. Gerla and L. Kleinrock, "Flow control: A comparative survey," *IEEE Trans. Commun.*, vol. COM-28, pp. 553–574, April 1980.
35. L. Pouzin, "Methods, tools, and observations on flow control in packet-switched data networks," *IEEE Trans. Commun.*, vol. COM-29, pp. 413–426, April 1981.
36. M. Reiser, "Performance evaluation of data communication systems," *Proc. IEEE*, vol. 70, pp. 171–196, February 1982.
37. S. Lam and M. Reiser, "Congestion control of store-and-forward networks by input buffer limits —An analysis," *IEEE Trans. Commun.*, vol. COM-27, pp. 127–134, January 1979.
38. D. W. Davies, "The control of congestion in packet-switched networks," *IEEE Trans. Commun.*, vol. COM-20, pp. 546–550, June 1972.
39. W. L. Price, "Data network simulation: experiments at the National Physical Laboratory," *Computer Networks*, vol. 1, pp. 199–210, May 1977.
40. P. G. Harrison, "An analytic model for flow control schemes in communication network nodes," *IEEE Trans. Commun.*, vol. COM-32, pp. 1013–1019, September 1984.
41. "Congestion control in computer networks," Special Issue of *IEEE Trans. Commun.*, vol. COM-29, April 1981.
42. W. Bux and D. Grillo, "Flow control in local area networks of interconnected token rings," *IEEE Trans. Commun.*, vol. COM-33, pp. 1058–1066, October 1985.
43. R. Varakulsiripunth, N. Shiratori, and S. Noguchi, "A congestion control policy on the internetwork gateway," *Computer Networks*, vol. 10, pp. 43–58, 1986.
44. G. Bernard, "Interconnection of local computer networks: Modeling and optimization problems," *IEEE Trans. Software Eng.*, vol. SE-9, pp. 463–470, July 1983.
45. ECMA Standard 89, "Local area network token ring technique."
46. ANSI/IEEE Standard 802.5, "Token ring access method and physical-layer specifications," 1985.
47. ANSI/IEEE Standard 802.2, "Logical link control," 1985.
48. C. H. Saner and E. A. MacNair, *Simulation of Computer Communication Systems*, Prentice-Hall, Englewood Cliffs, NJ, 1983.
49. A. Giessler, A. Jaegemann, E. Maeser, and J. O. Haenle, "Flow control based on buffer classes," *IEEE Trans. Commun.*, vol. COM-29, pp. 436–443, April 1981.
50. A. G. Konheim and M. Reiser, "A queueing model with finite waiting room and blocking," *J. Assoc. Comput. Mach.*, vol. 28, pp. 328–341, April 1976.
51. M. F. Neuts, "Two queues in series with a finite intermediate waiting room," *J. Appl. Prob.*, vol. 5, pp. 123–142, 1968.

CHAPTER
8

NETWORK
RELIABILITY

When conceiving any type of network, whether long-haul or local-area, the network designer has available a set of switches, transmission lines, repeaters, nodal equipment, and terminals with known performance ratings. The design problem is to arrange these components in such a way that a given set of traffic requirements are met at the lowest cost. This is known as *network optimization*. Within a given cost constraint, the main parameters for network optimization are throughput, delay, and reliability. Having covered throughput and delay in Chaps. 6 and 7, we now turn our attention to reliability.

Reliability is the probability that a network, or element thereof, will perform satisfactorily for a given period of time when used under specified operating conditions. The four key factors here are probability, satisfactory performance, time, and specified operating conditions. Their importances are as follows:

1. *Probability* refers to the mathematical tool we use to measure performance. When a number of supposedly identical devices operate under similar conditions, failures can be expected to occur at different points in time; thus we describe failures in terms of probability theory.

2. *Satisfactory performance* indicates that we need to specify a combination of qualitative and quantitative factors which define the functions the system is to accomplish. These are usually the system specifications such as bit error rate, throughput, and delay.

3. *Time* is obviously one of the most critical factors in making reliability measurements since we need to be able to predict the probability of a system being operational at specific points in time when we wish to use it.

4. *Specified operating conditions* include factors such as geographical location of the system, weather extremes to which the system is exposed (e.g., temperature, wind, humidity), vibration, shock, and potential damage by rodents.

From a general point of view, the topological connectivity largely determines the network reliability. Thus in Secs. 8.1 and 8.2 we examine network reliability in terms of network connectivity. These sections address connectivity in terms of topology and path or node failure, respectively. From a detailed point of view, reliability is described by the rate of breakdown of lines and nodal equipment, together with the mean time needed to repair these faults. Reliability models for this are set up in Sec. 8.3. As a final topic we examine several techniques in Sec. 8.4 for achieving fault-tolerant networks.

8.1   CONNECTIVITY THROUGH REDUNDANCY

One way to achieve high reliability in the event of line or nodal equipment failure is to require the network to have line and/or equipment redundancy. A sufficiently redundant network can then lose a few lines or nodes and still continue to function, although possibly at a lower performance level.

One of the simplest measures of reliability is whether or not the network is completely connected. To analyze the degree of redundancy in a network, designers have used ideas from graph theory.[1-7] In this representation the collection of network nodes and their connecting lines form a graph as is shown in Fig. 8.1. Although here we will not go into the details of using graph theory for network optimization, in the following sections we examine some of the terminology and analysis techniques that are commonly used.

8.1.1   Definitions and Concepts

We measure connectivity by how much a network will resist disconnection (being split into two or more parts) upon removal of certain nodes or lines. For example, the network in Fig. 8.1 will disconnect if we remove nodes 3 and 6. It will not disconnect upon removal of fewer nodes. Thus we say the network has a *node connectivity* of 2.

Now if we remove lines (which are also known as *arcs*) instead of nodes, the network will disconnect upon removal of three lines. The measure of the

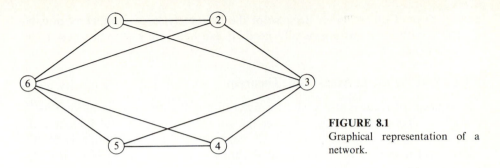

FIGURE 8.1
Graphical representation of a network.

number of lines that need to be removed to split the network is called the *arc connectivity*.

The set of lines whose removal isolates node *A* from node *B* is called an *A-B cut* (or *cutset*). The number of lines in a cut may vary from one to all the lines in the network. Since each network line has a certain capacity, the *capacity of a cut* is the sum of all the link capacities in that cut. The cut with the lowest capacity between a pair of nodes is called the *minimum cut*. A cut is *saturated* if the traffic load in every line of the cut equals the capacity of that line.

The arc connectivity of a network as a whole is the minimum of the arc connectivities of all pairs of nodes. If the two most weakly connected nodes have only *k* arc-disjoint paths (i.e., paths having no arcs in common) between them, then the network has a connectivity of *k*, or alternatively, the network is *k*-arc connected. The network in Fig. 8.1 thus has an arc connectivity of three, or alternately, is 3-arc connected.

The number of lines connected to a particular node determines the *degree* of that node. Figure 8.2 shows an example of network with a node connectivity of one, an arc connectivity of two, and a degree of two.

One way to find the arc connectivity of a network, is to do a straight-forward calculation of the arc connectivity of each pair of nodes and then take the minimum value. Although this can be done for a small number of nodes, this approach is intractable for large networks since each node can be connected to

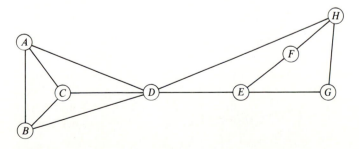

FIGURE 8.2
A network with a nodal connectivity of one, an arc connectivity of two, and a degree of two.

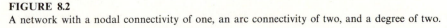

any number of other nodes. Because of the extremely large number of possible alternate paths, designers generally need to use heuristic methods when a network has many nodes.[6–9]

8.1.2 The Min-Cut Max-Flow Theorem

The concept of a cut is also useful for determining the mean information flow in a network. To see this, let us consider the network shown in Fig. 8.3 where the number next to each line indicates its capacity. (*Note:* Each node is both a source and a sink of information, so the flow does not balance at each node.) For illustrative purposes, we look at nodes A and J. Four sample cuts which separate these two nodes are drawn in Fig. 8.3. The capacities of cuts 1 through 4 are 16, 17, 13, and 11, respectively.

Although not all possible A-J cuts are drawn, the reader can easily verify that cut 4 is the minimum cut. Since all information that flows between nodes A and J must pass through the three links indicated by cut 4, the maximum possible flow between A and J is 11 units of data (the capacity of the minimum cut). This very important result, which is known as the *Min-Cut Max-Flow Theorem*,[10–11] states that *the maximum flow between a pair of nodes cannot exceed the capacity of the minimum cut separating these two nodes.*

A variety of algorithms for finding the maximum flow and the minimum cut have been developed and can be found in the literature.[6,12]

8.1.3 The Cut-Saturation Algorithm

A heuristic method that has been successfully used in the network-connectivity design problem is the cut-saturation algorithm.[8,13] Any network in general has a

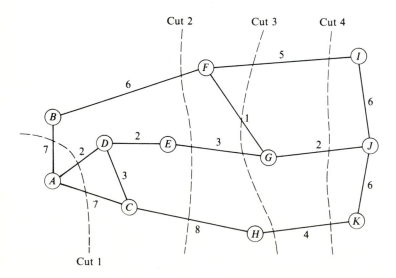

FIGURE 8.3
Possible cuts for separating nodes A and J.

large number of cuts. As the traffic level in a network grows, the lines in one of these cuts will approach saturation. At this point there are individual lines in which the traffic flows cannot be increased without creating excessive delay. The only way the capacity of the network can be made larger is to increase the capacity of one or more links within this cutset, or add more lines to the cut. This is the basis of the cut-saturation algorithm. It attempts to keep the network throughput within specified bounds while iteratively reducing overall line cost, maintenance needs, delay, and reliability constraints.

A basic simplifying assumption we will use here for the cut-saturation algorithm is that all of the links have the same capacity. The objective of the optimization algorithm is to achieve a desired network throughput at the lowest possible cost, but consistent with high reliability. Given a typical network configuration which is at least two-connected, we carry out the following steps:

1. Order all the links according to the volume of traffic they carry, for example, some lines will be highly utilized (80 to 90 percent is a suitable figure) whereas others see little traffic.

2. Conceptually remove links in sequence from the network, beginning with the most utilized ones, until the network has been separated into two disjoint groups of nodes, as is shown in Fig. 8.4. In this figure we denote all nodes that are adjacent to the cut as *primary nodes* (nodes E, F, H, and K). These are shown as solid circles. The dotted circles adjacent to the primary nodes are called *secondary nodes* (nodes B, C, G, and J). All other nodes are indicated by open circles. The minimal set of highly used lines that disconnects the network is called a *saturated cutset*. Because of the way it was derived, this cutset clearly reveals a weak spot in the topology.

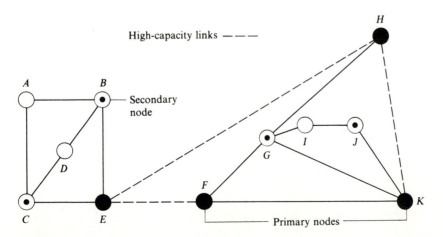

FIGURE 8.4
Example of the removal of links (denoted by dashed lines) to disjoin the network by means of the cut-saturation algorithm. The solid circles are called primary nodes and the dotted circles are secondary nodes.

To alleviate this weakness, the next step of the cut-saturation algorithm consists of adding and deleting links between the two disjoint parts of the network that are separated by the saturated cutset. Let us first consider the addition of links. If we choose to replace the lowest-cost link, this will usually rejoin primary nodes only. In practice, this is found to shift the cutset slightly without greatly improving network performance.

A simple heuristic criterion known as *distance 2* has been found to work better, since it effectively connects the so-called *centers of traffic* of the two disjoint parts of the network in Fig. 8.4. This criterion states that end points of new links should be placed at least two hops away from the primary nodes, that is, at least two hops away from the nodes adjacent to the cuts. This means connecting open-circle nodes in the two network parts. Figure 8.5 shows an example of this, where two open-circle nodes (*D* and *I*) are now directly connected (illustrated by the dashed line). Prior to installing this link, the traffic between the two newly connected nodes had to make at least five hops (two hops to the primary node in the left component of the nodes, one hop for the cutset line, and two hops in the right nodal component). The insertion of this link is thus likely to improve throughput, since it provides an alternate path to saturated lines.

We can continue adding lines by the cut-saturation method until the throughput exceeds the network requirements. At this point we can then consider link deletion. If the network is fully connected but expensive, links can be deleted from the cut. The two main criteria used for line removal are utilization and cost. Thus we can first remove the most costly, least-used link. This link is the one that maximizes the quantity[8]

$$E_i = \frac{D_i(C_i - f_i)}{C_i} \tag{8.1}$$

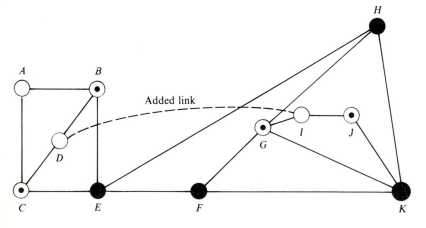

FIGURE 8.5
Addition of links through the distance-2 criterion.

where D_i, C_i, and f_i are, respectively, the cost, capacity, and flow in link i. The quantity $(C_i - f_i)/C_i$ is the relative excess capacity. Basically the parameter E_i represents the amount of money being needlessly spent on unused capacity for link i.

In removing links, we place a two-connectivity constraint on the network to ensure reliability. Thus a line is not deleted if its removal results in an isolated node or a pendant section. High-cost links having a maximum E in a saturated cutset are also not removed.

8.2   PROBABILITY OF CONNECTIVITY

To ensure reliability, networks are invariably designed so that more than one path exists between any given source-destination pair of nodes. However, even with this redundancy multiple failures of nodes or lines can break communications between various node pairs. Thus in designing maximally reliable networks, subject to fixed cost constraints, the objective is to maximize the probability that the network is operational based on a specific probability of failure for each of its nodes and lines.

In this section we examine techniques for assessing these probabilities. We start by considering a network having L links and N nodes which are at least two-connected. The main problem that has been extensively dealt with in the literature is the calculation of node-pair reliability.[11,14–21] In this problem, given a network with known failure probabilities of its nodes and lines, the objective is to find the probability that at least one complete path exists between a source and a destination node.

In the most general case, one would need to take into account simultaneous line and node failures, with each line and node having its own unique failure probability. The computation of the reliability measure requires the enumeration of all simple paths between all pairs of nodes. Clearly the complexity of this problem increases very rapidly with network size and topological connectivity. Thus for practical calculation purposes we first assume that all communication link failures and node breakdowns are statistically independent. Further, we assume that all links fail with the same probability p and that nodes break down with probability q.

8.2.1   Node-Pair Failure Probability

The most elementary performance measure is to calculate the probability of one node in the network becoming isolated. We refer to this as the *probability of the network becoming disconnected*. For ease of calculation we consider line and node failures separately. That is, in one case we assume that the probability of node failure q is zero, and in the other case that the line-failure probability p is zero.

Let us first consider the probability of successful communication between node pairs. Given that node failures are negligible compared to line failures

$(p \gg q)$, let $A_L(i)$ designate the number of ways that a network can be connected when i links are operational and the remaining $L - i$ links have failed. The probability of any particular set of i links being operational is then $(1 - p)^i p^{L-i}$. Summing over all values of i, the probability $P_c(p)$ of successful communication between any pair of operating nodes I and J is then approximated by[15]

$$P_c(p) = \sum_{i=0}^{L} A_L(i)(1 - p)^i p^{L-i} \tag{8.2}$$

Now let us consider the case when failures can occur in any of the $N - 2$ nodes that can be traversed by paths linking two arbitrary nodes I and J. For the case when line failures p are negligible compared to node failures q ($p \ll q$), the probability that k of the $N - 2$ nodes are operational while the remaining $N - 2 - k$ nodes have failed is $(1 - q)^k q^{N-2-k}$. Then the probability of successful communication is

$$P_c(q) = \sum_{k=0}^{N-2} A_N(k)(1 - q)^k q^{N-2-k} \tag{8.3}$$

where the coefficients $A_N(k)$ denote the number of combinations of k nodes such that if they are operational (and the others have failed), there is at least one communication path between nodes I and J.

Alternately, we can examine the probability of a communication *failure* between any pair of operative nodes. The probabilities corresponding to line and node failures, $P_f(p)$ and $P_f(q)$, respectively, are given by

$$P_f(p) = \sum_{i=0}^{L} C_L(i)p^i(1 - p)^{L-i} \tag{8.4}$$

and

$$P_f(q) = \sum_{k=0}^{N-2} C_N(k)q^k(1 - q)^{N-2-k} \tag{8.5}$$

Here the coefficients $C_L(j)$ and $C_N(j)$ denote the number of ways that a network can become disconnected given that j links or nodes, respectively, are not operational. Thus, $C_L(j)$ is equal to the total number of cuts of size j with respect to nodes I and J. A similar definition holds for $C_N(j)$.

An important point to note here is that for any network having a line connectivity equal to d, $C_L(i) = 0$ for all $i < d$. Therefore the dominant term for $P_f(p)$ in Eq. (8.4) is given by

$$C_L(d)p^d(1 - p)^{L-d}$$

for $p < \frac{1}{2}$. Since for small values of p (much less than 0.5) this term is reduced for increasing values of d, the ideal network should be maximally connected. A similar argument holds for the coefficients $C_N(k)$ in Eq. (8.5) for networks having a node connectivity of d.

8.2.2   Probability Bounds

In analyzing the reliability of a network, it is desirable to calculate the minimum value of the connectivity probability or the maximum value of the failure probability. For simplicity of discussion, let us concentrate here on the line-failure probability $P_f(p)$ given in Eq. (8.4). To find this we need to compute the parameter $C_L(i)$.

The exact calculation of the maximum value of $P_f(p)$ requires the examination of all I-J cuts for all I-J node pairs. This can only be done with algorithms run on a computer.[15,20-22] However, by using some simplifying arguments, upper and lower bounds on $P_f(p)$ can be established.[22] We first observe that given N nodes, at least $N - 1$ links are required to connect them. If there are fewer links, the network will be disconnected. For this minimum number of $N - 1$ links, we have that the number of ways the network can be disconnected if i links are not operational is given by

$$C_L(i) = \binom{L}{i} = \frac{L!}{i!\,(L-i)!} \qquad \text{for } i = 0, 1, 2, \ldots, N - 2 \qquad (8.6)$$

The network can also obviously be disconnected for $i = N - 1$, but we will ignore this here since we are looking for a lower bound. Using Eq. (8.6) in Eq. (8.4) then gives a lower bound of

$$P_f(p) \geq \sum_{i=0}^{N-2} \binom{L}{i} p^{L-i}(1-p)^i \qquad (8.7a)$$

or, alternately,

$$P_f(p) \geq \sum_{k=L-N+2}^{L} \binom{L}{k} p^k (1-p)^{L-k} \qquad (8.7b)$$

We now consider the upper bound. Let M be the minimum number of links that need to be removed for the network to be disconnected. Then clearly $C_L(i)$ is zero for any number of failed links less than M; that is,

$$C_L(i) = 0 \qquad \text{for } i = 0, 1, 2, \ldots, M - 1 \qquad (8.8)$$

We note here that these M links are generally not an arbitrary selection of lines and, in addition, more than M links may be needed to disconnect the network. That is, it is possible that the network may not become disconnected for a random selection of $i = M, M + 1, \ldots, L$ links. However, we discount these possibilities here in seeking an upper bound on $P_f(p)$. Using Eq. (8.8) in Eq. (8.4) then yields

$$P_f(p) \leq \sum_{k=M}^{L} \binom{L}{k} p^k (1-p)^{L-k} \qquad (8.9)$$

For values of p close to one, $P_f(p)$ is approximated by Eq. (8.7). At the other extreme, for p near zero, $P_f(p)$ is close to the limit given by Eq. (8.9).

A variety of other reliability analyses which go beyond the simple examples given here have been carried out. These include the consideration of simultaneous link and node failures,[21,23] network performance bounds based on link reliability,[17] evaluation of networks with dependent failures,[24,25] and reliability measures based on system availability.[26,27]

8.3 RELIABILITY MODELS

Having looked at network layout considerations for reliability and the probability of network connectivity, let us now see how to analyze the reliability and availability of a network having various failure and repair states. The main purpose here is to establish some simple time-dependent reliability models that are of general interest in the design and performance evaluation of a network. In doing this, we consider networks having two-state elements (node connections, transmission lines, terminals, and other devices), where an element is said to have two states if it either operates or fails. We also assume that the system can be repaired if elements in it fail. One considers network repair whenever the average repair cost of a piece of equipment is a fraction of its initial cost. If such a system can be quickly returned to service, the effect of a failure is minimized.

To start, we define some basic functions and commonly used terms. These are the reliability function, the mean time to failure (MTTF), the mean time to repair (MTTR), the mean time between failures (MTBF), and the availability function. We first look at these expressions for single two-state elements, and then separately consider networks with elements connected in series and in parallel.

8.3.1 The Reliability Function

Given that a network was fully operational at time $t = 0$ (with no failed elements), the reliability of the system is the probability that it has operated over the time interval $[0, t]$. A number of component failures could occur after $t = 0$, but the network remains operational through the interval $[0, t]$. The *reliability function* $R(t)$ is defined as[28–32]

$$R(t) = 1 - F(t) \tag{8.10}$$

Here $F(t)$ is the probability that the system will fail by time t, and is thus called the *failure distribution function* or the *unreliability function*. The temporal distribution of failures can be defined in terms of a failure density function $f(t)$ where

$$F(t) = \int_0^t f(t)\, dt \tag{8.11}$$

It follows from Eqs. (8.10) and (8.11) that

$$f(t) = \frac{dF(t)}{dt} = -\frac{dR(t)}{dt} \tag{8.12}$$

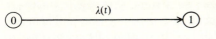

FIGURE 8.6
State-transition diagram for the reliability model of a simplex, one-unit system.

To derive an expression for the reliability function, we use a Markov state-transition model as was done in Chap. 5 when estimating message traffic flow. We first consider Fig. 8.6 which is the state-transition diagram for the reliability model of a simplex, one-unit system. Shown here is the transition between the initial operating state 0 and the final failed state 1. The failure rate (the transition rate from state 0 to state 1) is given by $\lambda(t)$.

The differential equations describing the transition between states are

$$\frac{dP_0(t)}{dt} + \lambda(t)P_0(t) = 0 \tag{8.13a}$$

$$\frac{dP_1(t)}{dt} - \lambda(t)P_0(t) = 0 \tag{8.13b}$$

Using the boundary conditions $P_0(0) = 1$ and $P_1(0) = 0$, we obtain the reliability function

$$R(t) = P_0(t) = 1 - P_1(t) = \exp\left[-\int_0^t \lambda(\tau)\,d\tau\right] \tag{8.14}$$

Under the condition that the failure rate $\lambda(t)$ is a constant λ, we have

$$R(t) = e^{-\lambda t} \tag{8.15}$$

This means that the arrivals of failures are Poisson. For the remainder of this chapter we will assume that failures occur at a constant rate λ.

8.3.2 Reliability Measures

Three commonly used measures of reliability are the mean time to failure, the mean time to repair, and the mean time between failures.

The *mean time to failure* (MTTF) is the average time in which the element enters the failed state, given that it was fully operational at time $t = 0$. This means that the MTTF is the mean life of the element. The MTTF is related to the reliability function through the expression

$$\text{MTTF} = \int_0^\infty R(t)\,dt = \frac{1}{\lambda} \tag{8.16}$$

where we have assumed that the failure rate is constant.

Analogous to the failure rate derivation, we assume that repair times are exponentially distributed and that repairs occur at a constant rate μ. Then, following the same derivation as for Eq. (8.16), we have that the *mean time to repair* (MTTR) for a single element is given by

$$\text{MTTR} = \frac{1}{\mu} \tag{8.17}$$

For an element that is repairable, the *mean time between failures* (MTBF) is the average time between successive failures of that element. This is obviously given by the expression

$$\text{MTBF} = \text{MTTF} + \text{MTTR} \tag{8.18}$$

8.3.3 The Availability Function

The term *availability* describes the performance benefits of repair in a system that tolerates shutdown times. The *availability function* $A(t)$ is the probability that an element (or system) is *operating at time t*. In contrast, the reliability function $R(t)$ is the probability that the element has operated *over* the interval $[0, t]$. To see this difference, let us look at an example. Consider 100 devices which operated for 500 hours. If $A(500) = 0.95$ then on the average, 95 devices will be working when 500 hours are reached and 5 will be undergoing some type of repair. Note that the availability function does not indicate how many repair cycles were made prior to time $t = 500$ hours.

On the other hand, $R(500) = 0.95$ says that if 100 devices are operated for 500 hours, then on the average 95 will have run without failure and five will have broken down at some time in the 500-hour interval. Thus the requirement $R(500) = 0.95$ is much stricter than the specification $A(500) = 0.95$ so that, in general, $R(t) \le A(t)$.

To derive the availability function, we examine the state-transition diagram shown in Fig. 8.7. The element goes from an operating state to a failed state at a rate λ, and through repair it transitions back to the operating state at a rate μ. From this Markov model the differential equations describing the state transitions are (with λ and μ constant)

$$\frac{dP_0(t)}{dt} + \lambda P_0(t) = \mu P_1(t)$$

$$\frac{dP_1(t)}{dt} + \mu P_1(t) = \lambda P_0(t) \tag{8.19}$$

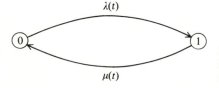

FIGURE 8.7
State-transition diagram for the availability model of a simplex, one-unit system.

Using the boundary conditions $P_0(0) = 1$ and $P_1(0) = 0$, we obtain the availability which is the probability $P_0(t)$ that the element is good at time t

$$A(t) = P_0(t) = \frac{\mu}{\lambda + \mu} + \frac{\lambda}{\lambda + \mu} \exp\left[-(\lambda + \mu)t\right] \tag{8.20}$$

As another difference between $A(t)$ and $R(t)$, let us examine their steady state behavior. When t becomes very large, $R(t)$ approaches zero, whereas $A(t)$ reaches some nonzero steady state value. From Eq. (8.20) the steady state value $A_{ss}(t)$ is

$$A_{ss}(t) = \lim_{t \to \infty} A(t) = \frac{\mu}{\lambda + \mu} \tag{8.21}$$

Using Eqs. (8.16) and (8.17), we can rewrite this as

$$A_{ss}(t) = \frac{\text{MTTF}}{\text{MTTF} + \text{MTTR}} \tag{8.22}$$

Basically $A_{ss}(t)$ measures the fraction of time the element is operational.

8.3.4 Series Network

Having looked at individual elements, let us now see what the overall reliability is when a number of elements are connected in series, as would occur in a ring or bus network, for example. The series configuration is one of the simplest to analyze. As illustrated by the series-connected units in Fig. 8.8, all the components in the network must work satisfactorily if the system is to operate properly. If the units do not interact, the failures are independent and the system reliability $R_s(t)$ is the product of the reliabilities of the individual constituent units

$$R_s(t) = \prod_{i=1}^{k} R_i(t)$$

$$= \prod_{i=1}^{k} \left[1 - F_i(t)\right] \tag{8.23}$$

where $R_i(t)$ and $F_i(t)$ are the reliability function and failure distribution function, respectively, of the ith system unit.

FIGURE 8.8
Network elements connected in a series configuration.

If the ith component has a constant failure rate λ_i, then from Eq. (8.15) we have

$$R_s(t) = \prod_{i=1}^{k} e^{-\lambda_i t} = \exp\left[-(\lambda_1 + \lambda_2 + \cdots + \lambda_k)t\right] \tag{8.24}$$

This gives the overall reliability of a k-element series-connected network that is expected to operate for a specified time period t.

For the series configuration, the mean time to failure MTTF_s can be found from Eq. (8.16). Substituting Eq. (8.24) into Eq. (8.16) we have

$$\text{MTTF}_s = \int_0^{\infty} R_s(t)\,dt = \left(\sum_{i=1}^{k} \lambda_i\right)^{-1} \tag{8.25}$$

8.3.5 Parallel Network

In a parallel network a number of similar individual components are connected in parallel. This provides redundancy and improves network reliability since the system will only fail if all its components break down. A parallel network with k units is shown in Fig. 8.9. To derive the reliability function $R_p(t)$ for the parallel network, we make the following two assumptions: (1) all units are active and share the network load, (2) all components are statistically independent. For nonidentical components, the failure distribution function $F_p(t)$ at time t is

$$F_p(t) = \prod_{i=1}^{k} F_i(t) \tag{8.26}$$

where $F_i(t) = 1 - R_i(t)$ is the failure distribution of the ith component.

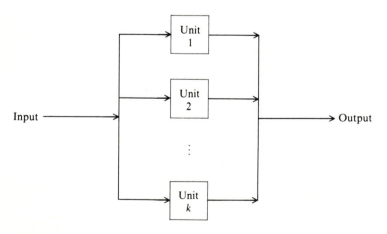

FIGURE 8.9
Network elements connected in a parallel configuration.

Since $R_p(t) + F_p(t) = 1$, the parallel-configuration reliability is

$$R_p(t) = 1 - F_p(t)$$

$$= 1 - \prod_{i=1}^{k} [1 - R_i(t)] \tag{8.27}$$

The mean time to failure, MTTF_p, for the parallel network can again be found from the relationship

$$\text{MTTF}_p = \int_0^\infty R_p(t)\, dt \tag{8.28}$$

As an example, consider a parallel system consisting of two nonidentical units having constant failure rates λ_1 and λ_2. Then from Eqs. (8.27) and (8.15) we have

$$R_p(t) = 1 - (1 - e^{-\lambda_1 t})(1 - e^{-\lambda_2 t})$$

$$= e^{-\lambda_1 t} + e^{-\lambda_2 t} - e^{-(\lambda_1 + \lambda_2)t} \tag{8.29}$$

Substituting Eq. (8.29) into Eq. (8.28) yields

$$\text{MTTF}_p = \int_0^\infty [e^{-\lambda_1 t} + e^{-\lambda_2 t} - e^{-(\lambda_1 + \lambda_2)t}]\, dt$$

$$= \frac{\lambda_1 + \lambda_2}{\lambda_1 \lambda_2} - \frac{1}{\lambda_1 + \lambda_2} \tag{8.30}$$

8.4 RELIABILITY IMPROVEMENT TECHNIQUES

The reliability and availability of a network can be enhanced by keeping active electronics in the transmission path to a minimum, reducing the number of repeaters or line amplifiers between stations, and by distributing the control electronics throughout the network. Reliability can also be improved by providing redundancy of transmission paths and nodal equipment. This is of particular interest for ring, or loop, networks since these can be relatively vulnerable and unreliable. An extreme case is the simple loop, where all terminals are connected in series. The failure of any link element or active repeater in the simple ring can disrupt the entire network.

Two fundamental techniques for improving reliability by using a redundant standby loop in parallel with the main ring have been analyzed by Zafiropulo.[33] Various implementations of these schemes have been carried out.[34-37] The first method is known as the *bypass technique*. As shown in Fig. 8.10, here both the main and standby rings transmit in the same direction. When a catastrophic failure occurs, a bypass element routes the signal stream onto the standby ring.

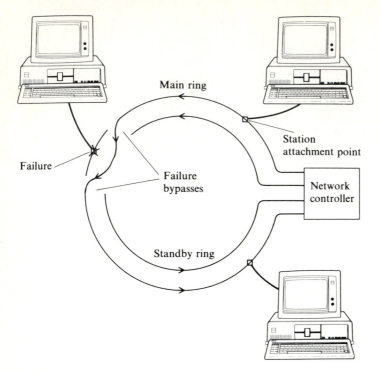

FIGURE 8.10
Schematic of the failure-bypass technique.

The second method is the *self-heal technique* shown in Fig. 8.11. Here the main and standby loops transmit in opposite directions. In the event of a catastrophic failure, a reconfiguration switch reroutes the signal stream so that it bends back on itself (via the standby loop) at either side of the failure. A hybrid network using a combination of either the bypass or the self-heal methods can also be implemented. In this case the standby loop must have bidirectional capability.

In this section we first look at the analyses of Zafiropulo for these two techniques, and then examine some fail-safe methods for fiber-optic networks.

8.4.1 Availability Performance

Let us first consider the general ring model shown in Fig. 8.12. Here a ring has *m* terminals, or stations, attached to it via terminal-to-ring interface couplers. In addition there is a network controller which may be an independent terminal or which could reside in one or more stations. For generality, we chose it to be an independent node. Some functions of the network controller could include initiating network start-up procedures, monitoring network status, remotely triggering diagnostic processes, and providing a link to other networks in the outside world.

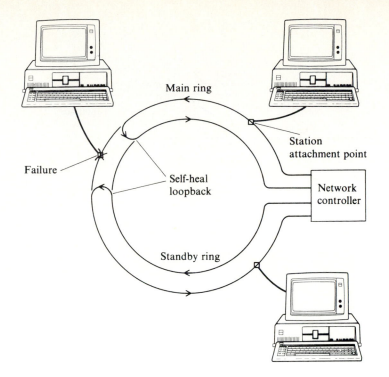

FIGURE 8.11
Illustration of the self-heal method.

As we noted earlier, the *availability* A of a particular element in a network is the probability that the element is operational. The probability D that a unit is not operational is then given by

$$D = 1 - A \tag{8.31}$$

The parameter D is the fraction of time that an element has failed and is thus referred to as the *down-time ratio* or DTR (the ratio of the length of time the element has failed to a specific time duration the network is in use). We use this parameter as a convenient measure for comparing the relative performance of different reliability enhancement techniques.

A variety of impairments can occur in the network shown in Fig. 8.12. First, a terminal could fail within the dashed box denoted by E at node j. Since this breakdown does not affect the performance of the other terminals on the link, we will assume that the DTR parameter D_E associated with it is small compared to failures which disrupt the entire ring.

A failure could also occur at the terminal-to-ring interface. The loss of this interface is catastrophic since it disables all communications on the ring. A rupture in the transmission line between two stations has exactly the same effect on

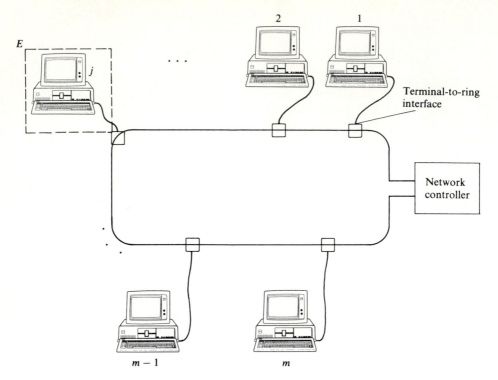

FIGURE 8.12
General model of a ring network.

network performance as a breakdown at a node attachment point. For simplicity of analysis, we combine these two disruptions and denote their DTR by D_T. (Alternately, we could take the finite cable reliability into account by defining pseudoterminal interfaces whose DTRs are equal to those of the cable sections.)

Failures in the network controller can be accounted for through the D_{NC}. This DTR encompasses both faults related to control of the ring and all impairments in the network controller that would disconnect the entire ring from the outside world.

To compare the simple one-loop m-terminal ring to one having redundancy, we introduce the concept of a terminal-attachment point and associate a down-time ratio $D_p(m)$ with it. We define a terminal-attachment point to be operational (that is available for use) if communications can be established from that point to any other terminal-attachment point on the ring or in the outside world. From 8.12, the factor $D_p(m)$ is then given by

$$D_p(m) = 1 - (1 - D_{NC})(1 - D_E)(1 - D_T)^m \qquad (8.32)$$

where $(1 - D_{NC})$ is the availability of the network controller, $(1 - D_E)(1 - D_T)$ is the probability the terminal connection point under consideration is operational, and $(1 - D_T)^{m-1}$ is the probability that there are no catastrophic failures in the remaining $m - 1$ terminals of the ring.

The expression $D_P(1)/D_P(m)$ compares the failure-induced degradation of an m-terminal network with respect to a one-terminal system. This degradation is shown in Fig. 8.13 for the case where $D_E \ll D_T$, $D_{NC} \ll D_T$, and $D_T = 10^{-4}$. The parameters D_E and D_{NC} were chosen small relative to D_T to prevent their values from masking the terminal degradation effect for small m (see Prob. 8.17).

8.4.2   The Bypass Technique

The failure bypass technique is illustrated in Fig. 8.14. To realize this technique, special bypass devices called *reconfiguration units* are added into the loop. Here

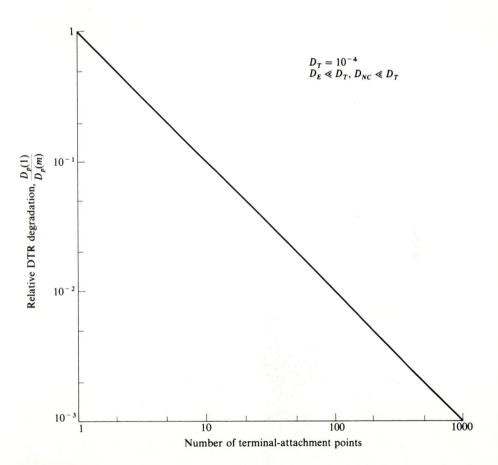

FIGURE 8.13
Relative failure-induced degradation of an m-terminal network with respect to a one-terminal system.

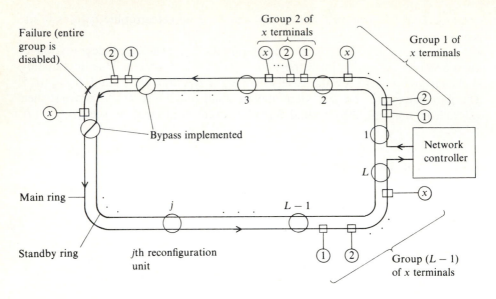

FIGURE 8.14
Implementation of the failure-bypass technique.

L units are added to the ring so $L - 1$ groups of X terminals are formed, where

$$X = \frac{m}{L - 1} \tag{8.33}$$

Two different failure possibilities must be taken into account. These are failures of nodes within a terminal group and failure of the reconfiguration unit. If a catastrophic failure occurs in a terminal group, that entire group is disabled and must be bypassed. If failures occur in several different groups, then each of these groups must be bypassed. For the reconfiguration unit, we assume for simplicity of analysis that any failure is catastrophic. That is, loss of this unit disrupts operation of the entire ring. Thus we let D_s be the down-time ratio associated with a failure in the reconfiguration unit or switch.

Similar to the derivation of Eq. (8.32), we can now define the DTR of a terminal-attachment point on a ring with failure-bypass capability. First recall that a terminal-attachment point is defined to be operational if a communication link can be established between it and any other functioning node. To achieve this, the following conditions must hold:

1. The terminal-attachment point must be operational. The probability of this is $(1 - D_E)(1 - D_T)$.
2. There can be no catastrophic failures among the other $X - 1$ terminals in the same group. The probability of this is $(1 - D_T)^{X-1}$.

3. All reconfiguration units must be operational, which occurs with a probability $(1 - D_S)^L$.

4. The network controller must be functioning with an availability $(1 - D_{NC})$.

Combining these four factors gives the availability A_B for a terminal-attachment point

$$A_B = (1 - D_E)(1 - D_T)(1 - D_T)^{X-1}(1 - D_S)^L(1 - D_{NC}) \qquad (8.34)$$

where the subscript B refers to a ring with bypass capability. From Eq. (8.31) the probability that a terminal-attachment point is nonoperational is

$$D_B(L, m) = 1 - A_B$$

$$= 1 - (1 - D_E)(1 - D_T)^X(1 - D_S)^L(1 - D_{NC}) \qquad (8.35)$$

To see what improvement the bypass technique offers over the simple ring network we examine the ratio $D_P(m)/D_B(L, m)$ where $D_P(m)$ is given by Eq. (8.32). Plots of this for $m = 49$, 256, and 400 terminals are given in Fig. 8.15 as a function of the number of reconfiguration units L. In each case we take $D_T = D_S = 10^{-4}$ and assume that $D_E \ll D_T$ and $D_{NC} \ll D_T$. These curves show that for each m there are optimum values L_{opt} at which a minimum D_B (denoted by $D_{B, opt}$) occurs. The value of L_{opt} is given by (see Prob. 8.18)

$$L_{opt} = \left[m \frac{\ln (1 - D_T)}{\ln (1 - D_S)} \right]^{1/2} + 1 \qquad (8.36)$$

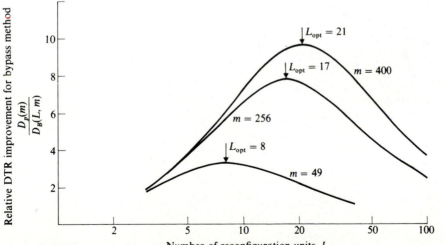

FIGURE 8.15
Relative DTR improvement of the bypass technique as a function of the number of configuration units for 49, 256, and 400 terminals.

If we use this value in Eq. (8.35) and write the expression in an exponential form (see Prob. 8.19), we have

$$D_{B,\,opt}(m) = 1 - \exp\left\{-[2(mD_T D_S)^{1/2} + D_S]\right\} \exp\left[-(D_E + D_{NC})\right] \quad (8.37)$$

This optimum results from two factors. First, if there are too few reconfiguration units, the bypass feature is insufficiently applied since a failure in a terminal-attachment point will still isolate a large portion of the network. If there are many reconfiguration units relative to the number of terminals, then the probability that one of these units fails begins to degrade the advantage of the bypass mechanism. This of course depends on the value of D_S. As the failure probability of the reconfiguration unit decreases, L_{opt} increases for a fixed number of terminals. In fact, for a highly reliable bypass unit, L_{opt} is equal to m; that is, the minimum value of $D_{B,\,opt}$ is reached when each terminal has a bypass unit (see Prob. 8.20).

8.4.3   The Self-Heal Technique

Figure 8.16 illustrates the concept of the self-heal technique. Reconfiguration switching units are employed analogous to the bypass technique. In this scheme, however, a reconfiguration unit loops the signal path back on itself via the auxiliary channel on each side of a failure.

The methods by which the self-heal technique handles different failure cases that could arise here are shown in Figs. 8.16 and 8.17. First, in Fig. 8.16, if a terminal-attachment point fails, the entire group to which the terminal belongs

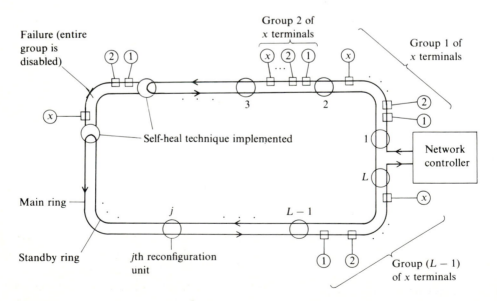

FIGURE 8.16
Implementation of the self-heal technique.

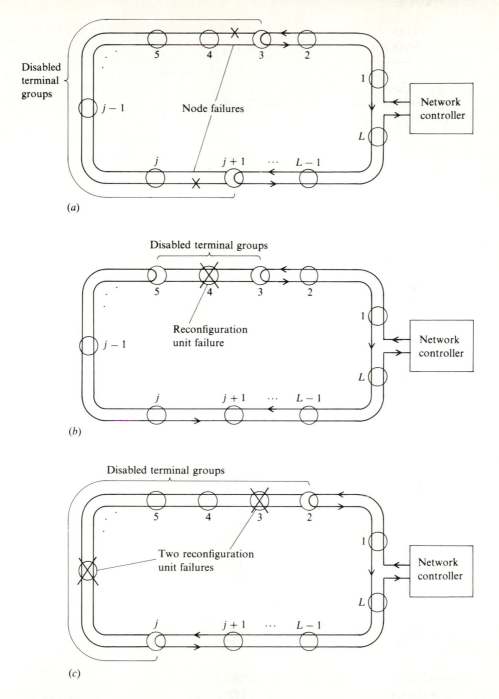

FIGURE 8.17
Handling of three different failure modes by the self-heal technique: (*a*) Failures in two different terminal groups, (*b*) Breakdown of one reconfiguration unit, (*c*) Loss of two reconfiguration units.

is disabled. Secondly, if terminals in two different groups are impaired, then not only are the two affected groups disabled, but also the entire ring section between the two groups is circumvented as Fig. 8.17a shows. Breakdown of a reconfiguration unit affects only the two adjacent terminal groups as Fig. 8.17b illustrates. Figure 8.17c depicts the effect of losing two reconfiguration units. Here all terminal groups between the affected units plus the two adjacent terminal groups are inactivated.

The worst-case down-time ratio in the self-heal technique occurs for a terminal that has the largest number of reconfiguration units between it and the network controller. Zafiropulo[33] shows this worst-case DTR is given by

$$D_{SH}(L, m) = 1 - (1 - D_E)(1 - D_{NC})$$
$$\cdot [2(1 - D_T)^{(m/2)L/(L-1)}(1 - D_S)^{L/2} - (1 - D_T)^m(1 - D_S)^L] \quad (8.38)$$

for L even, and

$$D_{SH}(L, m) = 1 - (1 - D_E)(1 - D_{NC})$$
$$\cdot [(1 - D_T)^{(m/2)(L+1)/(L-1)}(1 - D_S)^{(L+5)/2}$$
$$+ (1 - D_T)^{m/2}(1 - D_S)^{(L+3)/2} - (1 - D_T)^m(1 - D_S)^L] \quad (8.39)$$

for L, odd, where the subscript SH refers to a ring with self-heal capability.

The improvement of the self-heal technique over that of a primitive loop is given by $D_p(m)/D_{SH}(L, m)$ where $D_p(m)$ is Eq. (8.32). This is shown in Fig. 8.18 as a function of L for $m = 256$ terminals. Again there is a unique value L_{opt} which minimizes D_{SH}.

8.4.4   Fail-Safe Fiber-Optic Nodes

As an example of a bypass technique, let us continue to look at the topic we started in Sec. 4.2 concerning some fail-safe nodes that have been used in fiber-optic local area networks.[34-42] The characteristics of these nodes are that in a network containing a string of active repeaters, the network keeps functioning when power is lost at one or more nodes. Figure 8.19 shows a ring network consisting of a transmitter and receiver pair, a regenerator connecting this pair, and a passive lightwave coupler. The nodes are connected by optical fibers. A similar scheme can be envisioned for a linear bus network.

In normal operation each node actively monitors the transmission line and regenerates (amplifies and retransmits) information flowing in the network. When a node wishes to transmit, it turns off its regenerator and inserts its information into the network at the transmitter. Thus, in case the node fails electronically or if components are removed for maintenance, the lightwave coupler provides optical-line continuity for uninterrupted network operation.

To operate properly, the fail-safe network must meet sensitivity and interference constraints. The *sensitivity constraint* is that any receiver must be sensitive enough to detect the signal from a preceding transmitter when several nodes

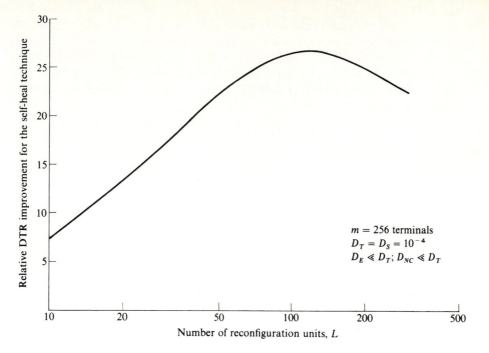

$m = 256$ terminals
$D_T = D_S = 10^{-4}$
$D_E \ll D_T; D_{NC} \ll D_T$

FIGURE 8.18
Relative DTR improvement of the self-heal technique as a function of the number of reconfiguration units.

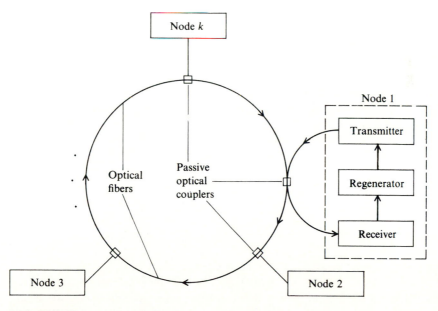

FIGURE 8.19
General schematic of a fiber-optic ring network.

between the transmitter and the receiver are off. The exact allowed number of adjacent failed nodes is derived from the system requirements. The *interference constraint* states that when two nodes are transmitting simultaneously, a downstream node should receive the signal from the closer node. This means that the less intense signal from the more distant transmitter must be below the threshold level of the receiver.

Each fail-safe node can have one or two optical couplers, depending on the particular operation desired. Figure 8.20 shows the concept of a one-coupler node. Here P_{in} is the optical power entering the coupler from the ring, and P_t is the optical power entering the coupler from the transmitter. In this configuration the receiver must be off when the transmitter is on to avoid saturation of the receiver. This is accomplished with a signal format having a duty cycle less then 50 percent, and having the transmitter operate out of phase from the receiver.

As we noted in Fig. 4.20, the coupler is characterized by a four-port device. Its basic parameters are C_T which represents the fraction of power removed from the ring, F_i which is the fraction of power lost in the coupler, and E which is the coupling efficiency of optical power onto the ring. For simplicity of analysis, here we will ignore the factor F_c which is the fraction of power lost at each port of the coupler (this is essentially the connector loss).

Under the condition that the transmitter is off, the optical power P_r entering the receiver is

$$P_r = C_T P_{in} \tag{8.40}$$

When the transmitter is on, the optical power leaving the coupler and entering the ring is

$$P_{out} = (1 - F_i)(1 - C_T)P_{in} + EP_t \tag{8.41}$$

where P_{in} and P_t fall in different time slots.

Now suppose Q adjacent upstream nodes have failed and are off. Given that the fibers between nodes have a length L and an attenuation α_f, the power received after these Q nodes is $P_S + P_I$.

Here

$$P_S = C_T \alpha_f^{Q+1}(1 - F_i)^Q(1 - C_T)^Q EP_t \tag{8.42}$$

is the power received from the closest active transmitter, and

$$P_I = \sum_{j=Q}^{\infty} C_T \alpha_f^{j+2}(1 - F_i)^{j+1}(1 + C_T)^{j+1} EP_t$$

$$= \frac{\alpha_f^{Q+2}[(1 - F_i)(1 + C_T)]^{Q+1} C_T EP_t}{1 - (1 - F_i)(1 - C_T)\alpha_f} \tag{8.43}$$

is the sum of the powers from all the other upstream active transmitters that could cause interference.

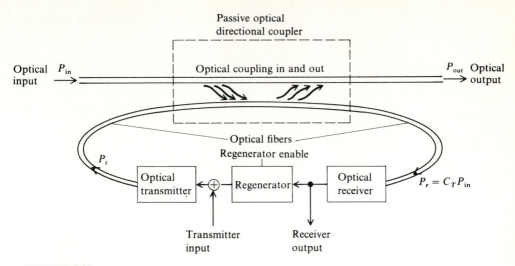

FIGURE 8.20
Concept for connecting to a fiber-optic ring or bus using one passive coupler.

Equation (8.43) takes into account the worst case of interference. The sensitivity and interference constraints are fulfilled when the effective received power, which is given by the difference of Eqs. (8.42) and (8.43), is greater than the sensitivity S of the receiver

$$P_S - P_I \geq S \tag{8.44}$$

Figure 8.21 shows a two-coupler arrangement. In this case the receiver can always be on because it does not receive optical power from the collocated transmitter.

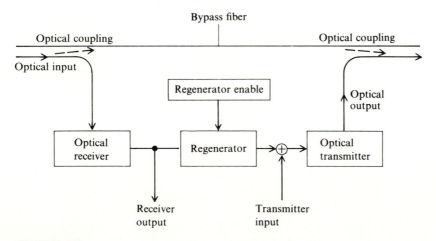

FIGURE 8.21
Concept for connecting to a fiber-optic ring or bus using two passive couplers.

A similar analysis as in Eqs. (8.40) to (8.44) can be carried out for the two-coupler node. The only difference is that we replace $\beta = (1 - F_i)(1 - C_T)$ in Eqs. (8.42) and (8.43) by β^2.

8.5 SUMMARY

In defining network reliability, we need to examine a variety of qualitative and quantitative factors. One important consideration is the topological arrangement of a network, since the simplest measure of reliability is whether or not a network is completely connected. If the geographical location and layout permits it, then redundancy of either transmission or nodal equipment can be used to achieve higher overall reliability in the event of failures. The cut-saturation algorithm is one analytical tool a designer can use to determine which alternate lines should be added to increase reliability.

In any given network consisting of a number of identical components, individual transmission lines and nodal devices will generally fail at different times when operated under similar conditions. To predict network performance, we therefore resort to probability theory. The most straightforward performance measure is to calculate the probability of one node in the network becoming disconnected. In this analysis it is desirable to calculate the minimum value of the connectivity probability or the maximum value of the failure probability. Although the concept is straightforward, for most networks of interest which consist of a large number of nodes and lines, the exact calculation requires the use of computer algorithms.[17,21–27]

Probability theory is particularly useful in analyzing the reliability and availability of a network having various failure and repair states. In doing this, we consider networks having two-state elements (e.g., node connections, transmission lines, and terminals), where the states are either operational or failed. Network repair is worthwhile whenever the average cost of a piece of equipment is a fraction of its initial cost. The basic parameters used in the analytical models are the reliability function, the mean time to failure (MTTF), the mean time to repair (MTTR), the mean time between failures (MTBF), and the availability function.

The reliability and availability of a network can be enhanced by keeping active electronics in the transmission path to a minimum, reducing the number of repeaters or line amplifiers between stations, and by distributing the control electronics throughout the network. Reliability can also be improved by providing redundancy of transmission paths and nodal equipment. Two fundamental techniques exist for improving reliability in a ring, which can be a relatively vulnerable configuration. These are the node-bypass and the self-heal techniques that are used in conjunction with reconfiguration switches and a redundant standby loop in parallel with the main ring.

PROBLEMS

Section 8.1

8.1. Consider the network shown in Fig. 8.2.

(a) Removing which node would disconnect the network?
(b) Which pairs of lines must be cut to disjoin the network?
(c) What nodes need to be joined to change the degree of the network to 3?

8.2. For the network shown in Fig. P8.2,

(a) Find all two-line cuts that would disconnect nodes A and F.
(b) Which nodes would be isolated by themselves through two line cuts?

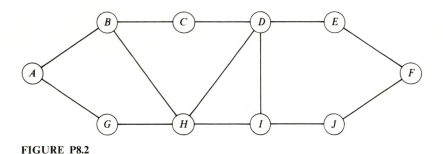

FIGURE P8.2

8.3. Consider a network having 13 nodes and 18 links. Assume these links have the following traffic load-to-capacity ratios:

AB	9/10	EG	18/30	CJ	3/15
BC	7/10	EF	4/10	JL	5/15
CM	5/15	FH	2/20	ML	2/10
AD	2/15	GH	12/30	KL	3/20
AE	7/30	GI	19/20	BK	29/30
DF	2/10	BI	15/40	IK	5/10

Use the cut-saturation algorithm to determine which pairs of nodes could be connected to improve throughput.

Section 8.2

8.4. Figure P8.4 shows a simple four-node, five-line network. Considering only line failures and assuming the same failure probability for each line:

(a) Find a binomial expression in which the probabilities of all failed states are summed to unity. State what each term in this expression means;
(b) Derive the coefficients $A_L(i)$ in Eq. (8.2);
(c) Derive the coefficients $C_L(i)$ in Eq. (8.4).

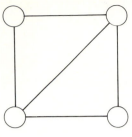

FIGURE P8.4

8.5. For typical network lines the failure probability p is small. Thus it is often sufficient to use only the first term of the series expansions given in Eqs. (8.2) to (8.5). Using Fig. P8.2, find the leading term for Eq. (8.4).

8.6. Consider the network shown in Fig. P8.6.

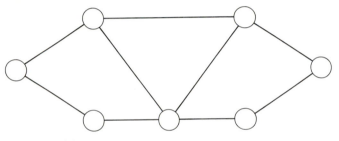

FIGURE P8.6

(*a*) Calculate the upper and lower bounds for the probability of the network becoming disconnected as a function of the link failure probability p.

(*b*) If $p = 0.1$, how much larger is the upper bound than the lower bound?

Section 8.3

8.7. In using the Markov model, we are interested in the transition probability from one state to another in a small time interval Δt. The transition probabilities must obey the following two rules: (1) the probability of transition from one state to another is $z(t)\,\Delta t$ where $z(t)$ is the transition rate, (2) the probability of more than one transition occurring during the interval Δt is negligible.

With these rules in mind, derive Eqs. (8.13), which describe the transitions from state 0 to state 1 shown in Fig. 8.6 (no repair) by using the following considerations:

(*a*) The probability $P_0(t + \Delta t)$ of being in state 0 at time $(t + \Delta t)$ is the probability $P_0(t)$ that the system is in state 0 at t multiplied by the probability $[1 - \lambda(t)\,\Delta t]$ of *no* failures during the interval Δt, plus the probability of being in state 1 at t multiplied by the probability of repair (which is zero here).

(*b*) The probability $P_1(t + \Delta t)$ of being in state 1 at time $(t + \Delta t)$ is the probability of the system being in state 0 at t multiplied by the probability of a failure during the interval Δt, plus the probability of being in state 1 at t multiplied by the probability of no repair during the interval Δt (which equals one here).

8.8. Derive Eq. (8.14) from Eqs. (8.13a) and (8.13b) using the stated boundary conditions.

8.9. Using the expression for $R(t)$ given in Eq. (8.15), plot $f(t)$ given by Eq. (8.12) as a function of t. Make the plot in terms of arbitrary values of λ. Indicate which areas of the curve represent $F(t)$ and $R(t)$.

8.10. Using the state-transition diagram shown in Fig. 8.7 for a system with repair, derive the differential equations given in Eq. (8.19). Follow the arguments given in Prob. 8.7.

8.11. Derive Eq. (8.20) from Eqs. (8.19) using the stated initial conditions.

8.12. A local area network operates 24 hours a day over an average of 20 days per month. Suppose the network fails once a month and that the breakdown takes 4 hours to repair.

(*a*) What is the MTTF?

(*b*) What is the steady state availability?

(*c*) Find the probability of failure in an 8-hour shift.

8.13. Consider a system that consists of four series-connected components, which is expected to operate for 2000 hours. Suppose the components have individual MTTFs of 6000, 4500, 12,000, and 3000 h.

(*a*) Find the value of the reliability function for $t = 2000$ h.

(*b*) What is the system MTTF_s?

(*c*) What is the system reliability if the required operating time is reduced to 1000 h? to 500 h?

8.14. Suppose a system has two identical units connected in parallel. Let each unit have a reliability of 95 percent.

(*a*) What is the reliability of the system?

(*b*) What is the reliability when a third identical unit is added in parallel?

8.15. Suppose we have two nonidentical units connected in parallel which have failure rates of $3 \times 10^{-4}/\text{h}$ and $2 \times 10^{-4}/\text{h}$.

(*a*) What are the component reliabilities at $t = 1000$ h?

(*b*) What is the system reliability at $t = 1000$ h?

8.16. Derive reliability expressions in terms of the unit reliabilities R_i for the three systems shown in Fig. P8.16. *Hint:* First evaluate the reliability of the parallel elements.

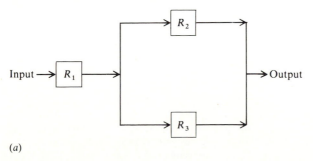

(*a*)

FIGURE P8.16   (*Continued*)

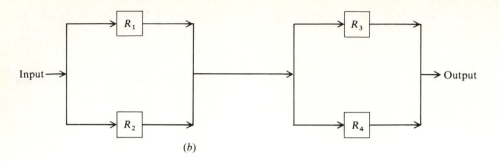

(b)

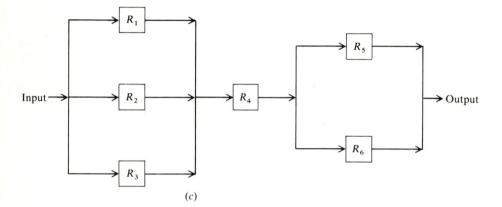

(c)

FIGURE P8.16 (*continued*)

Section 8.4

8.17. Compare the relative DTR degradation shown in Fig. 8.9 with the degradation occurring for the following cases:

(a) $D_E = D_{NC} = D_T = 10^{-4}$;
(b) $D_E = D_{NC} = 3D_T$ and $D_T = 10^{-4}$.

8.18. Using Eq. (8.14), derive the expression in Eq. (8.15) which gives the value of L at which a minimum of $D_B(L, m)$ occurs.

8.19. For very small values of X, we have that $e^X \sim 1 + X$. Using this relationship, derive Eq. (8.16) from Eqs. (8.14) and (8.15).

8.20. Given that $D_T = 10^{-4}$, find the values of D_S for which L_{opt} is equal to m when there are:

(a) 100 terminals, (b) 256 terminals.

REFERENCES

1. C. Berge, *The Theory of Graphs and Its Applications*, Wiley, New York, 1962.
2. F. Harary, *Graph Theory*, Addison-Wesley, Reading, MA, 1969.
3. D. J. Kleitman, "Methods for investigating connectivity of large graphs," *IEEE Trans. Circuit Theory*, vol. CT-16, pp. 232–233, May 1969.

4. M. Gerla and L. Kleinrock, "On the topological design of distributed computer networks," *IEEE Trans. Commun.*, vol. COM-25, pp. 48–60, January 1977.
5. S. Even, "An algorithm for determining whether the connectivity of a graph is at least k," *SIAM J. Comput.*, vol. 4, pp. 393–396, September 1975.
6. A. S. Tanenbaum, *Computer Networks*, Prentice-Hall, Englewood Cliffs, NJ, 1981, chap. 2.
7. D. W. Davies, D. L. A. Barber, W. L. Price, and C. M. Solomonides, *Computer Networks and Their Protocols*, Wiley, New York, 1979, chap. 10.
8. R. Boorstyn and H. Frank, "Large-scale network topological optimization," *IEEE Trans. Commun.*, vol. COM-25, pp. 29–47, January 1977.
9. H. Frank and W. Chou, "Topological optimization of computer networks," *Proc. IEEE*, vol. 60, pp. 1385–1397, November 1972.
10. L. R. Ford and D. R. Fulkerson, *Flows in Networks*, Princeton Univ. Press, Princeton, NJ, 1962.
11. H. Frank and I. Frisch, *Communication, Transmission and Transportation Networks*, Addison-Wesley, Reading, MA, 1971.
12. V. M. Malhotra, M. P. Kumas, and S. N. Maheshwari, "An $O(|V|^3)$ algorithm for finding maximum flows in networks," *Inf. Proc. Lett.*, vol. 7, pp. 277–278, October 1978.
13. M. Gerla, H. Frank, and J. Eckl, "A cut-saturation algorithm for topological design of packet switched communication networks," *Proc. Nat. Telecommun. Conf.*, pp. 1074–1085, December 1974.
14. R. F. Moore and C. E. Shannon, "Reliable circuits using less reliable relays," *J. Franklin Inst.*, part 1, vol. 262, pp. 191–208, September 1956; part 2, vol. 262, pp. 281–297, October 1956.
15. R. S. Wilkov, "Analysis and design of reliable computer networks," *IEEE Trans. Commun.*, vol. COM-20, pp. 660–678, June 1972.
16. W. H. Debany, Jr., P. K. Varshney, and C. R. P. Hartmann, "Network reliability evaluation using probability expressions," *IEEE Trans. Reliability*, vol. R-35, pp. 161–166, June 1986.
17. V. O. K. Li and J. A. Silvester, "Performance analysis of networks with unreliable components," *IEEE Trans. Commun.*, vol. COM-32, pp. 1105–1110, October 1984.
18. Y. F. Lam and V. O. K. Li, "An improved algorithm for performance analysis of networks with unreliable components," *IEEE Trans. Commun.*, vol. COM-34, pp. 496–497, May 1986.
19. M. O. Ball, "Computing network reliability," *Operations Research*, vol. 27, pp. 823–838, July-August 1979.
20. M. O. Ball, "Computational complexity of network reliability analysis: An overview," *IEEE Trans. Reliability*, vol. R-35, pp. 230–239, August 1986.
21. E. Haensler, "A fast recursive algorithm to calculate the reliability of a communication network," *IEEE Trans. Commun.*, vol. COM-20, pp. 637–640, June 1972.
22. J. F. Hayes, *Modeling and Analysis of Computer Communication Networks*, Plenum, New York, 1984, chap. 13.
23. E. Haensler, G. K. McAuliffe, and R. S. Wilkov, "Exact calculation of computer network reliability," *Networks*, vol. 4, pp. 95–112, 1974.
24. Y. F. Lam and V. O. K. Li, "Reliability modeling and analysis of communication networks with dependent failures," *IEEE Trans. Commun.*, vol. COM-34, pp. 82–84, January 1986.
25. J. D. Spragins, "Dependent failures in data communication systems," *IEEE Trans. Commun.*, vol. COM-25, pp. 1494–1498, December 1977.
26. ———, J. D. Markov, M. W. Doss, S. A. Mitchell, and D. C. Squire," Communication network availability prediction based on measurement data," *IEEE Trans. Commun.*, vol. COM-29, pp. 1482–1491, October 1981.
27. (*a*) M. J. Johnson, "Reliability mechanisms of the FDDI high bandwidth token ring protocol," *Computer Networks and ISDN Sys.*, vol. 11, pp. 121–131, February 1986.
(*b*) M. J. Johnson, "Proof that timing requirements of the FDDI token ring protocol are satisfied," IEEE Trans. Commun., vol. COM-35, pp. 620–625, June 1987.
28. M. L. Shooman, *Probabilistic Reliability, An Engineering Approach*, McGraw-Hill, New York, 1968.
29. B. S. Dhillon, *Reliability Engineering in Systems Design and Operation*, Van Nostrand Reinhold, New York, 1983.

30. I. Bagovsky, Sr., *Reliability Theory and Practice*, Prentice-Hall, Englewood Cliffs, NJ, 1960.
31. S. W. Ng, "Reliability and availability of duplex systems: Some simple models," *IEEE Trans. Reliability*, vol. R-35, pp. 295–300, August 1986.
32. C. S. Raghavendra and S. V. Makam, "Reliability modeling and analysis of computer networks," *IEEE Trans. Reliability*, vol. R-35, pp. 156–160, June 1986.
33. P. Zafiropulo, "Performance evaluation of reliability improvement techniques for single-loop communications systems," *IEEE Trans. Commun.*, vol. COM-22, pp. 742–751, June 1974.
34. A. Albanese, "Fail-safe nodes for lightguide digital networks," *Bell Sys. Tech. J.*, vol. 61, pp. 247–256, February 1982.
35. J. P. Van Dooren, "Local area networks on optical fiber," *Fourth World Telecom Forum*, Geneva, Switzerland, paper 3.13.7, November 1983.
36. P. A. Bulteel and J. Tillemans, "New directional coupler and connecting device for fiber optic local area networks," *SPIE Conf. on Fiber Optic Couplers, Connectors, and Splice Tech.*, Arlington, Virginia, May 1-2 1984.
37. R. Rom and N. Shacham, "A reconfiguration algorithm for a double-loop token-ring local area network," *IEEE Trans. Computer*, vol. 37, pp. 182–189, February 1988.
38. B. S. Kawasaki and K. O. Hill, "Low-loss access coupler for multimode optical fiber distribution networks," *Appl. Opt.*, vol. 16, pp. 1794–1795, July 1977.
39. M. M. Nassehi, F. A. Tobagi, and M. M. Marhic, "Fiber optic configurations for local area networks," *IEEE J. Selected Areas Commun.*, vol. SAC-3, pp. 941–949, November 1985.
40. G. Keiser, *Optical Fiber Communications*, McGraw-Hill, New York, 1983, chap. 8.
41. S. F. Su, L. Jou, and J. Lenart, "A review on classification of optical switching systems," *IEEE Commun. Mag.*, vol. 24, pp. 50–55, May 1986.
42. A. R. Tebo, "Fiber-optic couplers: Directional and otherwise," *Electro-Optic Sys. Design*, vol. 13, pp. 25–45, November 1981.

CHAPTER
9

NETWORK
SECURITY

As a result of the rapidly growing use of local area networks and their interactions will all types of other networks (often on a worldwide basis), the problem of protecting the confidentiality and integrity of the information transmitted on these networks started to attract widespread attention[1-6] in the late 1970s and early 1980s. Local area networks are particularly vulnerable to security compromise, since they are by definition designed to provide many user access points. Since a feature of LANs is that additional access points can be easily added without having any effect on other network users, these connections could be used by an unauthorized person to gain access to proprietary or classified information.

To protect both equipment and information, network security must consider a wide range of administrative, physical, and technical issues. To select an appropriate set of network security measures, one first needs to evaluate the threat environment and assess the security risks in that environment. For example, the threat environment determines whether the main concern is to physically protect the hardware from accidental or intentional damage and access, to ensure that only trustworthy people are operating and using the network, or to protect programs and user data from accidental or malicious modification, disclosure, and destruction. Once the threat has been established, appropriate security techniques can be selected and applied.

In this chapter we first address some of the general issues concerning local area network security. We then consider mechanisms for achieving security, with particular emphasis on encryption since this is a fundamental tool for ensuring security in data communications.

9.1 ISSUES IN NETWORK SECURITY

To get an idea of where security fits into a LAN, let us examine Fig. 9.1. Here we see a variety of interfaces to a LAN, including individually attached users, multiple users connected through a host computer, a bridge connecting a similar LAN, a gateway connecting a dissimilar LAN or a public network, and other equipment such as printers, memory banks, and shared computers. The transmission medium connecting the various elements and networks could be

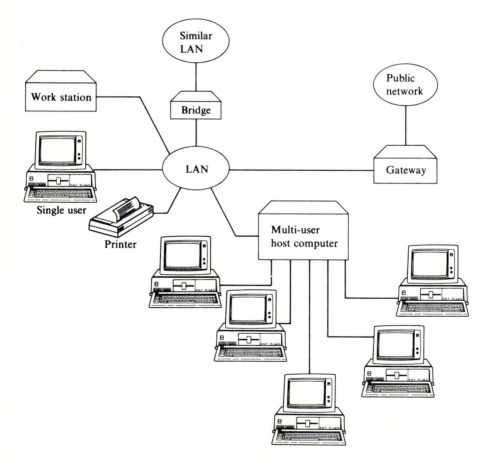

FIGURE 9.1
Security environment for a local area network.

twisted-pair wires, coaxial cables, optical fibers, leased phone lines, microwave links, or satellite links.

9.1.1   Threats to Network Security

Depending on the quantity and value of the information being carried in the network, an adverse party may find it desirable to intercept the information transmission. This interception has traditionally been referred to as *wiretapping.* In considering network security, one generally assumes that an intruder can be located at some point in the network through which all information of interest must pass. Referring to Fig. 9.1 this could be at any point in the network, including the transmission link, at a multiple-user host computer, in a bridge, or in a gateway. Thus, the wiretapper could be located outside of the LAN user community or be an otherwise legitimate user of the network.

Wiretapping can be done in either a passive or an active manner. In *passive wiretapping* an intruder simply monitors the messages at some point without interfering with the information flow. Such unauthorized observation of information is referred to as *release of message content* and is the most basic type of passive wiretapping.

The most obvious objective of this covert data observation is to learn the contents of the messages. However, even if the observed information is not intelligible to the unauthorized user, the protocol control information contained in the message header can reveal the locations and identities of the communicating parties. Furthermore, when the message content is not available, the wiretapper can examine the quantities, lengths, and frequencies of the message transmissions to learn about the character of the data being exchanged. These types of passive attacks are referred to as *traffic analysis.*

Whereas passive wiretapping does not interfere with the message flow, in *active wiretapping* some type of message processing is performed on the information stream that passes the tapping point. For example, messages could be selectively modified, deleted, delayed, reordered, duplicated either immediately or at a later time, or be allowed to pass through unaffected. In addition, bogus messages can be created. These types of activities are referred to as *unauthorized message stream modification.*

Denial of service to a user by a temporary or permanent incapacitation of the LAN is another form of active wiretapping. Here the adversary can discard all messages that pass the connection point, or can delay all messages going in either one or both directions. Attacks of this nature are classified as *unauthorized denial of message service.*

A point to note here is that active and passive wiretapping require different defense mechanisms. The passive attacks of release of message contents and traffic analysis usually cannot be detected, but they can effectively be prevented. Conversely, active attacks such as message stream modification, denial of message service, and message playbacks cannot be prevented but they can be readily detected.

9.1.2   Approaches to Network Security

Secure communication in physically vulnerable networks depends on the disciplines of cryptography to protect the confidentiality and integrity of material passing between machines. Cryptography, which comes from the Greek words *kryptos* or "hidden" and *graphein* or "to write," is the science of secret communication. It is a methodology for transforming the representation or appearance of a message through a position-scrambling process or through some method of transformation of letters or characters without changing its information content. The original message is called *plaintext* or *cleartext* and the transformed message is known as *ciphertext*, which is also sometimes called a *cryptogram*.

Military and intelligence organizations have used many forms of cryptographic techniques to protect sensitive and secret information for thousands of years. For example, in Sec. 9.2 we discuss a message-encoding methodology used by Julius Ceasar when sending messages to his general. The process of changing plaintext to ciphertext is called *enciphering* or *encryption*. The inverse operation which changes ciphertext to plaintext is known as *deciphering* or *decryption*. We discuss the fundamentals of these techniques in Sec. 9.2. Although its primary purpose is to provide secrecy as a countermeasure for preventing unauthorized information disclosure under passive attacks, encryption can also detect active attacks such as message-stream modification, denial of service, and fraudulent initial connection.

To see where security fits into a communication network, let us look back at the seven-layer OSI Model described in Chap. 2. Although, in principle, encryption can be done in any of the seven layers of the OSI Model, it is usually only implemented in several of them. The two fundamental approaches to communication security are link-oriented and end-to-end encryption measures.

As its name implies, *link-oriented security measures* protect message traffic passing over an individual transmission link between two nodes, regardless of the original source and the ultimate destination of that information. The general scheme is shown in Fig. 9.2 where encryption is performed independently on each communication link between successive modems. The encryption is done by means of a function called a *key*. Each link corresponds to a data-link layer association in the OSI Reference Model. An advantage of link-oriented security is that, depending on the encryption method used, it can mask origin-to-destination information flow patterns and can completely prevent all forms of traffic analysis by hiding message frequency and length patterns. A weakness of link-oriented security is that since information is encrypted only on the links, the network nodes must be both physically secure and capable of isolating information from each of the various independent data streams that could pass through the node.

In contrast to this protection of individual links, *end-to-end security* uniformly protects each message along its entire route from source to destination as is shown in Fig. 9.3. Thus messages pass through the entire network of transmission links, local computers, intermediate nodes, and switches in an encrypted

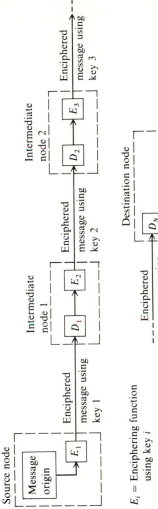

E_i = Enciphering function using key i

D_i = Deciphering function using key i

FIGURE 9.2
Link-oriented security measures.

325

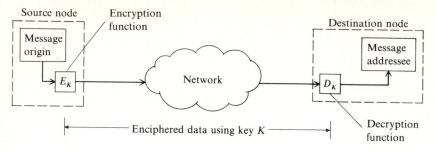

FIGURE 9.3
End-to-end security scheme.

form as provided by the encryption device at the message originator. However, only the *user data* can be encrypted since the network control information must remain unencrypted to be processible by the network nodes. Ideally then a combination of link-oriented and end-to-end encryption techniques would be desirable.

Encryption to implement end-to-end security is usually done in the host-to-host levels above the OSI network layer. The higher the layer at which encryption is performed, the greater security it provides to the user. A major advantage of end-to-end security measures is that an individual user or host computer can use them without affecting other users or hosts. Consequently the cost of implementing these measures can be fairly apportioned among the participating users of the service. Some caution must be exercised though when discussing end-to-end security, since there is a fair amount of flexibility in identifying exactly at which endpoints the security measures are implemented. For example, the end-to-end measures can run from host to host, from terminal to service host or process, or from process to process.

9.2 DATA ENCRYPTION

In this section we first examine the basic concepts of data encryption and then describe two fundamental data encryption techniques.[1,7-11] These are transposition ciphers and simple substitution ciphers. We examine two further encryption methods in Secs. 9.3 and 9.4. These are product ciphers as exemplified by the Data Encryption Standard (DES) and exponential ciphers, an example of which is the Rivest-Shamir-Adleman (RSA) scheme.

9.2.1 Basic Concepts

The fundamental encryption and decryption processes are represented pictorially in Fig. 9.4. The encryption function has two inputs, one of which is the plaintext and the other is called a *key*. The key consists of a finite number of bits which

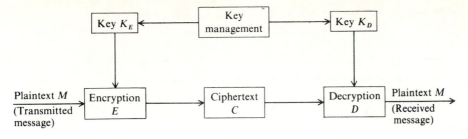

FIGURE 9.4
Fundamental encryption and decryption processes.

are usually expressed as decimal, hexadecimal, or alphanumeric character strings. Although the length of the key may be of the same order of magnitude as the plaintext, it is commonly eight characters long for practical reasons.

As depicted in Fig. 9.4, the function of the encryption key K_E is to perform some mathematical operation (denoted by E) on the plaintext to transform it into ciphertext. This encryption algorithm must be *invertible*. That is, there must be a decryption algorithm D that reverses the encryption transformation when presented with the appropriate decryption key K_D. In mathematical notation, if

$$M = \text{plaintext message}$$
$$C = \text{ciphertext}$$
$$K = \text{key}$$
$$E = \text{encryption function}$$
$$D = \text{decryption function}$$

then for encryption

$$C = E_K(M) \tag{9.1}$$

and for decryption

$$M = D_K(C)$$
$$= D_K[E_K(M)] \tag{9.2}$$

The effectiveness of the encryption technique does not depend on whether or not the encryption algorithm is secret. Instead, its success in preventing information-security breaches depends on the degree of difficulty required to decipher it without having knowledge of the decryption key. A property of the decryption key is that it should not be derivable by anyone who has knowledge of the encryption key, the ciphertext, *and* the plaintext. The amount of work required by an adversary to break the code should be prohibitively expensive compared to the value of the information being protected.

The theory and practice of uncovering a secret from either ciphertext or encryption keys without the authorization of the sender is known as *cryptanalysis.*[12-14] The means of doing this is called the *method of attack*. A cryptanalyst could make one of the three following kinds of attacks:

1. *Ciphertext only.* The cryptanalyst has only one or more cryptograms that are known to have been encrypted with the same key.
2. *Known plaintext.* In addition to an undeciphered cryptogram, the cryptanalyst has available one or more plaintexts *and* their resulting cryptograms that are known to have been created by the same key.
3. *Chosen plaintext.* For any desired plaintext, the cryptanalyst can obtain their resulting cryptograms using the same key from which the undeciphered cryptogram of interest was created.

The designer of any encryption system should ideally make it secure against a chosen-plaintext attack. If this is not possible then it should be secure against a known-plaintext attack. Failing this, it should at the very least be immune to a ciphertext-only attack.

The encryption ciphers can be either secret or public.[15] In a *conventional* (*secret*) *cipher* the same key is used to encrypt and decrypt a message. Such a key must obviously be kept secret. This type of system is alternately referred to as a *classical, symmetric,* or *one-key cryptosystem.*

On the other hand, in a *public-key cipher* (which is also known as an *asymmetric* or a *two-key cryptosystem*) different keys are used to encrypt and decrypt a message.[16] These keys define a pair of transformations, each of which is the inverse of the other and neither of which is derivable from the other. The encryption key is made publicly known, whereas the corresponding decryption key is kept secret.

Keys held for long periods of time are referred to as *master, primary,* or *key-encryption* keys. Keys used during the course of a single association between communicating parties are known as *working, secondary,* or *data-encryption* keys. Master keys are used to verify the authenticity of the communicating parties and to safely transmit working keys. Working keys are used exclusively to encrypt information on a single association.

An important aspect is the management of these keys.[11,17-19] Key management encompasses all the procedures for generating, distributing, storing, entering, using, and destroying or archiving cryptographic keys. For systems employing a small number of keys, manual management techniques are used. However, in large computer networks automated distribution is needed to allow keys to be exchanged quickly and transparently in an efficient, flexible, low-cost, and secure manner.

9.2.2 Transposition Ciphers

Transposition ciphers are based on the rearrangement of each character in the plaintext message to produce a ciphertext. These encryption techniques include reversing the entire message, reforming the message into a geometrical shape, rearranging the plaintext by scrambling a sequence of columns, and periodically permuting the characters of the plaintext. Let us now look at some simple examples to illustrate these techniques.

Encryption using *message reversal* means that the plaintext is written backwards to produce a ciphertext. If the plaintext message is

LOCAL AREA NETWORK SECURITY

then the encrypted message reads

YTIRUCES KROWTEN AERA LACOL

This is one of the simplest encryption methods. Obviously it is not very secure, since to decipher it one merely reads the ciphertext in reverse.

In *geometrical pattern encoding* the message is rearranged with the aid of some type of geometric figure, a typical example being a two-dimensional array or matrix. First the plaintext message is written into the figure according to a particular pattern. The ciphertext is then created by taking the letters off the figure according to a different path. For example, suppose the plaintext word LIECHTENSTEINER is written into a 3×5 matrix by rows as follows

Column number	1	2	3	4	5
Ciphertext	L	I	E	C	H
	T	E	N	S	T
	E	I	N	E	R

If the letters are taken off by columns in the order 2 4 1 3 5, the resulting ciphertext is IEICSELTEENNHTR.

In *columnar transposition*, one first transposes the plaintext message into a rectangular form by columns. The columns are next rearranged and the letters are then taken off in a horizontal fashion. For example, consider the plaintext message "The Product Brochure is Ready," which we write into a 5×5 matrix by columns as follows

Column number	1	2	3	4	5
Ciphertext	T	O	B	U	R
	H	D	R	R	E
	E	U	O	E	A
	P	C	C	I	D
	R	T	H	S	Y

Since there are five columns, they can be rearranged in $5! = 120$ different ways. To enhance the security of the plaintext message, we can thus choose one of these rearrangements.

If we shift the columns into the position 3 5 2 4 1, we have

Column number	3	5	2	4	1
Ciphertext	B	R	O	U	T
	R	E	D	R	H
	O	A	U	E	E
	C	D	C	I	P
	H	Y	T	S	R

Reading the letters off in a horizontal fashion then yields the ciphertext

BROUT REDRH OAUEE CDCIP HYTSR

Note that here we show the ciphertext in groups of five letters only for reader clarity. The actual encrypted message would be sent as a continuous stream of characters to hide the encryption periodicity.

A drawback in using columnar transposition ciphers for computer applications is that entire matrices of characters must be generated for encryption and decryption. A more efficient method is one which permutes the characters of the plaintext with a *fixed period d*. If the function f is a permutation of a block of d characters, then the encryption key is represented by $K(d, f)$. Thus a plaintext message

$$M = m_1 m_2 \cdots m_d m_{d+1} \cdots m_{2d} \cdots \qquad (9.3)$$

where the m_i are individual characters, is encrypted as

$$E_K(M) = m_{f(1)} m_{f(2)} \cdots m_{f(d)} m_{d+f(1)} \cdots m_{d+f(d)} \cdots \qquad (9.4)$$

where $m_{f(1)} m_{f(2)} \cdots m_{f(d)}$ is a permutation of $m_1 m_2 \cdots m_d$.

As an example, let $d = 5$ and suppose f permutes the sequence i: 1 2 3 4 5 into $f(i) = 3\ 5\ 1\ 4\ 2$. As shown in Fig. 9.5, this means that the first entry in a block of five characters is moved to the third position, the second character moves to the fifth position, and so on. The plaintext word GROUP for example, becomes OPGUR. Using Fig. 9.5, the plaintext message

I LOVE BEETHOVENS MUSIC

Starting position	Permutation position	Word	Result
1	3	G	O
2	5	R	P
3	1	O	G
4	4	U	U
5	2	P	R

FIGURE 9.5
Example of a permutation transposition with a period $d = 5$.

is then encrypted as

OEIVL EHBTE ESONV SCMIU

where again we have left spaces in the ciphertext for clarity.

In discussions on cryptography, the process of shuffling the positions of binary digits is often illustrated by means of a permutation box or a *P* box, such as the one shown in Fig. 9.6.

9.2.3 Substitution Ciphers

Substitution enciphering involves the replacement of each character in the plaintext by some other character. This can be either a letter, a number, or a symbol. The four basic classes of substitution ciphers are as follows:

1. *Simple substitution.* Each character of plaintext is replaced by a corresponding character of ciphertext; a single one-to-one mapping from plaintext to ciphertext is used to encrypt an entire message.
2. *Homophonic substitution.* Each plaintext character is encrypted with a variety of ciphertext characters; the mapping from plaintext to ciphertext is thus one-to-many.
3. *Polyalphabetic substitution.* Multiple cipher alphabets are used to change plaintext to ciphertext; the mappings are usually one-to-one as in simple substitution, but can change within a single message.
4. *Polygram substitution.* These are the most general ciphers; they permit arbitrary substitutions for groups of plaintext characters.

For illustrative purposes, we only discuss simple substitution ciphers here. The interested reader should consult the literature[8,9] for further details. First let us look at some notation. Suppose A is a *plaintext n-character alphabet* ordered as $\{a_0, a_1, a_2, \ldots, a_{n-1}\}$. A simple substitution cipher then replaces each character

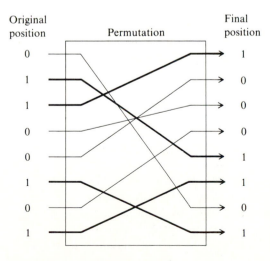

Original position — Permutation — Final position

Original position	Final position
0	1
1	0
1	0
0	0
0	1
1	1
0	0
1	1

FIGURE 9.6
Concept of a permutation box or *P* box.

of A by a corresponding character from an ordered *cipher alphabet* C denoted by $\{f(a_0), f(a_1), \ldots, f(a_{n-1})\}$. Here the function f represents a one-to-one mapping of each character of A to the corresponding character of C. A plaintext message

$$M = m_1 m_2 \cdots \qquad (9.5)$$

is then written in ciphertext as

$$E_K(M) = f(m_1) f(m_2) \cdots \qquad (9.6)$$

where m_i is a character of A. Typically C is simply a rearrangement of the characters in A.

One of the most well-known simple-substitution ciphers is the Morse code in which letters of the alphabet are replaced by a series of dots and dashes. The ASCII code shown in Table 2.5 is also a simple-substitution cipher. For example, the letter A is represented by the binary number 1000001 or 65 in decimal notation, B is given by 1000010 or 66, and so forth up to 1011010 or 90 for Z.

Another popular simple-substitution cipher is a *shifted alphabet*. Here the letters of the alphabet are shifted to the right by k positions, modulo the size of the alphabet. That is, if a represents both a letter of A and its position in the alphabet, then

$$f(a) = (a + k) \bmod n \qquad (9.7)$$

where n is 26 for the standard English alphabet. This type of cipher is also known as a *Caesar cipher* since Julius Caesar used it with $k = 3$ to send messages to his general.

As an example, if $k = 3$ then we have

Plaintext
  alphabet   A B C D E F G H I J K L M N O P Q R S T U V W X Y Z
Ciphertext
  alphabet   D E F G H I J K L M N O P Q R S T U V W X Y Z A B C

Using this Caesar cipher, the plaintext word

LIECHTENSTEINER

becomes

OLHFKWHQVWHLQHU

in ciphertext.

9.3   THE DATA ENCRYPTION STANDARD (DES)

In 1971 the U.S. National Bureau of Standards announced a Data Encryption Standard (DES) to be used in unclassified United States Government applications.[20] The encryption algorithm was developed at IBM and was an outgrowth of the LUCIFER cipher designed by Feistel.[21]

The DES algorithm converts blocks of 64 bits of plaintext to 64 bits of ciphertext under the action of a key. The key consists of 64 binary digits, 56 of which are used directly by the encryption algorithm and the other 8 bits are used for error detection. A block of data to be encrypted is subjected to an initial permutation, then to a complex key-dependent computation involving sixteen iterations of a function f that combines substitution and transposition, and finally to a permutation which is the inverse of the initial permutation.

Before going into the details of the DES operation, let us first look at some concepts relating to it. These are product ciphers and block ciphers, which we address in Secs. 9.3.1 and 9.3.2, respectively.

9.3.1 Product Ciphers

A product cipher involves a combination of transposition (permutation) and substitution to produce a ciphertext.[22-23] The origin of this method is the 1949 paper by Shannon[24] which connects cryptography with information theory. Shannon suggested using products of the form $B_1 M B_2 M \cdots B_n$ where M is an unkeyed mixing transformation or permutation and the B_i are simple cryptographic transformations. Thus, a product cipher is the application of a sequence of n enciphering functions $f_1, f_2, \ldots, f_n$ where each f_i can be a permutation cipher P or a substitution cipher S.

Figure 9.7 illustrates the application of the basic principle to a 12-bit message block $M = (m_1 m_2 \cdots m_{12})$. We should note that this example is for concept illustration purposes only, since in practice longer blocks should be used. The enciphering scheme alternately applies k substitutions S_i and $k-1$ permutations P_i yielding

$$C = E_K(M) = S_k P_k S_{k-1} \cdots S_2 P_1 S_1(M) \tag{9.8}$$

where each S_i is a function of the key K.

The 12-bit plaintext block is divided into four 3-bit subblocks each of which is acted on by a different invertible 3-bit to 3-bit mapping or substitution cipher S_{ij}. The resulting 12 bits are scrambled by the permutation box P_i and input to the next round of enciphering. The permutation mixes bits from different S_{ij} boxes to prevent the overall transformation from degenerating into a substitution on 3-bit blocks.

9.3.2 Block Ciphers

Block ciphers involve encrypting and decrypting messages in blocks of information bits.[9] Given that M is a plaintext message, a block cipher breaks M into successive blocks $M_1, M_2, \ldots$ and enciphers each M_i with the same key K, that is,

$$E_K(M) = E_K(M_1) E_K(M_2) \cdots \tag{9.9}$$

We have seen examples of this earlier. For example, in simple substitution the block is one character long, and in transposition ciphers with period d, the block is d characters long. In general, each block is several characters long.

Block ciphering has the same basic structure as block coding for error control that is described in Chap. 3. Both transform a block of uncoded or

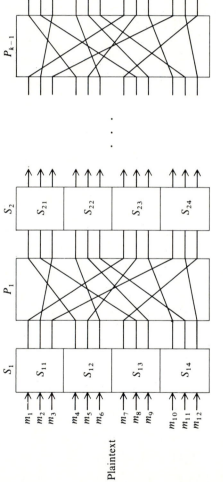

FIGURE 9.7
Product enciphering applied to a 12-bit message block.

334

plaintext message into a block of coded or encrypted message. The difference between the two methods is that block ciphering is done with encryption keys, whereas most block coding schemes rely on parity checking.

The level of secrecy in message transmission with block ciphering can be increased either by (1) partitioning the plaintext into blocks, and then encrypting and decrypting them separately, (2) repeating or iterating the block encryption a number of times, or (3) using a combination of (1) and (2).

The basic concept of block ciphering with partitioning and iteration is shown in Fig. 9.8. A block of message to be transformed iteratively $i = 1, 2, \ldots,$ r times is divided equally into left and right halves denoted as L_i and R_i. If the block is n bits long, then L_i and R_i each have $n/2$ bits. Encryption and decryption is carried out by means of the set of iteration-dependent keys K_{i+1} and a transformation function f. This transformation function depends on R_i and K_{i+1} for encryption and on L_{i+1} and K_{i+1} for decryption.

As shown in Fig. 9.8, for the $(i + 1)$th iteration the encryption yields

$$L_{i+1} = R_i$$
$$R_{i+1} = L_i \oplus f(K_{i+1}, R_i)$$

(9.10)

where $\oplus$ denotes modulo-2 addition. For decryption the order of K_{i+1} is reversed, that is

$$L_i = R_{i+1} \oplus f(K_{i+1}, L_{i+1})$$
$$R_i = L_{i+1}$$

(9.11)

9.3.3 The DES Algorithm

The essential functions of the encryption algorithm used in the DES are partitioning, iteration, permutation, shifting, selection, and modulo-2 addition. Figure 9.9 outlines the enciphering computation of the algorithm, which is used

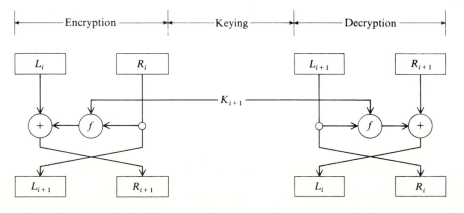

FIGURE 9.8
Basic concept of block enciphering with partitioning and iteration.

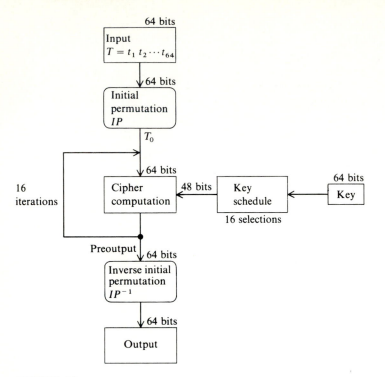

FIGURE 9.9
Outline of the enciphering and deciphering process.

for both enciphering and deciphering. The algorithm processes input blocks of 64 bits. An input $T = t_1 t_2 \cdots t_{64}$ is first transposed under an initial permutation IP giving $T_0 = IP(T)$. This permuted input is then passed through sixteen iterations of a cipher computation function that combines substitution and permutation, where a different key K_i is used for each iteration i. Finally it is transposed under the inverse initial permutation IP^{-1} to give the output ciphertext. Let us now look at the details.

INITIAL PERMUTATION. The enciphering algorithm is shown in Fig. 9.10. The 64 bits of the input block T are first transposed according to the initial permutation IP shown in Table 9.1. This table (as well as other permutation tables shown later) should read from left to right and from top to bottom. This means that the permuted block T_0 has bit 58 of the input T as its first bit, bit 50 as its second bit, and so on with bit 7 as its last bit; that is

$$T_0 = t_{58} t_{50} t_{42} \cdots t_{23} t_{15} t_7 \tag{9.12}$$

This permuted block is the input to the iterative enciphering process.

THE ITERATION FUNCTION $f(R_{i-1}, K_i)$. The 64-bit block T_0 is first broken into a right block R_0 and a left block L_0 of 32 bits each, that is

$$T_0 = L_0 R_0 \tag{9.13}$$

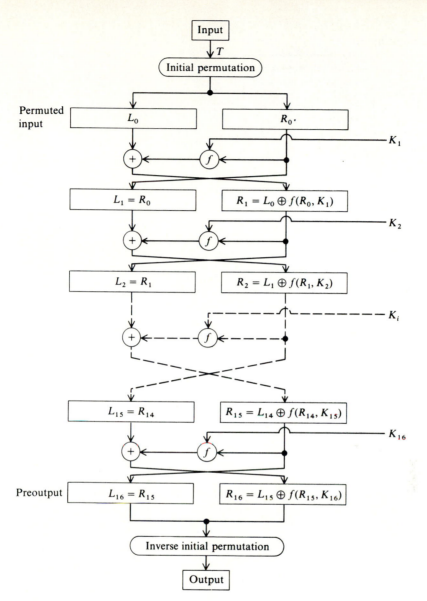

FIGURE 9.10
DES enciphering algorithm.

TABLE 9.1
Initial permutation IP

Original bit position	New positions of bits resulting from the *Initial Permutation* IP							
1–8	58	50	42	34	26	18	10	2
9–16	60	52	44	36	28	20	12	4
17–24	62	54	46	38	30	22	14	6
25–32	64	56	48	40	32	24	16	8
33–40	57	49	41	33	25	17	9	1
41–48	59	51	43	35	27	19	11	3
49–56	61	53	45	37	29	21	13	5
57–64	63	55	47	39	31	23	15	7

where

$$L_0 = t_{58}\, t_{50}\, t_{42} \cdots t_{16}\, t_8$$

$$R_0 = t_{57}\, t_{49}\, t_{41} \cdots t_{23}\, t_{15}\, t_7$$

If T_i denotes the result of the ith iteration, and letting L_i and R_i be the left and right halves of T_i, respectively, then from Eq. (9.10)

$$L_i = R_{i-1}$$

$$R_i = L_{i-1} \oplus f(R_{i-1}, K_i) \tag{9.14}$$

where each K_i is a different 48-bit key that is chosen from a 64-bit starting key.

Figure 9.11 shows the operation of $f(R_{i-1}, K_i)$ in more detail.[20] First R_{i-1} is expanded to a 48-bit block $E(R_{i-1})$ by shuffling the bits according to the bit-selection method E shown in Table 9.2. Note the repetition of various bit positions in Table 9.2 (such as 1, 4, 5, 8, 9, etc.) which makes the 32- to 48-bit expansion possible. This table is used in the same way as the permutation tables, except that some of the bits of R_{i-1} are selected more than once. Thus, for example, the first three bits of $E(R)$ are those in positions 32, 1, and 2 of R, and the last three bits of $E(R)$ are those in positions 31, 32, and 1.

Next $E(R_{i-1})$ and K_i are modulo-2 added and the result is written as eight 6-bit blocks $B_1, B_2, \ldots, B_8$ where

$$E(R_{i-1}) \oplus K_i = B_1\, B_2 \cdots B_8 \tag{9.15}$$

Each 6-bit block B_j is transformed into a 4-bit block using the selection functions S_j shown in Table 9.3. The transformations are done as follows. Consider the 6-bit block $B_1 = b_1\, b_2\, b_3\, b_4\, b_5\, b_6$ used for selection box S_1. The first and last bits of B_1 (that is, $b_1\, b_6$) represent a base-2 number in the base-10 range 0 to 3. The number, which we call r, selects the row of S_1. The middle four bits of B_1 (that is, $b_2\, b_3\, b_4\, b_5$) represent a base-2 number in the base-10 range 0 to 15. This number, which we call q, selects the column of the table. Thus looking up the number in the rth row and qth column yields a base-10 number in the range 0

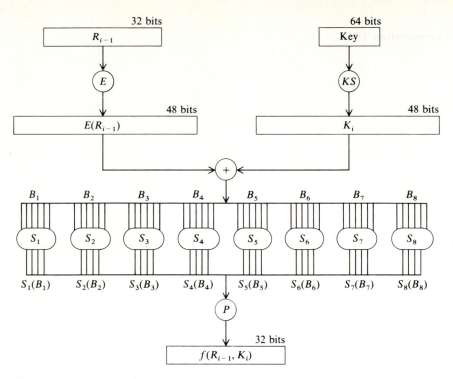

FIGURE 9.11
Calculation of the function $f(R_{i-1}, K_i)$.

to 15. This number is uniquely represented by a 4-bit base-2 block. We can let each entry $S_j(B_j)$ of S box S_j be represented by the function

$$S_j(B_j) = S_j^{b_1 b_6}(b_2\, b_3\, b_4\, b_5) \tag{9.16}$$

for the input block $B_j = b_1\, b_2\, b_3\, b_4\, b_5\, b_6$. Following the transformation, the eight 4-bit blocks $S_j(B_j)$ are then concatenated and the resulting 32-bit block is

TABLE 9.2
E bit-selection table

Original bit position	E bit-selection table					
1–6	32	1	2	3	4	5
7–12	4	5	6	7	8	9
13–18	8	9	10	11	12	13
19–24	12	13	14	15	16	17
25–30	16	17	18	19	20	21
31–36	20	21	22	23	24	25
37–42	24	25	26	27	28	29
43–48	28	29	30	31	32	1

TABLE 9.3
Selection functions (S boxes)

Function	Row	0	1	2	3	4	5	6	7	8	9	10	11	12	13	14	15
S_1	0	14	4	13	1	2	15	11	8	3	10	6	12	5	9	0	7
	1	0	15	7	4	14	2	13	1	10	6	12	11	9	5	3	8
	2	4	1	14	8	13	6	2	11	15	12	9	7	3	10	5	0
	3	15	12	8	2	4	9	1	7	5	11	3	14	10	0	6	13
S_2	0	15	1	8	14	6	11	3	4	9	7	2	13	12	0	5	10
	1	3	13	4	7	15	2	8	14	12	0	1	10	6	9	11	5
	2	0	14	7	11	10	4	13	1	5	8	12	6	9	3	2	15
	3	13	8	10	1	3	15	4	2	11	6	7	12	0	5	14	9
S_3	0	10	0	9	14	6	3	15	5	1	13	12	7	11	4	2	8
	1	13	7	0	9	3	4	6	10	2	8	5	14	12	11	15	1
	2	13	6	4	9	8	15	3	0	11	1	2	12	5	10	14	7
	3	1	10	13	0	6	9	8	7	4	15	14	3	11	5	2	12
S_4	0	7	13	14	3	0	6	9	10	1	2	8	5	11	12	4	15
	1	13	8	11	5	6	15	0	3	4	7	2	12	1	10	14	9
	2	10	6	9	0	12	11	7	13	15	1	3	14	5	2	8	4
	3	3	15	0	6	10	1	13	8	9	4	5	11	12	7	2	14
S_5	0	2	12	4	1	7	10	11	6	8	5	3	15	13	0	14	9
	1	14	11	2	12	4	7	13	1	5	0	15	10	3	9	8	6
	2	4	2	1	11	10	13	7	8	15	9	12	5	6	3	0	14
	3	11	8	12	7	1	14	2	13	6	15	0	9	10	4	5	3
S_6	0	12	1	10	15	9	2	6	8	0	13	3	4	14	7	5	11
	1	10	15	4	2	7	12	9	5	6	1	13	14	0	11	3	8
	2	9	14	15	5	2	8	12	3	7	0	4	10	1	13	11	6
	3	4	3	2	12	9	5	15	10	11	14	1	7	6	0	8	13
S_7	0	4	11	2	14	15	0	8	13	3	12	9	7	5	10	6	1
	1	13	0	11	7	4	9	1	10	14	3	5	12	2	15	8	6
	2	1	4	11	13	12	3	7	14	10	15	6	8	0	5	9	2
	3	6	11	13	8	1	4	10	7	9	5	0	15	14	2	3	12
S_8	0	13	2	8	4	6	15	11	1	10	9	3	14	5	0	12	7
	1	1	15	13	8	10	3	7	4	12	5	6	11	0	14	9	2
	2	7	11	4	1	9	12	14	2	0	6	10	13	15	3	5	8
	3	2	1	14	7	4	10	8	13	15	12	9	0	3	5	6	11

transposed by the permutation P shown in Table 9.4. This table is used sixteen times for every input block.

INVERSE INITIAL PERMUTATION. Following the sixteenth iteration, we have 64 output bits $L_{16} R_{16}$ which are known as the *preoutput* as shown in Fig. 9.10. These 64 bits are then transposed by the inverse initial permutation IP^{-1} according to the bit position reordering shown in Table 9.5. As an example, the output of the algorithm IP^{-1} has bit 40 of the preoutput block as its first bit,

TABLE 9.4
Permutation function P

Original bit position	Permutation function P			
1–4	16	7	20	21
5–8	29	12	28	17
9–12	1	15	23	26
13–16	5	18	31	10
17–20	2	8	24	14
21–24	32	27	3	9
24–28	19	13	30	6
29–32	22	11	4	25

bit 8 of the preoutput as its second bit, and so on until bit 25 of the preoutput is the last bit of the ciphertext output.

KEY CALCULATION. The 48-bit keys K_i used in each iteration are derived from a 56-bit key K, which is kept secret by the sender and the receiver. (Some controversy exists as to whether a 56-bit key is sufficiently strong to withstand cryptanalysis attacks. The interested reader is referred to the literature for this discussion.[8,9,25–27]) The function KS used to generate the different keys K_i is known as a *key schedule*. The concept used in the DES is shown in Fig. 9.12. First K is input as a 64-bit block, designated as KEY, which has eight parity bits in positions 8, 16, ..., 64. The function KS takes an integer n between 1 and 16 and the 64-bit block KEY as input to yield a 48-bit output block K_n which is a permuted selection of bits from KEY. That is

$$K_n = KS(n, \text{KEY}) \tag{9.17}$$

The bit selection is done as follows. First a permutation PC-1, known as *permuted choice 1*, discards the parity bits and shifts the 56 key bits to the

TABLE 9.5
Final permutation IP^{-1}

Original bit position	Inverse initial permutation IP^{-1}							
1–8	40	8	48	16	56	24	64	32
9–16	39	7	47	15	55	23	63	31
17–24	38	6	46	14	54	22	62	30
25–32	37	5	45	13	53	21	61	29
33–40	36	4	44	12	52	20	60	28
41–48	35	3	43	11	51	19	59	27
49–56	34	2	42	10	50	18	58	26
57–64	33	1	41	9	49	17	57	25

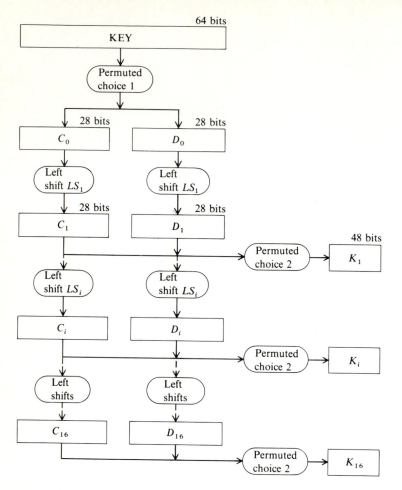

FIGURE 9.12
Key schedule calculation for the DES.

positions indicated by Table 9.6. The result is then divided into two equal 28-bit halves C_0 and D_0. Each of the 28-bit blocks is shifted to the left by one bit as indicated by the *key schedule of left shifts* shown in Table 9.7. That is, in each block bit 2 moves to position 1, bit 3 moves to position 2, and so on with bit 1 shifting to position 28. The result is the two blocks C_1 and D_1. The 56-bit block $C_1 D_1$ then gets shuffled and reduced to a 48-bit block by means of the permutation *PC-2* shown in Table 9.8, which is known as *permuted choice 2*. The result is the key K_1.

For the *i*th iteration, the blocks C_{i-1} and D_{i-1} are then successively shifted to the left as designated by the left-shift functions shown in Table 9.7 to derive each key K_i. This is represented as

$$C_i = LS_i(C_{i-1})$$

TABLE 9.6
Permuted choice 1 ($PC - 1$)

Bit position				$PC - 1$				
1–7	57	49	41	33	25	17	9	
8–14	1	58	50	42	34	26	18	Left block
15–21	10	2	59	51	43	35	27	C_0
22–28	19	11	3	60	52	44	36	
1–7	63	55	47	39	31	23	15	Right block
8–14	7	62	54	46	38	30	22	D_0
15–21	14	6	61	53	45	37	29	
22–28	21	13	5	28	20	12	4	

TABLE 9.7
Key schedule for left shifts LS

Iteration number	Number of left shifts
1	1
2	1
3	2
4	2
5	2
6	2
7	2
8	2
9	1
10	2
11	2
12	2
13	2
14	2
15	2
16	1

TABLE 9.8
Permuted choice 2 (PC-2)

Bit position				PC-2		
1–6	14	17	11	24	1	5
7–12	3	28	15	6	21	10
13–18	23	19	12	4	26	8
19–24	16	7	27	20	13	2
25–30	41	52	31	37	47	55
31–36	30	40	51	45	33	48
37–42	44	49	39	56	34	53
43–48	46	42	50	36	29	32

and

$$D_i = LS_i(D_{i-1}) \qquad\qquad (9.18)$$

The key K_i is given by

$$K_i = PC\text{-}2(C_i D_i) \qquad\qquad (9.19)$$

9.3.4   Summary of the DES Procedure

To tie all of the above discussion together, we examine here a general step-by-step procedure of the DES method. A numerical example of the first iteration is given in Sec. 9.3.5.

Initialization

1. Specify the 64-bit cryptographic key $K = k_1\, k_2\, k_3 \cdots k_{63}\, k_{64}$. This is externally supplied and consists of 56 key bits and 8 nonkey parity bits.
2. Using K, construct sixteen 48-bit key vectors K_1, K_2, ..., K_{16} which are used for iteration rounds 1 through 16, respectively. (This is illustrated in Fig. 9.12.)
3. Select the 64-bit, externally supplied plaintext input $X = x_1\, x_2 \cdots x_{63}\, x_{64}$.
4. As is illustrated in Fig. 9.10, using the initial permutation IP, construct the 32-bit vectors L_0 and R_0 given by Eq. (9.13).
5. Set iteration counter to $i = 1$.

Iterations $i = 1$ through 16

6. For each iteration i, expand R_{i-1} to a 48-bit block $E(R_{i-1})$ according to the bit-selection method E shown in Table 9.2.
7. If enciphering is being done, choose the key K_i; for deciphering select $K_{17\text{-}i}$.
8. Modulo-2 add $E(R_{i-1})$ and K_i. Let the resulting 48-bit vector be $B = b_1\, b_2 \cdots b_{47}\, b_{48}$.
9. The results of $E(R_{i-1}) \oplus K_i$ are inputs to the selection functions S_1 through S_8 given in Table 9.3. This then defines the 32-bit vector $A = a_1\, a_2 \cdots a_{31}\, a_{32}$.
10. Derive $P(A)$ by applying the permutation function P shown in Table 9.4 to the vector A.
11. Modulo-2 add $P(A)$ to L_{i-1} and let the result be R_i.
12. Define $L_i = R_{i-1}$.
13. Increment the iteration counter i by 1. If $i < 16$, repeat steps 6 through 13. Otherwise go to step 14.
14. Using the inverse initial permutation IP^{-1} shown in Table 9.5, transpose the 64-bit preoutput $L_{16}\, R_{16}$ to yield the final 64-bit output.

9.3.5 Numerical Example of Iteration 1

Let us now use these steps to derive the 32-bit blocks L_1 and R_1 for a particular plaintext message. We first select the 64-bit initial key K shown in Fig. 9.13. Here all bits from 9 through 32 and from 41 through 64 are zero. Using the sequence illustrated in Fig. 9.12, the key K_1 becomes the bit sequence shown in Fig. 9.14 (see Prob. 9.9). Here the 24 left-hand bits represent C_1 and the 24 right-hand bits are D_1.

Now let the plaintext message X in hexadecimal notation be

$$X = E\,A\,C\,W\,7\,9\,5\,2$$

We convert this to binary notation using a 7-bit ASCII code with even parity (that is, the first entry in an eight-bit block is the parity bit) to get the binary sequence for X shown in Fig. 9.15 (see Table 2.5). Using the initial permutation IP given by Table 9.1, we construct the 32-bit vectors L_0 and R_0 given by Eq. (9.13). These are shown in Fig. 9.16. Next we expand R_0 using Table 9.2 to get the expression for $E(R_0)$ shown in Fig. 9.17. Here the arrows indicate the bit repetitions which create the expansion. Adding $E(R_0)$ and K_1 modulo-2 then yields the 48-bit vector B depicted in Fig. 9.18.

Using the selection functions S_1 through S_8 given in Table 9.3, we transform the 48-bit vector B into a 32-bit vector A. Let us first look at the function S_1 in detail. Recall that bits 1 and 6 locate the row in the S box, and bits 2 through 5 locate the column. Thus from B we have

$$S_1^{b_1 b_6}(b_2\, b_3\, b_4\, b_5) = S_1^{01}(1101)$$

where the superscript 01 denotes the base-2 row number of S_1 in Table 9.3 and the base-2 number 1101 denotes the column number. In base 10 these are row 1 and column 13, respectively, which yields the base-10 number 5 or, equivalently, the base-2 number 0101. We follow a similar procedure for S_2 through S_8 to get the entries listed in Table 9.9.

Concatenating the base-2 numbers in Table 9.9 yields the 32-bit vector $A = a_1 a_2 \cdots a_{31}\, a_{32}$ shown in Fig. 9-19a. Applying the permutation P given in Table 9.4 to A gives the value for $P(A)$ listed in Fig. 9.19b. Finally, the modulo-2 addition of $P(A)$ with L_0 produces the 32-bit right-half output R_1 depicted in Fig. 9.19c.

Bit no.	1 2 3 4 5 6 7 8 9 $\cdots$ 31 32 33 34 35 36 37 38 39 40 41 $\cdots$ 64
K	1 1 1 0 0 1 1 1 0 $\cdots$ 0 0 1 1 1 0 0 1 1 1 0 $\cdots$ 0

FIGURE 9.13
Values of the 64-bit initial key K.

FIGURE 9.14
Bit sequence for the 48-bit key K_1.

(48-bit sequence)

1	2	3	4	5	6	7	8	9	10	11	12	13	14	15	16	17	18	19	20	21	22	23	24	25	26	27	28	29	30	31	32	33	34	35	36	37	38	39	40	41	42	43	44	45	46	47	48
0	0	1	0	1	0	0	0	1	0	1	0	0	0	1	1	0	0	0	0	1	0	0	0	0	0	1	0	0	0	0	0	0	0	0	0	0	0	1	0	0	0	0	0	0	0	0	0

$\underbrace{\qquad\qquad}_{C_1\ (24\ \text{bits})}$ $\underbrace{\qquad\qquad}_{D_1\ (24\ \text{bits})}$

FIGURE 9.15
Binary sequence of for the plaintext message EACW7952.

1	2	3	4	5	6	7	8	9	10	11	12	13	14	15	16	17	18	19	20	21	22	23	24	25	26	27	28	29	30	31	32	33	34	35	36	37	38	39	40	41	42	43	44	45	46	47	48	49	50	51	52	53	54	55	56	57	58	59	60	61	62	63	64
1	1	0	0	0	1	0	1	0	1	0	0	0	0	0	1	1	1	0	0	0	1	1	1	0	0	0	1	1	1	1	0	1	1	1	0	0	1	1	0	1	1	0	1	1	1	0	0	1	0	0	0	1	0	1	0	1	1	1	0	0	1	0	0

$X = \underbrace{\quad}_{E}\underbrace{\quad}_{A}\underbrace{\quad}_{C}\underbrace{\quad}_{W}\underbrace{\quad}_{7}\underbrace{\quad}_{9}\underbrace{\quad}_{5}\underbrace{\quad}_{2}$

FIGURE 9.16
Values of the blocks L_0 and R_0.

Bit no.	1	2	3	4	5	6	7	8	9	10	11	12	13	14	15	16	17	18	19	20	21	22	23	24	25	26	27	28	29	30	31	32
L_0	0	0	0	0	1	1	1	1	1	1	1	1	0	0	0	0	1	0	0	1	1	0	0	1	0	1	0	1	1	1	1	1
R_0	1	0	0	1	1	0	1	1	1	0	1	1	1	1	0	0	0	0	0	0	1	0	0	0	1	0	0	1	1	1	0	0

346

Bit no.	1	2	3	4	5	6	7	8	9	10	11	12	13	14	15	16	17	18	19	20	21	22	23	24	25	26	27	28	29	30	31	32	33	34	35	36	37	38	39	40	41	42	43	44	45	46	47	48
R_0	1	0	0	1	1	1	0	1	1	1	1	1	0	0	0	1	1	1	0	0	0	1	0	0	0	1	0	0	1	1	0	0																
E																																																
$E(R_0)$	0	1	0	0	1	1	1	1	1	0	1	1	1	0	1	0	0	0	0	1	0	0	0	0	0	1	0	0	1	0	0	0	0	0	0	1	0	1	0	0	1	0	1	1	1	1	0	1

FIGURE 9.17
Expansion of R_0 to yield the expression for $E(R_0)$.

Bit no.	1	2	3	4	5	6	7	8	9	10	11	12	13	14	15	16	17	18	19	20	21	22	23	24	25	26	27	28	29	30	31	32	33	34	35	36	37	38	39	40	41	42	43	44	45	46	47	48
B	0	1	1	0	1	0	1	0	0	1	0	1	1	0	1	0	1	1	0	1	1	0	0	0	0	0	1	1	0	0	0	0	0	0	1	0	1	1	0	1	1	0	1	1	1	0	0	1
Operated on by:	S_1						S_2						S_3						S_4						S_5						S_6						S_7						S_8					

FIGURE 9.18
The 48-bit vector resulting from adding $E(R_0)$ and K_1.

347

TABLE 9.9

Tabular procedure for deriving the 32-bit vector A from the 48-bit vector B

Function derived from B	Row Base 2	Base 10	Column Base 2	Base 10	Table entry Base 10	Base 2
$S_1^{01}(1101)$	01	1	1101	13	5	0101
$S_2^{01}(1001)$	01	1	1001	9	0	0000
$S_3^{00}(0111)$	00	0	0111	7	5	0101
$S_4^{10}(1000)$	10	2	1000	8	15	1111
$S_5^{00}(0110)$	00	0	0110	6	11	1011
$S_6^{01}(0000)$	01	1	0000	0	10	1010
$S_7^{01}(1101)$	01	1	1101	13	15	1111
$S_8^{11}(1100)$	11	3	1100	12	3	0011

Bit no.	1	2	3	4	5	6	7	8	9	10	11	12	13	14	15	16	17	18	19	20	21	22	23	24	25	26	27	28	29	30	31	32
A	0	1	0	1	0	0	0	0	0	1	0	1	1	1	1	1	1	0	1	1	1	0	1	0	1	1	1	1	0	0	1	1

(a)

Bit no.	1	2	3	4	5	6	7	8	9	10	11	12	13	14	15	16	17	18	19	20	21	22	23	24	25	26	27	28	29	30	31	32
$P(A)$	1	0	1	1	0	1	1	1	0	1	1	1	0	0	1	1	1	0	0	1	1	1	0	0	1	1	0	0	0	0	1	1

(b)

Bit no.	1	2	3	4	5	6	7	8	9	10	11	12	13	14	15	16	17	18	19	20	21	22	23	24	25	26	27	28	29	30	31	32
R_1	1	0	1	1	1	0	0	0	1	0	0	0	1	0	1	1	1	1	0	0	0	1	0	1	1	0	1	1	1	1	0	0

(c)

FIGURE 9.19
Steps leading to the derivation of the right-hand block R_1.

The first iteration is thus completed since the 32-bit left half is $L_1 = R_0$ that was calculated above. As noted in Fig. 9.12, this block $L_1 R_1$ is then used as the input for the next iteration.

9.4 PUBLIC KEY CRYPTOGRAPHY

Conventional cryptographic systems, such as the DES, use a single key for enciphering and deciphering a message, so that both the sender and the receiver must know the key and keep it secret. A major problem with these techniques is how to securely distribute the keys. In military systems, a courier service is traditionally used, whereas registered mail might be employed in a commercial system. For either case, key distribution is slow, expensive, and an impediment to secure communications.

Consequently, various researchers[16,28–30] examined a different approach to the key distribution problem. This approach, which is known as *public key cryptography*, uses two separate keys. One key is used for message enciphering and is made publicly known; the other key is used for message deciphering and is kept secret. Although the two keys perform inverse operations and are therefore related, there must be no easily computed method for deriving the deciphering key from the encryption key. This can be achieved through the use of special mathematical formulations known as *trapdoor one-way functions*. The inverse of these functions cannot be derived solely from a description of the function. Instead, to derive the inverse, one must know how the function was constructed. This special knowledge that makes the inverse easy to compute results in the *trapdoor*.

Hellman[31] likens a public key cryptosystem to a mathematical strongbox with a special resettable combination lock which requires one type of combination to lock it and another to open it. By making the locking combination (which is analogous to the enciphering key) public, anyone can lock up the information. However, only the intended recipient who knows the unlocking combination (the deciphering key) can unlock the strongbox to recover the information.

9.4.1   Mathematical Concepts

Before we examine public key cryptography schemes, we need to review some mathematical concepts and definitions. The principal mathematical concepts relating to public key cryptography are prime and composite numbers, factoring, and modular arithmetic. We treat each of these topics briefly here. More comprehensive treatments are given in Refs. 32–36.

PRIME AND COMPOSITE NUMBERS. An integer $p > 1$ is defined as a *prime number* (or a *prime*) if it is divisible only by one and itself. If an integer is not a prime, it is a *composite number* which can be expressed as a product of primes. For small integers, primes can be obtained by striking out all the composite numbers from the list of integers. If an integer is very large, it is difficult to determine whether it is a prime. This is particularly true for the approximately 100-digit-long numbers used in public key cryptography. We describe a test for primality of a number at the end of this section.

EULER FUNCTION. The Euler function $\phi(m)$ denotes the number of positive integers less than or equal to m that are relatively prime to m, that is, having no common factor with m. For a prime p, the number of integers less than p which are relatively prime to p is simply given by

$$\phi(p) = p - 1 \tag{9.20}$$

As an example, for $m = 31$, we have $\phi(31) = 30$ since every integer less than 31 is relatively prime to 31.

Now let us consider composite numbers. Given two prime numbers p and q, then for their product $n = pq$ we have

$$\phi(n) = \phi(p)\phi(q) = (p - 1)(q - 1) \tag{9.21}$$

For example, if $p = 3$ and $q = 5$, then

$$\phi(15) = \phi(3)\phi(5) = (3 - 1)(5 - 1) = 8$$

Thus there are eight numbers that are relatively prime to 15. These are the set $\{1, 2, 4, 7, 8, 11, 13, 14\}$.

In general, for an arbitrary composite number n, $\phi(n)$ is given by

$$\phi(n) = \prod_{i=1}^{r} p_i^{\alpha_i - 1}(p_i - 1) \tag{9.22}$$

where

$$n = p_1^{\alpha_1} p_2^{\alpha_2} \cdots p_r^{\alpha_r}$$

is the prime factorization of n with the positive integers α_i indicating the number of occurrences of the prime p_i.

FACTORING: GREATEST COMMON DIVISOR. The *greatest common divisor* (gcd) of a pair of integers is the largest integer that divides *both* numbers of the given pair. Thus 3 is the greatest common divisor of the pair (12, 15).

This is expressed as

$$\text{gcd } (12, 15) = 3$$

One way to find the gcd is to list all the divisors of each number and pick out the largest one common to both lists. For example,

Divisors of 12: 1, 2, 3, 4, 6, 12
Divisors of 15: 1, 3, 5, 15
gcd (12, 15) = 3

A simpler method is to use *Euclid's algorithm*.[32-35] This technique eliminates the need to list all the divisors and is therefore particularly useful for large numbers. We examine the methodology through an example. Given two numbers, say 34 and 704, divide the *smaller* (34 in this case) into the larger. Doing so yields a remainder of 24. We write this as

$$\text{gcd } (34, 704) = \text{gcd } (24, 34)$$

This process is then repeated until we arrive at the step before a divisor comes out even with no remainder. In this case

$$\text{gcd } (34, 704) = \text{gcd } (24, 34) = \text{gcd } (10, 24) = \text{gcd } (4, 10) = 2$$

We stopped at the point gcd $(4, 10) = 2$, since in the next step 4 divided by $2 = 2$ *with no remainder*. Thus the gcd of 34 and 704 is 2.

CONGRUENCES: MODULAR ARITHMETIC. The arithmetic notion of congruence can be easily understood by considering the commonly used 12-hour clock. In giving the time of day it is customary to count only up to 12 and then begin over again. We say two integers are *congruent modulo 12* if they differ only by an integer multiple of 12. As an example, the numbers 7 and 19 are congruent modulo 12, which is written as $7 = 19$ modulo 12 or $7 = 19$ mod 12.

   We thus have the following definition of congruences: given integers a, b, and $n \neq 0$, then a is congruent to b modulo n if the difference $(a - b)$ is an integer multiple of n. This relationship is written as

$$a = b \bmod n \tag{9.23}$$

   The advantage of using modular arithmetic is that it restricts the size of the numbers occurring at intermediate steps when carrying out an arithmetic operation. This results from the fact that computing in modular arithmetic (wherein one reduces each intermediate result modulo n) yields the same answer as computing in ordinary arithmetic and reducing the final answer modulo n. This correspondence is based on the following *principle of modular arithmetic*:

   Letting op denote one of the arithmetic functions, $+$, $-$, or $*$ (addition, subtraction, or multiplication) then, for integers a_1 and a_2,

$$(a_1 \; op \; a_2) \bmod n = [(a_1 \bmod n) \; op \; (a_2 \bmod n)] \bmod n \tag{9.24}$$

This principle is illustrated in Fig. 9.20.

   Note that in applying this theorem to repeated multiplication, each intermediate step must be reduced modulo n. Thus, for example, to calculate the expression $4^5 \bmod 7$, we repeatedly apply Eq. (9.24) to get

$$4^5 \bmod 7 = \{[(4^2 \bmod 7)(4^2 \bmod 7)] \bmod 7 \, (4 \bmod 7)\} \bmod 7$$

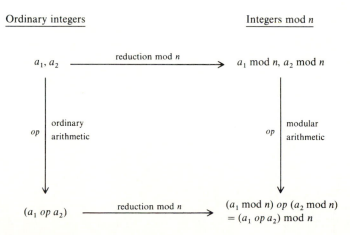

FIGURE 9.20
Basic principle of modular arithmetic.

To evaluate this we would perform the following steps:

1. Square 4 $(4 * 4) \bmod 7 = 2$
2. Square the result $(2 * 2) \bmod 7 = 4$
3. Multiply by 4 $(4 * 4) \bmod 7 = 2$

Using ordinary arithmetic and carrying out the same sequence of repeated squaring and multiplication followed by mod 7 reduction at the end we have

1. Square 4 $4 * 4 = 16$
2. Square the result $16 * 16 = 256$
3. Multiply by 4 $256 * 4 = 1024$
4. Reduce the answer mod 7 $1024 \bmod 7 = 2$

The reduction in size of the intermediate numbers using the modular arithmetic approach is dramatically obvious.

We can also use modular arithmetic to easily calculate expressions of the form $a^x \bmod n$ for large values of a, x, and n without creating enormous intermediate numbers. In particular, public key cryptosystems use exponentials of this form where $0 < x < n - 1$.

TEST FOR PRIMALITY. To securely implement a public key cryptosystem, it is necessary to generate large prime numbers, which are approximately 100 digits long. A major factor is how to test the primality of such a large randomly selected number. Several straightforward methods exist which will determine with absolute certainty whether a number is prime or composite.[11,36] However, for large numbers these approaches are not computationally feasible since too many multiplications are required.

Thus, less reliable but highly probable approaches have been considered.[37-39] In these techniques a trade-off is made between computation time and the risk of assuming that a number is prime when it is really composite. A popular test is the algorithm of Solovay and Strassen[37]. In this method, to test a number p for primality one picks a random number b from a uniform distribution $[1, p - 1]$ and checks whether it satisfies the conditions

$$\gcd (b, p) = 1$$

and
$$J(b, p) = b^{(p - 1)/2} \bmod b \tag{9.25}$$

where $J(b, p)$ is the Jacobi symbol,[33,34] which is defined recursively by

$$J(b, p) = \begin{cases} 1 & \text{if } b = 1 \\ J\left(\dfrac{b}{2}, p\right)(-1)^{(p^2 - 1)/p} & \text{if } b \text{ is even} \\ J(p \bmod b, b)(-1)^{(p - 1)(b - 1)/4} & \text{otherwise} \end{cases} \tag{9.26}$$

If p is prime, then Eq. (9.25) always holds. If p is composite, Eq. (9.25) will be false with a probability of at least 50 percent for each b selected.

MULTIPLICATIVE INVERSES. For certain cases in modular arithmetic, it is possible to compute multiplicative inverses.[9,32-35] The case in point is, given an integer a in the range $[0, n - 1]$, it may be possible to find a unique integer x in the range $[0, n - 1]$ such that

$$ax \bmod n = 1 \tag{9.27}$$

For example, 3 and 11 are multiplicative inverses mod 8 since 33 mod 8 = 1. This characteristic makes modular arithmetic very useful and appealing in cryptographic applications. When a and n are relatively prime, that is, gcd $(a, n) = 1$, then the solution to Eq. (9.27) is

$$x = a^{\phi(n)-1} \bmod n \tag{9.28}$$

where $\phi(n)$ is Euler's function.

Solutions can also be found to the general equation

$$ax \bmod n = b \tag{9.29}$$

when gcd $(a, n) = 1$. The solution is

$$x = bx_0 \bmod n \tag{9.30}$$

where x_0 is the solution to

$$ax_0 \bmod n = 1 \tag{9.31}$$

If gcd $(a, n) \neq 1$, Eq. (9.29) will either have no solution or will have more than one solution in the range $[1, n - 1]$. First let $g = \text{gcd} (a, n)$. If $b \bmod g = 0$ (that is, if g divides b exactly), then Eq. (9.29) will have g solutions of the form

$$x = \left(\frac{b}{g} x_0 + t \frac{n}{g}\right) \bmod n \tag{9.32}$$

for $t = 0, 1, \ldots, g - 1$ where x_0 is the solution to

$$\frac{a}{g} x \bmod \frac{n}{g} = 1 \tag{9.33}$$

Otherwise it will have no solution.

9.4.2 The Rivest-Shamir-Adleman (RSA) Algorithm

In 1978 Rivest, Shamir, and Adleman[29] proposed a method for realizing public-key encryption as suggested by Diffie and Hellman.[16] The RSA algorithm makes use of the fact that it is easy to generate two large prime numbers and multiply them, but it is extremely difficult to factor the product. The product of two large secretly kept numbers can thus be made public without giving a clue to the factors which effectively constitute the deciphering key.

In the RSA algorithm each station independently and randomly chooses two large primes p and q, and multiplies them to produce $n = pq$ which is the modulus used in the arithmetic calculations of the algorithm. By making each of the primes about 100 decimal digits long, the product can be calculated in a fraction of a second. However, factoring n, which is 200 digits, would require billions of years at the rate of one step per microsecond using the fastest known factoring algorithm of Schroeppel.[29] This states that it takes

$$S = \exp\left[(\ln n)\ln(\ln n)\right]^{1/2} \qquad (9.34)$$

steps S to factor n into p and q.

Next Euler's function

$$\phi(n) = (p-1)(q-1) \qquad (9.35)$$

is computed. Given $\phi(n)$, the station randomly selects an integer K between 3 and $\phi(n) - 1$ such that the greatest common divisor is one,

$$\gcd\left[K, \phi(n)\right] = 1 \qquad (9.36)$$

The parameter K is defined as either the secret key D or the public key E depending on the desired usage in the network. Here we assume it is the public key. The multiplicative inverse of K modulo $\phi(n)$ is then calculated using Euclids' algorithm. This quantity is defined to be the secret key D (since we took K to be the public key E); that is, given the number E, the integer D is that unique number which satisfies the condition

$$ED \bmod \phi(n) = 1 \qquad (9.37)$$

The public information then consists of E and n with all other quantities kept secret.

To form the ciphertext C, a plaintext message is first represented as a sequence of integers each between zero and $n - 1$. Denoting this sequence by P, the ciphertext C is formed by raising P to the power of E modulo n, that is,

$$C = P^E \bmod n \qquad (9.38)$$

where C is also in the range from zero to $n - 1$.

To recover the plaintext at the receiving end, the parameters D and n are used as the deciphering key via the relationship

$$P = C^D \bmod n \qquad (9.39)$$

The procedures for selecting the keys and performing the steps of encipherment and decipherment are shown in Fig. 9.21. The various quantities used are summarized in Table 9.10.

Let us consider an example using the different steps shown in Fig. 9.21. Here we use small numbers for simplicity of illustration.

Step 1   Choose $p = 5$ and $q = 7$
Step 2   Calculate $n = pq = 35$
Step 3   Calculate $\phi(n) = (p-1)(q-1) = 24$

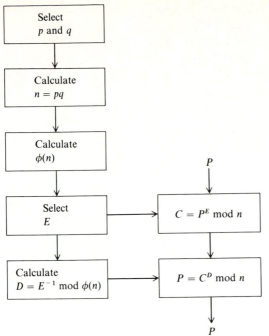

FIGURE 9.21
Various steps in the RSA algorithm.

Step 4   Select $E = 5$ since gcd $(5, 24) = 1$

Step 5   Then $D = E^{-1} \bmod 24 = 5$ since $ED \bmod \phi(n) = 5 \times 5 \bmod 24 = 1$

Step 6   Given that the plaintext $P = 2$, calculate C:

$$C = P^E \bmod n = 2^5 \bmod 35 = 32$$

Step 7   Use Eq. (9.39) to recover the plaintext P from C:

$$P = C^D \bmod n = 32^5 \bmod 35 = 2$$

which is the original message

TABLE 9.10
Quantities used in the RSA
public key encryption algorithm

Quantity	Status
Primes p and q	Secret
$n = p \cdot q$	Nonsecret
$\phi(n) = (p - 1)(q - 1)$	Secret
Public key E	Nonsecret
Private key D	Secret
Plaintext message P	Secret
Ciphertext C	Nonsecret

To encipher an alphanumeric message in practice, the plaintext message characters would be represented by their 8-bit ASCII codes shown in Table 2.5 (seven-bit code plus one parity bit). A simpler example and exercise using a two-digit code for the alphabet is given in Prob. 9.20.

9.4.3 Comparison of Cryptographic Techniques

Although the RSA public-key cryptographic scheme makes the key distribution problem easier than in the DES method, the RSA technique is costly and relatively slow. Whereas encryption times of a few microseconds are needed for the DES, the RSA designs require encryption times of a few milliseconds, thus limiting their throughput rate to about 50 kb/s using current technology. Although faster public-key cryptographic methodologies are being investigated,[40,41] they still need to be implemented and scrutinized for resistance against attack.

9.5 SUMMARY

Network security has become an important issue for protecting the confidentiality and integrity of information transmission in communication networks. Encryption of transmitted information is a fundamental tool for ensuring security in networks. To encrypt a plaintext message, one uses a finite-bit encryption key to perform some mathematical operation on the plaintext to transform it into ciphertext. At the receiving end a decryption algorithm reverses the encryption transformation when presented with the appropriate decryption key. The effectiveness of a particular encryption technique does not depend on whether or not the encryption algorithm is secret, but depends instead on the degree of difficulty required to decipher an encrypted message without having knowledge of the deciphering key.

The encryption ciphers can be either secret or public. In a conventional (secret) cipher, the same key is used to encrypt and decrypt a message. Such a key must obviously be kept secret. A popular implementation of a conventional one-key cryptosystem is the Data Encryption Standard (DES), which is now a Federal standard.

In a public key cryptosystem one key is used for encryption and a different key for decryption. The encryption key is made publicly known, whereas the corresponding decryption key is kept secret. In 1978 Rivest, Shamir, and Adleman proposed a viable method for implementing a public-key cryptosystem. The algorithm, which is known as the RSA technique, uses the fact that it is easy to generate two large prime numbers and multiply them, but it is extremely difficult to factor the product. Such a product can thus be made publicly known without giving a clue to its factors which contain the required information for the deciphering key.

In addition to securely sending information across a communication channel, public-key cryptosystems can also be useful for implementing legally binding *digital signatures* in an electronic mail and/or funds transfer network environment.[11,18,29,42,43] Such a signature assures the recipient that the sender was really the authorized person making the request.

PROBLEMS

Section 9.1

9.1. Tapping information off a wire line can often be simply done by monitoring the electromagnetic emanations outside of the cabled wire. In contrast, tapping information off of an optical fiber is extremely difficult, since one needs to have direct access to the bare fiber contained inside the cable.

Supposing a skillful agent has managed to gain access to a bare fiber section, one way to tap optical power off the line (without breaking it and inserting a repeater and/or tap-off device) is to bend the fiber, thereby inducing higher-order modes to scatter out of the core. A sensitive optical receiver can then monitor the information on the line.

Based on a simple analysis,[44,45] the fraction F of modes lost in a bent graded-index fiber is

$$F = \frac{2a}{R\Delta}$$

Here a is the core radius, R is the bending radius, and $\Delta = 1 - (n_2/n_1)^2$ is the core-to-cladding index difference where n_1 and n_2 are the refractive indices of the fiber core center and cladding, respectively. Given that $n_1 = 1.005n_2$, what bending radii are needed to scatter 1, 5, and 10 percent of the light out of a 50-micrometer core diameter fiber?

9.2. Consider the network architect's layout of the LAN given in Fig. P9.2. Shown here is the main LAN in building 1 and various gateways (some of which could be

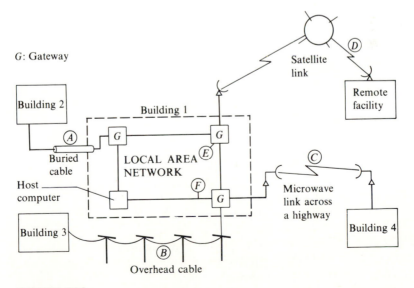

FIGURE P9.2

bridges) connecting several nearby buildings and one remotely located facility. Describe the security vulnerabilities at points A through E, and suggest ways to alleviate them.

Section 9.2

9.3. Decipher the following cryptogram which was enciphered by geometrical pattern encoding using a 5-by-5 matrix with letters taken off in the columnar order 2 3 1 5 4:

  L A T E S S S O T U E H R H A E A T E E I P F R R

9.4. Using a permutation cipher with a fixed period $d = 5$ which permutes the sequence i: 1 2 3 4 5 into $f(i)$: 2 4 5 3 1, show that the message "Why do I have so many homework problems now" becomes

  H D O Y W H V E A I O A N M S H M E O Y O K P O W O L E B R S O W N M

9.5. Decrypt the following message which was encrypted using the shifted alphabet cipher $f(a) = (a + 4) \bmod 26$:

  X L M W T V S F P I Q K E Z I Q I E L I E H E G L I

9.6. How many different columnar transpositions are possible with a six-column matrix?

Section 9.3

9.7. Let

  R_i = 1010101010101010101011100011011

Using the bit-selection matrix E given in Table 9.2, find the expanded block $E(R_i)$. For simplicity, write the result as an 8-row, 6-column matrix.

9.8. Let Y = 11001001111010101011100110000101 be the 32-bit input block to the permutation matrix P given in Table 9.4. Show that rearranging Y according to P yields

  $P(Y)$ = 00110001110010011110100111100101

9.9. Following the procedure illustrated in Fig. 9.12, show that the 48 elements in the first iterative key K_1 are given by the following selected bit positions from the 64-bit starting key K shown in Fig. P9.9.

9.10. Verify the steps shown in the numerical example of the DES algorithm given in Sec. 9.3.5.

9.11. Using the eight-level EBCDIC code given in Table 2.6 and the same key K_1 given in Fig. 9.14, show that after one DES iteration the plaintext input message ILY41087 yields the block given by L_1 and R_1 in Fig. P9.11.

Section 9.4

9.12. Use Euclid's algorithm to find the greatest common divisor of

(a) (14, 35)   (d) (2873, 6643)
(b) (11, 15)   (e) (4148, 7684)
(c) (180, 252)   (f) (1001, 7655)

Bit no. in K_1	1	2	3	4	5	6	7	8	9	10	11	12	13	14	15	16	17	18	19	20	21	22	23	24	25	26	27	28	29	30	31	32	33	34	35	36	37	38	39	40	41	42	43	44	45	46	47	48
Bit from K	10	51	34	60	49	17	33	57	2	9	19	42	3	35	26	25	44	58	59	1	36	27	18	41	22	28	39	54	37	4	47	30	5	53	23	29	61	21	38	63	15	20	45	14	13	62	55	31

FIGURE P9.9

Bit position	1	2	3	4	5	6	7	8	9	10	11	12	13	14	15	16	17	18	19	20	21	22	23	24	25	26	27	28	29	30	31	32
L_1	1	1	1	0	0	0	1	1	1	0	0	1	1	1	0	0	1	1	0	0	1	1	0	0	1	1	1	0	1	1	1	1
R_1	0	0	0	1	0	1	1	0	0	1	1	0	0	0	1	0	0	1	1	0	0	0	1	0	0	0	0	1	0	1	1	0

FIGURE P9.11

9.13. Write a program to determine if an integer is prime. Use the program to check which of the following numbers are prime:

(a) 51, (b) 71, (c) 103, (d) 317, (e) 903.

9.14. Write a program to solve for a when $a = b$ mod n. Solve the following expressions using this program:

(a) 13 mod 11   (c) 2594 mod 48
(b) 87 mod 9   (d) 2^7 mod 21

9.15. First solve the expression 3^7 mod 5 using ordinary arithmetic followed by mod 5 reduction at the end. Next solve 3^7 mod 5 using modular arithmetic. Compare the number sizes used in the two methods.

9.16. Solve the following congruences for X in the range $[0, n - 1]$;

(a) $3X$ mod 7 $= 1$ (c) $3X$ mod 7 $= 2$
(b) $5X$ mod 17 $= 1$ (d) $5X$ mod 8 $= 3$

9.17. Consider a linear substitution cipher that uses the transformation $f(a) = ak$ mod 26. (a) Find k if the plaintext letter G (letter number 7) corresponds to the ciphertext letter Q (letter number 16). (b) Find k if the plaintext letter D becomes the cipher-text letter S.

9.18. Find all solutions to the equation $6X$ mod 10 $= 4$ in the range $[0, 9]$.

9.19. Based on Schroeppel's factoring algorithm, how many years would it take to factor a 200-digit long number?

9.20. For the RSA algorithm let us choose $p = 47$ and $q = 61$. Then $n = pq = 2867$ and $\phi(n) = 2760$. Select a secret key $D = 167$ which is relatively prime to $\phi(n)$.

(a) Calculate the multiplicative inverse of D mod $\phi(n)$ to derive the public key $E = 1223$.

(b) To encipher a message, first divide it into a series of blocks such that the value of each block does not exceed $n - 1$. One way to do this is to substitute the following two-digit numbers for each letter in the alphabet: blank $= 00$, $A = 01$, $B = 02, \ldots, Y = 25, Z = 26$.

Using this code, write the message "RSA ALGORITHM" in blocks of 4 bits:

$$b_1 b_2 b_3 b_4 \ \ b_5 b_6 b_7 b_8 \cdots b_{25} b_{26} b_{27} b_{28}$$

(c) Encipher each 4-bit block by raising it to the power D, dividing by n, and taking the remainder as the ciphertext. Show that the ciphertext becomes

2756 2001 0542 0669 2347 0408 1815.

REFERENCES

1. J. H. Saltzer and M. D. Schroeder, "The protection of information in computer systems," *Proc. IEEE*, vol. 63, pp. 1278–1308, September 1975.
2. S. T. Kent, "Security in computer networks," in *Protocols and Techniques for Data Communication Networks*, F. F. Kuo (ed), Prentice-Hall, Englewood Cliffs, NJ, 1981.
3. W. Diffie and M. E. Hellman, "Privacy and Authentication: An introduction to cryptography," *Proc. IEEE*, vol. 67, pp. 397–427, March 1979.
4. M. D. Abrams and H. J. Podell (eds.), *Computer and Network Security*, IEEE Computer Society, Washington, DC, 1987.
5. S. C. Kak, "Data security in computer networks," *Computer*, vol. 16, pp. 8–10, February 1983.

6. D. K. Branstad, "Security of computer communication," *IEEE Comm. Mag.*, pp. 33–40, November 1978.

7. V. L. Voydock and S. T. Kent, "Security in high-level network protocols," *IEEE Comm. Mag.*, vol. 23, pp. 12–24, July 1985.

8. B. Bosworth, *Codes, Ciphers, and Computers*, Hayden, Rochelle Park, NJ, 1982.

9. D. E. Denning, *Cryptography and Data Security*, Addison-Wesley, Reading, MA. 1982.

10. A. G. Konheim, *Cryptography: A Primer*, Wiley, New York, 1981.

11. C. H. Meyer and S. M. Matyas, *Cryptography: A New Dimension in Computer Data Security*, Wiley, New York, 1982.

12. D. Kahn, *The Codebreakers*, Macmillan, New York, 1967.

13. H. F. Gaines, *Cryptanalysis*, Dover, New York, 1956.

14. A. Sinkov, *Elementary Cryptanalysis: A Mathematical Approach*, Random House, New York, 1968.

15. G. J. Simmons, "Symmetric and asymmetric encryption," *Computing Surveys*, vol. 11, pp. 305–330, December 1979.

16. W. Diffie and M. E. Hellman, "New directions in cryptography," *IEEE Trans. Info. Theory*, vol. IT-22, pp. 644–654, November 1976.

17. D. M. Balenson, "Automated distribution of cryptographic keys using the Financial Institution Key Management Standard," *IEEE Commun. Mag.*, vol. 23, pp. 41–46, September 1985.

18. D. E. Denning, "Protecting public keys and key signatures," *Computer*, vol. 16, pp. 27–35, February 1983.

19. R. C. Merkle, "Protocols for public-key cryptosystems," in *Advances in Computer System Security*, R. Turn (ed.), Artech House, Dedham, MA., 1981, pp. 299–311.

20. "Data Encryption Standard," *Federal Information Processing Standards Publication 46*, National Bureau of Standards, Washington, DC, January 1977.

21. H. Feistel, "Cryptography and computer privacy," *Scientific American*, vol. 228, pp. 15–23, May 1973.

22. J. B. Kam and G. I. Davida, "A structured design of substitution-permutation encryption networks," in R. A. DeMillo, D. P. Doblin, A. K. Jones, and R. J. Lipton (eds.) *Foundations of Secure Computation*, Academic, New York , 1978, pp. 95–113.

23. H. Feistel, W. A. Notz, and J. Smith, "Some cryptographic techniques for machine-to-machine data communications," *Proc. IEEE*, vol. 63, pp. 1545–1554, November 1974.

24. C. E. Shannon, "Communication theory of secrecy systems," *Bell Sys. Tech. J.*, vol. 28, pp. 656–715, October 1949.

25. W. Diffie and M. E. Hellman, "Exhaustive Cryptanalysis of the NBS Data Encryption Standard," *Computer*, vol. 10, pp. 74–84, June 1977.

26. M. E. Hellman, "DES will be totally insecure within ten years," *IEEE Spectrum*, vol. 16, pp. 32–39, July 1979.

27. W. Tuchman, "Hellman presents no shortcut solutions to the DES," *IEEE Spectrum*, vol. 16, pp. 40–41, July 1978.

28. R. C. Merkle, "Secure communication over an unsecure channel," *Commun. Assoc. Comput. Mach. (ACM)*, vol. 21, pp. 294–299, April 1978.

29. R. L. Rivest, A. Shamir, and L. Adleman, "On digital signatures and public key cryptosystems," *Commun. ACM*, vol. 21, pp. 120–126, February 1978.

30. S. C. Pohlig and M. E. Hellman, "An improved algorithm for computing logarithms over $GF(p)$ and its cryptographic significance," *IEEE Trans. Inform. Th.*, vol. IT-24, pp. 106–110, January 1978.

31. M. E. Hellman, "An overview of public key cryptography," *IEEE Commun. Soc. Mag.*, vol. 16, pp. 24–32, November 1978.

32. A. V. Aho, J. E. Hopcroft, and J. D. Ullman, *The Design and Analysis of Computer Algorithms*, Addison-Wesley, Reading, MA., 1974.

33. I. Niven and H. Zuckerman, *An Introduction to the Theory of Numbers*, Wiley, New York, 1972.

34. W. J. LeVeque, *Fundamentals of Number Theory*, Addison-Wesley, Reading, MA., 1977.

35. D. Knuth, *The Art of Computer Programming: Vol. 2, Seminumerical Algorithms*, 2d ed., Addison-Wesley, Reading, MA. 1981.

36. O. Ore, *Number Theory and Its History*, McGraw-Hill, New York, 1949.

37. R. Solovay and V. Strassen, "A fast Monte-Carlo test for primality," *SIAM J. Computing*, vol. 6, pp. 84–85, March 1977.

38. M. O. Rabin, "Probabilistic algorithms," in J. F. Traub (ed.), *Algorithms and Complexity*, Academic, New York, 1976.

39. J. M. Pollard, "Theorems on factorization and primality testing," *Cambridge Phil. Soc. Proc.*, vol. 76, pp. 521–528, 1974.

40. R. M. F. Goodman and A. J. McAuley, "A new trapdoor-knapsack public-key cryptosystem," *IEE Proc.*, vol. 132, part E, pp. 289–292, November 1985.

41. S. C. Kak, "Secret-hardware public-key cryptography," *IEE Proc.*, vol. 133, part E, pp. 94–96, March 1986.

42. S. M. Matyas, "Digital signatures—An overview," *Computer Networks*, vol. 3, pp. 87–94, 1979.

43. P. R. Zimmermann, "A proposed standard format for RSA cryptosystems," *Computer*, vol 19, pp. 21–34, September 1986.

44. D. Gloge, "Bending loss in multimode fibers with graded and ungraded core index," *Appl. Optics*, vol. 11, pp. 2506–2512, November 1972.

45. G. Keiser, *Optical Fiber Communications*, McGraw-Hill, New York, 1983.

CHAPTER 10

APPLICATIONS
OF
LAN
TECHNOLOGY

In this chapter we examine application aspects of some popular LANs which are being widely used in a variety of commercial networks. In particular we consider the following:

1. Three variations of the IEEE-802.3 Standard for baseband CSMA/CD bus LANS.
2. Optical fiber versions of Ethernet.
3. The IEEE 802.4-based Manufacturing Automation Protocol (MAP) and the IEEE 802.3-based Technical and Office Protocols (TOP) used for communicating in the factory and the office, respectively.
4. Token ring local area networks as described by IEEE 802.5.
5. The 100-Mb/s Fiber Distributed Data Interface (FDDI), which is a high-speed fiber-optic token ring.
6. Protocols for integrating voice and data on local area networks.

10.1 VARIATIONS ON IEEE 802.3

Several variations on IEEE 802.3 now exist. The original implementation is the popular Ethernet system. This operates at 10 Mb/s and offers a wide range of application variations. A more limited abbreviated version of Ethernet is known as Cheapernet or Thinnet. Like Ethernet, Cheapernet operates at 10 Mb/s but uses a thinner, less expensive coaxial cable aimed at interconnecting low-cost stations such as personal computers and workstations. A third variation is called StarLAN, which was developed by AT&T. This works at 1 Mb/s and uses unshielded, twisted-pair cable which is often already installed in office buildings for telephone lines.

10.1.1 The Ethernet Specification

The Ethernet specification (known as IEEE 802.3 Type 10-Base-5, where the 10 refers to the data rate in Mb/s and the 5 refers to the cable segment length in 100-m units) covers the data-link and physical layers of the OSI Model, and the medium access control (MAC) and physical layers of the IEEE 802.3 Standard for CSMA/CD bus networks.[1-3] It specifies a bus having a 2.5-km maximum length connected in 500-m segments, a 10-Mb/s data rate, and a maximum of 1024 connected stations. Although the CSMA/CD access procedure can use any physical transmission medium including radio channels, twisted-pair wire, coaxial cable, or optical fibers, Ethernet is designed specifically for baseband transmission over coaxial cable. (Section 10.2 describes optical-fiber versions of Ethernet).

An example of a medium-sized Ethernet layout is given in Fig. 10.1. This shows two bus segments connected with a repeater. A repeater consists of two

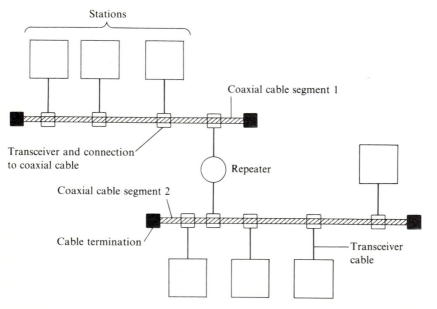

FIGURE 10.1
Example of a medium-sized Ethernet layout.

transceivers, one for each direction of transmission. The station attached to the Ethernet cable is typically a computer or a cluster of terminals that interface to the network via a communications server. Individual terminals are generally not connected directly to the network. Certain physical limits (in terms of length) have to be placed on the cable. This is done to meet maximum allowable signal propagation times through the network (see Chap. 3). The Ethernet specification thus imposes the following restrictions:

1. A coaxial cable segment may be a maximum of 500 meters long.
2. A maximum of two repeaters is allowed between any two stations. Repeaters can be located anywhere on a cable segment, since they are basically viewed as transceivers by the network.
3. The maximum total cable length between any two transceivers is 1500 m.
4. The maximum transceiver cable length is 50 m.

A general Ethernet implementation for a station is shown in Fig. 10.2. The physical layer performs the following two functions that are generally associated with physical channel control:

Data encoding which includes the generation and removal of preamble for synchronization, and bit encoding and decoding (translation from one data format to another).

Channel access which includes transmission and reception of encoded data bits, carrier sensing, and collision detection. These functions are carried out by the transceiver.

The two main functions of the data-link layer are:

Data encapsulation which includes framing, handling of source and destination addresses, and detection of errors on the physical channel.

Link management which includes channel allocation to avoid collisions, and collision-contention resolution.

The frame format of an Ethernet packet is given in Fig. 10.3. Each packet is a sequence of 8-bit bytes wherein the least significant bit for each byte (starting with the preamble) is transmitted first. The functions of the various fields are as follows:

Preamble. This is a 56-bit (7-byte) synchronization pattern consisting of alternating ones and zeros, which is used to ensure receiver synchronization.

Start-Frame Delimiter. The 1-byte start-frame delimiter is similar to the preamble, except that it ends with two consecutive one bits.

Destination address. This 48-bit field specifies to which station the packet is addressed. The address can be either a unique station on the Ethernet, or it can

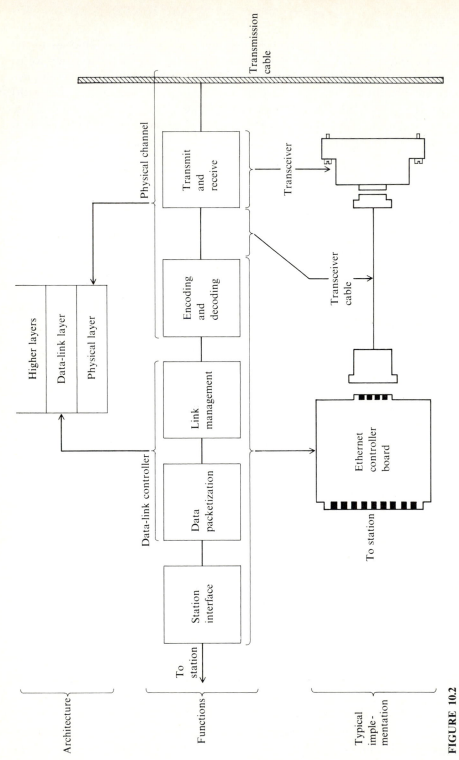

FIGURE 10.2
A general Ethernet implementation for a network station.

					46–1500		
7	1	6	6	2	≥ 0	Variable	4
Preamble	Start-frame delimiter	Destination address	Source address	Length	Information field	Pad	Frame-check sequence

Bytes

FIGURE 10.3
Frame format for an Ethernet packet.

be a multidestination address. The first bit indicates the type of address: if it is a 0, the field gives the address of a unique station; if it is a 1, the field specifies a logical group of recipients.

Source address. The unique address of the originating station is specified in this 48-bit field.

Length. This two-byte field indicates the number of information bytes being supplied by the LLC layer for the data field.

Data field. The IEEE-802 Standard recommends that the data field has a length between 46 and 1500 bytes. If the data supplied by the LLC layer is less than the 46-byte minimum required for proper operation of the Ethernet protocol, then an integer number of padding bytes are added to the end of the data field to bring the length to 46.

Frame check sequence. This last part of the frame contains a 32-bit (4-byte) cyclic-redundancy-check (CRC) code for error detection as defined in Sec. 3.7. The CRC covers the destination address, source address, length, and data fields.

The maximum and minimum packet sizes are as follows:

Maximum: 1526 bytes
(8-byte preamble + 14-byte header + 1500 data bytes + 4-byte CRC)

Minimum: 72 bytes
(8-byte preamble + 14-byte header + 46 data bytes + 4-byte CRC)

10.1.2   Ethernet Controller

A number of integrated-circuit chips are commercially available for controlling an Ethernet LAN.[4] As an example, let us consider Fig. 10.4 which shows the implementation of an Ethernet chip set made by Intel.[5] These include an 82586 LAN coprocessor, an 82C501 Ethernet serial interface, and an 82502 Ethernet transceiver chip. The 82586 is an intelligent peripheral that completely manages the processes of transmitting and receiving frames over a CSMA/CD network. It performs the full set of IEEE-802.3 CSMA/CD media-access-control functions

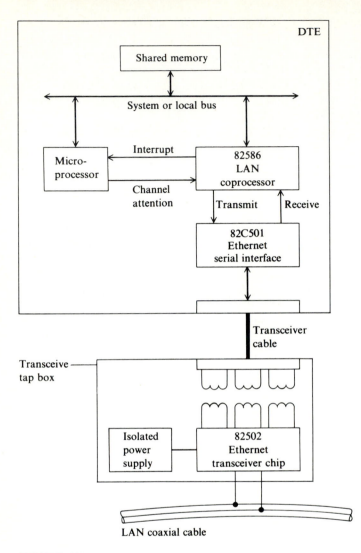

FIGURE 10.4
Ethernet (IEEE 802.3 10-Base-5) station-attachment configuration using an integrated-circuit chip set.

including framing, preamble generation and stripping, source address generation, destination address checking, CRC generation and checking, and short-frame detection.

The primary functions of the 82C501 are to perform Manchester encoding and decoding, provide the required 10-MHz transmit-clock to the 82586, recover clock from the received signal, generate carrier-sense collision-presence signals, and interface to the transceiver cable. A diagnostic loopback control for network-node fault detection and isolation enables the 82C501 to take the signal coming from the 82586, route it through the Manchester encoding and decoding circuitry, and return it the 82586. The combined loopback capabilities of the 82586 and 82C501 result in efficient fault detection and isolation by providing sequential testing of the communications interface. An on-chip watchdog timer circuit (which is defeatable) prevents a station from locking up in a continuous transmit mode.

The main functions of the 82502 transceiver chip are insertion of data onto the network coaxial cable, reception of data from the coaxial cable, collision detection, and interfacing to the transceiver cable. The Ethernet specification requires that the 82502 transceiver chip can be located in a tap box attached directly to the coaxial cable of the network, and that a dc isolated power supply be used for the transceiver chip.

Numerous other IEEE-802.3 controllers are also available from manufacturers such as Advanced Micro Devices (AMD), Exar Corp., National Semiconductor, Seeq Technology, Thomson-Mostek, and Western Digital Corp. For example, in contrast to the single-address controller described above, the 8005 Ethernet controller made by Seeq[6] can handle up to six addresses per connection.

10.1.3 Cheapernet (Thinnet)

Not all local area network implementations require the full capabilities of an Ethernet system. This is particularly true for small businesses. Therefore the IEEE 802.3 LAN Standards Committee has created a new standard called *Cheapernet* or *Thinnet*. This standard (which is known as IEEE 802.3 Type 10-Base-2) is a simple, low-cost, and user-manageable network. It is an abbreviated version of the Ethernet standard as is shown in Table 10-1.

TABLE 10.1
Comparison of fundamental Ethernet and Cheapernet parameters

Parameter	Ethernet	Cheapernet
Data rate	10 Mb/s	10 Mb/s
Segment length	500 m (1600 ft)	185 m (600 ft)
Network span	2.5 km (8000 ft)	925 m (3000 ft)
Nodes per segment	100	30
Nodes per network	1024	1024
Node spacing	2.5 m	0.5 m
Network cable	0.4-in diameter 50-Ω coax cable; N-series connector	0.25-in diameter 50-Ω coax cable; BNC connector
Transceiver cable	Up to 50 m (165 ft) of 0.38-in diameter multiway cable; 15-pin D-series connector	No transceiver cable

The major differences between the two networks are that the single-segment Cheapernet cable is limited to 600 m and only 30 nodes are permitted on a segment. The biggest change from the standard CSMA/CD LAN is the physical integration of the transceiver function into the Cheapernet data terminal equipment (DTE). This construction technique results in significant cost savings. The medium interconnecting the Cheapernet DTEs is a thin (0.25-inch diameter) RG-58 coaxial cable. Cheapernet thus preserves the high data transfer rate of Ethernet, but reduces the per node cost considerably.

The implementation of a Cheapernet node is shown in Fig. 10.5 using the same integrated-circuit chip set as described in Sec. 10.1.2. In contrast to Ethernet, the 82502 transceiver chip is now located inside the DTE, so that there is no transceiver cable. Three miniature pulse transformers between the transceiver chip and the serial interface chip provide the electrical isolation required within the data terminal equipment. Again, as is the case with Ethernet, the IEEE spec-

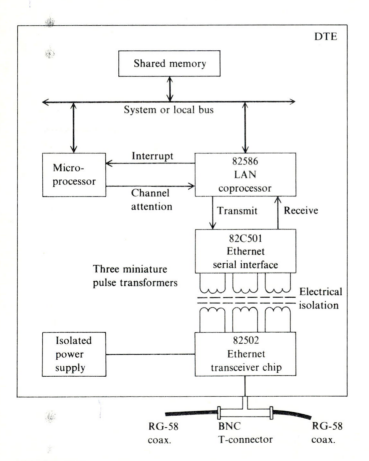

FIGURE 10.5
Cheapernet (IEEE 802.3 10-Base-2) station-attachment configuration.

ifications require that a dc isolated power supply be used for the transceiver chip.

10.1.4   StarLAN

A third variation on the IEEE-802.3 specification is the Type 1-Base-5 StarLAN, which was developed by AT&T.[7,8] This network operates at 1 Mb/s and uses unshielded, twisted-pair cable, which generally already exits in most buildings for telephone applications. These cables usually come in bundles of 25 to 50 pairs of wires. Each telephone requires four wires: two for analog voice transmission and two for powering the phone. The StarLAN architecture allows voice and data to coexist on the same cable bundle without interference.

The topology of a StarLAN network is a hierarchical tree-like configuration in which stations connect to local hubs, or concentration points, that act as telephone-switching stations. This configuration may contain up to five upward levels of hubs. An example with three levels is illustrated in Fig. 10.6. Transmitted messages first propagate to all higher-level hubs until they reach the header hub. From there they are broadcast down to all the terminal stations on the network.

When data passes in the upstream direction, all hubs generate collision-signaling waveforms when they detect a collision. The hubs also retime signals, start interframe-spacing timing, and watch for stations that do not stop transmitting (this is known as a jabber-timing function). In the downstream direction, a hub merely retimes signals and propagates them to all lower level outputs.

Two types of transceiver chip and controller chip implementations for StarLAN are shown in Fig. 10.7. In the top half, a two-circuit (XR-T82515 and XR-T82C516) transceiver chip set made by Exar[8] links the LAN cable with an 82586 communication controller. In the bottom half of Fig. 10.7 an 82588 communication controller chip from Intel is used. The 82588 controller costs about half as much as the 82586 and can do all the required link functions for a low-cost 1-Base-5 compatible station. The 82586, however, is much more powerful since it functions as a coprocessor that can easily link to bus microprocessors such as the 8-bit 80188 or the 16-bit 80186.

The transceiver has digital and analog sections. The transmitter section consists of a Manchester encoder, a wave shaper, and a line driver. When the controller is ready to deliver data, the digital XR-T82C516 chip encodes the NRZ-formatted messages from a station into a Manchester data stream and feeds it through an RC filter (integrator) to be clipped by the analog XR-T82515 chip. The clipping creates a trapezoid-shaped signal having a lower harmonic content than a sharply rising one such as the NRZ signal coming from the 82586. Consequently, the trapezoidal signal produces less cross talk interference. The analog XR-T82515 chip then drives the twisted-pair LAN line with the resulting Manchester-encoded signal going to all stations.

The receiver circuitry consists of a buffer amplifier, receive filter, energy detector, received-data digitizer, Manchester decoder, and clock-recovery system.

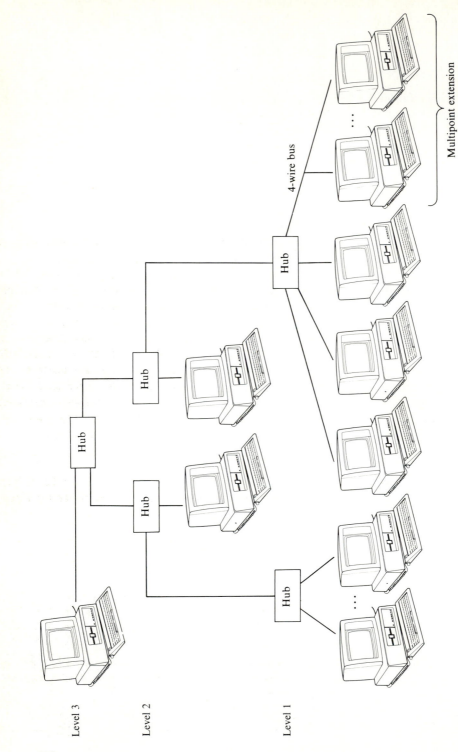

Level 3

Level 2

Level 1

4-wire bus

Multipoint extension

Hub

FIGURE 10.6
Hierarchical tree-like configuration of a StarLAN network.

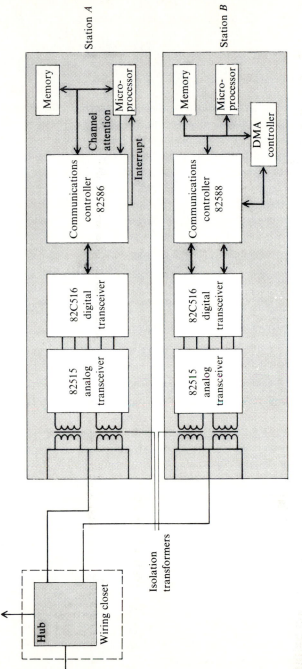

FIGURE 10.7
Two types of transceiver-chip and controller-chip implementations for StarLAN.

373

The receiver can extract data and clock over a cable segment having as much as 14-dB attenutation at 1 MHz in a bus system (having a maximum of 48 stations and 4000 ft of cable) or 20 dB in a star configuration having a 2400-ft maximum cable length.

10.2 OPTICAL FIBERS IN CSMA/CD LANs

Although CSMA/CD LANs such as Ethernet were initially developed and implemented with coaxial cable, fiber-optic versions of these networks offer a number of advantages.[9-11] These advantages, which come about from the dielectric nature of optical fibers, include immunity to electromagnetic interference (EMI), freedom from ground loops, small cable size, low weight, and high transmission security.

To implement an optical-fiber version of an IEEE 802.3-compatible CSMA/CD LAN, the following four criteria must be satisfied:

1. The bit error rate (BER) must be less than 10^{-9}
2. The LAN must accommodate up to 1024 data terminal equipment (DTE) sets
3. The transmission distance between DTEs can be up to 3 km
4. All collisions on the network must be detectable

10.2.1 Topology

Coaxial-based CSMA/CD LANs are implemented as passive buses. However, a straight one-for-one replacement of a coaxial bus with an optical-fiber bus is not possible because of the different physical characteristics of optical fibers and coaxial cables. By using high-impedance cable taps, up to 1024 stations can be attached to a single coaxial cable which allows data to be sent bidirectionally.

Such a configuration is not possible with optical fibers because of the lack of an optical equivalent of the electrical high-impedance tap. To see this, consider Fig. 10.8 which shows a passive optical coupler. This coupler has an insertion loss of I dB and taps off T dB of the optical power in the trunk line. Although a variety of bus-type optical couplers have been developed,[12-17] in all cases the fiber must be cut so that the device can be inserted into the line. This generally introduces an insertion loss of 0.5 to 1 dB per device, in addition to the coupling loss itself. Typically couplers are made to tap off from 10 to 50 percent of the optical power in the trunk line, thus yielding a 0.5 to 3-dB coupling loss. If one considers that the optical dynamic range of a receiver is on the order of 30 to 35 dB, then the number of passive couplers that can be attached to the bus is nominally less than 20 for symmetric couplers having a 20 percent tapoff. This number could be increased two- or threefold by using asymmetric couplers, but it is still far from the 1024 number that is desired.

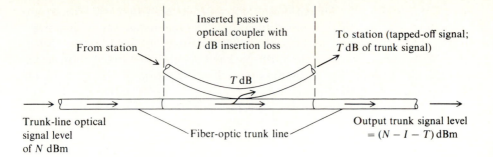

FIGURE 10.8
Characteristics of a passive optical-fiber in-line coupler.

The attenuation limit can be overcome by using active coupling devices at each bus interface. In this case the optical power is regenerated and amplified at each coupler, so that inexpensive LED sources and PIN photodetectors can be used. With this configuration collisions are simply detected through the simultaneous transmission and reception of data. As we noted in Sec. 8.4, the lower reliability of active components as compared to passive devices can be mitigated through the use of bypass switches at each node. Although the active coupler overcomes the optical power limitation problem, the accumulation of edge jitter in the transmitted serial bit stream that passes through each coupler can limit the number of active taps on the fiber bus to less than 1024.

The limitations imposed by the linear bus configuration can be overcome with either a passive or an active star coupler topology,[12-14,18] An example of an optical-fiber Ethernet using a passive star coupler is shown in Fig. 10.9. As

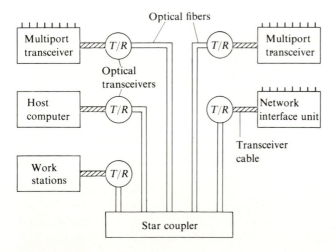

FIGURE 10.9
Example of an optical-fiber Ethernet using a passive star coupler.

we noted in Sec. 4.2.2 the optical power losses associated with a star coupler are the insertion loss and the power-splitting loss. The major loss factor is power-splitting which is 10 times the logarithm of the number of output ports. Thus a 32-by-32-port star coupler has a 15-dB splitting loss, and a 64-by-64 coupler has an 18-dB splitting loss. The excess loss typically ranges from 3 to 6 dB depending on the coupler type and construction.

In the fiber-optic Ethernet shown in Fig. 10.9, a star segment is the equivalent of a coaxial Ethernet segment. Owing to loss and manufacturing considerations, star couplers are generally 64-by-64 or less in size. By using an Ethernet or IEEE-802.3 repeater, up to 4000 nodes can be accommodated without exceeding the round-trip delay-time budget.

10.2.2 Collision Detection

In a coaxial-cable Ethernet, collision detection is achieved by placing dc information on the line along with the data. Since the coax cable has a very low dc resistance over a single 500-m segment span, and since the output level of each transmitter is made uniform by design, all stations connected to the line will see the same level. Thus a collision can readily be detected by a station as a change in the dc signal level.

The situation is different for an optical network. Although an optical fiber itself has a low attentuation, there can be large variations in the attenuations of different paths. This results from the differences in cable lengths to various transceivers, differences in path loss through the fiber-optic star coupler, and variations in transmitter output power. Thus a strong signal could mask out a weaker signal, thereby preventing a collision from being detected.

A variety of collision-detection methods for fiber optic CSMA/CD LANs have thus been proposed[11,19-20] using either a passive star or an active star coupler. Among the passive-star methods are monitoring average optical power levels, detecting pulse-width violations, comparing transmitted and received data packets, time-delay violations, and hybrid star configurations. However in general most of these passive-star methods are either unreliable in that they do not guarantee the detection of a collision, or they are very complex to implement.

Thus let us look at schemes for collision in active star couplers. A schematic of an active-star network is shown in Fig. 10.10. This consists of point-to-point fiber-optic links running from each station to a centralized hub of electronics equipment called the *star repeater*. In the star repeater the input fibers are terminated in an electro-optic receiver and are electrically bused together. Collision detection thus takes place in the electrical domain.

The point-to-point link topology allows the use of only one active star repeater to interconnect up to 1024 DTEs having distances of up to 3 km between them. However, in practice many active stars would be interconnected by means of IEEE-802.3 repeaters to minimize the total length of optical fiber cable.

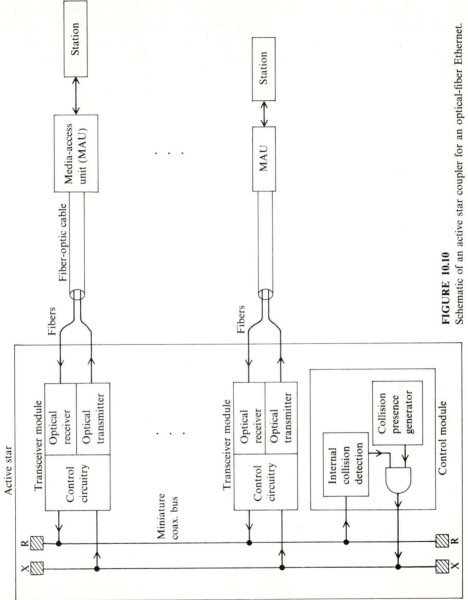

FIGURE 10.10
Schematic of an active star coupler for an optical-fiber Ethernet.

377

In the active star shown in Fig. 10.10, the transmitter and receiver modules are connected via a miniature coax backplane bus. For each fiber optic line coming into the star, a receiver module converts the optical input signals into electrical signals, and places the bit stream on the receive (R) backplane bus. A control module next transfers the data from the R bus to the transmit (X) bus. This module also detects collisions and substitutes a jam signal in place of the data signal when a collision occurs. The transmitter then takes the electrical information from the X bus and optically transmits either the bit stream or an easily detectable jam signal over all the fiber-optic output lines.

Alternately, collision detection can be done in the fiber-optic media access unit (FOMAU). In this method the active star distributes the data arriving from any station to all other stations except the transmitting one. Consequently, if data arrives at the receiver of a transmitting station then a collision has occurred.

10.3 MAP/TOP

The lack of effective communications among programmable tools, instruments, controls, and robots has traditionally been a key roadblock to large-scale automation of the factory floor. Thus in 1980 the General Motors Corporation initiated a study of the Manufacturing Automation Protocol (MAP) to reduce production costs while improving quality control.[21,22] A similar effort was launched by the Boeing Computer Services Company to address communication problems among engineering work stations, computers, and peripheral devices, and for general office applications.[23] Their development, which is known as the Technical and Office Protocols (TOP) specification, will ultimately provide common communications methods and related services for applications such as electronic mail, word processing, file transfer, graphics, database management, and business analysis tools.

10.3.1 Comparison of MAP and TOP

Both MAP and TOP follow the seven-layer OSI Model described in Chap. 2. A comparison of the MAP and TOP network architectures is given in Fig. 10.11. Both use the same protocols for layers 2 through 6 for the OSI Model. The differences between the two specifications occur only for the physical layer (layer 1) and for the application layer (layer 7).

The physical layer of the MAP network is based on a token-passing bus architecture as specified in IEEE Standard 802.4. Since the equipment that is to be interconnected can have either voice, data, or video signals, MAP uses a broadband backbone cable linking carrierband subnets as is shown in Fig. 10.12. The backbone medium is a 75-ohm coaxial cable having nondirectional impedance-matching taps that are used to connect stations, bridges, and gateways to the trunk cable. The backbone provides three data rates: 1 Mb/s which

Layer	TOP Protocols	MAP Protocols
7	ISO File Transfer, Access, and Management (FTAM) (DP) 8571 • File Transfer, limited file management (ASCII and binary data only)	ISO FTAM (DP) 8571 • File Transfer Protocol • Manufacturing Messaging Format Standard (MMFS) • Common Application Service Elements (CASE)
6	Null: only provides a logical path for the flow of network data and control (ASCII and binary encoding)	
5	ISO Session (IS) 8327 Session kernel, full duplex	
4	ISO Transport (IS) 8073 Class 4	
3	ISO Internet (DIS) 8473 Connectionless and X.25 Subnetwork Dependent Convergence Protocol (SNDCP)	
2	ISO Logical Link Control (DIS) 8802/3 (IEEE 802.2) Type 1, Class 1	
1	ISO CSMA/CD (DIS) 8802/3 (IEEE 802.3) CSMA/CD media access control, 10 Base 5	ISO Token-Passing Bus (DIS) 8802/4 (IEEE 802.4) Token-passing-bus media access control

FIGURE 10.11
A comparison of the MAP and TOP network architectures.

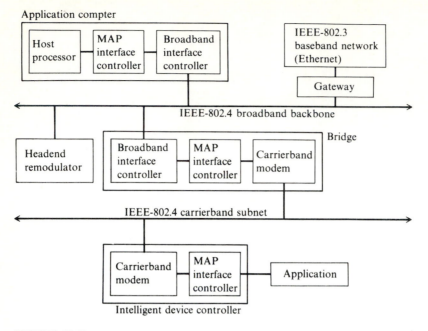

FIGURE 10.12
The hierarchical structure of MAP.

occupies a 1.5-MHz channel, 5 Mb/s in a 6-MHz channel, and 10 Mb/s in a 12-MHz channel. The carrierband subnets are low cost networks used by localized controllers which are dedicated to specific testing or manufacturing functions. The data rates on the subnets are 5 and 10 Mb/s. The subnets use phase-coherent FSK, which is a single-channel carrierband.

The physical layer of the TOP network follows the IEEE-802.3 CSMA/CD specification and operates at a 10-Mb/s data rate. The physical medium is a shielded 50-ohm coaxial cable. The main reason for selecting the IEEE-802.3 specification for TOP is the ease of interfacing similar Ethernet LANs to the network, and the wide availability of compatible network components that were developed for Ethernet networks.

Since the MAP and TOP networks are compatible above layer 1, interconnections can be made across a wide geographic boundary as is shown in Fig. 10.13. For example within a TOP network a repeater can be used to physically extend the network. The common use of the IEEE-802.2 logical link control at layer 2 for both MAP and TOP allows the use of bridges to interconnect these networks, provided they have a consistent addressing scheme and frame size, and identical-link protocols.

10.3.2 MAP Token-Bus Controller

A relatively simple interface to a token bus can be accomplished by using one of several available VLSI-circuit token-bus controller chips. As an example, let us

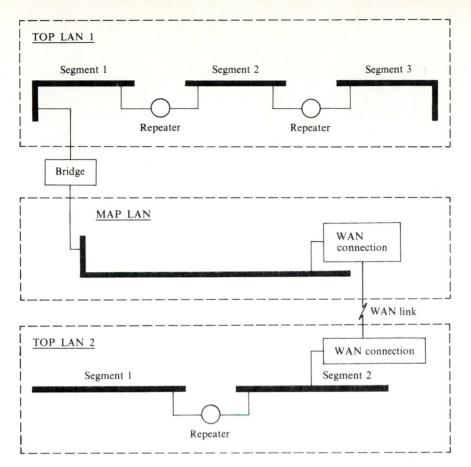

FIGURE 10.13
Interconnections of MAP and TOP networks.

consider the MC68824 chip made by Motorola.[24–26] The implementation of the 68824 bus-controller chip is shown in Fig. 10.14. This chip has a 32-bit address bus and can handle four priority levels. In addition to providing all the services called for in the IEEE-802.4 MAC sublayer, the token-bus controller also monitors the network and carries out diagnostics. The functions which the device handles above the MAC sublayer are implemented in software and firmware running on local and host processors.

Since the controller must operate with either the carrierband or the broadband signaling scheme, its serial interface to the physical layer has been designed to send and receive generic, encoded data symbols. Each symbol represents the unit of data transmitted or received within one bit time.

The MC68824 can pass or accept pointers to buffer areas, data, and parameters contained in the memory of the host processor. The direct-memory-access (DMA) channel can then transfer the appropriate data, without any

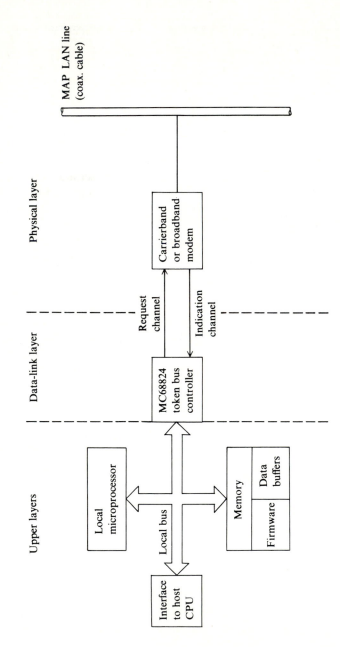

FIGURE 10.14
Implementation of an MC68824 MAP bus-controller chip.

intervention by the host, at the highest rate that the bus and memory of the host can support.

The IEEE-802.4 protocol denotes an option for four levels of message priority. The controller chip supports these four classes, any or all of which can be disabled. In an operating network, critical information such as a warning of catastrophic failure might be assigned the highest priority. The lowest priority could be given to less important frames, such as those containing batch information. The controller executes the priority mechanism by linking together frames of the same priority through their frame descriptors.

10.4 TOKEN-RING NETWORKS

The IEEE Standard 802.5 for token-ring local area networks evolved from work initiated at the IBM Research Laboratory in Zurich, Switzerland. Details of the access method of the token ring are given in Sec. 6.2 and its performance characteristics are discussed in Sec. 6.3. Here we examine the topology, network components, and the architecture of the IBM token-ring network.[27-30]

To overcome the vulnerability of network degradation due to component or node failures in a ring topology, ring networks can be installed using a star configuration. This concept is shown in Fig. 10.15 where all stations are wired to one of a number of different possible wire centers. The wire centers themselves are connected by point-to-point links. Each wire center contains a series of electronic relays that are used for structuring the star network, such as inserting into or removing nodes from the ring. One interesting feature of this type of configuration is that since the transmission medium is segmented at the wire center, rather than being one continuous cable, it is possible to intermix copper and optical fiber cables in the same network.

As depicted in Fig. 10.15, the token-ring network can also employ repeaters, bridges, and gateways. If the distance between stations exceeds the 770-meter length of the IBM specification, either a copper-cable repeater can be used to extend the distance another 770 m, or an optical repeater can be implemented to drive the signal up to 2 km. Multiple token rings can be interconnected via bridges, and gateways are used to interface a token-ring LAN and a wide-area network for establishing long-distance communications.

10.4.1 Token-Ring Frame Formats

There are two basic frame formats for a token ring: one for information frames and one for the control token. These are given in Figs. 10.16a and 10.16b, respectively. The encoding procedure specified by the token-ring standard is differential Manchester encoding.

The general data-frame format for transmitting information on the token ring is shown in Fig. 10.16a. The length of the information field is variable and contains the data that the sender is transferring to the receiver. This field is preceded by a variable-length header, and is followed by a 6-byte trailer. The

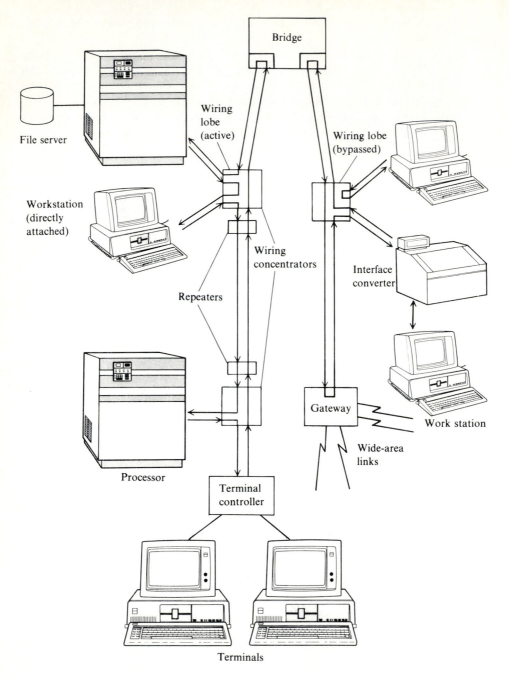

FIGURE 10.15
Concept of a token-ring network (*Reproduced with permission from Strole,*[28] *copyright 1983, IBM*).

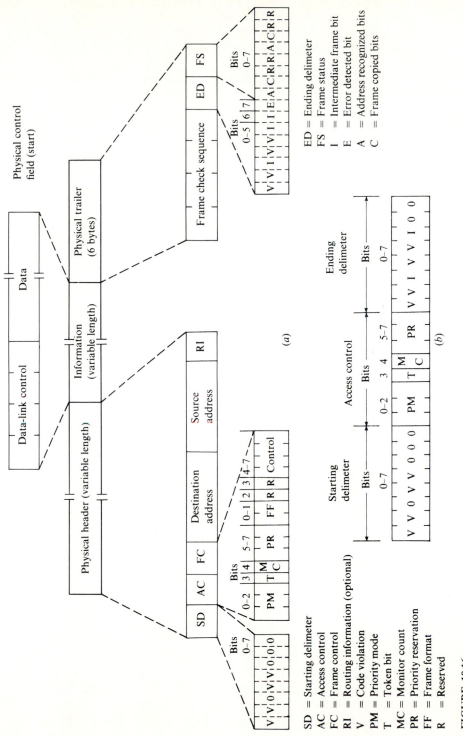

SD = Starting delimeter
AC = Access control
FC = Frame control
RI = Routing information (optional)
V = Code violation
PM = Priority mode
T = Token bit
MC = Monitor count
PR = Priority reservation
FF = Frame format
R = Reserved

ED = Ending delimeter
FS = Frame status
I = Intermediate frame bit
E = Error detected bit
A = Address recognized bits
C = Frame copied bits

FIGURE 10.16
General data-frame format of a token-ring network (*Reproduced with permission from Strole,*[28] *copyright 1983, IBM*).

385

first byte is the starting delimiter (SD) which identifies the beginning of the frame. Likewise the 8-bit ending delimiter (ED) denotes the end of the frame. These two fields contain special bit sequences which are used to achieve data transparency.

The second byte is the access control (AC) field which controls the ring-access protocol. It contains three priority mode (PM) bits, a token (T) bit, a monitor-count (MC) bit, and three priority reservation (PR) bits, some of which are used for a token and others of which apply to information frames. In a token the PM bits provide up to eight levels of priority in accessing the ring, and indicate those frames a DTE may transmit upon receipt of a token. The token bit T is set to zero in a token frame and to one in an information frame. The monitor-count bit MC is used by a device called the *active monitor* to prevent a frame from circulating around the ring continuously. When a station which has information to send detects a token having a priority less than or equal to that of its waiting data unit, it removes the token and sends its data. The three PR bits in the AC field are used to request that the next token be issued at the requested priority.

The one-byte frame control (FC) field tells whether the data field contains medium-access control information or user data. If the frame format bits (FF) define a MAC frame, all stations on the ring interpret and, if necessary, act on the control bits (Z); if the FF bits indicate an information (I) frame, then the control bits are only interpreted by those stations identified in the destination-address field.

The destination address (DA) and source address (SA) are either two or six octets long. Either individual stations, groups of stations, or all stations can be addressed. The source address is always an individual address which identifies the station originating the frame. An optional routing information (RI) subfield may follow the address fields when a frame must traverse more than one ring to reach the destination node.

The information (INFO) field contains either data or additional control information when it is part of a MAC frame. Although no maximum length is specified for the INFO field, in practice its length is limited by the maximum allowed station transmission time. A typical maximum length is 132 octets (1056 bits).

The information field is followed by a 32-bit cyclic redundancy check (CRC) frame check sequence (FCS) used for error detection. The error check at the receiver covers the FC, DA, SA, INFO, and FCS fields. Finally, there is a frame status (FS) field. The FS field contains address-recognized (A) and frame-copied (C) bits that are set by the destination station to indicate when it recognizes a frame addressed to the station, and whether or not it copied the frame. Both the A and C bits are set to zero by the DTE of the station originating the frame. DTEs to which the frame is addressed set the A bits to one and also, if it copies the frame, it sets the C bits to one. This way the originating station can determine if the addressed station is nonexistent or switched off, is active but did not copy the frame, or is active and copied the frame. The reserved (R) bits are

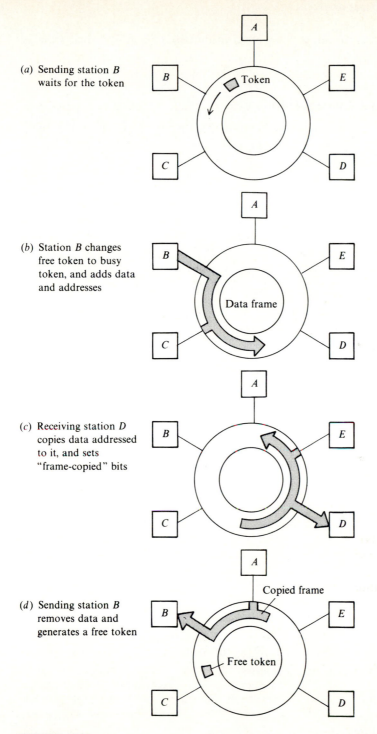

(a) Sending station *B* waits for the token

(b) Station *B* changes free token to busy token, and adds data and addresses

(c) Receiving station *D* copies data addressed to it, and sets "frame-copied" bits

(d) Sending station *B* removes data and generates a free token

FIGURE 10.17

Token-access control mechanism.

387

saved for future standardization. They are transmitted as zeros, but their value is ignored by the receiver.

10.4.2 Token-Ring Access Control

The token-access control mechanism is illustrated in Fig. 10.17. A single token circulates on the ring, sequentially giving each node an opportunity to transmit information when it receives the token. When a node wishes to transmit, it captures the token when it comes by, changes the token status in the AC field to indicate a frame, and then begins transmission. Immediately following the AC byte, the transmitting node appends the remainder of the header (FC, destination address, source address, and RI fields), the information field, and the trailer. A transmitting node is responsible for removing its frame from the ring and issuing a new token once it receives the header and completes the frame transmission. If a node finishes transmitting the entire frame before receiving its own header, it continues to transmit idle characters (contiguous zero bits) until the header is recognized. This ensures that only one token or frame is on the ring at any time.

A complete integrated-circuit chipset for connecting equipment to a token-ring LAN has been developed by Texas Instruments.[31] It is known as the TMS380 LAN adapter chipset, and consists of five integrated circuit chips as shown in Fig. 10.18. The chipset operates at 4 Mb/s using telephone twisted-pair

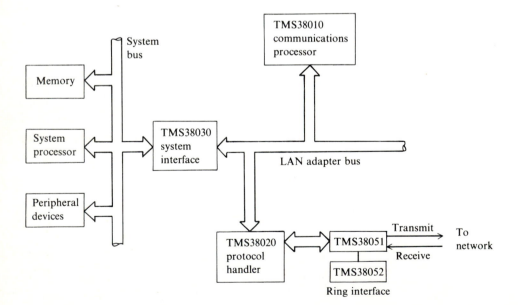

FIGURE 10.18
TMS380 LAN adapter chipset for token passing rings.

wire, shielded twisted-pair wire, or optical fibers. The integrated architecture of the TMS380 chipset combines a high-speed DMA host-to-system bus interface, a 16-bit central-processing unit (CPU) with on-chip buffer random-access memory (RAM), a protocol handler with on-chip read-only memory (ROM) for protocol software, and a pair of chips for interfacing to the physical medium. The integrated circuits for implementing these functions include the TMS38030 system-interface chip, the TMS38010 communications-processor chip, the TM38020 protocol-handler chip, and the TMS38051 and TMS38052 ring-interface chip pair.

10.5 FIBER DISTRIBUTED DATA INTERFACE (FDDI)

The Fiber Distributed Data Interface (FDDI) is a fiber-optic based counter-rotating token-ring architecture with a throughput of 100 Mb/s. FDDI is under development as a standard by the American National Standard Institute (ANSI) and is the result of work initiated in 1980–1981 by the Sperry Corporation.[32–36]

The FDDI design allows a maximum configuration of 500 stations connected with 100 km of optical fiber. This is in contrast to a maximum of 50 nodes linked by 10 km of cabling for the 4-Mb/s IEEE-802.5 token-ring network. The FDDI protocol largely follows the IEEE-802.5 Standard, deviating only where required to by its higher data-throughput rate.

A large-scale implementation of FDDI is conceptualized in Fig. 10.19. This figure shows that FDDI satisfies the throughput requirements of the following three fundamental LAN categories:

1. Back-end networks that support communications among mainframe computers, super minicomputers, and their associated high-speed storage devices
2. Backbone networks that tie together various types of LANs such as a token ring, Ethernet, a MAP token bus, or StarLAN
3. Front-end networks that operate through a wiring concentrator to link equipment such as engineering workstations

10.5.1 Operational Concept

The counterrotating ring concept is shown in Fig. 10.20. Two rings are connected to each station, with one ring transmitting clockwise and the other one transmitting counterclockwise. Thereby a redundant path is provided so that the ring remains functional in the event of any single failure. If a link fails, the stations on either side of the fault reconfigure internally to provide a loopback path as is described in Sec. 8.4. When the network is in operation, one of the rings may be designated as a standby ring only, or it may be used for concurrent transmission. Thus it is possible to have data flowing on both channels for an

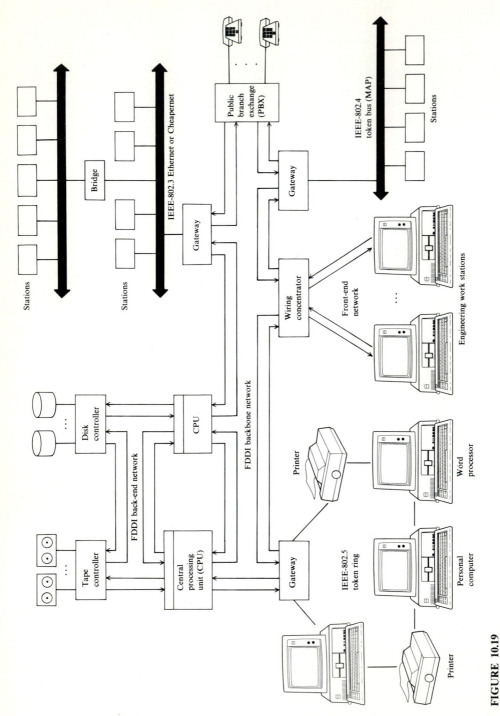

FIGURE 10.19
Large-scale implementation of FDDI which satisfies the needs of backbone, backend, and frontend networks.

390

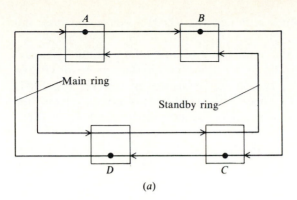

(a)

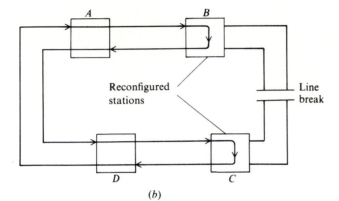

(b)

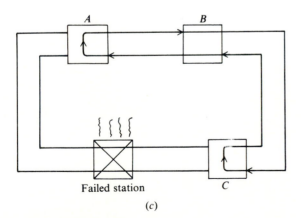

(c)

FIGURE 10.20
Counterrotating ring concept for FDDI (a) All stations in operation; (b) Loopback due to a line break; (c) Loopback due to a station failure.

aggregate throughput of 200 Mb/s, although the FDDI specification does not recommend doing this.

Figure 10.21 shows the main components of an FDDI station. These are the physical-medium-dependent (PMD) function, the physical protocol (PHY), the media-access control (MAC), and station management (SMT). The PMD defines the characteristics of the fiber-optic transmitters and receivers, the medium-dependent code requirements, cables, connectors, power budgets, optical bypass provisions, and other hardware related specifications. The PHY establishes clock synchronization and specifies encoding and decoding functions between the physical bit stream and the higher layers. The MAC controls nodal access to the medium. Some of its functions include address recognition, removal of frames from the ring (this is done by the MAC at the originating station), transmitting frames, repeating frames addressed to other stations, and removing and inserting tokens.

The station management (SMT) monitors and controls the overall activity of a station. This covers connection management (including inserting stations into the ring and removing them), station initialization, configuration management, fault isolation and recovery, administration of addressing, allocation of network bandwidth, and network control.

The choice of fiber-optic cable as the transmission medium makes FDDI attractive from the point of view of large bandwidth, low attenuation, immunity from electromagnetic interference, and inherent physical security of the transmitted information. In the interest of keeping down the cost and complexity of the

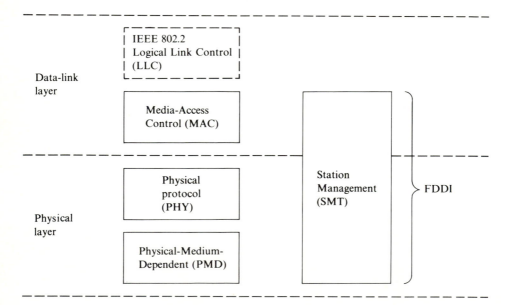

FIGURE 10.21
Main protocol components of an FDDI station.

network interfaces, FDDI uses light-emitting diodes (LEDs) in the transmitters and *pin* photodiodes in the receivers.[37] The nominal operating wavelength is 1300 nm. In choosing a fiber, a trade-off must be made between the amount of optical power that needs to be coupled into the fiber and the fiber bandwidth. The best overall compromise for FDDI thus specifies that fibers having core/cladding diameters of 62.5/125 or 85/125 micrometers be used. For building applications the recommendation is that the fibers have a 400-MHz-km bandwidth and an attenuation of no greater than 2.5 dB/km.

10.5.2 Station Implementation

One of the first implementations of the FDDI standard is a five-chip family of integrated circuits from Advanced Micro Devices (AMD).[38] An application of these chips is shown in Fig. 10.22. The AM7984 encoder-decoder receiver and AM7985 encoder-decoder transmitter chips are fast bipolar devices which physically interface to the 100-Mb/s fiber-optic LAN medium. The other three ICs are slower-speed CMOS devices. These are the AM79C83 fiber-optic-ring media-access controller (Formac), the AM79C82 data-path controller (DPC), and the AM79C81 RAM buffer controller (RBC). The first chip manages the access to the media, whereas the latter two control and manage the buffer memory, respectively.

The AM7985 transmitter serializes eight-bit-wide parallel data from the MAC sublayer of the data-link layer to produce NRZ code for transmission on the fiber-optic ring. This conversion is done using 4B5B encoding (see Chap. 3).

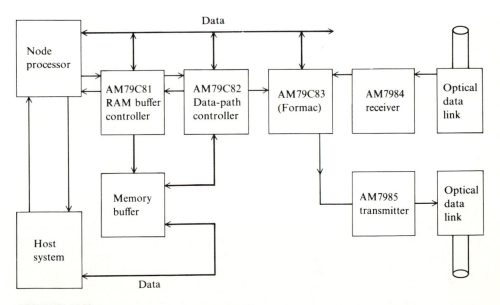

FIGURE 10.22
Application of a five-IC chipset for FDDI station control.

On the receiver side, the AM7984 chip converts the incoming 5-bit code back to 4-bit code, establishes the symbol-to-byte boundary, and presents the data to the MAC sublayer.

The functions of the AM79C83 Formac chip include packet transmission, reception, repetition and removal from the ring, address recognition, generation and checking of frame-check sequences, ring-recovery control, and network and frame status handling. Access to the fiber-optic ring is controlled by a timed-token protocol. When the chip has a pending request for transmission and has time left in which to transmit, it captures the token off the ring. The station that holds the token then has permission to transmit.

Both the AM79C82 DPC and the AM79C81 RBC manage the data flow in and out of the local buffer memory. The RBC generates address and control signals for the buffer memory. It directly supports 256 kbytes of address space and also includes five independent DMA channels that are used by three sources. The DPC uses two of the channels to transmit and receive data to and from the Formac. The host processor uses two other channels to read and write into the buffer memory.

10.6 VOICE AND DATA INTEGRATION IN LANs

Although LANs were developed for transmitting data among terminals and host computers in the office environment, the evolution of office automation has created a great interest in the integration of voice and data on the same network.[39-41] This is of particular interest in that voice traffic is still a dominant factor in office communications. The problem in realizing this, however, is that voice and data have different traffic characteristics and require different types of service from a network. For example, voice is stream traffic that has a long holding time, requires real-time delivery, and is tolerant of errors. On the other hand, data is bursty traffic that can tolerate long delays but which is very sensitive to errors.

To see the difficulties in the integration of voice and data, let us look at some of the technical characteristics of these two technologies. For telephone applications the voiceband is considered to encompass analog signals in the 300- to 3400-Hz range (although the frequency band of the human voice actually ranges from around 0 Hz to over 5000 Hz). The transmission lines used for telephones are usually 24-gauge 2-wire twisted-pair wires. These lines must carry 48 volts dc and up to 120 volts ac.

On the other hand, data signals are generally digital outputs from computer network equipment. The cables are typically only a few hundred meters long, and the wire sizes range from 18 to 20 gauge. In these wires the dc voltages are less than 15 volts and there are no ac requirements. This allows the use of higher-speed but more complex and delicate terminal-to-computer line-interface components. Consequently the terminal equipment for computer networks generally cost at least several hundred dollars, whereas telephone terminal equipment costs run in the tens of dollars.

We need to consider a variety of factors in the integration of voice and data on a local area network. These include choosing the networking scheme that can best accommodate these two traffic types, formulating an appropriate transmission protocol for handling both voice and data, and devising a good flow-control scheme that will not cause a degradation in the quality of the voice traffic.

The first step in making the two traffic types compatible is to digitize the voice signals. As we saw in Chap. 3, this is standardly done by sampling the voice signal 8000 times per second and then using an 8-bit per sample quantizing method to produce a PCM bit stream. A voice encoder operating at V bits per second combines several samples to produce a voice packet that is L_v bits long. A header which is L_h bits long is also added to each packet before it is transmitted. Since a packet usually experiences a network access delay before it can be sent out, it is temporarily buffered before transmission takes place.

In selecting a networking scheme for implementing integrated voice and data, we have a choice between a CSMA/CD network, as is exemplified by Ethernet, and a token-passing methodology. CSMA/CD networks do not guarantee a finite channel-access delay. Thus either the basic operation of the CSMA/CD protocol has to be modified[42] or a complex voice-handling algorithm needs to be implemented.[43-44] However, channel-access delay is finite when the token-passing protocol is used.[39,45-46] Since the question of exactly which methodology to implement is under consideration by standards organizations such as the IEEE 802.9 Committee (Integration of Voice and Data), the latest recommendations of these studies should be consulted for up-to-date information.

10.7 SUMMARY

The expansion of LAN technology into all conceivable types of applications has progressed from a relatively simple, moderate-speed, coaxial bus topology to sophisticated, high-speed fiber-optic-based networks. Commercial applications of LAN technology include both coaxial and fiber-optic Ethernets which follow the IEEE 802.3 Standard, IEEE 802.4 token bus implementations such as the Manufacturing Automation Protocol (MAP), coaxial token-ring LANs as described by the IEEE 802.5 Standard, and the Fiber Distributed Data Interface (FDDI) which is a 100-Mb/s fiber-optic token ring network.

Also of increasing interest is the integration of voice and data traffic onto the same network. The goal here is to combine two types of traffic which have rather different characteristics. This effort and other perhaps as yet unthought of applications are bound to keep communication equipment and network developers challenged for many years to come.

REFERENCES

1. R. M. Metcalfe and D. R. Boggs, "Ethernet: Distributed packet switching for local computer networks," *Commun. ACM*, vol. 19, pp. 395–404, June 1976.
2. J. F. Shoch, Y. K. Dalal, D. D. Redell, and R. C. Crane, "Evolution of the Ethernet Local Computer Network," *Computer*, vol. 15, pp. 10–27, August 1982.
3. *The Ethernet: A Local Area Network: Data Link Layer and Physical Layer Specifications*, Version 2.0, Digital Equipment Corp., Intel, Xerox, November 1982.
4. J. Wiegand, "LAN ICs for IEEE-802 networks," *EDN*, vol. 32, pp. 131–140, April 30 1987.
5. Intel. Corp., *Microcommunications Handbook*, Santa Clara, CA, 1987.
6. (*a*) N. Mokhoff, "Enhanced Ethernet controller recognizes up to six stations," *Electronic Design*, vol. 35, pp. 51–52, June 25, 1987.
   (*b*) G. Rauh, "Network interface makes efficient use of bus bandwidth," *Electronic Design*, vol. 36, pp. 126–128, June 9, 1988.
7. ANSI/IEEE Standard 802.3a, b, c, e-1988, *Supplements to Carrier Sense Multiple Access with Collision Detection (CSMA/CD)*, 1988.
8. J. Paetau, "StarLAN transceiver makes easy connections for office PCs," *Electronic Design*, vol. 36, pp. 79–85, Feb. 4 1988.
9. R. V. Schmidt, E. G. Rawson, R. E. Norton, Jr., S. B. Jackson, and M. D. Bailey, "Fibernet II: A fiber optic Ethernet," *IEEE J. Sel. Areas Commun.*, vol. SAC-1, pp. 702–711, November 1983.
10. E. G. Rawson, "The Fibernet II Ethernet-compatible fiber-optic LAN," *IEEE J. Lightwave Tech.*, vol. LT-3, pp. 496–501, June 1985.
11. S. Moustakas, "The standardization of IEEE 802.3 compatible fiber optic CSMA/CD local area networks: physical topologies," *IEEE Commun. Mag.*, vol. 25, pp. 22–29, February 1987.
12. G. Keiser, *Optical Fiber Communications*, McGraw-Hill, New York, 1983.
13. H. H. Witte and V. Kulich, "Branching elements for optical data buses," *Appl. Optics*, vol. 20, pp. 715–718, February 1981.
14. J. Strauss and B. Kawasaki, "Passive optical components," in *Optical Fiber Transmission* (E. E. Basch, ed.), H. W. Sams & Co., Indianapolis, 1987.
15. M. Kieli and P. P. Herczfeld, "Asymmetric fiber-optic coupler for LAN applications," *IEEE J. Lightwave Tech.*, vol. LT-4, pp. 1729–1731, December 1986.
16. T. H. Wood, "Increased power injection in multimode optical-fiber buses through mode-selective coupling," *IEEE J. Lightwave Tech.*, vol. LT-3, pp. 537–543, June 1985.
17. H. S. Huang, H. C. Chang, and J. S. Wu, "Power transfer between single-mode and multimode optical fibers," *IEEE Microwave Theory and Tech. Symp. Digest*, pp. 519–522, June 1986.
18. Y. Hakamada and K. Oguchi, "32-Mb/s star-configured optical local area network design and performance," *IEEE J. Lightwave Tech.*, vol. LT-3, pp. 511–524, June 1985.
19. J. W. Reedy and J. R. Jones, "Methods of collision detection in fiber optic CSMA/CD networks," *IEEE J. Sel. Areas Commun.*, vol. SAC-3, pp. 890–896, November 1985.
20. S. Moustakas, H.-H. Witte, V. Bodlaj, and V. Kulich, "Passive optical star bus with collision detection for CSMA/CD-based local area networks," *IEEE J. Lightwave Tech.*, vol. LT-3, pp. 93–100, February 1985.
21. M. A. Kaminski, Jr., "Protocols for communicating in the factory," *IEEE Spectrum*, vol. 23, pp. 56–62, April 1986.
22. R. Allan, "Factory communication: MAP promises to pull the pieces together," *Electronic Design*, vol. 34, pp. 102–112, May 15 1986.
23. S. A. Farowich, "Communicating in the technical office," *IEEE Spectrum*, vol. 23, pp. 63–67, April 1986.
24. T. Balph, R. A. Dirvin, and Y. Shvager, "Token bus controller uses monolithic structure to chip away MAP costs," *Electronic Design*, vol. 33, pp. 151–156, Nov. 14 1985.
25. I. Erickson, "Token bus controller simplifies network design," *EDN*, vol. 32, pp. 159–168, April 30, 1987.
26. P. Polansky, "Token-bus-controller interface must resolve family disparities," *EDN*, vol. 33, pp. 167–178, March 17, 1988.

27. *Token-Ring Network Architecture Reference.* IBM Publication 6165877, 1986.
28. N. C. Strole, "A local communications network based on interconnected token-access rings: A tutorial," *IBM J. Res. Develop.*, vol. 27, pp. 481–496, September 1983.
29. N. C. Strole, "The IBM token-ring network—A functional overview," *IEEE Network Mag.*, vol. 1, pp. 23–30, January 1987.
30. R. C. Dixon, "Lore of the token ring," *IEEE Network Mag.*, vol. 1, pp. 11–18, January 1987.
31. *TMS380 Adapter Chipset User's Guide—1986*, Texas Instruments, Dallas, TX, 1986.
32. Draft ANSI Standard, *FDDI Token Ring Media Access Control (MAC)*, ASC X3T9.5, Rev. 10, Feb. 28, 1986.
33. Draft ANSI Standard, *FDDI Token Ring Physical Layer Protocol (PHY)*, ASC X3T9.5, Rev. 14, Oct. 20, 1986.
34. Draft ANSI Standard, *FDDI Token Ring Physical Layer Medium Dependent (PMD)*, ASC X3T9.5 Rev. 6, July 10, 1986.
35. F. E. Ross, "FDDI—A tutorial," *IEEE Commun. Mag.*, vol. 24, pp. 10–17, May 1986.
36. V. Iyer and S. Joshi, "FDDI's 100 Mb/s protocol improves on 802.5 spec's 4 Mb/s limit," *EDN*, vol. 30, pp. 151–160, May 2, 1985.
37. W. E. Burr, "The FDDI optical data link," *IEEE Commun. Mag.*, vol. 24, pp. 18–23, May 1986.
38. N. Mokhoff, "Five-chip token-passing set operates LANs at 100 Mb/s," *Electronic Design*, vol. 36, pp. 45–50, Sept. 17, 1987.
39. O. C. Ibe and D. T. Gibson, "Protocols for integrated voice and data local area networks," *IEEE Commun. Mag.*, vol. 24, pp. 30–36, July 1986.
40. T. V. Russotto, "The integration of voice and data communication," *IEEE Network*, vol. 1, pp. 21–29, October 1987.
41. IEEE Standard 802.9 Committee, "Integrated Voice and Data LANs."
42. N. F. Maxemchuk, "A variation on CSMA/CD that yields movable TDM slots in integrated voice/data local networks," *Bell. Sys. Tech. J.*, vol. 61, pp. 1527–1550, September 1982.
43. S. Q. Li and J. C. Majithia, "Performance analysis of a DTDMA local area network for voice and data," *Computer Networks*, vol. 8, pp. 81–91, April 1984.
44. R. K. Goel and A. K. Elkakeem, "A hybrid FARA/CSMA/CD protocol for voice-data integration," *Computer Networks and ISDN Sys.*, vol. 9, pp. 223–240, March 1985.
45. W. Bux, F. H. Closs, K. Kuemmerle, H. J. Keller, and H. R. Mueller, "Architecture and design of a reliable token-ring network," *IEEE J. Select. Areas in Commun.*, vol. SAC-1, pp. 756–765, November 1983.
46. J. W. Wong and P. M. Gopal, "Analysis of a token-ring protocol for voice transmission," *Computer Networks*, vol. 8, pp. 339–346, August 1984.

AN
OVERVIEW
OF
UNITS

A.1 INTERNATIONAL SYSTEM OF UNITS

TABLE A.1

Quantity	Unit	Symbol	Dimensions
Length	meter	m	
Mass	kilogram	kg	
Time	second	s	
Temperature	kelvin	K	
Current	ampere	A	
Frequency	hertz	Hz	$1/s$
Force	newton	N	$kg \cdot m/s^2$
Pressure	pascal	Pa	N/m^2
Energy	joule	J	$N \cdot m$
Power	watt	W	J/s
Electric charge	coulomb	C	$A \cdot s$
Potential	volt	V	J/C
Conductance	siemens	S	A/V
Resistance	ohm	Ω	V/A
Capacitance	farad	F	C/V
Magnetic flux	weber	Wb	$V \cdot s$
Magnetic induction	tesla	T	Wb/m^2
Inductance	henry	H	Wb/A

A.2   DECIBEL DEFINITION

In designing and implementing a transmission link, it is of interest to establish, measure, and/or interrelate the signal levels at the transmitter, at the receiver, at coupling devices, and in the cable. A convenient method for this is either to reference the signal to some absolute value or to a noise level. This is normally done in terms of a power ratio measured in *decibels* (dB) defined as

$$\text{Power ratio} = 10 \log \frac{P_2}{P_1} \tag{A.1}$$

where P_1 and P_2 are electric or optical powers.

Recalling that in terms of current I, voltage V, and resistance R, we have $P = IV = V^2/R$, then for the same resistance R, Eq. (A.1) becomes

$$\text{Power ratio} = 20 \log \frac{V_2}{V_1} \tag{A.2}$$

This is widely used when defining a signal-to-noise ratio in a device in terms of the signal voltage and the noise voltage levels.

The logarithmic nature of the decibel allows a large ratio to be expressed in a fairly simple manner. Power levels differing by many orders of magnitude can be readily compared when they are in decibel form. Some very helpful figures to remember are given in Table A.2. For example, doubling the power means a 3-dB gain (the power level increases by 3 dB), halving the power means a 3-dB loss (the power level decreases by 3 dB), and power levels differing by factors of 10^N or 10^{-N} have decibel differences of $+10N$ dB and $-10N$ dB, respectively.

The decibel is used to refer to ratios or relative units. For example, we can say that a certain cable has a 6-dB loss (the power level gets reduced by 75 percent in going through the cable) or that a particular element has a 1-dB loss (the power level gets reduced by 20 percent in the device). However, the decibel gives no indication of the absolute power level. A common derived unit for doing this is the *dBm*. This is the decibel power level referred to 1 mW. In this case the power in dBm is an absolute value defined by

$$\text{Power level} = 10 \log \frac{P}{1 \text{ mW}} \tag{A.3}$$

An important relationship to remember is that 0 dBm = 1 mW. Other examples are shown in Table A.3.

TABLE A.2
Examples of decibel measures of power ratios

Power ratio	10^N	10	2	1	0.5	0.1	10^{-N}
dB	$+10N$	$+10$	$+3$	0	-3	-10	$-10N$

TABLE A.3
Examples of dBm units (decibel measures of power relative to 1 mW)

Power (mW)	100	10	2	1	0.5	0.1	0.01	0.001
Value (dBm)	+20	+10	+3	0	−3	−10	−20	−30

APPENDIX
B

USEFUL MATHEMATICAL RELATIONS

Some of the mathematical relations encountered in this text are listed for convenient reference. More comprehensive listings are available in various handbooks.[1-4]

B.1   TRIGONOMETRIC IDENTITIES

$$e^{\pm j\theta} = \cos\theta \pm j\sin\theta$$

$$\sin(\alpha \pm \beta) = \cos\alpha\cos\beta \pm \sin\alpha\sin\beta$$

B.2   INTEGRALS

$$\int \sin x \, dx = -\cos x$$

$$\int \cos x \, dx = \sin x$$

$$\int u \, dv = uv - \int v \, du$$

$$\int e^{ax} \, dx = \frac{1}{a} e^{ax}$$

$$\int_{-\infty}^{\infty} e^{-p^2x^2 + qx} \, dx = e^{q^2/4p^2} \frac{\sqrt{\pi}}{p}$$

$$\int_0^{\infty} \frac{1}{1 + (x/a)^2} \, dx = \frac{\pi a}{2}$$

$$\frac{2}{\sqrt{\pi}} \int_0^t e^{-x^2} \, dx = \text{erf}(t)$$

$$\int_0^{\infty} x^n e^{-ax} \, dx = n! \, a^{-n-1} = \Gamma(n + 1)a^{-n-1}$$

B.3 SERIES EXPANSIONS

$$\sum_{k=1}^m k = \frac{m(m+1)}{2}$$

$$\sum_{n=0}^{\infty} x^n = \frac{1}{1-x} \qquad x < 1$$

$$\sum_{k=1}^{\infty} kp^{k-1} = \frac{1}{(1-p)^2}$$

$$\sum_{i=1}^s aq^{i-1} = \frac{a(q^s - 1)}{q - 1}$$

$$(1 + x)^n = 1 + nx + \frac{n(n-1)}{2!}x^2 + \frac{n(n-1)(n-2)}{3!}x^3 + \cdots \quad \text{for } |nx| < 1$$

$$e^x = 1 + x + \frac{x^2}{2!} + \frac{x^3}{3!} + \cdots$$

REFERENCES

1. R. S. Burington, *Handbook of Mathematical Tables and Formulas*, 5th ed., McGraw-Hill, New York, 1973.
2. J. J. Tuma, *Engineering Mathematics Handbook*, 2d ed., McGraw-Hill, New York, 1982.
3. M. Abramowitz and I. A. Stegun, *Handbook of Mathematical Functions*, Dover, New York, 1965.
4. I. S. Gradshteyn and I. M. Ryzhik, *Table of Integrals, Series, and Products*, Academic, New York, 1980.

APPENDIX
C

ETHERNET
TECHNICAL
SUMMARY

C.1 PACKET FORMAT

Stations must be able to transmit and receive packets on the common coaxial cable with the packet format and spacing shown in Fig. C.1. Each packet is a sequence of 8-bit bytes. The least significant bit of each byte (starting with the preamble) is transmitted first. The fields are defined as follows:

Preamble. This is a 56-bit (7-byte) synchronization pattern consisting of alternating ones and zeros, which is used to ensure receiver synchronization.

Start-Frame Delimiter. The 1-byte start-frame delimiter is similar to the preamble, except that it ends with two consecutive one bits. Thus the preamble and starting delimiter together are given by

10101010 10101010 10101010 10101010 10101010 10101010 10101010 10101011

Destination address. This 48-bit field specifies to which station the packet is addressed. The address can be either a unique station on the Ethernet, or it can be a multidestination address. The first bit indicates the type of address: if it is a

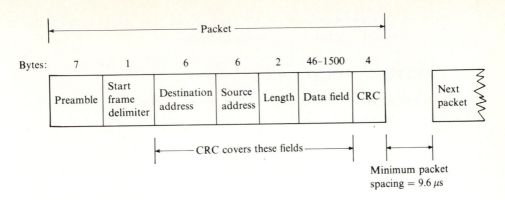

FIGURE C.1   Packet format and packet spacing for Ethernet.

0, the field gives the address of a unique station; if it is a 1, the field specifies a logical group of recipients.

Source address. The unique address of the originating station is specified in this 48-bit field.

Length. This two-byte field indicates the number of information bytes being supplied by the LLC layer for the data field.

Data field. The IEEE-802 Standard recommends that the data field has a length between 46 and 1500 bytes. The 48-byte minimum ensures that valid packets will be distinguishable from collision fragments. If the data supplied by the LLC layer is less than the 46-byte minimum required for proper operation of the Ethernet protocol, then an integer number of padding bytes are added to the end of the data field to bring the length to 46.

Frame check sequence. This part of the frame contains a 32-bit (4-byte) cyclic redundancy check (CRC) code for error detection as defined by the generating polynomial

$$G(x) = x^{32} + x^{26} + x^{23} + x^{22} + x^{16} + x^{12} + x^{11} + x^{10}$$
$$+ x^8 + x^7 + x^5 + x^4 + x^2 + x + 1$$

The CRC covers the destination address, source address, length, and data fields. The CRC algorithm uses a linear feedback register which is initially preset to all ones. After the last bit is transmitted, the contents of this register are inverted and sent as the CRC field. After receiving a good packet, the shift register contains 11000111 00000100 11011101 01111011.

Maximum packet size. 1526 bytes (8-byte preamble + 14-byte header + 1500 data bytes + 4-byte CRC).

Minimum packet size. 72 bytes (8-byte preamble + 14-byte header + 46 data bytes + 4-byte CRC).

Minimum packet spacing. The minimum time that must elapse after one transmission before another transmission is started is 9.6 μs.

Collision filtering. Any received bit sequence smaller than the minimum valid packet size is discarded as a collision fragment.

C.2 CONTROL PROCEDURE

The control procedure defines when and how a station may transmit packets.

Defer. A station must not transmit when a carrier is present or within the minimum interpacket spacing time.

Transmit. A station may transmit if it is not deferring. It may continue transmitting until either the end of the packet is reached or a collision is detected.

Abort. If a collision is detected, transmission of the packet must terminate, and a jam signal (4 to 6 bytes of arbitrary data) is transmitted to ensure that all involved participants are notified of the collision.

Retransmit. After a station has detected a collision and aborted, it must wait for a random retransmission delay, defer as usual, and then attempt to retransmit the packet.

Backoff. Retransmission delays are computed using the truncated binary exponential backoff algorithm, with the aim of resolving contention among up to 1024 stations.

C.3 CHANNEL ENCODING AND DATA RATE

Manchester encoding is used on the coaxial cable as shown in Fig. C.2. This has a 50 percent duty cycle and ensures a transition in the middle of every bit cell. The data rate is 10 Mb/s, so that the bit cell is 100 ns $\pm$ 0.01%.

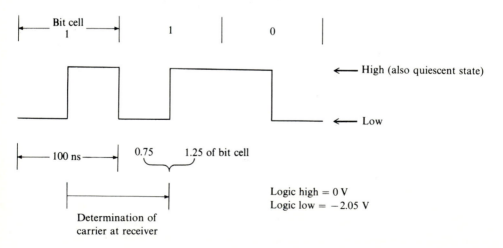

FIGURE C.2   Manchester encoding used on an Ethernet coaxial cable.

C.4 CARRIER

The presence of data transitions indicates that a carrier is present. If a transition is not seen between 0.75 and 1.25 bit times since the center of the last bit cell, then carrier has been lost, indicating the end of a packet. For purposes of deferring, carrier means any activity on the cable independent of the signal being properly formatted. Specifically, it is any activity of either receive or collision-detect signals in the last 160 ns.

C.5 COAXIAL CABLE

Impedance. 50 ohms ± 2 ohms. This impedance tolerance includes batch-to-batch variations. Periodic impedance variations of up to ±3 ohms are permitted along a single piece of cable.

Cable loss. The maximum end-to-end loss of a cable segment is 8.5 dB at 10 MHz.

Shielding. The physical-channel hardware must operate in an ambient field of 2 volts per meter from 10 kHz to 20 MHz, and 5 V/m from 30 MHz to 1 GHz. The shield has a transfer impedance of less than 1 milliohm per meter over the frequency range 0.1 to 20 MHz.

Ground connections. The coaxial cable shield must not be connected to any building or ac ground along its length. If for safety reasons a ground connection of the shield is necessary, it must be in only one place.

C.6 TRANSCEIVER CONNECTION RULES

Up to 100 transceivers may be placed on a cable segment, with no two being closer than 2.5 m together. This placement rule gives a very low probability that objectional standing waves will result.

C.7 TRANSCEIVER TO COAX-CABLE INTERFACE

Input impedance. The resistive component of the input impedance must be no greater than 50 kΩ. The total capacitance must be less than 4 pF.

Nominal transmit level. The important parameter is an average dc level with a 50 percent duty cycle waveform input. The dc level must be −1.024 V (41 mA) nominal with a range of −0.9 to −1.2 V (36 to 48 mA). The peak-to-peak ac waveform must be centered on the average dc level and its value can range from 1.4 V peak-to-peak to twice the average dc level. The voltage must never go positive on the coax. The quiescent state on the coax is logic high (0 V). Voltage measurements are made on the coax near the transceiver with the shield as reference. Positive current flows out of the center conductor of the coax.

Rise and fall time. 25 ns ± 5 ns with a maximum of 1 ns difference between rise and fall time in a given unit.

Signal symmetry. Asymmetry on the output should not exceed 2 ns for a 50 percent duty-cycle square wave to either the transmit or the receive section of the transceiver.

C.8   TRANSCEIVER TO TRANSCEIVER-CABLE INTERFACE

Signal pairs. Both the transceiver and the station shall drive and present at the receiving end a 78-ohm balanced load. The differential signal voltage shall be 0.7 volts nominal peak with a common mode voltage between 0 and +5 volts using power return as reference.

Collision signal. The active state of the collision line is a 10-MHz waveform and its quiescent state is a logic high. It is active if the transceiver is transmitting and another transmission is detected, or if two or more other stations are transmitting, independent of the state of the local transmit signal.

Power. +14 to +16 volts dc at the controller. The maximum current available to the transceiver is 0.5 A.

C.9   TRANSCEIVER CABLE

The maximum signal loss should be 3 dB at 10 MHz. This is equivalent to about 50 m of either 20 or 22 AWG twisted-pair wire.

AN
OVERVIEW
OF
PROBABILITY
THEORY

In this appendix we review selected topics from probability theory. This will basically consist of important definitions. For details, the interested reader should consult the vast array of literature available on this topic.

D.1 NOTATION

The following symbols are commonly used in probability theory:

1. $A \cup B = $ *union* of A and $B = $ at least one of A or B occurs
2. $A \cap B = A, B = $ *intersection* of A and $B = $ both A and B occur
3. $P\{J\} = $ probability of event J
4. $P\{A|B\} = $ conditional probability of A given B
5. $\varnothing = $ the null set (or null event)

D.2 STATISTICAL INDEPENDENCE

Events A and B are said to be *statistically independent* if and only if

$$P\{A, B\} = P\{A\}P\{B\} \tag{D.1}$$

This theorem extends to N events. That is, if

$$P\{A, B, C, \ldots, N\} = P\{A\}P\{B\}P\{C\} \cdots P\{N\} \tag{D.2}$$

then the events A, B, $C, \ldots, N$ are statistically independent.

D.3 CONDITIONAL PROBABILITY

It is often useful to calculate the probability that an event A occurs when it is known that an event B has occurred, where B has positive probability. The symbol for this probability is $P\{A|B\}$ which reads "the conditional probability of A, given B." In general, to calculate the probability that A occurs given that B has occurred, means that we are only interested in that part of A which occurs with B, which is $A \cap B$. Thus we have the formula

$$P\{A|B\} = \frac{P\{A \cap B\}}{P\{B\}} \tag{D.3}$$

where $P\{B\} \neq 0$. If A and B are independent, then

$$P\{A|B\} = \frac{P\{A \cap B\}}{P\{B\}} = \frac{P\{A\}P\{B\}}{P\{B\}} = P\{A\} \tag{D.4}$$

D.4 MUTUALLY EXCLUSIVE EVENTS

If the events A and B have no points in common, that is, if $A \cap B = \emptyset$, then A and B are *mutually exclusive events*. Thus, given that A and B are mutually exclusive, then

$$P\{A \cup B\} = P\{A\} + P\{B\} \tag{D.5}$$

Given that the events A_1, A_2, $A_3, \ldots$ are mutually exclusive (that is, $A_i \cap A_j = \emptyset$ if $i \neq j$), then

$$P\left\{ \bigcup_{n=1}^{\infty} A_n \right\} = \sum_{n=1}^{\infty} P\{A_n\} \tag{D.6}$$

For example, for n mutually exclusive events A_1, A_2, $A_3, \ldots, A_n$

$$P\{A_1 \cup A_2 \cup A_3 \cup \cdots \cup A_n\} = P\{A_1\} + P\{A_2\} + \cdots + P\{A_n\} \tag{D.7}$$

D.5 COMBINATORIAL ANALYSIS

Combinatorial analysis is the science of counting. For example, this could be the number of elements in prescribed sets, or the number of ways a particular selection can be made. One important concept is that of a permutation. A *permutation of order k* is an ordered selection of k elements. The number of permutations of n elements taken k at a time, without repetition, is

$$P(n, k) = \frac{n!}{(n-k)!} \tag{D.8}$$

Related to this is the *binomial coefficient* defined by

$$\binom{n}{k} = \frac{P(n, k)}{k!} = \frac{n!}{k! \, (n-k)!} \tag{D.9}$$

APPENDIX
E

A REVIEW OF MARKOV CHAIN THEORY

This appendix gives a brief summary of Markov chain theory. The interested reader should consult books on stochastic processes for detailed discussions.

Let $X(t)$ be a random variable depending on a continuous parameter $t \geq 0$ and taking values in the set of nonnegative integers $\{0, 1, 2, \ldots\}$. We can think of t as time and of $X(t)$ as the system state at time t. The collection of random variables $\{X(t), t \geq 0\}$ is a *stochastic process*. That collection is said to be a *Markov process* if the probability distribution of the state at time $t + y$ depends only on the state at time t regardless of its history prior to arriving at t.

The behavior of a Markov process can thus be described as follows: at time $t = 0$ the process starts in some state, say i, where it remains for an exponentially distributed interval of time. The process then enters state j with probability P_{ij} and remains there for an exponentially distributed interval of time. From there it enters state k with probability P_{jk}, etc. The successive states

412

visited by the process form a *Markov chain*; that is, the next state depends on the one immediately before it, but not on all the previous ones. This Markov chain is said to be *embedded* in the Markov process.

In probability notation, for all $n > 0$, $i_{n-1}, \ldots, i_0, i, j$,

$$P_{ij} = P\{X_{n+1} = j \mid X_n = i, X_{n-1} = i_{n-1}, \ldots, X_0 = i_0\}$$
$$= P\{X_{n+1} = j \mid X_n = i\} \tag{E.1}$$

where $\{X_n \mid n = 0, 1, 2, \ldots\}$ is a discrete-time stochastic process that takes values from the set of nonnegative integers (that is, we write X_n for $X(t_n)$). The parameters P_{ij} are the *one-step transition probabilities*, which must satisfy the conditions

$$P_{ij} \geq 0 \text{ and } \sum_{j=0}^{\infty} P_{ij} = 1 \qquad \text{for } i = 0, 1, 2, \ldots \tag{E.2}$$

These transition probabilities can be exhibited as a square matrix

$$P = \begin{bmatrix} P_{00} & P_{01} & P_{02} & \cdots \\ P_{10} & P_{11} & P_{12} & \cdots \\ \vdots & & & \\ P_{i0} & P_{i1} & P_{i2} & \cdots \\ \vdots & & & \end{bmatrix} \tag{E.3}$$

which is called the *transition probability matrix* of the chain. If the number of states n is finite, this will be an $n \times n$ matrix; otherwise, the matrix is infinite.

We define the *n-step transition probabilities* by

$$P_{ij}^n = P\{X_{m+n} = j \mid X_n = i\} \qquad \text{for all } m \geq 0 \text{ and } n \geq 0 \tag{E.4}$$

The P_{ij}^n can be computed using the Chapman-Kolmogorov equations, which are

$$P_{ij}^{m+n} = \sum_{k=0}^{\infty} P_{ik}^n P_{kj}^m \qquad \text{for all } m, n, i, j \geq 0 \tag{E.5}$$

This shows that the parameters P_{ij}^n are the elements of the matrix P^n, the transition probability matrix P raised to the nth power.

State j of a Markov chain is said to be *reachable* from (or *communicate* with) state i if for some m and n we have $P_{ij}^n > 0$ and $P_{ij}^m > 0$. If every state is reachable from every other state, we say the chain is *irreducible*. Furthermore, a chain is *aperiodic* if for every state i there is no integer $d \geq 2$ such that $P_{ii}^n = 0$ except when n is a multiple of d.

A probability distribution $\{\pi_j \mid j \geq 0\}$ is a *stationary distribution* for the Markov chain if

$$\pi_j = \sum_{i=0}^{\infty} \pi_i P_{ij} \qquad \text{for } j \geq 0 \tag{E.6}$$

Such a probability distribution is called stationary because if $\pi_j^0 = \pi_j$ then $\pi_j^n = \pi_j$ for all n and j; this means the probabilities π_j^n do not change with time but are stationary. For such a chain

$$\pi_j = \lim_{n \to \infty} P_{jj}^n \quad \text{for } j \geq 0 \tag{E.7}$$

When this limit exists and when $\pi_j > 0$, then $1/\pi_j$ equals the expected number of transitions between two successive visits to state j, or alternately, the proportion of time the process visits j on the average.

The limits given in Eq. (E.7) consititute a probability distribution

$$\sum_{j=0}^{\infty} \pi_j = 1 \tag{E.8}$$

The following theorem thus arises:

Theorem. Exactly one of the following holds in an irreducible, aperiodic Markov chain:

1. All states are recurrent null, that is, $\pi_j = 0$ for all $j \geq 0$ in which case the chain has no stationary distribution
2. All states are positive recurrent, that is, $\pi_j > 0$ for all $j \geq 0$ in which case $\{\pi_j | j \geq 0\}$ is the unique stationary distribution of the chain.

Case 2 is of interest here. For queueing systems we have

$$\pi_j \sum_{\substack{i=0 \\ i \neq j}}^{\infty} P_{ji} = \sum_{\substack{i=0 \\ i \neq j}}^{\infty} \pi_i P_{ij} \tag{E.9}$$

These equations, which are known as the *global balance equations*, state that in equilibrium the probability of a transition out of state j equals the probability of a transition into j. A discrete Markov chain which is irreducible, aperiodic, and for which all states are positive recurrent is said to be *ergodic*. This basically says that the statistics of a particular process can be determined from a single observation, which means that its dependence on time t can be dropped.

INDEX